T O

ABSENT FRIENDS

"Red Smith was the top man in his profession. He had to be because every newspaperman I ever talked to placed him in that category." —Paul Brown, *Cincinnati Bengals*

"Red Smith was a serious man, but never heavy. He wreathed himself, as he wreathed his writing, in wit and grace, courtesy and kindness." —Roger Kahn, author of *The Boys of Summer*

"To know Red Smith was to know greatness. To read Red Smith was to know the heart and mind of a consummate professional. I never finished one of his columns but what I wished there was more." —George Halas, *The Chicago Bears*

"Eloquent isn't often the word used to describe the style of a sportswriter, but it does belong to Red Smith. I appreciated Red Smith's columns, not only because of his style, but from personal experience I knew he was telling the truth."—Roger Staubach

"Red Smith was not only an outstanding sportswriter, he was a true gentleman. Over the years, he accumulated a multitude of friends. It was a privilege and a pleasure to be included among them." —Joe DiMaggio

TO

ABSENT FRIENDS

WALTER W. (RED) SMITH was born in Green Bay, Wisconsin in 1905. The papers he wrote for included the *Milwaukee Sentinel*, the *St. Louis Star*, the *Philadelphia Record*, the *New York Herald Tribune*, and finally, *The New York Times*. His earlier books included *Out of the Red* and *Views of Sports*. His last column appeared shortly before his death on January 15, 1982. His many awards included an Honorary LLD from his alma mater, Notre Dame, the George Polk Award, and in 1975, long overdue, the Pulitzer Prize.

BOOKS BY RED SMITH

TO
ABSENT FRIENDS
FROM
RED SMITH

A PLUME BOOK
NEW AMERICAN LIBRARY
TIMES MIRROR
NEW YORK AND SCARBOROUGH, ONTARIO

Designed by Harry Ford

SIGNET, SIGNET CLASSIC, MENTOR, PLUME, MERIDIAN
and NAL BOOKS are published *in the United States* by
The New American Library, Inc., 1633 Broadway, New York, New York 10019,
in Canada by The New American Library of Canada Limited,
81 Mack Avenue, Scarborough, Ontario M1L 1M8

Library of Congress Cataloging in Publication Data

Smith, Red, 1905-1982.
  To absent friends.

  Reprint. Originally published: 1st ed. New York:
Atheneum, 1982.
    1. Athletes—Biography—Addresses, essays, lectures.
2. Farewell sermons—Addresses, essays, lectures.
I. Title.
GV697.A1S55 1983   796'.092'2 [B]   83-8211
ISBN 0-452-25443-4 (pbk.)

First Plume Printing, September, 1983

1 2 3 4 5 6 7 8 9

PRINTED IN THE UNITED STATES OF AMERICA

PUBLISHER'S NOTE

TO ABSENT FRIENDS was conceived some years ago by Edward Fitz-gerald, chairman of the Book-of-the-Month Club who, in an earlier incarnation, was not only editor of *Sport* magazine but the author of books about such athletes as Althea Gibson, Johnny Unitas and Yogi Berra. It took some gentle persuasion to convince Red that this would be a worthy project, but two years ago Red signed the contract. Because his own file of columns was far from complete, and especially since those that appeared in the New York *Herald Tribune* went back to the late forties, fifties, and sixties, before the *Trib* folded and Red went to the *Times,* Joel Cohen spent months going through microfilm copies of the papers picking out the appropriate columns, and supplying us with white-on-black xeroxes, which of course had to be retyped. Red took the entire manuscript—some five hundred columns—up to Martha's Vineyard last summer, picked out the ones he wanted in the book, and edited many of them. He did not want to see the final copy-edited manuscript, only the proofs, but alas he died before this book was in type. Phyllis, his wife, and Terry, his son, went through the proofs with great care, and this is the final version. We are immensely grateful to them, and to Dave Anderson of the *Times,* not only for his introduction but for the enormous help he gave us prior to publication.

INTRODUCTION
BY DAVE ANDERSON

SEVERAL YEARS AGO, Red Smith agreed to deliver the eulogy at the funeral of his long-time friend, Fred Corcoran, the golf impresario. When the Mass ended, Red Smith walked up near the sanctuary and turned to face those assembled in the pews.

"Dying is no big deal," he began. "The least of us will manage that. Living is the trick."

Put that on Red Smith's tombstone. And sprinkle a vodka-and-tonic over his grave. But no lime, thank you.

"No fruit," he would always tell the bartender. "Just the vodka and tonic and the ice."

When he was awarded the 1976 Pulitzer Prize for commentary, he was toasted at a champagne party in the office of A. M. Rosenthal, the *Times*'s executive director.

"I didn't have the champagne," he said later. "I held out for vodka-and-tonic."

His Pulitzer Prize, of course, was about a quarter of a century over-due. More than any other sportswriter, Red Smith made sportswriting important. Unlike many other famous sportswriters before him, he never deserted the sports page.

If being a sportswriter was good enough for Red Smith, it had to be good enough for anybody. Red Smith was, quite simply, the best sportswriter. Put the emphasis on writer.

Of all those who have written sports for a living, nobody else ever had the command of the language, the turn of the phrase, the subtlety of the skewer as he did. And perhaps nobody else ever enjoyed it more. All he ever wanted to be was a "newspaper stiff," as he often identified himself.

"I never wanted to be an actor, never wanted to sell insurance, never wanted to drive a truck," he once said. "All I wanted to do is what I'm doing."

In his thirty-seven years as a New York sports columnist at the *Times* and earlier with the *Herald Tribune*, his columns entertained his readers and nurtured his disciples. Virtually all of today's sportswriters grew up reading Red Smith's column. He was their idol and their inspiration. And their friend. Young sportswriters would flock around him to listen to his stories, to have a drink with him, to hope somehow that some of his talent would rub off on them. And he would sit there over a vodka-and-tonic and entertain them. Educate them really. He was seventy-six when he died, but his memory of all his stories never wavered. Year after year, he would tell those same stories word for word.

His memory was better than a computer's. But he took no credit for it.

"You don't get a memory, you are born with it," he once said. "When I was young, I could commit to memory, almost at one reading, certainly at two, almost anything I enjoyed reading. I knew all 101 verses of the *Rubaiyat*."

His memory helped make him what he was. The mere mention of a sports personality invariably stirred a story, if not two or three.

But perhaps his most important attribute was his integrity. Early in 1980 he was the first sports columnist to call for a boycott by the United States of the Moscow Olympics because of what he branded the Soviet Union's "bloody work" in Afghanistan.

"I was thinking in terms of common decency," he later said. "How can you go over and play games with these people when they're committing a naked act of aggression against a neighboring country? It's simply a matter of withdrawing from Ivan's playground."

Not many people remember that soon after the column appeared President Carter began to talk about a boycott.

In his later years, Red Smith's columns had two favorite targets—Bowie Kuhn, the baseball commissioner, and George M. Steinbrenner III, the Yankees' principal owner. Whenever either was in the news, he could expect to be the subject of a Smith column.

Writing about the split season caused by the 1981 baseball strike, he describes it as having been cut by a "Bowie knife."

When roasting the Yankees' principal owner, he often merely referred to "George III" as if writing about a king.

But his criticism was always professional, not personal. Those he criticized seemed to understand that and accept it. He would say hello to them and they would say hello to him, without any apparent hard feelings. He might not hold a conversation with Kuhn or Steinbrenner beyond a quick hello, but there was always that hello. And that too was part of his perspective on sports.

"I'm just writing about games that little boys play," he often said.

With that perspective, he saw what other writers did not see. He wrote of baseball players "in knickers" and of milers "in their underwear." But of all the spectator sports, horse racing was his favorite.

"There were more stories at a racetrack," he liked to say, "than anywhere else."

At the Kentucky Derby or the Belmont, he often would find a story that others missed. The week before the Derby, while other writers stayed in Louisville, he preferred to visit the horse farm where the Derby favorite had been foaled. He wrote about horses as if they were people. Personally, his favorite sport was fishing. During the Montreal Olympics, he went off to northern Quebec for trout.

"Leaving the Olympics for a fishing trip might not work for anybody else," he said with a smile, "but it works for me."

Two days later, he returned with a fishing column that his readers probably appreciated more than another column about an Olympic event. Not that he deserted the big events often. Throughout his career, he was always where he should be—at the World Series, the Super Bowl, the big fights, the big horse races. But he had to miss the 1979 World Series to travel to South Africa for a heavyweight championship fight.

"I'd never covered a fight in Africa before," he explained later. "I've been to all the continents now."

He was seventy-four then. Some people of seventy-four won't go around the block but Red Smith went to Africa to add another continent to his list. Another column, too. In his later years, he naturally emerged as the dean of his profession. But he was never comfortable in that role. When he arrived in Manila for the Ali-Frazier heavyweight title fight there in 1975, he thought his hotel room was a little small, until he realized that it connected to the sitting room of a suite.

"It's nice," he grumbled, "but I hate the dean treatment."

On the long flight across the Pacific to Manila, another sportswriter had slept for several hours and now was strolling brightly about the cabin. Looking up with eyes bleary from having been unable to sleep on a plane, Red Smith glared with envy.

"Look at him," he said of the sportswriter who had slept. "He's like Amelia Earhart: you take off and you never hear from him again."

As colleagues for a decade on the *Times,* we often checked with each other to avoid writing about the same subject. Only once was there a mix-up. Looking ahead to a Tuesday column a few years ago, I requested a Monday working-press ticket to the Westminster Dog Show at Madison Square Garden, but the next day Red asked for a Tuesday ticket.

"The ticket's no problem," Red was told, "but I think Dave's going to do a dog-show column for Tuesday's paper."

Red backed off. Two consecutive columns on the dog show, he knew, would be overkill. But just as I wasn't aware that Red had been thinking about a dog-show column, Red wasn't aware that I had decided, instead, to write a hockey column for Tuesday's paper. Tuesday morning Red was having breakfast with a friend, who happened to ask him something about which many people had wondered.

"How do you know," the friend asked, "what the other guy is writing about?"

"No problem," Red said. "We check with each other, or the office tells us. Like today, I know that Dave is writing about the dog show. Here, let me show you."

He had opened to the sports page. When he discovered I had written a hockey column, his reaction was true to the vocabulary of a dog show.

Every so often, Red Smith would find himself well-stocked with column subjects. But more often than not, he would wait until the day he had to write to decide what he would write about.

"God is good," he would say. "God will provide."

At the end, God indeed was good to him. Red Smith never thought about retiring. During a brief illness in 1980 a friend suggested that maybe he should think about retiring, about not writing anymore.

"No, never," Red Smith said. "If I don't write, I'll die."

As it turned out, he wrote until he died. His last column appeared in the *Times* four days before his death of heart failure on January 15, 1982, a haunting flashback on his role as a sports columnist. In retrospect, that last column was virtually his own obituary.

"I want to go like Granny Rice did," he often said, referring to the famous sports columnist of another generation who was his friend. "I just want to fall into my typewriter."

Red Smith was never quite as famous as some of the athletes he wrote about, but the famous ones respected him as the best sports columnist. Muhammad Ali would look out over a gathering of sportswriters and see this little white-haired man and call, "Red Smith, you wrote about me at the Rome Olympics in 1960 and you're still writing about me; maybe you are the greatest." The day that Reggie Jackson's candy bar appeared, the slugger noticed Red Smith across the Yankees' locker room.

"Hey, Red," he called with a grin, "you ever have a pen named for you?"

Red Smith laughed and shook his head. But the next time he visited Yankee Stadium, he strolled over to Reggie Jackson's locker. He reached into his briefcase and took out one of those fat pens.

"Remember when you asked me the other day if I ever had a pen named for me?" he said. "Here it is, the Big Red."

His peers treated Red Smith as if he were a patron saint. He and Mo Siegel, then a sports columnist with the *Washington Star*, once were leaving the Texas Stadium press box when a few sportswriters began heckling them good-naturedly.

"Leave us alone," Mo Siegel said, putting an arm around Red Smith, "don't you guys know that between us, we've won one Pulitzer Prize?"

So if you've enjoyed Red Smith through the years, say a prayer for him. Not that he needs it. Toast him, too. Preferably with a vodka-and-tonic. But no lime, thank you.

FOREWORD

PETE ROSE, the ball player, translates anything he can into baseball terms. Ask when he was born and he will tell you, "The year of DiMaggio's streak," meaning 1941, when Joe DiMaggio hit safely in fifty-six consecutive games.

"How long have you been writing?" Pete asked me.

"Well," I said, "I got my first regular job on a newspaper in 1927."

"The year Babe Ruth hit sixty home runs," he said.

Although I never won a plaque for arithmetic, my years as a newspaper stiff seem to count up to more than half a century, time enough to get around and about and meet some interesting people. If I have had the good fortune to know more than some do, that is not evidence of my irresistible charm. It goes with the territory.

My job has taken me around the world and put me in contact with thousands of individuals. They have varied widely as to size, shape, color, creed and previous condition of servitude but virtually all have had one quality in common—they have been men and women of action. What they did commanded attention and when they died their deaths touched many.

This book introduces some of them. Most of these were friends of mine; some were among my dearest friends.

I hope I avoided mawkishness writing about them but if emotion sometimes tugged at the typewriter, I suppose it couldn't be helped.

The reader will find many described by adjectives like "sweet" or "great." This may be unfortunately repetitious but it is also true. I have never subscribed to the *de mortuis nil nisi bonum* school. Dr. Sam Johnson, noting discrepancies between the character or behavior of the living man and the sentiments graven on his tombstone, observed that "in lapidary inscriptions a man is not upon oath." Nevertheless, I have tried to level. If I write that somebody was a great guy, that's how I found him.

Rereading these pieces, I find frequent mention of the gift of laughter. I suppose that is because the memories I treasure most warmly have to do with happy occasions, days and nights enriched by laughter. I suspect that I have enjoyed such days and nights more often than some do in other jobs, and if that is so I am grateful. Maybe the world I have traveled is a merrier world than some others.

I recall an interview with Primo Carnera long after that snaggle-toothed ogre had turned the heavyweight boxing championship over to Max Baer and gone home to Italy. Now he was back on these shores performing as a professional wrestler. I asked him to relive for me some of his happiest memories of the days of his ascendancy.

He tried, but shook his head in defeat.

"There were so many money," he said, "so many fun."

RED SMITH
Martha's Vineyard
September 1981

A FOOTNOTE TO THE FOREWORD

HERE IT IS, *then, the way he assembled it, tossing columns into a box almost as they came to hand. Where there were several concerning the same absent friend he tried to keep those together, but otherwise neglected sequence. Where stories overlapped, he left them alone.*

In the fall of 1973, when we sat on Martha's Vineyard warming our vacation evenings by the fire and going through columns for Strawberries in the Wintertime, *he made some effort to polish and arrange them. After all, he said, a columnist on deadline is likely to repeat explanations or useful phrases in a number of newspaper pieces without realizing it, or heeding. Between hard covers, he cares about making them neat.*

Last summer at the Vineyard, when he was reading through these stories—pulled from the collected years of clippings—he was not on vacation and was feeling very weary. If he gave less attention to this finished volume than to the last, it doesn't matter. What shows is his special way of seeing people, his true affection for his multifarious friends, and his ability to convey it all so vividly to us.

PHYLLIS W. SMITH (*Mrs. Walter*)

CONTENTS

T O

ABSENT FRIENDS

SOCIETY KID

SOCIETY KID HOGAN was hurrying through the Illinois Central pedestrian tunnel under Michigan Avenue on June 9, 1930, when a man in the crowd put a gun to the head of Jake Lingle, a grafting crime reporter, and it went *blooie*.

The Kid kept right on walking.

"Why?" the Law asked him later.

"The last train was leaving for the racetrack," he said reasonably.

"Did you see the killer?" they asked.

"Sure."

"Could you identify him?"

The Kid drew a hand across the knot in his flashy necktie.

"Only up to here," he said.

The Kid was born Salvatore de Lorenzo in Palermo, Italy. He boxed as a lightweight, if you could call it boxing, and Hogan was his nom de guerre. Chances are it was Damon Runyon who hung the "Society Kid" tag on him, for he was a snappy dresser and a blithe spirit, well-known and universally liked in the joints where café society gathered in Prohibition days.

Above all, he was a horse player. It was at the races that he met Runyon, who knew just about everybody in the fight mob and around the horse parks. Wherever you saw Damon, in New York or Chicago or Philly or L.A., there'd be these lobbygows around him—Frisco Legs, Swifty Morgan, Camden Moishe, Society Kid.

Withdrawn and rather dour himself, Runyon could sit all night with these guys, saying little but listening a lot, and later on they would be gratified to recognize themselves in his short stories—even if the fictional character was by no means an exact image and likeness.

The Kid was a special favorite of Runyon's and he did a few bits in films based on Runyon's stories. For that matter, he was a favorite with many. He got around. There was a night, for instance, when somebody tossed a bon voyage party in either the Stork or "21" for Bing Crosby, who was going abroad to make a picture. Society Kid was there, naturally.

He was almost always on hand for a championship fight or a big race or a World Series. One year he arrived in Louisville for the Kentucky Derby with no hotel reservation. He had $400 in the kick.

He got a furnished room within walking distance of Churchill Downs, a pleasant and comfortable room, he said, in the home of a motherly old doll. She talked a lot, but that didn't bother the Kid, who didn't plan to spend his waking hours there.

About Thursday of Derby Week he showed up in the clubhouse restaurant with a sad tale. Seems he'd waked about noon and couldn't find his roll. He could hear his landlady somewhere about the house humming a happy tune. When he got downstairs he told her he'd been clipped for $400. Said he'd had it when he came in last night and couldn't find it now.

The shock and distress of his hostess was touching to see. That such a thing could happen in her house! That any one could be so shamelessly, so selfishly, so—so downright dishonest! Her sweet old face brimmed with compassion for Mr. Hogan, such a quiet, polite guest.

After a moment, however, her natural cheerfulness reasserted itself. After all, she pointed out, this was Derby time. "And at Derby time in Louisville," she said brightly, "everybody steals from everybody else."

"I am practically sure," the Kid said, telling about it, "that the old doll rolled me. But I don't have the guts to put the finger on her."

WORLD'S GREATEST SALOONKEEPER

THIS IS a holiday greeting to a friend who is spending Christmas in University Hospital, although he is not the university type. His name is Toots Shor. He is the greatest saloonkeeper in the world and for more than forty years he has been a major figure in sports in the Big Apple, friend and confessor and counsel to athletes, confidant of the sports hierarchy, fan, authority, raconteur. He ought to be designated a national landmark.

These days when he is on his feet he holds forth in Thirty-third Street across from Madison Square Garden in a joint that caters to the hit-and-run crowds attending games in the Garden. In a slightly earlier day, his joint, especially the brick house at 51 West Fifty-first Street, was the mother lodge. Attendance was practically compulsory. If you wanted to see anybody, you went there, and if the guy you sought had stepped out for a moment, you could settle for Ernest Hemingway or Chief Justice Earl Warren or Yogi Berra or Paul Draper or Edward Bennett Williams or Gene Fowler or Billy Conn or Frank Sinatra or Pat O'Brien or Robert Sherwood or Jackie Gleason or Abe Attell.

There never was a gathering place like it and it seems improbable there will ever be another. It wasn't necessarily the handsomest restaurant on the block and the cuisine never moved Craig Claiborne to ecstasy, but it was almost surely the most widely known saloon on earth. It was what it was for a single reason—Toots. It was an extension of the proprietor's personality: loud, loyal, laughing, sentimental, boisterous, generous, considerate and dead on the level.

Toots made the place and the place made him a celebrity, although he never knew he was one. In his eyes he was and is a saloonkeeper, and he has worked hard at it. In health, he was always there, at lunchtime, dinnertime and closing time. He made all the ball games, all the fights, all the black-tie functions like the Baseball Writers' dinner, but when they were over and the crowds went on to Shor's, they found the proprietor waiting for them.

Chances were he'd be waiting to insult them. In Shor's, all men were equal, which is to say everybody was a crumb-bum. The celebrated, accustomed to obsequious bowing and scraping, encountered a different reception in the brick house. There was the night Charles Chaplin was annoyed by an invitation to wait in line for a table.

"It'll be about a half-hour, Charlie," Toots bawled. "Be funny for the folks."

Chances are Toots never met a dignitary he respected and admired more than he respected and admired Owney Madden, one of his first bosses in New York. In Prohibition days, speakeasies were run by the mob and Toots worked in several of the joints owned by Madden and Big Frenchy La Mange. Later, when Toots was running Billy LaHiff's Tavern, he had a visit from Eddie Mead, manager of Henry Armstrong, who held the featherweight, lightweight and welterweight titles. Mead was feuding with Mike Jacobs. In fact, he got so furious at the promoter that he paid him $20,000 that he owed him because it was beneath him to be indebted to such a creep.

The trouble was, he told Toots, half the money belonged to Armstrong. "So now I've lost my fighter," Mead said. Toots dashed off a telegram to Madden. "Need ten," the wire read. "Need it now."

In an hour or so a messenger arrived with an envelope, which Toots handed to Mead unopened. Inside were ten big ones. "You didn't have to do that, Mr. Mead," Armstrong said when the manager paid him off. "I'd never leave you."

No doubt Mead eventually paid Toots back and he repaid Madden, but to tell the truth, it never occurred to me to ask.

Toots will argue with anybody, preferably when the other guy is an authority on the topic under discussion.

"On one point we disagree," he was told by Georges Carpentier, the old light-heavyweight champion from France whose classic encounter with Jack Dempsey drew boxing's first million-dollar gate. "You always say Jimmy McLarnin and Billy Conn were great fighters."

"They were great fighters!" Toots insisted.

Carpentier shook his head. "No. A man who cannot punch has no charm."

Not everybody in this world or this town is Toots's friend, but in his seventy-odd years he has ruled out only two men as ineligible for the role. One was Sherman Billingsley, who was a captain in the mob before he became proprietor of the Stork Club. The other was a man in Philadelphia named Paul Harron. Both had cost him jobs and, Toots believes, had tried to make sure he wouldn't get another.

"One word I can't stand," Toots said many years later, "is *hate*. I don't hate anybody and I don't use the word. I say dislike, and I've disliked a few guys but not many.

"Once my daughter, Kerry, was sick, in a coma. I prayed to God. I told God, 'If this little girl gets better, I'll never dislike anybody again in my life—except two guys.' "

Desperate though he was, he still had to level.

TOOTS'S GUYS WERE WAITING

TOOTS SHOR wept for so many guys we can all spare a tear for him now. Though it is not quite true that if you told him, "Chester A. Arthur is dead," he would break down sobbing, it is true that his capacity for affection was limitless and his sentimentality unabashed. His family and friends were his life. "If God told me I could have anything and do anything I wanted in life," he often said, "I would say I wanted to be a saloonkeeper, because where else could I make the friends I've got?"

Grantland Rice was deeply touched when on his seventieth birthday he received seventy red roses from Toots Shor. "That was generous and considerate of you," Toots was told. "You don't know how Granny appreciated it." The fat paw made a brush-off gesture. "Whisky," Toots said. "That's all you need in this world—whisky and heart."

Toots loved Billy Conn, who stayed in the Shors' duplex apartment the last night or so before his second fight with Joe Louis. It was common knowledge that when Louis knocked Conn out in the eighth round it cost Toots a gang of dollars but he never would tell how much he had bet. "I lost my heart," he said when pressed.

When Toots was out of action after running Billy LaHiff's Tavern, Grantland Rice was one who lent him walking-around money. Nobody but the two of them ever knew whether it was $5 or $500 or $5,000. When Toots got rolling in the brick house at 51 West Fifty-first Street, he went around paying off loans.

"How much do I owe you?" he asked, dropping into Granny's office.

"You owe me?" Granny said. "You owe me nothing."

"I know what it is," Toots said, counting out the bills, "and listen, you creep, this is a compliment. I saved you till last."

"Toots lives surrounded by celebrities," said Bill Veeck when he was operating the Cleveland Indians, or maybe it was when he owned the St. Louis Browns or Chicago White Sox for the first time. "What I don't forget is that when I was a busher in Milwaukee he treated me just the same as now when I'm in the majors—like a bum."

When his Indians were winning the 1948 World Series, Veeck joined a group at a table in the Cleveland press headquarters. Toots's greeting to his host was characteristic.

"Ya creepy bum, ya! You can't buy me a drink. Take this."

He tossed a $100 bill on the table.

Smiling gently, Veeck tore the bill into tiny pieces and dropped them in Toots's drink.

"Jiminy crickets!" Toots said. "How rich can a guy get?"

He fished the wet green shreds from his glass and tucked them carefully away in a pocket. Nobody was offended. Toots had been topped, but he would get his friend the next time.

In the late 1940s Joe Page, the relief pitcher, was a towering figure with the Yankees. During the season or in the World Series, he was the one the manager—Bucky Harris and then Casey Stengel—turned to when trouble threatened, and there was a conscious air of majesty about him when he strode in from the bullpen.

In 1950 the Yankees won another pennant but Page had a poor year. In the four-game World Series with the Phillies, Casey used Tom Ferrick the first time he needed a relief pitcher and in the fourth game he called in Allie Reynolds to wrap up the final victory. Page took no part in the Series, and had no stomach for the team's victory party afterward. That evening Toots was sitting with a friend in the dining room when a waiter told the boss that Page had just come into the bar alone. "Excuse me," Toots said, and hastened out.

A little while later the waiter came back smiling. "The boss gave him a hero's welcome," he reported.

It is comforting to believe that Toots himself got a hero's welcome last Sunday midnight when he stepped out of here to join his old gang. So many of them were waiting for him—Granny Rice, Frank Graham, Bill Corum, Bob Considine, Mark Hellinger, Gene Fowler, Harry Truman, Bob Hannegan, General Rosy O'Donnell. They had gone ahead of him and left him desperately lonesome.

Toots was too far gone to know it, but one of his best customers stepped out just ahead of him. Lillian Graham, Frank's widow, was buried last week. She was eighty-seven, and seven years ago her son, Frank Jr., had a story to tell. Encountered at Toots's bar—where else?—Frankie told of taping a television show with Bud Leavitt of the *Bangor News*. (Frank is a freelance writer living in Maine.)

"I'll be watching this show from home on Saturday night," Frank told Leavitt, "because it's my mother's eightieth birthday and we're having a family party."

They watched the show and at the end Bud Leavitt said, "Thank you, Frank Graham, Jr., and by the way, today is the eightieth birthday of Frank's mother. So happy birthday to you, Lillian Graham."

Listening, Lillian clutched her head. "On the air!" she said. "I'll lose my driver's license!"

Not for nothing had she been married to a sportswriter all those years. On her license she was using her baseball age, seventy-seven.

A GUY WHO MADE MISTAKES

THERE ARE probably a lot of stories that could be told about Jake Powell by people who knew him better. Here there is only one, which may help explain a couple of things. That is, it may furnish a little insight into the nature of a guy who never knew fear and never knew what was good for him, a guy who always acted on impulse and was wrong more often than not.

In the end, he was tragically wrong, of course. He killed himself. Jake Powell, who used to play the outfield for the Yankees and the Senators and any number of minor league clubs, got himself messed up the other day and gave up and shot himself. He didn't slip off and lock himself in a room and turn on the gas. He shot himself twice, once in the chest and then in the head, in a police station in Washington, D.C., with the cops looking on.

Now, as to that story. When Jake was playing ball in the American League a radio broadcaster grabbed him for one of those offhand, unrehearsed dugout interviews just before a game in Comiskey Park in Chicago. Answering questions without thinking, Powell made a thoughtless remark that offended thousands of Negroes.

A storm ensued. The American League office in Chicago was flooded with protests. There was talk of a boycott against any park where Powell might be playing. Jake had been wrong as wrong could be.

Well, the next time Powell got to New York he went up to the top end of Harlem. He went alone, after dark. He worked down from north to south, stopping in every saloon he came across.

In each he introduced himself. He said he was Jake Powell and he said that he had made a foolish mistake and that he was sorry. Then he ordered drinks for the crowd and moved on to the next joint.

He did that by himself, on his own initiative, after dark, in a section where he had reason to believe feelings ran high against him.

That's one story about Jake Powell. The only story here.

AFTER FIFTY YEARS

ON MARCH 31, 1931, a farmer near the village of Bazaar, Kansas, looked up from his plowing when he heard the motor of a transport plane faltering. Then he broke into a run. Within hours, headlines shouted the news across the land: "KNUTE ROCKNE KILLED IN CRASH."

For a few days the papers were full of it—obituaries, tributes, feature stories, some painfully sentimental like the one about the Atlanta newsboy shouting the news to passing crowds while tears rolled down his face. Then other and timelier matters took precedence, and you might have expected that Rockne would have been forgotten, as were the names of the seven who died with him.

After twenty-five years, that hasn't begun to happen. The name of Rockne is recognized as readily today as in 1930, when his last Notre Dame football team was barreling over Southern Methodist, and Navy, Pittsburgh and Pennsylvania, Army and Southern California to the national championship. His photograph would be known instantly, with the small, sharp blue eyes and the bent and flattened nose.

The nose, incidentally, had been remodeled by a baseball bat, and twelve-year-old Knute exhibited it triumphantly at home to parents who had forbidden him to play football. "You think football is rough," he told them, "look what I got in baseball."

This broke down parental objections to football, and when Rock was an end and captain of the Notre Dame team his mother went the whole way and attended a game against South Dakota. Rock had a spectacular day and his mother was impressed.

"Who," she asked, "was that boy who turned the cartwheel? He was wonderful." Her son never again was able to feel any special warmth for cheerleaders.

Knute Rockne was a great football coach, but there have been many.

He was a great man who happened to choose football as a career. It is likely that he would have had exceptional success in almost any other field, for he had exceptional qualities—an agile and original and keenly analytical mind, a quick wit, one of those incredibly retentive memories, and a tremendous gift for influencing people. He could address an assembly of middle-aged, pot-bellied automobile salesmen —this is eyewitness testimony—and, pretending this was a football dressing room, lift them shouting out of their chairs with an old-style fight talk. He would soar to a screaming crescendo and break it off there without warning, looking on mischievously while abashed listeners discovered that they were on their feet.

Tom Conley, captain of Rock's last team, and Herb Jones, the business manager of athletics who was Rock's secretary, spoke at a breakfast following a memorial mass at Notre Dame. If they said that in his forty-three years Rock did as much as any man to influence American youth, personally, and through the men he sent out across the country as coaches and through the legends still told about him, then they did not exaggerate. After fifty years, his influence has not ended.

BILL CANE AND GAYLE TALBOT

WILLIAM HENRY CANE, the man who made the Hambletonian, died at eighty-one in Miami Beach. Bill Cane was a racing official in New Jersey, New York and Michigan; a track operator and promoter; a breeder, owner and driver of harness horses; an owner of thoroughbreds; a bicycle rider and fight promoter and iceboat racer; and the construction man who built Boyle's Thirty Acres for the Dempsey-Carpentier fight of 1921.

He was one of the men who pioneered night harness racing in New York, and when he was seventy-five he leased the Empire City track to convert it into Yonkers Raceway. When he was close to eighty he sank a chunk in a great, crumbling homestead on a hilltop outside Goshen, New York, tore it apart and restored it as his residence. He was then a newlywed, for the second time.

When Yonkers was being readied for its first meeting, Bill Cane drove past a big cemetery in the neighborhood, and his eyes gleamed. "Customers," he said. "They still vote, so why can't they bet?" He was not a man who stood in awe of death.

Gayle Talbot, sportswriter for the Associated Press, loved life and left it too soon. He had suffered a severe heart attack last summer and another in Florida this spring when, perhaps, he should not have been pounding the sports beat, but he was a man accustomed to moving fast.

Several springs ago in Miami, Gayle sat with two companions at a bar. After a while the others became aware that Gayle's stool was unoccupied, but they paid no special heed, assuming he'd stepped into the washroom and would return. When he didn't come back they searched, couldn't find him, and walked back to their hotel.

Next day there was a story in the paper by Gayle Talbot. The dateline was Caracas, Venezuela.

ED BURNS OF THE *TRIB*

ED BURNS of the *Chicago Tribune* probably was the only sports reporter in America who was prodded into the craft by the muzzle of a sawed-off shotgun. This was a piece of rare good fortune for the sportswriting field, which he ornamented thereafter with a large, spherical silhouette and a delicate wit.

In the Prohibition Era of gang warfare in Chicago, Ed worked on the news side covering criminal courts or some such beat that threw him into contact with some of the city's most redoubtable marksmen. A conscientious reporter and a man of wide friendliness, he became personally acquainted with commanders, lieutenants and foot soldiers of the underworld's several clashing forces.

A character prominent in Al Capone's social circle, or perhaps Bugsy Moran's, fell into step with Ed one day as the newspaperman went billowing down Michigan Avenue. When their ways diverged, the character was reluctant to depart; for a considerable time he held Mr. Burns in conversation.

Next day Ed encountered a member of a rival faction who remarked, "You bumped into Big Tony yesterday, didn't you? Did you happen to notice a car following you along the curb?" Ed hadn't.

"Some of us boys were in it," the man said. "We were gonna take care of Big Tony but we didn't leave him have it because you were in line."

Five minutes later Ed was telling his managing editor, "I have come to the conclusion that sportswriting is my true metier."

It was, too. From that time on, Ed's agile typewriter brightened the paper's fun-and-games department, and if occasionally there were threats of violence from some ball player over what the athlete deemed an excess of candor, Mr. Burns remained undisturbed. A mere fungo stick held no terrors for a man with his early training.

He enjoyed the sports beat, though he was no hero-worshipper enshrining demigods on pedestals of prose. He could see deeper than a sweat shirt and, having measured an athlete's talents accurately, could sum up his judgment succinctly.

"What kind of club have the Cubs this year?" he was asked one spring during training exercises on the Pacific Coast.

"They're all nice boys," he said. "Nicest bunch of kids you ever met. They faint at the sight of blood."

Ed liked most people and they liked him, but he had no patience with professionals who came complaining when he'd written the truth about them, whining, "You're taking away my bread and butter." "How do they think I earn my bread and butter?" he would snort.

He needed more bread and butter than the ordinary infielder, whom he outweighed by one hundred pounds or so.

A Hoosier by birth, Ed was absentee owner of some rich bottomland in Indiana. For a man whose days and nights were lived in sports arenas, his choice of a crop was appropriate. He had the farm planted to peanuts.

Corpulent and sedentary, he liked his affairs to run smoothly in accustomed grooves. They didn't always, though. Traveling with the White Sox, he was boarding a train for Philadelphia when he heard himself paged in Washington's Union Station. It was a telephone call from his office warning him not to set foot in Pennsylvania or even to ride a train through the state, but to catch a nonstop plane to New York and await the team there.

It seemed J. David Stern, publisher of the *Philadelphia Record,* was suing the *Tribune*'s Colonel Robert McCormick for libel and McCormick had been advised not to accept service in Pennsylvania or permit anybody connected with the paper to risk encounter with a process server in the state.

For something like a year, Pennsylvania was off-limits to Ed Burns and his colleagues. When the Cubs or White Sox played in Philadelphia or Pittsburgh, the *Tribune* arranged for coverage by local correspondents. Traveling between Chicago and the Atlantic seaboard, Ed had to skirt Pennsylvania, which is a large state to get around, and he was not built for broken-field maneuvers.

Taking a train from Chicago to New York, Ed had to route himself by way of Canada. If he traveled by air the plane must make no scheduled stops in Pennsylvania. The order applied to all employees of the paper, but Ed was the most severely inconvenienced. A bachelor, he had a lady-love in Philadelphia.

When Dave Stern heard of this he was touched and promised safe convoy to Ed Burns, in the interests of romance. Ed didn't take advantage of the offer. Though he had been a sailor in World War I, valorous in defense of the Brooklyn Navy Yard, he was a good soldier to the end.

JOE H. PALMER

JOE PALMER made fun of all games that didn't employ horses but he liked football, when Kentucky or Michigan was winning. Way back when Kentucky used to go outside Pennsylvania for large students, Joe was an undergraduate and then a teacher of English courses there. Subsequently he taught at Michigan while working for his doctorate.

It must have been something to be in his classes, for he had a deep and affectionate respect for the language and a pure taste, and sacred cows moved him irresistibly to laughter, in literature as in a horse park. Yet for all the fun they must have had, there is evidence that he inspired a respect that endured among his students.

Years after Shipwreck Kelly's football days at Kentucky, when he was a big wheel in New York, former owner of the football Dodgers, a figure of some prominence in the Long Island social set, he knocked politely on the Palmer door in Malverne, Long Island.

"Is Professor Palmer in?" he inquired in the manner of a small boy asking for Mr. Chips.

There was another day when Joe was a placing judge at Keeneland in Lexington, his and the university's hometown. The customers dissented from a decision at the wire and undertook to recoup their losses out of the judges' hides. A task force was scaling the judges' stand, which in those precamera days stood open and undefended at the rail, when Joe recognized a former pupil as the leader.

"Bull," he snapped.

"Y-yes, sir, Mr. Palmer."

"Get down outta there."

"Y-yes, sir," Bull said, and the riot was quelled.

It was fun to tell people that Joe was the only Ph.D. writing horse racing in America, but that wasn't literally true. He had completed his work for a doctorate when a choice was presented: Should he write a thesis for the degree or write horses for the *Blood-Horse*? He made the only decision possible for one who had grown up on the banks of Elkhorn Creek.

It can be stated only as one man's opinion, yet unquestionably it is shared by thousands, that Joe Palmer could write better than anybody else in the world whose work appeared in newspapers. And that may be limiting the field too narrowly. In the field of racing, which he preferred, there never was another in his time or before to compare with him.

He knew his subject profoundly, he was scholarly without stuffiness, and he wrote as he talked, with wit and urbanity and grace and sure confidence. Years before we met, I was reading his stuff in the *Blood-Horse* aloud to my wife, and after he came to New York his column made Monday the brightest day of the week on the *Herald Tribune* sports pages.

"Did you read Palmer today?" was a question heard weekly, not only among admiring professionals who write for a living, not only among the racing crowd where he was loved and respected, but also among many whose interest lay in neither field but rather in the pure pleasure of reading.

Joe loved an argument and reveled in joyous contention, in his column and in person. He sank editorial barbs into the race crowd that would have had any other newspaperman burned in effigy, but the people Joe skewered didn't resent him because (*a*) he knew what he was talking about and (*b*) they appreciated his genuine enthusiasm for their sport.

His supple mind raced in an argument. After a program of amateur boxing at Saratoga one evening, Joe was holding forth on the fine old sport of cock-fighting. Just for the fun of stirring him up, objections to the pastime were raised. Indignantly, he inquired what was wrong with chicken-fighting.

"It's cruel. It's inhuman."

"Inhuman?" Joe shouted. "Of course it's inhuman. And that stuff we saw tonight—that's unchicken."

"You big stiff," I have told him enviously, "if you'd just write a poor column, just once. The only consolation is you don't have to do it every day."

But all along there was a haunting suspicion that if he did write a column every day, he'd be the best every day.

Professionally there will not be another like him. Personally, he was one of the best and dearest friends a man could have. We came to New York almost together and have worked and played and wrangled together ever since. There was a friendship that could have ended only one way. As it did yesterday.

THE LIFE JOE LOVED

THIS IS kind of a personal thing, if you don't mind. There was a lunch in the city which was still going on when the last race special started for Belmont Park; and a man said the quickest route for a late starter was the subway to Jamaica and a taxi from there. Thus it happened that the cab of Mr. Louis Steinberg was engaged at 179th Street and Hillside Avenue in Jamaica.

"Do you know anything good?" Mr. Steinberg asked.

"No. I'm only going out because they're running a race for a friend of mine who died last fall."

"That's too bad," Mr. Steinberg said. "Friend of yours?"

"Joe Palmer, who wrote racing for the *Herald Tribune*. They're calling it the Joe H. Palmer Handicap. Sixth race."

"Sixth race," Mr. Steinberg said. "Tom Fool, eh?"

There was a strong feeling that Joe Palmer would have liked this. To Joe, a horse race was a sporting event, an athletic contest among horses, but he didn't believe in forcing his own point of view on others. He felt strongly that it was a proper thing for taxi drivers to go to the races and bet their money on Tom Fool to win the sixth race, no matter what it might be called, because if they didn't go and bet that would be the end of racing and of the life Joe loved.

Mr. Steinberg, driving with his left hand, picked a paper off the seat alongside him. It was the *Morning Telegraph*, opened to the last page of the Belmont past performances.

"When I find something real good," he explained, "I try to get in for the seventh or eighth race. I can't make the sixth, too early for me."

"I think Tom Fool will win the sixth," it was suggested, "but he won't pay much. Not enough to justify parking the cab and losing a couple of fares."

"No," Mr. Steinberg said, "I can't make the sixth. But this Tom Fool, what a record they got for him in here! Won five of his last seven and second the other two. This Joe Palmer, he wrote for the *Herald Tribune*."

"Better than anybody else in the world."

"He was a wonderful writer," Mr. Steinberg said. "I read him when somebody left a paper in my cab. Wonderful writer."

"He was a wonderful guy."

"Must've been," Mr. Steinberg said, pulling into the Belmont gate. "Well, do yourself a lot of good."

Inside the park was a normal midweek crowd. As far as the sixth race was concerned, it held two major points of interest for the bulk of the 24,307 present: Who would win? What would he pay?

This would have been all right with Joe. What else, he would ask, should a man wish to know about a race? Yet there were some present for whom the race had another interest.

There were dozens of these present, scores, hundreds—trainers, owners, jockeys, track officials, writers, Pinkertons, barkeeps, ushers, attendants—guy and dolls who were Joe Palmer's friends because they enjoyed him and he enjoyed being with them.

It was one of those days, overcast but pleasantly warm and not too sultry, when just being at the races was pure pleasure. It was a day for the sort of sport that Joe conceived racing to be, a sport of grace and charm and comfort and leisure. "I am no authority on grace and charm," Joe used to say, "but with respect to comfort and leisure I bow to no man."

Joe's race was a six-furlong athletic contest among seven horses, and the athlete Tom Fool, carrying 130 pounds and giving from nine to twenty-five pounds to the others, ran off by himself in the stretch. Ted Atkinson eased him approaching the wire, so that his margin was only a length and a half when it might have been five.

It couldn't have been done more appropriately. Joe Palmer admired Tom Fool last year when the horse was a three-year-old, and Tom Fool's trainer, John Gaver, was one of Joe's best friends. It was Gaver who hunted Joe down in Kentucky years ago, found him on a fishing trip, and persuaded him to come to New York.

Joe would have enjoyed the sixth race and he would have approved the name given the fifth, which was called The Anecdote, because anecdotes were Joe's stock in trade. He could have told one about the winner of the first race, a horse named Blue Charger, owned by Fred B. Hicks.

Seems Mr. Hicks had two taxis operating out of Jamaica. He sold one cab and bought a horse named Flying Tuck, which so encouraged him by taking small pieces of small purses that he sold the other hack and bought Blue Charger. Which may explain why other hackies in that region carry form sheets in their cabs.

JOE PALMER'S FRIENDS

IN THE dining room at Belmont, Joe Palmer's friends were swapping stories about him. It seemed only a little while ago that Joe was there, holding up his end of the conversation to say the very least, but the feature race this day was a handicap named in his memory, and it was not the first or the second or the third so titled. If figures matter, it will be five years, come Halloween, since the *Herald Tribune's* wonderful racing writer left an unfinished column in his typewriter.

"It keeps happening all the time," one fellow was saying, "that something comes around the track and I think, 'What a shame Joe isn't here to write about that.' For instance, I guess the two forms of animal life that he loathed most were state racing stewards and people who watered down whisky.

"Well, since he died there's been a man around who lost his license for cutting the whisky he served, and he was also a state steward. If Joe had been around to work him over—"

"That reminds me," another began, and while he told a story the others waited, with no special patience, to get in one of their own. As the day wore on, truth did not necessarily prevail, which would have been all right with Joe Palmer.

"This department," Joe wrote, "had a reputation for unswerving truthfulness until approximately the age of seven, and would no doubt have it still except for leaving Kentucky temporarily at that age. But since then various things have happened, and now a certain admiration is felt for a well-told falsehood. This is wrong, of course, but there you are."

Belmont is a pleasure place and this was a pleasant, uncrowded day. Some millions were spent on physical improvements since last season, but the changes hardly show. To the casual eye this old cavalry post looks just about as it did when Joe temporarily shared Greentree Cottage there with John Gaver and would occasionally watch the morning works before bedtime.

Actually, the most noticeable change isn't on the course at all, but on Creedmoor, the big mental hospital beyond the far turn. There've been additions there, a skyscraper construction that gives the patients an unimpeded view of all the racing, even that on the Widener Chute. Almost certainly, Joe would have approved.

Conn McCreary dropped by to chat. He was one of Joe's favorite guys, though they were relentless adversaries at poker. The broken leg Conn suffered this summer when a horse banged him against the starting gate has just about repaired itself.

Joe DiMaggio, an infrequent visitor, was in a box with friends, taking a somewhat more modest profit than he used to get from an afternoon in Yankee Stadium. "I only wish," he said, "that I'd do as well as I know the Yankees are doing."

At that moment the Yankees were playing the White Sox but there had been no report as to the score. They won, of course.

Sammy Renick, the little man who does television at the races, said he and DiMaggio had just paid a call to the jockeys' quarters.

"I took Joe in there a couple of years ago," Sammy said, "and one of the jocks looked up and said, 'Here comes God.' Today when he walked in, one of 'em said, 'Here comes God—with Renick.' Do you think that moves Joe up, or back?"

"A man who spends his life poking around racetracks," Joe Palmer wrote, "gets in addition to a view of human nature which is at once more tolerant and less rosy than any warmly endorsed by the clergy, a rather unreasonable fondness for certain places. I say unreasonable, because it does not seem to be dependent upon architectural or horticultural attractiveness, on setting, on comfort, or even on the quality or cleanliness of the racing at these places."

There were five fillies and mares in the Joe Palmer Handicap, all connected with somebody who had been Joe's friend. Jimmy Jones had two from Calumet Farm, just down the Versailles Pike from Joe's home in Lexington, Kentucky. These were Amoret and Beyond.

Attica was running in the silks of Kentucky's Hal Price Headley, and George B. Widener, president of Belmont in Joe's time, had Rare Treat. Jack Skirvin saddled the other, named Gay Life.

"On Joe's account," a man said, frowning on past performances, "I've got to bet Gay Life. I can't find any excuse for it here, though, and there are some awful nasty comments about his races."

The comments were justified. Gay Life ran out of speed early.

Attica and Rare Treat ran Amoret down in the stretch and raced to a rousing finish, with Rare Treat the winner in a photo.

Joe's friends tore up their tickets and went downstairs for a bourbon —even those who preferred Scotch. They lifted their glasses silently.

LOVE IN THE BARN

THERE WAS this television movie titled *Thoroughbreds*, which is perhaps all the description anybody really needs. However, for the benefit of any reader who has been living in a cave since the invention of the magic lantern, it went something like this:

Sireson is strictly a man's horse, but that doesn't mean he hasn't an eye for a neatly turned fetlock. He meets up with this cute little filly named The Princess and in practically no time he's nickering sweet nothings into her shapely ear, romping with her in the paddock and, on moonlit nights, taking her out back of the barn for an oat and a spot of bran mash.

The doll in the picture is training The Princess for the great Springvale Steeplechase, and Sireson is being prepped for the same race by the guy who rode him in the cavalry. The guy and the doll don't know it yet, but before the next commercial, something's going to come about that will be too big for either of them.

Carrying the trainer on a morning gallop, The Princess raps a fence with a foreleg and knocks herself out of training. The guy helps the doll to her feet, brushes a speck of loam off her nose, and—honest to gawd—says, "I hope you'll help me train Sireson now. That's how The Princess would want it."

This may be the warmest line of dialogue since Aristophanes, but it is more than that. Joe Palmer would say it was the supremely perfect manifestation of horse love according to the classic definition.

Thus we arrive tardily at our text: There is now in the stores a new book, *This Was Racing*, by Joe H. Palmer (A. S. Barnes & Co., New York). It is pure Joe Palmer, which means there is no more joyous reading on any shelf.

In a space like this, one ordinarily hesitates to crow about a book bearing his own name as editor, and I was implicated in this, though only as driver of the getaway car. In this case I feel no sense of impropriety; rather, a failure to mention *This Was Racing* would be an injustice to those who love laughter and wit and grace and the enriching fun which only a few men could wring from the English language.

In the year and more since death brought an end to Joe's work for the *Herald Tribune*—his pieces appeared under the general heading of racing comment, but they dealt freely with other necessities of life, like women and money and television and jellied martinis—letters have not ceased to arrive asking, "Can't we have a book of Joe Palmer's stuff?" Now we have one; the reader will appreciate what wonderful fun it was helping put it together.

It is a book that should be read at least twice—the first time at one gulp, in a rush of pleasure, and then bit by bit each evening either before or after the passage from the Bible. That way lines are discovered and savored which were missed the first time around because Joe slipped them in so deftly, like a dirk under the fifth rib.

Not that he was a devious writer. He declared flatly that he did not know how a man around the tracks had got the name of Lyin' Fitz, "for he would answer honestly when asked the time of day or whether he had a match." And of a certain Mr. Brownie Leach he wrote that "Mr. Leach has a great respect for the truth, and uses it sparingly."

He told, quite simply, the story of Eddie Murphy, a horse player whose regular bookmaker, Spike McManus, died, thus forcing Mr. Murphy to take his business to one Willie Branahan. Mr. Branahan was nettled at being second choice, and he answered grumpily when a doctor of his acquaintance phoned to say that Eddie Murphy, though critically ill, wanted ten across on Cavalcade.

"I'm going to operate on him today," the doctor said, "and he's no better than even money to make it. But he still wants ten across on Cavalcade."

"He does, does he?" said the bookie bitterly. "Tell him to hold the bet awhile and give it to Spike McManus."

The other day an admirer of Joe's writing ordered fifty copies of the trade edition and several of the leather-bound limited edition. "I'm going to send them around to my nonracing friends," his letter said, "to show them why I love the sport."

He will accomplish more than he knows. His friends will also discover why he loves to read. Strength to him and pleasure to them.

CONNIE, AS EVER WAS

IT IS NOT for mortals anywhere to suggest that another has lived too long, yet for those who knew and, necessarily, loved him it is difficult to regard Connie Mack's last years as part and parcel of a life that was a beacon in our time. Toward the end he was old and sick and saddened, a figure of forlorn dignity bewildered by the bickering around him as the baseball monument that he had built crumbled away.

That wasn't Connie Mack. Neither was the bloodless saint so often painted, a sanctimonious old Puritan patting babies on the skull and mumbling minced oaths and platitudes. As long as he was Connie Mack he was tough and human and clever. He was tough and warm and wonderful, kind and stubborn and courtly and unreasonable and generous and calculating and naive and gentle and proud and humorous and demanding and unpredictable.

Many people loved him and some feared him, everybody respected him and, as far as I know, nobody ever disliked him in the ninety-three years of his life. There may never have been a more truly successful man, for nobody ever won warmer or wider esteem and nobody ever relished it more.

Only the most fortunate men can appreciate their own success and enjoy it fully. Connie entered professional baseball when it was a game for roughnecks. He saw it become respectable, he lived to be the symbol of its integrity, and he enjoyed every minute of it.

He had an innocent vanity that could delight those who knew him. He liked going places and, of course, he was recognized everywhere. To see him introduced, say, at a fight in the Hollywood Legion Stadium was something to remember: He would spring through the ropes as nimbly as a preliminary boy and draw himself erect, hands clasped overhead, acknowledging the spontaneous cheers.

There were unexpected demonstrations of the affection felt for him in far places. It could be in Dallas or Houston or Fort Worth just before an exhibition game in the spring. All of a sudden, in the lull between infield practice and the first pitch, applause would go rippling through the stands, swelling to a roar, and the customers would be on their feet and here Connie would come hiking from dugout to dugout with his bouncy, long-legged stride, his scorecard waving high. For a moment, swallowing would be difficult.

He could laugh at himself. One winter he obtained title to the renowned orator and pitcher, Bobo Newsom, and brought Bobo up to Philadelphia for a formal signing. When the press was admitted to the tower office in Shibe Park, Connie was on his feet and Bobo relaxed in the swivel chair behind the desk, a big cigar in his face. A little later Newsom stepped outside to take a phone call and Connie dropped absentmindedly into the boss's seat.

As the door opened for his employee's return, Connie sprang up in mock alarm, reinstalling the great man with wonderfully exaggerated humility. Bobo was quite nice about it.

It is the little things one remembers most happily, the small foibles of his great humanity, like his sudden flash of real anger one day in San Francisco. It was a nippy morning and one of Connie's companions suggested closing the windows of a car that was taking them to San Quentin for an exhibition. He was astonished when his solicitude infuriated Connie.

"Dammittohell!" the old man exploded. "Don't worry about me! Dammit, everybody's always worrying. Mrs. Mack says, 'Con, wear your overcoat; Con, don't forget your rubbers!' So I put on my dam' coat and my dam' rubbers and go out to the drugstore to get medicine for her!

"And that Blackburne!" Lena Blackburne, coach with the Athletics, had a leg infection that had kept him in bed in Anaheim, California, when the team broke camp there. "That Blackburne!" Connie said. "It's 'Boss, are you comfortable? Boss, are you warm enough? Sit still, boss, and I'll get it for you.' And where's Blackburne? Down on his tail in Anaheim, dammit!"

So many little things. He could fight a player for the last dime at contract time and win. Yet he confessed that after fifty years two jobs still made him miserable—haggling with a player and telling a kid from the minors that he had to go back.

Little things. His unfailing gift for getting names wrong, from the day of the pitcher Addie "Josh" to the time of the young Cleveland manager "Mr. Bordiere." "It is a great pleasure," he told fans in Long

Beach, California, before an exhibition game with Gabby Hartnett's Cubs, "to be here in Long Branch playing my old friend, Pat Hartnett."

His Athletics are gone. Memories are his monument, and small things like the elevator built for him in Shibe Park before the place was renamed Connie Mack Stadium. The elevator was tailored to measure, eight feet tall and narrow as a phone booth, and there was an old press box attendant named Smitty assigned to take the lift to the ground floor each day in the eighth inning and hold it so Connie could ride up to his office directly after the game.

One day in 1945, the score was tied 1-all when Smitty went down in the eighth. It was still tied when the game was called after the twenty-fourth. Smitty stood with his foot in the door for sixteen innings.

FAREWELL IN THE RAIN

PHILADELPHIA. Thin cold rain fell steadily on the steep streets of East Falls that pitch down toward the Schuylkill River. In Midvale Avenue rain dripped from massed umbrellas, glistened on the slickers of policemen outside St. Bridget's Church where the Reverend John Cartin was singing requiem high mass for Connie Mack.

Police kept an aisle open up the middle of the gray stone steps to the packed vestibule. When the crowd overflowed the steps, clogged the sidewalk and spilled out over the curb, police herded the overflow across the street to keep traffic moving. There they stood in silence while the hour-long service went on inside. Mostly they were children or elderly. There was an old woman on crutches handling her umbrella with difficulty. On the curb across the way was a boy wearing a Phillies baseball cap. Rain fell more heavily and they held their ground.

Within the narrow vaulted church there were a few mink stoles but not many. The big men of baseball were there and Connie would have appreciated that because baseball was his whole life. His old players were there. He'd have felt at home with them. There were also three boys in Levi's, windbreakers and sneakers, two bobby-sox girls, one wearing blue jeans. Connie would have liked that best of all.

Probably there were days when the weather was pleasant and Connie Mack's Athletics drew crowds no larger than the one at his funeral. This time, this last time, it was the man who drew them, not the game. The stately liturgy moved on. In the choir loft were Phil Banabach, choirmaster of the Church of the Holy Child, and three members of his group. In the pews, Connie's friends bowed their heads and prayed or remembered, each according to his fashion.

Roberto Estalella was a Cuban outfielder who joined the Athletics in their wartime training camp in Wilmington, Delaware. It may have been his first day of those frostbitten exercises when players shivered on a street corner waiting in vain for the bus to take them to the ball park. Connie was the first to grow impatient.

"Come on, boys," he said, "let's walk." And he struck out first on the two-mile hike, stretching his long legs briskly and leaning into the wind. Estalella, the newcomer, watched with lifted brows, then swung into step behind him. "He eighty?" Bobby said. "Ho! He live to be a hundred. We win the pennant he live to two hundred."

To many in the church now it must have seemed strange to be present in these circumstances. They had known so many years when Connie, wearing his dignity lightly, had been the liveliest, keenest, most tireless of them all. The man they knew had moved in crowds, lived in excitement, glorying in it and seeming never to weary. They remembered the sweltering days in St. Louis, the hot sunshine of Florida or the southwestern plains, the tumult of World Series. Some had not expected ever to see this gray, quiet, solemn day. Chances are most of them had said at one time or another, only partly in jest, "He'll bury us all, that unbelievable old guy. They'll never kill him." Now at the head of the center aisle six tall candles burned and polished wood gave back their flickering beams.

"It is not the custom in our church at requiem mass to preach a sermon," Father Cartin said. For the Mack family, he expressed gratitude for the tribute paid by the presence of Connie's friends, of the men in government, in baseball, in civic and community affairs. "Those who know the greatness of this man can pay tribute to his greatness far better than I. . . . His memory is held sacred in the lives of our people in general, whose inspiration he was. . . . He will indeed be missed by our American people, generations young and old. . . ."

Slowly the church emptied. A long file of limousines drew up to the curb, drew away in the rain. All his life Connie loved best to go on trips. There was a time away back when he was seventy-five, when he was too ill to travel. He was desperately ill then. So sick—he said afterward—that he tried to die and couldn't. He also said that what he had missed most sorely in that time was making the trips with the team. Even if it was just across the river for an exhibition game in Camden, he wanted to go along with the other guys, was deeply disappointed if business or poor health kept him at home.

This was the last trip, two or three miles to the Cemetery of the Holy Sepulchre. A lot of the guys went along.

BILLY EVANS

THINGS GOT a bit thick in the White Stockings' park this afternoon in 1907. For five or six innings, every close decision had gone against the home team, and now glassware glittered in the April sunshine as Chicago's citizenry hurled invectives and pop bottles. Again and again Billy Evans, the rookie umpire on the bases, glanced nervously toward the plate for a signal to take cover, but his revered partner, Tim Hurst, seemed unaware of any unrest. The game rolled on to a conclusion without a direct hit from the stands.

"Whew!" young Evans sighed when he and Hurst were safe in their dressing room. He mopped a pale brow.

"Willie," said Tim, "you needn't worry about these boys in April or May. They got no control. When the warm weather comes, watch out. They're deadly at a hundred yards."

It was hot that September in St. Louis. A dispute on the field stirred up another crystal shower. As Hurst had predicted, marksmanship was greatly improved. A bottle shattered itself on Billy Evans's hairdo. They carried him away with a fractured skull, and for several days he teetered on the rim of death.

He didn't die for another forty-eight years. In the meantime he served out twenty-two years as an American League umpire, was an executive of the Cleveland Indians, Boston Red Sox, and the Detroit Tigers, president of the Southern Association, general manager of the Cleveland Rams football team, sports editor, columnist and author.

The title "Greatest of All Umpires" can't be awarded with confidence to one man. There's a select group bracketed at the top—Bill Klem, Tommy Connolly, Tim Hurst, Silk O'Loughlin, Jack Sheridan, the melodic Lord Bill Byron, Bill McGowan and, of course, Billy Evans.

Of all these, William George Evans was the last you'd have picked for the profession he dignified. In his fine book, *The Umpire Story,* Jim Kahn describes him as a big league rookie of twenty-two—a young man of grace and some learning, trim, fast, alert and fastidious in impeccable blue serge tailored to order.

The obituaries told how, on the death of his father, Billy gave up plans to study law after three years at Cornell and got a job at $12 a week as cub reporter for the Youngstown, Ohio, *Vindicator,* advancing to sports editor at $18 and in that capacity accepting $15 to work a game in the Ohio and Pennsylvania League when the regular umpire didn't show up.

Offered steady employment in the league, Billy doubled for two seasons as umpire and sports editor, and never got an unfavorable press notice. It wasn't his clippings, however, that enabled him to jump from Class D to the majors. He went into the American League over a back fence.

Playing in Niles, Ohio, Youngstown led by one run with two out in the ninth inning, three balls and two strikes on the batter, and three Niles runners on the bases. A hit would win the game and a walk would tie it. The Youngstown pitcher threw a curve, Billy Thomas, the batsman, fell over backward, got up and started for first base. "Strike three," Billy Evans said.

Here came the mob giving off strange animal cries. Charley Crowe, the Niles manager, rescued the umpire and got him into a hotel but an hour and a half later, an angry crowd was still waiting outside. While Crowe showed himself at the front door, Billy slipped out the back, dragged his suitcase over a fence and caught an interurban train back to Youngstown.

Jimmy McAleer, manager of the St. Louis Browns, was scouting a Youngstown player. He recommended the umpire to Ban Johnson, founder of the American League, and Billy became the fifth man on Johnson's staff.

In those days one man worked a game and when he had to rule on a play that occurred behind him he relied on what Dick Nallin called "the animal instinct of the umpire." As fifth man in the league, Billy teamed with Jack Sheridan and Tim Hurst for most of his first two seasons before going out on his own.

He considered Sheridan the greatest of them all and imitated him assiduously. Riding from Chicago to New York for his first big league assignment, he received from Sheridan one piece of advice that remained the cardinal principle of his career: "Never lose sight of the ball."

Billy had boxed at Cornell besides playing basketball and football and running on the track team. Hardly a ball player ever lived who could handle a boxer equipped with a straight punch, but when the young umpire did get into a baseball fight it wasn't the sort in which science plays a major part.

He went to it with the redoubtable Ty Cobb under the grandstand in Washington, both clawing, gouging, lashing out with spike-shod feet. Players who broke it up scored it as a draw.

Naturally it was understood that no report of the affair was to go to the league president and Billy kept the bargain. Naturally, Ban Johnson heard about the fight through unofficial channels. He told Ed Barrow that he was sorry he had missed it.

SAM LANGFORD AND THE LEGENDS

JUST ABOUT everything worth saying about Sam Langford has been said, in the record books and the obituaries and the sports columns and on the editorial pages. A lot of it is true and no doubt some of it is important.

There have been pieces telling what a great fighter old Sam was— written mostly by men who never saw him, for he quit more than thirty years ago and it has been close to forty since he did any real fighting in the East. A lot of the pieces repeated the old statement that he lived before his time, when Negroes got little but the worst of it in the ring and, consequently, Sam was often forced to wear handcuffs in order to get any work at all.

As to that, a fellow has to wonder. Tom Molineaux, who was black, fought Tom Cribb for the title almost a century before John L. Sullivan invented the "color line" and drew it against Peter Jackson. Barbados Joe Walcott and Joe Gans and George Dixon and Jack Johnson won championships in Sam's day or earlier, and it does not appear that any racial barriers impeded Sam McVey or Joe Jeannette or Jack Blackburn.

Chances are there were occasions when Sam did go into the ring manacled, but one is entitled to mental reservations on the question of whether he did so through necessity or merely because it seemed sound business at the time.

It is often said that the bars didn't go down until Joe Louis's day, and certainly it is true that Joe greatly increased the stature of the Negro in the ring. Still, Kid Chocolate and Battling Siki and Tiger Flowers had known some success before that, and Henry Armstrong was on his way when Joe was still in the amateurs.

Anyhow, Sam Langford is pictured as a fellow who had a bad time of it while he was fighting and a worse time afterward. The tale is re-told how Sam dropped out of sight and was forgotten until Al Laney found him in 1944, old and penniless and blind and alone in a squalid room in Harlem.

The stories make him a tragic figure, and that furnishes a text for sermons about the need for reforms that will protect fighters in their youth and insure them in age. That would be fine. Everybody, includ-ing sportswriters, should be protected against exploitation and insured against error and extravagance and foolhardiness. All the fighter would need is a split personality—recklessly impetuous in the ring, prudent outside the ropes.

The fact is, Sam Langford wasn't a tragic figure in his own blind eyes or in Al Laney's clear ones. "I fought maybe three, four hundred fights," he told Al, "and every one was a pleasure." There was a gladiator.

Almost a year later, when Laney's story had brought gifts and dona-tions of almost $10,000 to old Sam, Al paid him a Christmas Eve call. "I got a geetar," Sam said, "and a bottle of gin and money in my pocket to buy Christmas dinner. No millionaire in the world got more than that, or anyhow they can't use more." Tragic?

HE'D QUIT A JOB TO SEE THE CIRCUS

WHEN ART SMITH worked on the *Chicago Times* the paper was run by Louis Ruppel, a big, hard-nosed and aggressive editor whose speech was redolent of Brooklyn. On some assignment in the northern Wisconsin woods, Art wrote a line about a log cabin "among the towering tamaracks," no doubt because the alliteration pleased him. In the first edition this caught the eye of some tree freak in the city room, who protested to Ruppel that tamaracks didn't tower, reaching a height of only twenty or twenty-five feet. "Don't hire no more of them little guys," Ruppel told the city editor. "Everything looks big to 'em."

That wasn't why Art lost that job, though. Patti was. She was the food editor, a smashing young widow with a small daughter. An artist, she would write about how to cook turnips in beer, and illustrate the piece with pen-and-ink sketches. Ruppel fired Art for marrying her. "He took my cooking editor," Ruppel said. "I'll fix it so they got nothing to cook."

Art got another job. He could always get another job. His obituary in the *New York Daily News* said he had worked on twenty-one newspapers before he landed on the *News* in 1942. How anybody managed to count them, it is hard to say. Some that were shot from under him during the Depression are almost completely forgotten today, like the *Detroit Mirror*.

When that one folded, Art went down to St. Louis, where nobody was hiring anybody. The *Star* wasn't even sending anyone to Florida to cover the Cardinals and Browns in training camp. Arrangements had been made for Clarence Lloyd, a reformed sportswriter who was the Cardinals' traveling secretary, to file a daily story from his camp. The *Star* was going to pay $15 a week.

"Give me the fifteen dollars," Art said, "and I'll file."

So for the next six weeks or so he was a sportswriter. In those days the newspapers, except for the *Post-Dispatch* in St. Louis, let the ball club pick up the tab for writers traveling with the team. So food and lodging were free, the $15 a week took care of cigarettes, and Sam Breadon, who owned the club, loved parties and poured with a heavy hand. Thus all necessities of life were provided, Clarence Lloyd was relieved of a chore he didn't want, and everybody was happy.

When that assignment ended, Art went somewhere else. He was always going somewhere else—Milwaukee, Chicago, Denver, Philadelphia. Sometimes he would hit two or three different hitches on the same paper.

He could always get a job because he was a hell of a good newspaperman, an enterprising and imaginative reporter whose writing was lively and professional. He used to say he was one of the best bad writers around. A lead comes back to mind, done when he was on rewrite at the *News*: "The firepower of martinis was effectively demonstrated at the New York Athletic Club last night when a guest sprang across the table and bit off his host's nose."

When Art was in Detroit the Purple Mob was riding high. He got to meet some interesting people with names like Singin' in the Nighttime Sam (Salvatore Nottecantare). He covered the police beat in the Chicago of Al Capone and Bugs Moran. He never really got over the notion that the best possible news story was a good gangster funeral.

Once when he was in Milwaukee between newspapers he took a job on a magazine called the *Wisconsin Banker*. Art never had more than a quarter, and that only until he could get rid of it. It was pleasant to think of this master of finance tellings banks how to handle money.

The *Wisconsin Banker* didn't make Art's fortune but it did lead, in a roundabout way, to the gold fields of the Yukon. On the magazine he made friends with a colleague, one Mort Stevens, an older man who had been in the Klondike gold rush of 1898. Later, in St. Louis, Art had a letter from Stevens, then working as a private eye in Southern California. He had talked a couple into grubstaking a prospecting expedition and he suggested that Art join up.

For $20 Art got a hot pass to Los Angeles from the son of an official on the Santa Fe. (The young man did a small business renting out his father's pass.) Art and Stevens were joined by Ray Powers, a newspaperman who had gone down with Art when the *Detroit Mirror* sank. Alaska and the Yukon Territory seemed to be fresh out of nuggets, so Art worked for a while on the paper in Anchorage, caught ship for Seattle and hopped an eastbound freight. He was heard from next on the *Denver Post*.

He was light of heart and light of foot and he would quit a job to go to the circus. He drank a lot, too much and too often in the opinion of some editors. Once he landed in New York, however, he stayed put.

After seventeen years on the *News* he did a short turn on the *Daily Mirror*, then took over the rod and gun column on the *Herald Tribune*. He made such a hit on that job so fast that editors around town started asking who was that bright new boy on the *Trib*. He wrote the column until the *Herald Tribune* and its misbegotten offspring, the *World Journal Tribune*, were dead. Then he helped Robert Abplanalp launch the Eldred Preserve in the Catskills, a trout hatchery and fee fishing project. Fish interested Abplanalp before he took up bankrolling Richard Nixon.

Authorities from Euripides to Shakespeare assure us that the sins of the fathers are visited upon the children, yet Art's father was a sinless man who headed the family business—wholesale produce and retail groceries—in Green Bay, Wisconsin. Nevertheless, he had two sons who became newspapermen and each had a son who became a newspaperman, although Art's son, Patrick, escaped into television. It makes one wonder about sin.

GRANTLAND RICE

COMING HOME from vacation is different this time. New York isn't the same town at all. Grantland Rice isn't here. This isn't going to be maudlin but it has to be personal. Grantland Rice was the greatest man I have known, the greatest talent, the greatest gentleman. The most treasured privilege I have had in this world was knowing him and going about with him as his friend. I shall be grateful all my life.

I do not mourn for him, who welcomed peace. I mourn for us.

Granny was a restless sleeper. Sometimes he thrashed about and muttered in his sleep and sometimes he cried out in the dark. "No!" he would shout. "No, dammit, no! Frankie, help me! No, I say!"

Does that seem a curious thing to tell about him now? It isn't, really, because it was so characteristic. It required no dream book by Freud to help interpret those cries. All through his waking hours Granny was saying *yes, surely, glad to, of course, no trouble at all, certainly, don't mention it.* Not only to his friends, but to all the others who imposed on his limitless generosity. And so, when he slept . . .

The only thing greater than his talent was his heart—his gentle courtesy, his all-embracing kindness. And as great as that was his humility.

Once his working press ticket for the Army–Notre Dame football game went astray in the mail. This was Grantland Rice, who did as much for American football as any other man who ever lived; who practically invented the Army–Notre Dame game, who made it a part of American literature with his "Four Horsemen" story of 1924.

He went down Broadway and bought a ticket from a scalper and watched the game from the stands, with his typewriter between his knees. When it was over he made his way apologetically to the press box to do his work.

A friend who heard of this was aghast. "Why didn't you throw some weight around?" he demanded.

"Tell you the truth," Granny said, "I don't weigh much."

In 1944, when the whole World Series was played in St. Louis, the working press had one ticket for the Cardinals' home games and another for the Browns'. On the day of the last game Granny arrived at Sportsman's Park with the wrong ticket.

Nobody crashes the World Series. Granny was going to catch another cab, fight the traffic three or four miles to the Chase Hotel and return with his proper credentials. "You'd miss the first six innings," Frank Graham said. "Come with me."

Leading his reluctant friend through the press gate, Frank whispered to the man at the turnstile, "This is Grantland Rice behind me. He has the wrong ticket."

"Where?" the gateman said, his face lighting. "Come in, Mr. Rice, come in."

Now they were inside, but at the entrance to the press box proper another guard held the pass. Again the conspiratorial whisper, the thumb gesturing back over the shoulder.

"Grantland Rice!" the guard said. "Mr. Rice, how are you, sir. I've always wanted to meet you."

"Frankie, you are marvelous," Granny said as they took their seats. "How did you manage that?"

Perhaps it is not literally true that Grantland Rice put a white collar upon the men of his profession, but not all sportswriters before him were cap-and-sweater guys. He was, however, the sportswriter whose company was sought by presidents and kings.

When Warren Harding was president he asked Granny down to Washington for a round of golf and Granny invited his friend, Ring Lardner.

"This is an unexpected pleasure, Mr. Lardner," Harding said as they hacked around. "I only knew Granny was coming. How did you happen to make it, too?"

"I want to be ambassador to Greece," Lardner said.

"Greece?" said the President. "Why Greece?"

"Because," Lardner said, "my wife doesn't like Great Neck."

Granny and several friends were leaving Toots Shor's a few weeks before his death. There was some confusion just inside the revolving door and one of the group was aware, without looking back, of strangers hesitating behind him, uncertain whether to push through or wait for the way to clear. He heard a woman say, "A lovely man. Let them go."

The small sounds of departure covered the question that must have been asked, but the woman's reply came clearly to the sidewalk.

"Mr. Grantland Rice."

She spoke quietly, but her tone was like banners.

A LETTER ABOUT GRANNY

WHEN A great man dies [reads a letter from a man who loved Grantland Rice] everybody who was his friend says for the papers "We shall miss him," but it really takes a little while for this to happen.

I've realized this before [the letter continues; this whole column is the letter] because I'm getting old and so it is that too many of the good guys are stepping out of here and leaving me with one less friend who is hard to spare.

Like this morning. I get up early, real early, in the country and it was dark this morning while I sneaked around making barefoot coffee so as not to wake the family, who would get sore. When it was made and I was in the living room jolting it down and having the first smoke, all of a sudden it happened again. "Oh, gee, Granny is dead," I said to myself, alone in the living room at five in the morning.

It was as if I had just heard about Granny, although he died a month ago. All over again, I had to convince myself that no matter where I go, Saratoga, Belmont, Toots's place, Yankee Stadium, the table in the Chatham, the Dutch Treat, no matter where it is, I won't see Granny Rice again.

This thing of suddenly saying to yourself Granny is dead wouldn't be so bad if I could explain it. That is if something reminded me of him, like looking at the race entries and thus being reminded of how we used to go to the races together and have fun. But there never is any reminder. The thought comes popping out of itself, and each time I have to realize its truth all over again and it hurts.

So now I'm doing that—it's 5:45 A.M. now—and I think Granny was a saint who swore and drank and bet on horses, the kind of saint a person would love to be around with. The regularly enrolled saints I've read about in books would make me very nervous to have around, I think, but not Granny.

There were three of us used to go to the track together. We'd meet on the sidewalk in front of Granny's house at 97th Street and Fifth, and Charles Goering, his chauffeur, would be there with the car to take us out.

Granny was a big man in the world, but nobody had to be a big man to be his friend. The elevator men at the house would not hesitate to ask him nicely would he please take out a couple of bucks and buy them daily double tickets. And they'd give him crumpled bills and the names of the horses written down and he'd stuff it in any old pocket as only Granny could do it, such a way you'd think he'd never find the money again and often enough he couldn't, but don't think he didn't buy them the tickets anyway, because he did. Anyway, we'd get in the car and Granny would ask, "Has everybody got a badge?" and he'd give a badge to Charles and we'd roll along to the newsstand on the southwest corner of 96th and Lex, and Charles would stop. Granny would get out—he wouldn't let any of us get out and do it—and he'd buy all the afternoon papers, the *Morning Telegraph* and more scratch sheets than there were people in the car, and climb back in and pass the papers and scratch sheets around.

When we got to the track he'd hurry up and buy programs and pass them around as we went in. When we sat down to lunch he'd ask, "Anybody want daily doubles?" And we'd give him numbers to buy and off he'd go to the window. When he'd come back he'd give us each our own ticket and half the time he'd refuse to take the two bucks, and that's the way it went all day.

One day something delayed him as we got out of the car at the track and I was able to beat him to the program man and buy three programs for 45 cents, the first time in years I could do that with Granny. When I handed him his program he glared at me, real serious.

"You greedy bum," he said. "Do you want to pay for *everything?*"

I guess with a man like that, it is not too difficult to understand, after all, why every once in a while, without any reminder at all, I suddenly say to myself, "Oh gee, Granny is dead." Or why, when I go to the places we used to go, I find myself looking around, foolishly perhaps, and thinking, "Where's Granny, he ought to be here someplace."

HAPPY BIRTHDAY

SINCE IT was only Sunday evening when it began, chances are Grantland Rice's birthday party will be settling into stride about the time these pages become a shroud for some obsolete haddock. There've been some memorable wingdings in Mr. Toots Shor's fish and chips hutch, but none topped this and none ever could.

It wasn't the people present who made it the best. It was the man who was not there, though he wasn't really absent, either. What happened more than once since Grant died last July kept happening again and again Sunday night: you found yourself gazing around the merry room in absentminded questing, expecting to see Granny at the merriest table.

It was amusing to see men—who live all their lives in a swarm of autograph-seekers going around this time collecting signatures from others, signatures that would fill the register of a Hall of Fame in any sport or almost any other field from show business to politics.

Yet what else would you expect? Jack Dempsey, Gene Tunney, Earl Sande, Gene Sarazen, Vinnie Richards, the Four Horsemen, Johnny Weissmuller, Herman Hickman, Lou Little, Tommy Henrich, Yogi Berra, Eddie Arcaro, Ted Atkinson, Hank Greenberg—where else would they be on a night the clan was lifting a tall one to Granny?

Wherever they were, in Miami or Nashville, Cleveland, Chicago or California, they dropped what they were doing and came on. There wasn't one among them, however famous, however successful, who doesn't owe much to Grantland Rice.

It was the biggest haul of debtors this side of Old Bailey, and they were there to pay up in the only coin Granny would ever accept—affection and laughter.

This was the party Granny's friends had been planning for several years. It didn't come off earlier because they'd never got together on a date and, anyway, there was grave doubt that Granny would have attended an affair in his honor at gunpoint. This date sort of picked itself; it was the eve of the seventy-fourth anniversary of Grant Rice's birth and the night before publication of his memoirs, *The Tumult and the Shouting*.

There was nobody to sing "Happy Birthday" to, but they could have sung it loudly, for it was a happy occasion. Granny is missed but he is not mourned. There was no tear-jerking; that would have embarrassed Granny.

Rube Goldberg thought of this while watching Douglas Fairbanks, Jr., on Ed Sullivan's television show. (Some of the guests went to the studio before dinner and the others watched from the party.) Fairbanks was giving a graceful reading of Granny's moving verse, "Ghosts of the Argonne."

> You can hear them at night when the moon is hidden;
> They sound like the rustle of winter leaves. . . .

The party was quiet. "If Granny were here now," Rube said to Colonel Red Reeder of West Point, "he'd be talking."

"Right," another said, "he'd be asking Red here, 'Hey, how about that Virginia team pretty near beating Army?' Or he'd want to know what you thought about the election, Rube. Or he'd be talking about some book he'd just read, not his."

General Rosie O'Donnell was across the room. He and his West Point sidekick, General Blondie Saunders, were two of Granny's all-time favorites. Mrs. Kit Rice tells of the morning her squire got home showing traces of wear, but full of reassurances.

"Everything's all right, honey," he said, "I've been out with Rosie and Blondie."

Everything's still all right with Granny. Nothing can be said of him now that he didn't say better of somebody else. For example, there is a verse he addressed to Charon, the boatman of the Styx, after many of his friends had died:

> The flame of the Inn is dim tonight—
> Too many vacant chairs—
> The sun has lost too much of its light—
> Too many songs have taken flight—
> Too many ghosts on the stairs—
> Charon—here's to you—as man to man—
> I wish I could pick 'em the way you can.

GRANNY'S HORSE PARK

OLDSMAR, FLORIDA. The Sunshine Park that Grantland Rice knew was a Shoeless Joe among racetracks, a sort of slum-clearance project in a rattlesnake colony. The barns were sagging shanties of scrap lumber, the clubhouse and grandstand featured peeling paint, and there was a seedy, carpet-slippers informality that captivated Granny. The clubhouse dining room was bare, plain and tiny, but it served the superlative Stevens victuals, and immediately outside were the remaining necessities of life—an open-air bar and a mutuel battery maybe fifteen feet apart and not more than six paces removed from a view of the running strip.

There were horses but hardly any people, which is not good for management but wonderful for the clientele. Granny made no secret of his affection for the place.

"Mr. Rice," asked a bright young native son interviewing him in California, "what's your favorite racetrack? Santa Anita? Hollywood? Del Mar?"

"Sunshine Park," Granny said. The startled reporter never had heard of Sunshine and was not hugely gratified when Granny described its location about the middle of a triangle made by Tampa, St. Petersburg and Clearwater.

"Well, sir," the young man inquired, trying again, "what's your favorite city? For climate, I mean."

It happened to be a miserable winter of cold and smog in Los Angeles.

"Quebec," Granny said. "You go there for snow, you get it."

Aided by Granny's benedictions, Sunshine prospered modestly, and after Granny died it got a face-lift and hairdo, with fresh paint and glassed-in restaurant on the third level, elevator and so on.

"I'm not quite sure Granny would like it," the secretary, Milo Vega, confessed dubiously, "but it's progress."

More or less as a peace offering for scrubbing up the playground which Granny had regarded with something like a parent's feeling for a small, soiled child, Sunshine inaugurated with this year's meeting a Grantland Rice Memorial Handicap and also endowed two scholarships for senior journalism students at the University of Florida and Florida State.

The race's first running had nine horses of three years and older going a mile and a sixteenth for $3,500, the richest purse Sunshine has got up yet. There were, of course, some garden-variety horse players present, but at a casual glance it looked as though admission was by invitation only this day, for wherever you looked you saw Granny's mob.

George Weiss, the general manager of the Yankees, had a luncheon party for baseball writers covering the St. Petersburg camp and their wives; Everett and Petey Clay flew up from Hialeah; there were special friends of Granny like Dan and Norma Parker and Frank and Lillian Graham.

Sunshine has been having an uncommonly formful meeting with the program selector picking four or five winners a day and something like 37 percent of the favorites winning, but this day it was almost as though the results had been arranged for Granny, who doted on long shots. One after another, the outsiders came banging down to pay $47 or $55.

"Do you suppose," somebody asked, "that Granny's got a hand in this somehow?"

Stabbing through the early races, hunch players kept groping for a good thing for Granny's race. There was a tip out on Belldiver, and that was all right because Belldiver is a six-year-old son of Devil Diver, a horse that Granny admired when his friend John Gaver was training him for his friend Jock Whitney. The favorite at 2 to 1 in the morning line was a five-year-old gelding named Steppin Pappy. Nothing wrong with that for a hunch, either, considering how Granny was still stepping along at the top of his stride right down to the day when he collapsed at his typewriter.

"Me, though," a fellow said, "I like The Butcher, because if you ever pounded this asphalt here with Granny through nine races in the afternoon and then tried to keep up with him that night at the dog races, you know he could kill you."

Thus they joked through the balmy afternoon, who had to laugh lest they cry. They prowled the grounds, pausing at the bar to lift one in memory, strolling away up to the head of the stretch where the jockeys come whipping and war-whooping around the last turn.

Except for a few children playing in the dusty grass, and a few mothers watching them from parked cars, it was a place of deserted quiet up there. One little girl wearing patent leather Mary Janes had climbed a cyclone fence beside the parking lot and her mother was telling her to get down lest she scuff her new shoes. Two men wearing neckties walked past and the mother said, "Here comes the president. He'll knock you down." The little girl paid no attention.

In Granny's race a gray named Blue Ember, turned almost white in his sixth year, led for about three-quarters, but then the favorite, Steppin Pappy, took over and won. His trainer, K. J. Helsey, was excited in the winner's circle accepting the trophy, a handsome silver bowl with one of the finest pictures Granny ever had taken reproduced in the metal by some photographic process.

It was a simple and dignified little ceremony that Granny wouldn't have watched. He loathed winning favorites. He'd have been back at Scott Miller's mutuel window bucking for a good thing in the next race.

NEWS ABOARD SHIP

ABOARD M. V. BRITANNIC. The story made page one of the *Ocean Times* immediately below the bulletin about the Kremlin conversations. The headline read, "Death of Baseball Idol," and the dispatch announced that "Babe Ruth, baseball's beloved homerun king, died in his sleep last night. The fifty-three-year-old famed Sultan of Swat died after a week-end rally that had raised the fading hopes of his legions of admirers. The end came swiftly."

Even in midocean, news like that arrives punctually. It was news, too, in Japan and Pakistan and Johannesburg and Canberra. There are a great many places on this earth where baseball is not played, but very few indeed where the name of Babe Ruth was unknown. Which could be, if you liked, a way of saying how much bigger the man was than the game.

The end came swiftly, the dispatch said. Not swiftly enough. Not without years of unceasing, remorseless pain. Not so suddenly as to take anyone by surprise. Not anyone at all. "I haven't much farther to go," the Babe told his friend, Frank Stevens, in the hospital last winter, "but I'm not going to die in here. I'm going to get out and have some fun first."

The betting was against him on that, but he did get out as he said he would. How much fun he had only he could have said. It didn't look like fun being convoyed around Florida, where he'd had, in his time, some fun that really was fun. You'd encounter him in Miami and Tampa and St. Petersburg and Clearwater at the spring training games or maybe at a dinner, always with a squad of cops fending off the autograph hounds and a horde of junior executives chuffing and scurrying like tugboats around a liner.

There always seemed to be junior executives around him in those last few months. In Florida he had some sort of business tie-up with a motor company and later, back home, there was a great fuss about the launching of his autobiography into the market, and after that came the screening of the book in Hollywood. Seemed as though everyone had an idea how to make some more money, but there wasn't much time and it had to be hurry, hurry, hurry.

Always there was a pain that never went away. He was so dreadfully sick even to the layman's eye. There was a sadness even in the jauntiness of his tan cap and camel's-hair polo coat. Still, probably it was better than the hospital, and maybe he did have some fun of a sort.

There was a day at a ball game in St. Pete's Al Lang Stadium, the shiny new playground on the site of old Waterfront Park where Babe and the other Yankees used to tee off in the spring. Somebody asked him about the old days in St. Pete. He pointed to the weathered facade of the Gulf Coast Inn, which, when the old park was up, had stood an everlasting distance beyond the outfield wall. He remembered, he said in the husk of voice he had left, how he'd really got his *adjectival* shoulders into a swing and had knocked the *indelicacy* ball against the *Anglo-Saxon* hotel out there.

"Gee!" the other said. "Quite a belt!"

"Yeah," Babe said, "and don't forget the *adjectival* park was a block back this way then."

His eyes gleamed with something like pleasure. Some of the old joie de vivre remained, all right. But the end didn't come swiftly, really. The Yankees of Ruth's day who have gone, they didn't get many breaks at the end. There was the Babe with his intractable pain these last several years. There was Lou Gehrig dying by inches and knowing it and facing it. There was Tony Lazzeri alone in the dark when the finish came. Little Miller Huggins was luckier. He went tragically, but suddenly.

Now that Babe is gone, what's to be said that hasn't been said? Nothing, when you come down to it. Just that he was Babe Ruth. Which tells it all, for there never was another and never will be. Probably he was the greatest ball player who ever lived, Ty Cobb and Honus Wagner and the rest notwithstanding.

It's a typically shabby trick on history's part that, as time goes by, he will be remembered merely for his home runs. He was also, remember, a genuinely great pitcher, a genuinely great outfielder, a genuinely great competitor, a truly great personality.

Merely by being part of the game, he wrought lasting changes in its strategy, its financial standards, its social position and the public conception of it. Somebody else will come along to hit sixty home runs, probably very soon. That won't make somebody else a second Babe Ruth. Never another like him.

AFTER FIFTEEN YEARS

FIFTEEN YEARS AGO this week the obituary made Page One. "BABE RUTH DEAD AT 53," the headline read. "End Peaceful." At 8:30 P.M. tonight, the eve of the anniversary, ABC-TV presents a study of the man and the legend which, for faithful reporting, affectionate honesty and all-round literary excellence, sets a television record as valid as the Babe's sixty home runs in 1927.

Written by Roger Kahn, narrated superbly by Horace McMahon and brightened with anecdotes from the Babe's teammates, Waite Hoyt, Jumping Joe Dugan and Leo Durocher, it paints an extraordinary human being who lived every hour on earth, not a tin saint who never existed. Indeed, it even sins on the side of truth by employing words *verboten* in the wasteland, such as *bo-oze* and *da-mes.*

Putting fact before legend, McMahon says, "He liked children, but his life was not a dedication to healing sick little boys."

And again, regarding the mistaken notion that Babe was an orphan: "He was the unmanageable child of parents who were not dedicated to parenthood."

"I was a pallbearer," says Joe Dugan. "It was a hot, humid day, the service lasted two and a half hours. I whispered to Hoyt, 'I'd give my right arm for a cold beer.' 'So would the Babe,' Waite said."

Babe was the most highly paid ball player up to his time, and his old playmates make it clear that he needed the money. Durocher recalls a rainy Saturday in New Orleans during the training season when, with the exhibition game canceled, Babe went to the racetrack. Next day in the clubhouse, he tossed winnings of $8,000 or $9,000 on a trunk and the other players, unpaid in the spring, grabbed what they needed while Babe looked on.

Came the first payday in New York and the Babe visited every locker, his big bat in hand. "How much did you take?" he demanded of each. "Get it up."

Another time, Dugan, needing steak and beer, braced Ruth in the Hollenden Hotel in Cleveland. "Judge, your old pal is empty." Babe slipped him a banknote without looking at it. Picking up the dinner check later, Dugan threw the waiter into a tizzy by handing him a $500 bill. "They had to get the owner out of bed to change it, he came down and bought us a drink, and it was another tough night."

Back in New York Joe handed Babe five $100 bills. "What's this for?" "It's that money you lent me in Cleveland." "Thanks, kid. I was afraid I'd blown it."

There was another rough night in Philadelphia, and when Babe got to the park the next day Fred Merkle, a coach, told him he looked terrible. Just the same, Ruth said, he'd bet $50 he'd get a home run that day; he'd lay $100 to $50. Merkle took the odds.

Sam Gray's first pitch to the erring boy went upstairs.

There are photographs of the young Ruth, recalling a description once given by a waiter in Toots Shor's who, in his youth, had worked in Boston.

"There was a waitress in the place, a pretty little thing. Tell the truth, I was a bit sweet on her meself. But there was this young fella would come in, a big lummockin' fella, and she wouldn't look at anybody else. I found out he was Ruth, the new pitcher with the Red Sox." The waitress became Babe's first wife, who died in a fire.

BABE REMEMBERED

SEVERAL YEARS after Babe Ruth packed it in as a player, he signed on with the Brooklyn Dodgers as a coach whose principal duty was to hit home runs in batting practice to entertain the customers. By this time the Phillies had moved from old Baker Bowl, the only privy with a scoreboard in the big leagues, to Shibe Park, where the Babe had swatted them through all his seasons in the American League.

"What do you remember best about this park?" he was asked the first time he accompanied the Dodgers to Philadelphia.

"The *naughty-word* day I hit that *naughty-word* ball into that *naughty-word* street over there, Opal Street," he said, nodding toward right field.

As any good Philadelphian could tell you, Shibe Park is bounded on the right by Twentieth Street. Chances are, not many Philadelphians could tell you the name of the little street, hardly more than an alley, a short block east of Twentieth.

That is Opal Street, and yet they say the Babe couldn't even remember the names of his teammates. Well, he might call Bob Shawkey "Horse Nose" because he couldn't remember his square name, and he might call Waite Hoyt or Tony Lazzeri or Bob Meusel "Pal," for the same reason, but he wasn't a guy to forget the name of any *naughty-word* street a whole *naughty-word* block from the *naughty-word* ball park if he had hit a *naughty-word* home run into it.

So that was Babe Ruth's dearest memory of Shibe Park. A lot of other memories were stirred in a lot of other minds the other day when the Phillies' owner, Bob Carpenter, sold the old battleground as a housing project for bats and owls. Connie Mack Stadium, they call it now, though when Connie was alive he opposed changing the name because he felt that as long as the joint stood it should remain a memorial to Benjamin F. Shibe, the man who brought American League baseball to Philadelphia.

Perhaps Connie never knew it, but the chances are that when Ben Shibe built the joint in 1909 he had it in mind that some day he might want to rename it for his manager and partner. At any rate, along about World War II the plant got its first bath in thirty-five years, and as the sandblasters chewed away the grime it turned out that the facade was studded with gargoyles and such. Right over the main entrance at Twenty-first Street and Lehigh Avenue appeared a stone bust of Connie wearing a full crop of wavy hair and a trap-door collar, both parted in the middle.

None of the Shibes, Ben or his sons, John and Tom, ever sold advertising space on the fences. Almost the entire right-field wall in Baker Bowl was covered by a sign announcing that the Phillies bathed with Lifebuoy soap so they'd smell better—"and, brother, can they use it!" Shorty Levin, the telegraph operator, used to say—but no such intimate disclosures marred the handsome dark green of the Athletics' playpen.

Shibe Park was also distinguished as the only drydock in the major leagues. One of the Shibe sons, a yachting enthusiast, kept a whole fleet stored under the left-field stands, and when Jimmy Foxx or Al Simmons or Bob Johnson was smashing the furniture in that sector, the grounds crew used to say he had hit one into the boathouse.

Fans are forever arguing about who hit the longest home run ever— Ruth believed his longest was batted out of Plant Field in Tampa— but until Arthur Patterson introduced the tape measure in recent years, there was no sure basis of comparison. Still a stickout in personal memory is one that Foxx creamed in Philadelphia. It looked like a low line drive streaking over the infield, but it was still climbing when it clipped the very peak of the roofed upper deck in left and took off for the clouds. Three days later a small boy in Bustleton, on the northeast fringe of town, found a baseball with snow on it.

Even more vivid is the memory of a less violent smash that had louder repercussions. It was during the World Series of 1931, when the Cardinals' Pepper Martin was slugging pitchers like Lefty Grove and George Earnshaw as though they were Little Leaguers and stealing everything but Mickey Cochrane's drawers. The team had split the first four games and as it is recalled now, the fifth was tied when Martin came up about the seventh or eighth inning.

"Well," said a guy in the press box, "so far he has singled, doubled, tripled, bunted safely and stolen everything in sight. There's nothing left now except to belt one into—"

The sound of wood splintering in left field interrupted him. The next sound heard was the dull plop of Connie's three-time pennant winners falling on their heads.

FRANK GRAHAM

THE MOST important single change in my business in my lifetime came about in the early 1930s, when Joe Vila died and Frank Graham succeeded him as sports columnist on the *New York Sun*. At that time sports columns in America were cut to a pattern: they were highly personal essays of opinion and comment expressing the writer's own view of the passing scene.

For almost twenty years, Frank Graham had been a newspaperman in the purest sense, a digger for truth, a reporter of facts.

He rejected the notion that having his stuff published in two-column measure must change him from reporter to pundit. Anyhow, he was congenitally unable to preach or pontificate or force his own judgments on others; one quality of his greatness was what his friend Bob Kelley once described as "psychopathic modesty."

"My job," he told himself, "is to take the reader behind the scene where his ticket doesn't admit him—into the dugout and clubhouse, the football locker rooms, the jockeys' quarters, the fighter's dressing room —and let him see what goes on there and hear what is said."

If anybody had said in Frank's hearing that he invented the "conversation piece" column, he would have hooted. He only did it incomparably better than it ever was done before, or has been done since. His incredibly accurate ear and implausibly retentive memory (he almost never took notes), his faultless taste, his warmth and understanding, his zest, his laughter and the purity of his prose combined to produce—it says here—the finest sports column of all time.

Quietly, perhaps without even knowing it, he brought about a revolution in the approach to and technique of writing a sports column in this country. Gradually editorial opinion gave way to reporting, to conversation pieces and interviews and "mood" pieces that strove to capture for the reader the color and flavor and texture of the event. No other sportswriter in Frank's lifetime exerted such effect on his own business. None was imitated so widely, or so unsuccessfully.

The rest of this, if I may be forgiven, must be embarrassingly personal. Frank and I had been friends since 1929, when I was a rookie on the baseball beat, working out of St. Louis. Shortly after World War II, when I was new in New York, and had my first postwar car, we agreed to drive South together for the annual tour of the baseball camps. We met one bitterly cold morning in front of Toots Shor's and I drove across town to the *Herald Tribune*.

"Would you take the wheel a minute," I said, "while I pop in and leave this copy with the elevator man?"

"No," he said. That's when I found out the bum couldn't drive. It was later I heard about the time a friend named Bob Murphy, wearing ice-cream pants, had a flat tire driving Frank and Grantland Rice down the Tamiami Trail in Florida. Bob spread newspapers under the axle to protect his pants and while he struggled to change the tire, Frank and Granny, equally gifted in a mechanical sense, walked about flapping their hands helplessly. First they tracked tar all over the newspapers. Then they kicked the tire lugs into the canal beside the road.

It was later, too, that I heard about the time Frank undertook to replace a burned-out bulb in a ceiling fixture at home. I forget what the rewiring and replastering cost.

I like to believe that on that cold morning when I learned he couldn't drive, I had some foreknowledge of how it would be for almost two decades—the tens of thousands of miles we would travel together with me at the wheel, the fun we would have, the priceless education I would enjoy.

But of course I couldn't have known about that. It's only that it happened so naturally, the way we made a team, that it seems I should have known.

In those days, Granny Rice and Frank pounded the beat together, and they took me in. I have been luckier than most in this world ("Underpaid and overprivileged," Jim Roach of the *Times* used to say of guys in our dodge), and the rarest privilege of all was to go around and about with those two as their friend.

Then Granny died and Frank and I changed to double harness. Arriving in Florida years ago, we walked into the press box at Hialeah. Pat Lynch, Frank's colleague on the *Journal-American* by that time, looked up from his typewriter.

"Here come 1 and 1-A," he said. I am prouder to have been part of that entry than of anything else in the world.

JIM THURBER

THE OBITUARY described James Thurber as "shy, introverted, self-deprecatory." Chances are he wasn't any of these. His public manner was diffident until something caught his interest or stirred him to argument, and something almost always did. Then he spoke freely with force and vigor and wit and no trace of self-consciousness.

If he was an introvert, he did not betray it at a party, where he was almost sure to be the center of attention, controlling the conversation, dominating the discussion. Widely informed, he could smash an adversary in argument on practically any topic, including topics on which he only appeared to be informed.

"You are aware of course," he would say, "that the Throckmorton Report disposed of that point definitely, proving that on the circumstances you describe—" The adversary wouldn't be aware of this at all, partly because no Throckmorton Report ever existed, but inasmuch as he was pretending to some knowledge of the subject he could hardly admit that.

If Jim was self-deprecatory, it was only about his slight physique, his blindness, his not quite splendid grooming. He did not underrate himself professionally. No man of taste could have failed to know how good he was, and he was a man of rare taste.

Because virtually everything moved him to laughter—publishers were an exception; most of them moved him to rage—he poked fun at himself as freely as he might skewer any other target.

"Your drink's here, Jamie," Marc Simont, his artist neighbor in West Cornwall, Connecticut, said one night, setting a highball at his elbow. Jim said thanks, and a little later, groping for the glass as he talked, he knocked it over. He made no more of that than a person would who could see, but when it happened again with a fresh drink he sprang to his feet and delivered an impassioned protest to an imaginary House Rules Committee about the untidy habits of this member, Thurber, who persistently loused up the club premises on the flimsy pretense, the hollow excuse, that he was blind.

His witty eloquence made it funny, and like all his humor it was also bitterly poignant.

As a kid with the sight of only one eye, Jim tried to pitch in sandlot baseball, though he was no athlete. In his newspaper days he never was a member of a sports department, though as a correspondent in France after World War I he did cover events like a tennis match on the Riviera between Suzanne Lenglen and Helen Wills. He remembered and quoted a line written by his brother, who did a hitch in sports in the era when Wee Dickie Kerr was a twenty-game winner with the White Sox: "Little pitchers have big years."

Jim was an avid sports fan with catholic tastes in games. He loved to spin yarns of football days at Ohio State in the time of Chick "Gimme the Ball" Harley, who was more or less the prototype of a character in "The Male Animal." Jim was a member of a little tennis club in West Cornwall. As his sight failed, he turned to the radio to keep him abreast of baseball developments.

In "The Catbird Seat," one of his most inventive and savagely penetrating short stories, he borrowed the title and other cornpone expressions like "tearing up the pea patch," from the mother tongue of Red Barber, then voice of the Dodgers.

Everybody knows, of course, that he invented the midget whom Bill Veeck signed on some years later as a major league player with the St. Louis Browns.

Jim Thurber was the greatest humorist of his time and probably, as the obituary suggested, America's greatest since Mark Twain. He recognized and appreciated his enormous talent but resented the fact that in many minds the definition of humorist was "unserious." Mentioning this rather angrily on a television program recently, he said, "I except Great Britain and Continental Europe," where, apparently, he was accepted as the thoughtful and perceptive critic of humankind that all great humorists are.

JIM AND JOHN

JIM THURBER's *Credos and Curios,* collected by Helen Thurber after her husband's death, has just come to hand. In it is a piece about John McNulty, and it tore me up. Both Thurber and McNulty are dead now and that is why you don't hear people laugh the way they used to.

Thurber says it is difficult to describe McNulty but John himself found it easy one day during a Derby Week in Kentucky. We had come over to Louisville after a stay in the Blue Grass country around Lexington and one of our crowd showed McNulty a snapshot he had made on a horse farm.

It showed John in a paddock in the Norfolk tweed jacket and snap-brim hat that nobody else could wear so jauntily, and a foal no bigger than a boxer dog was nuzzling his hand. McNulty didn't try to conceal his delight.

"Look at that!" he said. "Imagine throwing a man like that out of the Social Register—John McNulty, heir to the McNulty rewrite millions!"

If there's anybody around here who doesn't know, McNulty was a great writer of memorable books, author of incomparable pieces in the *New Yorker* when the magazine was better than it is, but mostly he was a newspaper stiff, a sportswriter for a while, oftener a rewrite man. When he felt identification necessary he identified himself as a writer, "author of those best-sellers, 'Barking Dog Rouses Family, Saves 5 from Fire,' 'Hotel Thieves Get $45,000 in Gems.'"

Every story Thurber tells about McNulty reminds me of another. Jim describes a walk about the streets with McNulty: "Two men would pass by you, one of them saying, 'It's the biggest gorilla in the world. They call it Garganetta,' or a waiter in a cafe would tell him, 'We get stranglers come in here at all hours.'"

McNulty didn't invent these characters, he attracted them like a magnet. In a single afternoon with him in a saloon called Little Czechoslovakia, I met Gabriel the Horseplayer, a timid little man who was afraid to carry a *Racing Form* because then the cops always picked him up; a former fighter, who, John said, might have been light-heavyweight champion of the world except he hated to hit people; a German butler whom McNulty called the Clash Man because, though he seemed a fairly decent guy, his mild arrival in the saloon caused everybody to bridle and pretty soon there'd be a loud row; the nephew of the proprietor, a kid from a wartime prison camp with a face empty of feeling who played the piano so mechanically that John would rage at him, "Look, I'll show you how to play 'Some of These Days' and mean something," and the kid would look at him blankly and John would be ashamed of himself.

"This is Joe the Russian," McNulty said. "He was bartender here but he wasn't a good bartender. When he got to like somebody he wouldn't take any money from him."

When Joe denied this with spirit, John said, "You gave me plenty drinks."

"Sure," Joe said, "but you deserve it."

There was the newsdealer on the corner in John's neighborhood. "*Izvestia*," McNulty would say to him in a conspiratorial whisper, or "*Pravda*" or "*Straits Settlement Gazette*."

"Yessir," the newsdealer would say, and scurry around and slip him a *Racing Form*.

There would be letters from John or, rather, notes, often written at 5:00 A.M. when he was first up in the house and making what he called "barefoot coffee so's not to wake the family." Sometimes there would be just a line or so beginning, "This I remember about Grogan the horse player," and a small story would go with it.

There was this on the handsome, heavy bond stationery of an elegant club:

"I would not have you think I was a member here," a postscript read, "because I grew up in Lawrence, Massachusetts, where my mother kept a candy store and we lived in the back of it, and up to now no member of this club's mother ever kept a store where they lived in the back of it. The way it happened, I stopped in to use the men's room—"

Chances are this isn't a sports column. The way it happened, there was this book by Jim Thurber, who used to get those notes from McNulty, too. The last one, Thurber says, began, "Dear Jimmy: I think maybe that threescore years and ten is subject to change without notice."

McNulty was sixty at the time. I'm not sure what year it was. I remember I was in a motel in Buffalo and in the morning paper there was a one-sentence obituary under a one-line head. The copyreader who wrote the head would not get my vote as the most meticulous craftsman in the business. It read:

"John McCarthy, Writer."

JOHN McNULTY AND HARRY MENDEL

AFTER VACATION there was sadness in the homecoming. In Buffalo the paper announced the death of John McNulty. Then from an Albany station the car radio brought word that Harry Mendel had died. Two treasured friends, Harry the great press agent and John the great writer; in their special ways, two rare talents.

John McNulty and Harry Mendel may or may not have known each other. Harry was the best press agent who ever handled the fight camp of an underdog, which was the camp they always gave him because nobody else was as good as he at building up a fighter who had no chance.

He was the best partly because he worked at it and was unfailingly reliable and tirelessly considerate, and partly because he knew the game so well, but especially because he was such a dead-honest guy. In line of duty, his typewriter turned out white lies faithfully every day but, when it came to his personal convictions, well, there was that day in Archie Moore's camp in North Adams, Massachusetts.

Sam Taub, who was working with Harry there, truly believed Moore was going to win Rocky Marciano's heavyweight championship. "If you tied me down and stuck knives in me," Sam said, "if you lit matches under my nails, I'd still believe it, and I know Harry feels the same way."

"Speak for yourself, Sam," said Harry without looking up from his luncheon plate.

A big-town guy, Harry was not always enchanted by the rural charm of fight camps. During his many weeks in North Adams he read up on local history and discovered that in the 1890s John L. Sullivan had been run out of town for being drunk and disorderly.

"It is my ambition," Harry said quietly, "to have the same thing happen to me."

If Harry and John did know each other, chances are they met at the track. Why are so many wonderful guys horse players, or so many horse players wonderful guys? Is it that the game breeds a kind of humorous fatalism that is a little like the essence of courage? Only a long-shot fancier could have composed the telegram that a newspaper in Columbus, Ohio, received after several days of unexplained silence from its reporter, McNulty, on an out-of-town assignment.

"Have been invited to join Marietta Lodge of Elks. Please send birth certificate and more expense money."

When John died, a girl who didn't know him but did know his stuff said a sentimental thing. "Maybe it was time," she said. "They tore down the Third Avenue El and the street isn't the same."

All the obituaries, of course, identify John as the chronicler of Third Avenue. All his friends—on newspapers and magazines and in the movies, the hack drivers and barkeeps and newsdealers and bootblacks and barbers and guys like Little Gabriel, the horse player, and Big Joe, the Russian, and the light-heavyweight who might have been champion but didn't like to punch people—they all thought of him as a horse player first of all.

When he wasn't speculating about how a rewrite man in Mecca would write a lead on a convention story ("Mecca became the New York of thousands today as the International Association of Pecan Growers gathered"), the stories he told were mostly about horse playing.

Like the time in Palm Springs or somewhere that he got $400 down to the local bookmaker. As John explained it, he had the money but it was in a joint checking account that he was reluctant to milk. Because the bookie was getting importunate, John telegraphed an Eastern publishing house asking $2,000 advance, by wire, on a novel whose manuscript he would deliver by such-and-such a date.

This went through channels, causing delay. By the time the check (for $1,000) arrived, John was $12 on top of the bookmaker. He sent the check back, explaining he wasn't going to write the novel, after all.

THE REAL LOMBARDI

IN THE BEGINNING the priest at Fordham is shown in the pulpit saying, "Vincent Lombardi not only believed in the gospel we read this morning, but lived it in his daily life." And a moment later Forrest Gregg, Green Bay's perennial All-Pro at tackle says, "After a loss he wasn't tough, he was ferocious."

Anybody who knew the man knows that both statements are the simple truth, and if the speakers seem to be talking about different men, that is because Vince Lombardi was many different men. Several of them are viewed with clarity and honesty and taste in a television documentary that is likely to be seen by the largest audience ever tuned in on a feature of its kind.

National Broadcasting Company will show it Sunday, starting at 12:30 P.M., Eastern time, as a preliminary to the world championship game between the Baltimore Colts and Dallas Cowboys, and NBC expects to have 67 million watching the game. Chances are the vast majority, being football fans, will welcome an opportunity to meet the real man behind the fiction and hyperbole and hearsay and legend that they have read and heard about him.

They will discover neither a saint nor a sadist but a human being who could sometimes seem to be one and sometimes the other. Vince Lombardi was a deeply moral man, pure of thought and speech and habit, who studied two years for the priesthood and was inwardly as violent as a crime of passion. He had the intelligence and drive and integrity to be—as his friend Wellington Mara suggests in the film—president or pope, and he chose to be a football coach teaching a game for boys.

A Man Named Lombardi was written and directed by Jerry Izenberg, the bright particular star of the *Newark Star-Ledger*, who knew

Vince Lombardi well. It was produced by George Flynn, who knew Vince well. Everybody who talks of him in the show: Bill Heinz, his collaborator on books and magazine pieces; his friend Well Mara; players he coached like Frank Gifford, Willie Davis, Bart Starr and Gregg—all knew Vince well.

They knew him, and they tell it the way it was. They do not let the fact of his death from a terribly virulent form of cancer frighten them into mealy-mouthed generalities. This is a show of quality, and the quality that illumines it most is truth.

"In 1959," Forrest Gregg says, remembering his apprehension approaching the first season of Lombardi's reign in Green Bay, "I came to camp with my bags packed."

"It was a vicious training camp," Bart Starr says.

Willie Davis explains why Vince drove them so mercilessly in camp, and why his training equipped them to play football better than anybody else.

"Coach Lombardi," Willie says, "made practice so difficult and so demanding that the game itself was fun."

Jerry Izenberg's writing is witty and perceptive, and the narration by George C. Scott, chosen the outstanding actor of 1970 by the National Society of Film Critics, is exactly right, low-keyed and sensitive.

The film traces Vince's career in football from his days as a 170-pound guard at Fordham—there is a remarkable shot of the play in a Fordham–St. Mary's game when an ungentle elbow permanently altered his smile—to his towering success as creator of Green Bay's superteams. It was a long difficult road up from a $1,700-a-year job teaching Latin, chemistry, physics, football, basketball and baseball to high school kids.

There is a striking contrast between the words that are spoken and the emotions they do not manage to disguise. The words are blunt—"vicious, ferocious, demanding, harsh, punishing"—yet the voices that speak them have an undertone of genuine affection.

The man named Lombardi was so competitive that he would drive ninety-five miles an hour just to reach a restaurant ahead of his friend Tony Canadeo and prove his route was better than Tony's. And winning was so important to him that Bill Heinz, who took the terrifying ride with him, was glad they got there first because "otherwise, it was going to be a terrible dinner."

Yet as Vince lay dying in a Washington hospital, the Redskins' veteran guard, Vince Promuto, would tell him, "I thank God that you came my way, even if it was for just a short year."

THE BIG TRAIN AND HIS BUDDIES

WASHINGTON, D.C. Walter Johnson, one of the most beloved of baseball players and perhaps the greatest of all pitchers, was buried today beside the grave of his wife in a little country cemetery. A funeral procession three blocks long wound through the thickets of Maryland to Rockville Cemetery after services in the National (Episcopal) Cathedral, which contains the crypt of an ardent Johnson fan, Woodrow Wilson.

"Big Barney's" casket was carried by eight of the men who were his comrades when he whipped the Giants in the deciding game of the 1924 World Series—Oscar Bluege, present manager of the club; Nick Altrock, now a coach; Muddy Ruel, new manager of the Browns; Joe Judge and Roger Peckinpaugh, who served with Bucky Harris and Bluege in Washington's finest infield; Sam Rice, outfielder; Tom Zachary, pitcher; and Mike Martin, who was the club trainer throughout Walter's twenty years with the Senators. All are graying or balding or both.

Bucky Harris, present manager of the Yankees, who was the "boy wonder" leader of the 1924 Senators, was an honorary pallbearer. So were Clark Griffith, president of the club; Edward Eynon, secretary; Clyde Milan, who roomed with Johnson for fourteen seasons; Jack Bentley, the Giant pitcher who lost that final World Series game; E. Lawrence Phillips, the Griffith Stadium announcer in megaphone days; Bill McGowan, dean of American League umpires; Spencer Abbott, scout and manager of Washington farm teams; Jim Shaw, a colleague of Johnson's on the pitching staff; and Lu Blue, former first baseman for Detroit and St. Louis. George Weiss, Yankee farm administrator, came down from New York, and Dick Nallin, a former American League umpire, from his farm near Frederick, Maryland.

"How he could pitch!" a man said. "How many bases on balls would you say he allowed in 1913 when he won thirty-six and lost seven games? Well, he had forty-three decisions that year and he walked thirty-eight men. In Hal Newhouser's best year, when he won twenty-nine, he walked one hundred and two."

"The best pitching I ever saw," Altrock said, "was in Detroit. The Tigers filled the bases on two boots and a walk with none out. Three left-hand hitters, Cobb, Veach, and Crawford, came up. Walter struck 'em out on nine pitches."

"That wasn't his best pitching," Griff said. "Neither was his game in the '24 Series or the time he beat New York three times in four days. The best of all was in 1912 against the Athletics with Eddie Collins, Home Run Baker, and the rest of that one-hundred-thousand-dollar infield. We'd been feuding with the A's all season and while we were fighting, the Red Sox slipped in and won the pennant.

"We had a three-game series in Philadelphia to close the season and the team that won the odd game would take second place. Jim Shaw over there started the series, the first game of a doubleheader, and led, three to nothing, until the seventh.. Then the A's tied the score and Johnson came in. He shut 'em out until the nineteenth, when his catcher got hurt. We put in Rippey Williams, who always wanted to catch Johnson, and the first pitch got by him and clipped Billy Evans, the umpire, on the ear. Billy clapped a hand to his ear and it came away blood.

" 'You're not gonna get me killed,' he told Williams. And he called the game on account of darkness, although it was only about four-thirty. Next day another doubleheader was scheduled and the same thing happened. Walter had to come in again with the score three to three after seven innings. This time it went to the twenty-first before we won, four to three. So he worked twenty-six innings against the greatest team of its time without allowing a run."

Johnson's eighty-year-old mother; his sons, Walter, Jr., and Edward and William, and his daughter, Barbara, were among the mourners. The simple services were conducted before a congregation of several hundred, mostly of middle age or older who packed one nave in the vast cathedral. Earlier in the day there had been a stream of visitors to the funeral home in suburban Bethesda, a few blocks from the house Johnson occupied until he moved to a Montgomery County farm.

These former neighbors stood in knots outside the funeral home, dropping in singly or in pairs, then lingering to talk of the plain, gentle man who is dead. A Montgomery County trooper came in alone and knelt before the casket. Walter was a member of the county commission, the only Republican. At each election, the voters would name four Democrats and Johnson.

"That woman," Griffith said, nodding, "was his nurse. She took care of him like a baby, and when she knew he couldn't get well she resigned. She couldn't bear to stay."

"See that man?" Griff said. "As long as Walter could eat anything, he took a quart of ice cream all the way out to the farm every day."

"Did you ever see such a guy for eating ice cream?" Bucky Harris said. "He hardly ever smoked or drank, except once in a while he'd take a few puffs out of a cigar, looking as awkward about it as a girl."

"What a sweet guy! My first year as manager I was young and I didn't know how some of the older players might take to me. We took the pitchers to Hot Springs for early training and Walter was the bellwether, setting an example that made 'em all work.

"You know, he pitched fifty-six consecutive scoreless innings for me. The last six innings of the streak he had St. Louis shut out, but then we scored six runs and I said to myself, 'Good night, here it goes.' I knew he'd coast on that lead, and I'd advertised him in Detroit, where we were going next, and Cobb had been promising to score on him and I knew we'd get a crowd up there.

"Sure enough, he threw a nothing ball to Ken Williams, who hit a triple. Joe Gedeon tripped Williams at second, fell on him, hollered for the ball and tagged him. But Billy Evans sent Williams on to third for interference, and he scored on a fly."

"Cobb," somebody said, "once confessed that if he hadn't been so sure of Walter's control and didn't know how careful Walter was not to hit anybody Ty couldn't have batted .100 against him. As it was Ty knew he could take a toehold."

Another said, "Henry Edwards once told me he asked Walter if he'd ever used a spitter. Walter said just once. It almost got away from him and he never tried it again for fear he'd kill somebody."

"When we had squad games in training camp with Walter pitching," Bluege said, "practically everybody that was supposed to hit against him would suddenly get sick or hurt."

Another said, "Remember the time Ruel and Milan were hurrying to a show with him and some fan spoke to him and held 'em up half an hour? They kept signaling him to break away and when he finally did they gave him hell. He said he was sorry, but the fan was a fellow who grew up in Kansas and knew his sister well and he didn't want to be rude.

"Milan said, 'I didn't know you had a sister.'

" 'I haven't,' Walter said. 'But he was a nice feller!' "

FRANK ERNE

WHILE ATTENTION was concentrated on the Marciano-Charles fight last week, boxing lost a great gentleman and distinguished ambassador. Frank Erne, lightweight champion of the world at the turn of the century, died in his eightieth year.

His last illness took his last dollar. He who had always made his way alone was broke at the end and he left Mrs. Erne in financial difficulty. She need not be. Boxing could take care of Frank Erne's widow without beginning to repay its debt to Frank Erne.

Erect, immaculate, courteous, he was a walking contradiction—a briskly striding refutation—of the ugly picture so often drawn of his sport. All those who imagine the pugilist, especially the pugilist of Frank Erne's day, as a muffin-eared bruiser in cap and sweater with a mouthful of marbles, should have had the experience of meeting and talking with this spritely gentleman.

Many did, for although Frank probably never thought of himself as an ambassador for boxing, he was just that, and he worked at it. When World War II was over for most of us, he remembered those for whom it would never end. Well along in his seventies, he continued his rounds of the veterans' hospitals, giving his time and strength as he had done during the war to visit Atlantic City, Northport, Castle Point in an effort to cheer the kids there.

Nobody could talk with more eloquent conviction of boxing as a pure science. A good punch, he would say, starts all the way down in the feet; it is an uninterrupted flow of power up from the legs, through the torso, delivered with arm and shoulder with the body's full weight behind it.

He would be on his feet demonstrating, this little old man. "You feint him this way, feint him that way, and then just as he starts a punch, you catch him coming in. It's like automobiles colliding head-on —sheer destruction."

Once in a while it might occur to a fascinated listener that Frank punched better at seventy-five than he had at twenty-five. He was a boxer rather than a slugger in his day, and although he scored his modest share of knockouts, nobody ever nicknamed him "Sheer Destruction."

"Do you go to the fights these days?" Benny Leonard asked Knockout Brown after they'd both quit the ring. Brown said he went regularly.

"Ever see anybody you couldn't lick?" Benny asked.

"Never."

"Good. So just stay there in your seat."

Sometimes when Frank Erne was talking you had a notion that he could still climb out of a ringside seat and take care of himself all right, he was that convincing. He could tell tales of men whose names are only legends today—Jim Jeffries and Bob Fitzsimmons; George Lavigne, the Saginaw Kid; George Dixon; Terrible Terry McGovern; Jack Skelly, who fought for the world championship in his first professional bout; Joe Gans, the old master.

Frank was one of the now-dwindling company that knew Gans, who may have been, pound for pound, the greatest that ever lived. Knew him? Frank fought him twice, although that wouldn't necessarily mean they really knew each other.

Chatting with Georges Carpentier in Paris some years ago, Frank Graham inquired about a fellow who had always interested him, Bombardier Wells, the punching Englishman with the crockery chin.

"What was he like?" Graham asked.

"I couldn't say, really," Carpentier said, "never knew the chap."

It could be that way sometimes. Man goes to Ghent and belts a guy out in four rounds, goes to London and belts him out again in one, never gets formally introduced.

Frank Erne knew Gans, though. They went twelve rounds together in 1900 and Gans quit with an injury, asking to have the bout stopped. That would be scored as a knockout today but in Erne's record it merely reads, "W-12."

Making weight became difficult, and Frank moved up one division to fight Rube Ferns for the welterweight championship but lost by a knockout. So he made the lightweight limit for a second bout with Gans, and was flattened in one minute, forty seconds.

That cost him the championship he had won from Kid Lavigne in 1899. Officially, he held no title after 1902. Actually, he was a champion up to last week.

GLENN SCOBEY WARNER

POP WARNER was a gruff old gent, kind and forthright and obstinate and honest. He was one of the few truly original minds in football coaching, and that made him a big man in his world. There is, however, a more important measure of a football coach than his contribution to and influence on the technique of the game. The quality of the man himself is revealed in the attitude of his former players after they outgrew the awed hero worship of undergraduate days.

After the boys who played for him had become men, Pop remained a hero to them. In later years, he was father confessor to many. Fellows like Fred Swan and Charley Winterburn, who played under him in college and were his assistants at Temple University in Philadelphia, felt more than affection and loyalty. To them he was almost a god.

Pop was always a stubborn man, and as he grew old in the game he resisted change, as old men are wont to do. In one season at Temple—memory stumbles, but it could have been his last year as a full-time head coach—his team seemed extraordinarily vulnerable to a forward passing attack. Fans and alumni grumbled that his pass defense was archaic, outmoded.

"I don't know what's wrong with it," Pop said. "It's worked for forty years."

He discerned in that one admission that perhaps his critics had a point.

As one of the great innovators of the game, he earned his distinction fairly. His single-wing and double-wing attack, behind a line unbalanced to concentrate power ahead of the ball, became the conventional system of offensive football. In the mid-twenties you could start a fight anywhere over the relative merits of Warner's power football and the Rockne system of man-for-man blocking. Ultimately the great majority of teams from sandlots to the professional leagues were playing Warner football, until the T-formation restored the balanced line.

Warner was still one of the most famous names in football when Temple hired Pop in 1933. Temple had resolved to set out boldly after the advertising and profits of big-time football and wanted a coach who could build a winning team and whose name would command national attention.

Scouts fanned out looking for players and brought in some that were first-class, guys named Dave Smukler and Swede Hanson. Pop gave full value on his last big job. It was his personal prestige, rather than the fame of his good teams, that put Temple in the national picture as a participant in the first Sugar Bowl game in 1935.

Before Pop's contract was completed in Philadelphia, Temple's enthusiasm for big-time football had abated. At the end, Pop wasn't getting the quantity or quality of material that had been provided at the beginning.

His own enthusiasm did not diminish, though. He would squat on the bench, a stocky and apparently imperturbable Buddha, but butterflies were doing loops and barrel rolls under his sternum. He remembered to the end a lesson he had learned in his youth, never to attempt anything heavier than toast and tea at lunch on Saturday.

There was a game in Fenway Park in Boston between Pop's Temple squad and a Boston College team coached by another member of football's rugged palace guard, Gil Dobie.

Nothing much is recalled about the game, except that it wasn't anything special by way of entertainment, and it ended in a tie. Afterward, though, there was a tableau in the Fenway Park press room that remains fresh in memory.

Pop and Gil sat having a bit of something to warm their bones, glowering stone-faced across a table, each telling the other how lucky he'd been to be let off with a tie. Gil said B.C. had worked all season on a long gainer which no defense could stop, but he hadn't the heart to use it against his old friend. Pop said that was good, because Temple had been prepared to retaliate with some dazzling forward laterals that never missed.

They made a picture—two tough old guys who probably had no wish to add to each other's troubles, positively had no taste for losing, and wouldn't admit how tickled they both were with the tie.

THOMAS OF THE ROSE BOWL

FRANK THOMAS was born in Indiana, coached football in Alabama and was so often in California that he could have voted there. Before the Pacific Coast Conference and the Big Ten were united in a shotgun wedding that turned the Tournament of Roses into a family picnic, it was not always easy to be sure whether Tuscaloosa, Alabama, or Pasadena's Arroyo Seco was the home base for Mr. Thomas and such operatives as Don Hutson, Dixie Howell and Harry Gilmer.

Alabama's football players received free board, lodging and tuition, and in return gave unquestioning obedience to the chunky gentleman whom they called "The Top Sergeant." At least, they did not question his authority more than once.

The Alabama player who fractured one of the coach's rules, and got caught, was ordered out at 6:00 A.M. every day thereafter to run under the baleful eye of an assistant coach until he had covered one hundred miles. The tale goes that one player, a trifle slow to learn, ran 250 miles before he got the idea.

Having studied discipline under a master, Alabama had no trouble at all making Southern California and Stanford behave in the Rose Bowl.

Frank Thomas belonged to a generation of coaches trained and taught by the incomparable Knute Rockne. In his day—he played quarterback in 1920, 1921 and 1922—young coaches were coming out of Notre Dame as though off an assembly line, and a celebrated company they were.

Hunk and Eddie Anderson, Clipper Smith, Buck Shaw, Harry Mehre, Jimmy Phelan, Slip Madigan, Chet Wynne, Jack Meagher—the list of Notre Dame players who turned to coaching in that era goes on and on. They fanned out across the country, carrying the gospel of Rockne football to both coasts and into the Deep South.

Chances are there never was before and has not been since so large and able a group produced from a single source within a comparably short period. Virtually all of them won distinction teaching a style of play which was—it must always seem to an aging fan—the most attractive and entertaining and colorful that we have seen.

Perhaps it was not the most efficient possible game, for the Rockne system is largely out of style now. Yet it was a thrilling thing to watch with its emphasis on split-second timing, the cadenced shift in the backfield, the explosive start synchronized with one-on-one blocks designed to make every play a potential touchdown shot.

Charley Caldwell, the Princeton coach, has recalled that during his undergraduate days at Nassau he was taught a bruising, smashing, head-to-head brand of power football that had precisely the quality of a collision of beer trucks.

"At the end of the game," he said, "we'd be completely exhausted, just drained. The time we played Rock's team, though, we weren't tired at all. We could have taken another sixty minutes right there. They didn't smash us. They just brushed us aside, tipped us off balance, and the ballcarrier would whip past barely out of reach.

"When it was over I thought, 'Holy mackerel, if this is football, then there is more to this game than we've ever suspected.'"

That was football as Rock taught it to fellows like Frank Thomas and as Thomas and his contemporaries taught it to thousands of others. Partly because of them and partly because of Rock's own unforgettable personality, the name of Knute Rockne remains today, twenty-three years after his death, a shining symbol.

Just the other evening at dinner, a man remarked that he supposed Rockne was tops among them all, but another at the table shook his head. This was John Minds, All-American fullback at Pennsylvania in 1897. No, he said, there never was another to compare with his coach, George Woodruff.

"The man who invented the famous guards-back formation?" one of the group said. "Yes, I suppose he was a wonder."

"Before he gave us guards-back," Jack Minds said, "he developed a much better play. If we were going to run a play to the left, our right tackle and right end would pull out of the line and swing around to lead the interference. Just before they hit the defensive line the ball would go into play, with that flying interference in front of it.

"Trouble was when our tackle and end pulled out the defensive players opposite them would charge across the neutral zone and follow them around and mess up the play before it got started. We never were able to make the officials honor the rules and call those men offside."

"I guess there'll always be trouble about rules," a man said. "I've just been reading some reminiscences by John W. Heisman, who played in the eighties and nineties, when you had to get hurt or fake an injury in order to make a substitution. 'In our game,' Heisman wrote, 'my captain whispered to me, "Get your neck broke, Heisman." ' Reading it, it seemed like yesterday, or last fall."

MR. PELLETERI'S HORSES

FOR A GUY who never met Tony Pelleteri, a surprising lot of memories were revived by the news of that horseman's death in New Orleans. Ordinarily when you read of the passing of a man you didn't know it doesn't mean a great deal, but if the man had horses and you knew them, that was something like knowing the man himself.

It was that way with regard to Mr. Pelleteri. A dozen years ago his name was so familiar that mention of it automatically suggested green silks with gold diamonds and a green and gold cap. Some pretty good horses had carried those silks, including one named Andy K. that was a kind of special favorite.

There was a girl who fell in love with Andy K. the day she saw him win the Kent Stakes at Delaware Park, and anybody who ever saw him win could understand why. He was an exciting horse, a bright bay who ran with his head high and his mane streaming in the wind the way Stymie's used to do, but you couldn't ever tell how he was going to do.

He had speed. At two he won the Arlington Futurity, and Johnny Longden brought him down the Widener Chute to win the Champagne Stakes at Belmont, but he had a tendency to go recklessly wide on turns and throw away races he could have taken easily.

After his four-year-old season he was retired to stud in Kentucky at a fee of $200. A couple of years ago he was advertised in the *American Racing Manual* as California's great sire of two-year-old winners, and his stud fee was $1,000. After that he dropped out of print.

Well, he was one of Tony Pelleteri's horses. Another was Bull Reigh, which looked like a live prospect for the Santa Anita Derby of 1941. Bull Reigh didn't do it, though. Charles Howard's colt Porter's Cap did, with the green and gold Pelleteri silks second.

That year the name Pelleteri was frequently in the news. That was the winter when the Fair Grounds in New Orleans went under water financially for the third time, and there seemed no hope for the old park where Black Gold and Pan Zareta had raced and died and found resting places in the infield.

That winter they enacted a scene snatched straight out of a showboat thriller like *East Lynne* or *Adrift in New York*. The Fair Grounds was under the auctioneer's hammer and the clubhouse chairs had already been sold off when an agent rushed in with papers that halted the sale.

He represented a syndicate created by Sylvester Labrot, Jr., the late William Helis and Tony Pelleteri, which bought up the old joint and kept it alive, as it is alive today.

That winter of 1941, a lot of things were happening in racing. A colt named Whirlaway was losing in Florida at odds of 3 to 10. A boy named Earl Dew, who had won the riding championship of America on the last day of 1940, was killed in a fall at Agua Caliente.

Racing was booming. Nobody knew Pearl Harbor would happen in the last month of that year. You go through the *Manual's* list of 1941 stakes winners and thrill to the names—Mioland, Roman, Sun Again, Omissions, Alsab, Attention, Level Best, Dit, Blue Pair, Requested, Haltal, Market Wise, Madigama, Shot Put, Big Pebble, Eight Thirty, Some Chance, Apache, Mar-Kell, Amphitheatre, King Cole, Ocean Blue.

That winter Tony Pelleteri had a four-year-old named Bay View, a spindly sort of horse without special distinction. He'd been a sprinter of no great account. In California they were telling a story that went like this:

Somebody had said Bay View had never won at a mile, and Mr. Pelleteri had said, "Wait 'til he goes a mile." He went a mile and won, and somebody said, "Well, he can't go any farther." Mr. Pelleteri had said, "Wait 'til he tries to go farther."

On February 21 he tried to go farther, set the pace for a mile and then tired, finishing third to Mioland and Hysterical in the San Antonio Handicap at a mile and a sixteenth. He was, as he deserved to be, ignored when the field paraded for the Santa Anita Handicap, $100,000 added, at a mile and a quarter on March 1.

Mioland, which had cleaned up practically everything in California that winter, was favored at even money. Bolingbroke, Royal Crusader, Can't Wait, General Manager, Sweepida, Hysterical, Porter's Cap, Challedon and Woof Woof all attracted more support than Bay View.

It was a miserable day, cold and rainy. Up in the Santa Anita Turf Club, the crowned heads of Hollywood turtled down into their minks and sables and probably saw nothing as Bay View belted out in front and stayed in front to the end of what was then the world's richest race.

When the tote board flashed the mutuel price of $118.40, a great, whistling sigh was heard in the press box. Mr. Ed Burns, of the *Chicago Tribune*, handed over a telegram he had received that morning from Mr. J. G. Taylor Spink, of the *Sporting News*, in St. Louis. It read: "Hope you have your umbrella. Don't overlook Bay View, no matter what price."

Mr. Burns had carried a modest sum to the track to bet on Bay View. Shortly before post he had glanced at the tote board and noted the price on Bay View, 60 to 1. "As a handicapper," Mr. Burns had told himself, "Spink stinks." And he thrust the money back into his pocket.

BO McMILLIN

THERE WAS the tale Bill Crowell used to tell about the memorable game between Harvard and little Centre College, when Bo McMillin and his playmates in Uncle Charley Moran's troupe of unknowns went up to Cambridge and perpetrated what was then a monumental upset. Bill Crowell was an official in Centre's famous victory.

"We'd all heard tell of Centre's 'Praying Colonels,' as they were called," Bill used to say, "and I suppose we all took it for granted the name was just a press agent's idea. Certainly it didn't occur to me that maybe these fellows actually did go in for prayers.

"I'd finished dressing for the game and I was passing the door of Centre's dressing room in the old Harvard fieldhouse when I heard a voice inside. Somebody was making a speech, and he really was letting go with the organ tones. The voice rose and fell, and now and then I thought I could hear sobs in the background.

"Then the voice stopped and a moment later a lot of voices joined in a kind of chant. 'By golly,' I thought, 'they are praying,' and I called the other officials to hear what I was hearing. We eavesdropped for a few moments and then the chanting ended and we slipped out of the fieldhouse and stepped aside to let the team file out past us.

"They came out looking grim and exalted. This one was rubbing his eyes with a big fist and that one's face was tear-streaked. Bo McMillin was the last out. He was blubbering a little. He saw us officials and stopped.

"'Mistah,' he said, 'out theh on that field today you're gonna see the God damndest bunch of prayin' Southern sons a bitches you've ever seen in your life!'"

"It's hard today," Bill used to say, "to appreciate the magnitude of that upset but it was a national sensation at the time. And those guys Charley Moran had, there never was a cockier bunch.

"Centre had a tall, rawboned end with big knobbly wrists that stuck this far out of his sleeves. When a Harvard play started he'd take one step forward and wait. If the play went away from him, he'd drop to one knee, rest his chin on a hand and watch with a pleased smile as the runner was smacked down. Then he'd call to the Harvard quarterback, 'Didn't do so good over there, youngster. Better come around and see me next time.'

"It was traditional with Harvard quarterbacks that they all called signals in the same way, accenting the second digit of each number. The quarterback would yell, 'Twenty-three! Forty-six' and on 'three' and 'six' his voice would be a shrill squeak. McMillin listened to this several times. Then he called time-out.

" 'What do you want?' one of us asked him.

" 'Jes' want to say,' he told us, 'that if that little old boy keeps on doin' that, I'm gonna kiss him.'

" 'You stop the game again like this,' I told him, 'and we'll kiss you for fifteen yards.' "

When Bo left Centre and went out coaching football, stories followed him. So did football players. It was a typical coincidence that when he quit as the Centenary College coach to take a job at Geneva College, the monstrous Cal Hubbard, whose ample torso had ornamented Centenary's line, suddenly became an undergraduate at Geneva.

It is related that on one occasion the late Jock Sutherland stumbled into a long-distance phone conversation between one of his players and Bo, who was describing the many attractions of Geneva.

Jock gently detached his athlete from the phone and spoke into it. "I didn't quite catch your proposition, Coach. Would you mind repeating it?"

Bo obliged.

"D'ye know who this is?" Sutherland demanded in his natural voice. There was a longish silence.

"Yessir, I do now, sir," a small voice answered, and the connection was broken.

WALTER O. BRIGGS

WALTER O. BRIGGS was, in the narrowest and best and most exacting sense of the term, a big leaguer. Among owners of baseball clubs, real big leaguers form a small and dwindling company, a company that has shrunk further with the death of the owner of the Detroit Tigers. Baseball cannot afford to lose his kind.

Mr. Briggs was a sportsman, one of the very few in a game that has become, over the years, more and more a business and less and less a sport. He was not in baseball to make money, which he didn't need. He wasn't in it for personal publicity, which he didn't want.

The opportunity to own a ball club did not represent to him an opportunity to preen and strut before the public, to air his opinions in the press and read his name in the headlines, to gratify his ego by gaining an almost dictatorial power over men's lives. If he had been, say, a radio comic, he would not have used his interest in baseball as the source of bad jokes written for him by hacks.

He did not look upon Briggs Stadium as a monument to himself. He considered it a place to play baseball, a place where fans like him could watch baseball, and because he was a fan and a big leaguer, he wanted it to be the best possible setting for the best possible baseball.

To be sure, he didn't need money or publicity or prestige and so he could afford to go first class. But there have been many men in baseball who were financially able to do things in big league style but didn't, because they weren't big league at bottom. Walter Briggs was.

His ball park was the handsomest in the American League and it rated one-two with Chicago's Wrigley Field as the most attractive in the majors. It was the most immaculately policed, provided the pleasantest working conditions for the players, the umpires, the office staff, the park help, the newspapermen who cover the games.

Detroit wage scales have been generally high, comparing favorably with any in baseball, and in some instances the salaries paid to Tigers of modest ability have been cited by executives of other teams in tones of consternation bordering on sheer horror.

Mr. Briggs endeavored to surround himself with able men and he placed complete faith in them. If Wish Egan, the late great scout for the Tigers, was willing to stake his reputation on an undergraduate like Dick Wakefield, Walter Briggs was prepared to stake his money on Wish's judgment. Wish did his best on every job. He landed a schoolboy named Hal Newhouser for a cash outlay of something like $400. Yet he never told the tale of that bargain transaction with half such relish as he took in the story of paying $52,000 for Wakefield, a failure.

When Jack Zeller was general manager of the Tigers he had a free hand which he employed so freely that Detroit lost title to ninety-one players who were declared free agents because of technical violations of the rules. Never publicly—and never privately, either, as far as is known here—did the owner of the Tigers offer a word of criticism of Zeller's judgment.

The passion for doing things in big league style embraced the smallest details. When exaggerating attendance figures was an almost universal practice in both leagues, Mr. Briggs ordered that the exact count be given to the press in Briggs Stadium, to the man. Anybody faking the figures would be discharged. Now and then an honest error would be discovered after the day's attendance had been announced, and then it was rare entertainment to watch the frantic scurrying to correct the mistake.

Spike Briggs, son of the owner, grew up in baseball in that tradition, surrounded by that atmosphere. Presumably Spike now becomes top man with the Tigers. He is candid, forthright, lively, enthusiastic.

Perhaps he will want to make some changes. For at least ten years, for example, he has been an outspoken admirer of Bucky Harris, whom he championed as manager and tried unsuccessfully to wangle into the post as general manager. Charley Gehringer, the general manager now, took the job with some reluctance. It is conceivable that Charley might have other plans for the future.

If so, it would hardly astonish anybody to see Harris move from the Washington dugout to the Detroit office. Only moderate physical strength would be required to wrench Bucky away from that curious and exotic assortment of imports whom he manages in Washington— manages but can't converse with because his Spanish stinks.

THE SWIFTEST HALFWIT

BEN JONES had been practically glowing with confidence when he saddled Whirlaway in the Kentucky Derby and Eddie Arcaro had been dubious because this was Eddie's first ride on the colt and in his short racing life Whirlaway had committed some deadly sins, like finishing behind things named Agricole and Cadmium and Little Beans and Pony in Florida and running wide into the Keeneland homestretch to kiss off the Blue Grass Stakes by six lengths.

Now, on May 10, 1941, at Pimlico, it was Ben who was stall-walking fretfully before the Preakness, and Arcaro was laughing at his fears. Having won galloping by eight lengths in the fastest Derby up to that time, Arcaro was positive nothing in this field could be close at the wire.

He was so blandly sure of his horse, in fact, that when the others came out of the gate, Eddie and Whirlaway didn't. Not right away. King Cole, Ocean Blue, Dispose, Curious Coin, Our Boots, Porter's Cap and Kansas, they came piling down past the stands with the jocks whipping and yelling and driving for position on the first turn. And away back, five lengths behind the field, Whirlaway came loping along counting the house with Arcaro sitting still as a bluepoint on the half-shell.

Eddie sat still down the backstretch as Whirlaway picked up horses in his own good time. Then with three still in front of him, Arcaro took the colt to the outside and clucked softly.

There was a curious sound from the crowd, a sort of deep bass "whuumph!" of exhaled breath—not a drawn-out "ooooohhh!" because the horse race didn't last that long.

"He moved around his field with a bold burst of speed," the chart reported afterward. Bold burst of speed? What he did to those horses was hard to believe even while you were seeing it. He cooked 'em, fried 'em. You could almost hear them sizzle, see them curl like froglegs in the pan.

The story was told later that Johnny Gilbert, setting the pace with King Cole, heard a rush of wind and glanced to his right, and Arcaro shouted, "So long, Johnny!" "So long, Eddie!" Gilbert shouted at the diminishing copper blur ahead of him.

That was all. Arcaro took hold of his horse and eased him in—five lengths behind the field going away, five lengths in front coming home.

"Johnny," Arcaro said to Gilbert as they dismounted, "wipe the jam off my mouth, will you? I been on a picnic."

That was Whirlaway, whose death was reported yesterday from France, where he had been in stud on lease to the French breeder Marcel Boussac. The beautiful chestnut son of Blenheim had passed his fifteenth birthday last week.

He wasn't the greatest horse that ever lived, but he was just about the most exciting. Every time he stepped on a track you knew that some time during the race you were going to see that breathless, blinding, tremendous burst which was as stirring a spectacle as any field of sports could produce.

He was Babe Ruth, Jack Dempsey, Bill Tilden, Bobby Jones—not just a champion but a champion who was also the most colorful figure in his game. Today the memory of him is so vivid it is difficult to believe that a dozen years have passed since his three-year-old season. So many pictures come back to mind.

Arcaro in the Lord Baltimore Hotel after that Preakness and a guy asking him what happened at the start and Eddie saying, "I got left."

"No, Eddie, not really left."

"Well," Arcaro said, "he dwelled. But when you cluck to this horse, he gets to other horses faster than any horse I ever rode. When you move on this horse, it's like moving in a Cadillac."

Whirlaway in the Narragansett Special, beaten by War Relic in a finish so unexpected that the management had prepared the winner's blanket of flowers in the colors of Calumet Farm, Whirlaway's home. And had Whirlaway's name engraved on the cup too, if memory serves.

He was favorite that day, of course. He ran sixty times and was favorite forty-nine times. In his last forty-five starts the only time he wasn't bet down to favoritism was the Pimlico Special of 1942, when he walked over by himself and there wasn't any betting.

This was the horse that had seemed such an unpredictable rockhead as a two-year-old that Grantland Rice said to Ben Jones, "I hear your colt is a halfwit."

And Ben said, "I don't know, Granny, but he's making a halfwit out of me."

LAWRENCE JAMES BENTON

THE DISPATCH from Cincinnati read: "Larry Benton, fifty-six, one of the New York Giants' all-time pitching greats, collapsed and died on a golf course here this afternoon." The obituary went on to state his claim to fame: Among the hundreds of men who have pitched for the Giants since 1900, only six won twenty-five games in a season—Christy Mathewson, Iron Joe McGinnity, Rube Marquard, Jeff Tesreau, Carl Hubbell and Larry Benton.

It is there in the records and the records do not lie, and so Larry Benton's place is secure in the company of the mighty half-dozen. Yet when there is talk of the old Giants—the swaggering, arrogant, turbulent Giants of John McGraw—whoever mentions the name of Lawrence James Benton? Hardly anybody. In Frank Graham's two great histories, *The New York Giants* and *McGraw of the Giants*, he is given scarcely more than a nod of acknowledgment.

The reasons aren't hard to find. Larry Benton came to the Giants and knew his greatest success in a day when almost all the Giants were more colorful figures than he. Something was always happening in the Polo Grounds in those days, something to excite the fans and make headlines and fill the sports pages with controversy, leaving only a little space down in the body of the stories for "Benton won another."

He had two good seasons, one great season, and then he was gone. Very soon, he was forgotten.

Larry Benton had been a truck driver in Cincinnati, but he didn't look like a truck driver. He wasn't especially big—an inch under six feet, weighing only 160 pounds. At twenty-two he was graduated from the sandlots to professional baseball, he advanced to the Boston Braves after three seasons, and on June 12, 1927, he was traded to the Giants along with Jim Taylor, a pitcher, and Herb Thomas, an infielder, for Hugh McQuillan, Kent Greenfield and Eddie Farrell.

A few months earlier, though, the Giants had made a vastly more exciting trade, sending Frank Frisch to St. Louis for Rogers Hornsby. In the spring, Eddie Roush had been a holdout. There'd been a great ruckus over Hornsby's ownership of stock in the Cardinals; John Heydler, president of the National League, had ruled that Hornsby couldn't play with the Giants until he sold his stock, the Giants threatened legal action against Heydler, and finally the whole league had to contribute money to meet Hornsby's price.

There was plenty of news to take precedence over the acquisition of a pitcher named Benton, a fourteen-game winner in Boston.

Winning seventeen games and losing seven in 1927, Benton had the best percentage in the league. His pitching would have been meat for much winter discussion, but that winter something else happened. Without warning or explanation, Hornsby was swapped to the Braves for the hungry catcher, Shanty Hogan, and Jimmy Walsh, an outfielder.

Nobody talked of anything else all winter. After Frisch and Hornsby, a young man named Andy Cohen was going to play second base for the Giants. Minnesingers at the annual dinner of the baseball writers jeered

> All your Walshes, Cohens and Hogans
> Won't begin to fill the brogans
> That Hornsby wore so well at second base.

And now, approaching Larry Benton's greatest season, Burleigh Grimes was traded to Pittsburgh. Everybody was talking about Cohen, who made a great start with the Giants, but it didn't take long to prove he was no Hornsby. Benton and Fred Fitzsimmons were pitching well, but down in Texas a bigger story was in the making.

One of McGraw's scouts, Dick Kinsella, was in Houston as a delegate to the National Democratic Convention. Bored with politics, he went to a ball game and saw a left-handed pitcher named Carl Owen Hubbell. A few weeks later Hubbell was with the Giants.

Larry Benton won twenty-five games in 1928 and lost nine. So what did they talk about as the season ended, with the Cardinals beating out the Giants in the last few days? About Benton's pitching?

No, they talked of Grimes, who had won twenty-five games for Pittsburgh. They talked of Hornsby, who had won the batting championship as a member of the Braves. And today when the season of 1928 is recalled, "That was the year Hubbell came up. Remember?"

Larry Benton never was the same pitcher again. He never again won as often as he lost. In May 1930, he was traded to Cincinnati for Hughie Critz, a brilliant defensive infielder. At last, the fans rejoiced, the Giants had a genuine major-league second baseman. Critz would give them the finest infield in the league, start them upward toward their first pennant in five years.

Benton? Well, he'd been fine while he had it. Nobody mourned his going.

JOSEPH FLOYD VAUGHAN

ARKY VAUGHAN was born ten years too soon. At the age of forty—which, of course, he would not have reached—he would still be busy in Ebbets Field or Pittsburgh playing shortstop or third base or second or the outfield, or at least pinch-hitting.

After fourteen seasons in the National League, Arky was released at thirty-five, having played out his best years against competition such as few of today's operatives ever met. A guy of his class could have gone on at least five years longer in the company that now peoples the majors.

Most of sports' rocking-chair jockeys believe that the game of their time, whatever it may have been—football in the days of the flying wedge, basketball in a cage, golf with a gutta percha ball—has deteriorated since their youth. Mostly they are mistaken.

Postwar baseball has had a few top men as good as ball players can get—the Rizzutos and DiMaggios and Henrichs and Musials and Slaughters. It is a provable fact, however, that never since Pearl Harbor has it regained the overall quality it achieved before World War II.

In his youth, Arky Vaughan was a star among stars named Pie Traynor and Paul Waner and Rogers Hornsby and Frank Frisch and Chick Hafey and Glenn Wright and Lefty O'Doul and Travis Jackson and Freddy Lindstrom and Hack Wilson and Riggs Stevenson and Gabby Hartnett and Charley Gelbert.

He was a .385 hitter and the Most Valuable Player in a league that included Bill Terry and Mel Ott and Babe Herman and Chuck Klein and Pepper Martin and Jim Wilson and Lloyd Waner and Rip Collins.

Never since then have there been so many so good. On every team in the league in those days there were men who could peel a pitcher like an orange, and not because the pitchers were below par. The pitchers were guys named Dizzy Dean and Carl Hubbell and Dazzy Vance and Freddy Fitzsimmons, who could face the Kleins and O'Douls and Otts and Terrys and Hermans and Vaughans and get everybody out and send the customers home inside a normal two-hour business day.

In such company Arky Vaughan was one of the best for fourteen summers. Even in such company, he could have been one of the best for seventeen summers, but for reasons that never were made entirely clear he did not choose to.

After ten big years in Pittsburgh, he was traded to the Dodgers in 1942. The following summer there occurred an incident that always pops into mind when Vaughan's name is mentioned. He was never a sulker or a clubhouse lawyer or a quarrelsome guy, but he did blow his stack once.

The way it came about, Leo Durocher, the Dodgers' manager, got into a noisy hassle with Bobo Newsom, who was serving one of his several terms at hard labor in Brooklyn. The quarrel between manager and pitcher raged through the clubhouse, involving other members of the team and the press and some rather free exchanges of personalities.

At length Arky Vaughan pulled off his uniform, bundled it up and handed it to Durocher together with a suggestion regarding its disposal. Such was the respect for Vaughan among other players that the whole club promptly went on strike. Feverish arbitration was necessary to wheedle them back to work for the next game.

When Durocher was rehired the following winter, he decreed group absolution for all the mutineers but in the same breath observed that there was one player whose magnetism and charm somehow eluded him. He mentioned no names and nobody else volunteered explanations, so it never was established that the reference was to Vaughan.

Just the same, Arky didn't return to the Dodgers in 1944. Branch Rickey, then operating in Brooklyn, visited him in California, but not even the Rickey eloquence could entice Vaughan off his ranch.

Possibly because he considered ranching a more useful wartime occupation than baseball, or perhaps for other reasons, Arky remained in the West through that season and the next.

The war ended, but Arky didn't come back in 1946, either. Apparently he made no application for reinstatement. There was no evidence that Brooklyn invited him back, although there were many in training camp that spring who believed, and said, that the Dodgers could make profitable use of the guy.

In 1947 he did come back, helped out when and where he was

needed, batted .325 as a part-time player and assisted in Brooklyn's successful race for the pennant. In two times at bat as a World Series pinch-hitter, he got a double.

It was the only World Series for one of the truly fine players of his time. At the end of the 1948 season, Arky was released. He departed from the majors with an average of .317 for fourteen seasons. It could just as well have been seventeen seasons. Had he elected to play through the war against the characters who were impersonating pitchers then, there's no telling what the lifetime average would have been.

WAITING ON JACOBS BEACH

THE WORD on Jacobs Beach was: "He may lick it yet. He's awful low but his blood pressure is down and they say he's coming around a little. They say he might lick it."

They stalled around, killing the slow time, talking. Saying how things like this always seem to happen in bunches, how it was Jimmy Johnston first and then Jimmy Walker and now Mike. And it was strange to think of that trio bracketed as an entry, for you couldn't find three other men quite so unlike personally; you couldn't go out and pick three men at random who wouldn't have a single small trait in common.

Still and all, you had to bracket them together because of the one big thing they shared, which was their stature in boxing. But then, of course, Jimmy Johnston and Jimmy Walker were gone but Mike might lick it yet. . . .

You don't ordinarily write obituaries about live men, but on the other hand there's no law that monuments may be erected only to the dead. And in his lifetime there've been no monuments reared to Mike. Decidedly on the contrary.

So there can't be anything particularly wrong about saying this of Mike Jacobs while the chance remains that he may get to read it: That although it is certainly true that nobody else ever exerted such absolute dictatorship as his over any sport and while it is probably true that no one else ever made such profits as he from boxing, it is emphatically true that no other man ever ran boxing as well as he, anywhere.

There must be a hundred things Mike has done in a business way which don't meet with everyone's approval and aren't necessarily good for the sport as a whole. But this is so and this is good: If anyone in the world has run fights on the level, Mike has. Undoubtedly there are guys who have slipped something across on Mike. But if he found out, they didn't do it again.

Insofar as one man is able, he has run fights on the square. Maybe this isn't because of any personal set of ethics or because of any high-minded love for clean sport. It could simply be that Mike is smart enough to know he can do better with square fights. During the war, when that abortive Louis-Conn promotion flopped, the customers didn't come clamoring for their money back. A solid year later they were still sending tickets in for refunds, knowing the money would be there and they'd get it.

So much for that. As for the man, well, the yarns they tell about him give the best picture. A classic tale is the one about the time he had a big outdoor fight coming up and decided to buy a recording machine so he could record a voice shouting, "This way to the bleachers, this way to the bleachers." That way he wouldn't have to hire guys with megaphones.

A sample machine was brought into the office and Mike said to one of the staff, "Say something into it," and went out to answer a call. The man recited a Shakespeare sonnet. Mike came back and sat down and played the record back:

> When in disgrace with fortune and men's eyes,
> I all alone beweep my outcast state,
> And trouble deaf Heaven with my bootless cries,
> And look upon myself and curse my fate . . .

"Ahh, for cat's sake," Mike said, "I heard that forty years ago."

The baseball schedule left no room for a postponement of the Buddy Baer–Joe Louis fight in Griffith Stadium, and on the afternoon of the match Washington was swept by a roaring cloudburst. Phones jangled incessantly in Mike's hotel suite and callers hammered on the door, flooding in to inquire whether the bout would go on. Mike sent out for sandwiches and sat there with his staff, spinning yarns in the midst of bedlam.

He talked about the old days when he started as concessionnaire on excursion boats and wound up owning the ships that plied the Hudson and ran from the Battery to Atlantic Highlands and other resorts. He told of the remedy he invented for seasickness, a vial of extremely weak tea that sold for twenty-five cents. He recalled how he peddled salted peanuts by the peck, and of course, there was no drinking water aboard, but Mike's soda pop sold right smart. Hard straw hats were the thing then, and Mike also sold his passengers a string to be run from hatband to lapel and thus tether the skimmer against the breeze.

Those were the yarns he told while the phones clamored and hail-stones rattled against the windows, threatening to wash maybe $150,000 down the drains. And afterward, when he was asked how he could take it that way, he said, "Me boy, I been battling the elements all me life."

He never kicks about a licking. His Lou Nova–Tony Galento fight in Philadelphia was a financial bust and when he left the stadium after-ward and couldn't find a cab, he sent Mushky Jackson to hunt one up while he sat on the curb and spun more yarns. Not a word of the fight, of the gate, of the bills to be paid. Not a word then or later.

When everyone was blasting him after the Louis-Conn match last spring, a man said, "Mike, why do you sit and take it? Why not point out that if Conn had thrown a half-dozen punches nobody would be yelling for anyone's scalp?"

Mike said, "Young feller, you're too dam' smart."

A few weeks ago he had guests in his home to watch the Notre Dame–Army football game on television. During a lull a guest got up and wandered around Mike's study glancing at the titles on the book-shelves.

"There's something I need," Mike said. "Gotta get me a carload of books."

RUSS CHRISTOPHER'S HEART

RUSS CHRISTOPHER was a "submarine ball" pitcher in the American League, tall, skinny, sallow, and a sweet guy. He was thirty-seven when his leaky heart gave out. He always knew that one of these days it would happen.

When he was a kid in the minors, doctors advised him to give up baseball and avoid physical exertion. He said that if his heart was going to stop he couldn't think of any other place where he'd rather have it happen than on a ball field, where he was happy.

When he started out to make a living as a ball player in El Paso, Texas, he was an outfielder like his brother Lloyd, who served hitches with the Red Sox and White Sox. As a pitcher, Russ batted like an outfielder, whipping his long arms through and getting pretty good power. If you knew about his heart, you quailed watching him run out a triple and slide into third base.

That's why the Yankees gave up on him. Sometime early in his travels from El Paso to Clovis, New Mexico, to Wenatchee, Washington, they got title to him, and in 1941 Russ won sixteen games for their Newark farm, losing only seven. His earned-run average was an excellent 2.82 per nine innings but because of his physical condition the Yankees left him on the draft list and the Athletics claimed him.

He used the conventional overarm pitching motion then but in his first or second Philadelphia season he got a sore arm and no longer was able to come over the top. Earle Brucker, the Athletics' pitching coach, schooled him in an underhand delivery.

Russ developed a malevolent pitch, a sinking fastball across the batter's knees. A witness familiar with Russ's work could tell within the first few pitches how good his stuff would be that day. If he was starting the ball down around his shoetops so it seemed to leap out of the grass, nobody was going to hit him. If he was delivering off his knee the pitch would reach the plate waist-high, and wouldn't reach the catcher at all.

You could tell how his stuff would be on any given day, but you couldn't predict what the game might hold in store for him, for there were some unpredictable guys with the A's of 1944 and 1945, and some fairly unbelievable things happened.

In one of those years there was a period of many weeks' duration when a hit off Christopher was an event and an earned run a phenomenon, yet he couldn't win a game. Even so, his 1944 record was fourteen won and fourteen lost and the next season it was thirteen–thirteen.

His last 1944 victory was his most memorable because it was achieved in Detroit when the Tigers and Browns were tied in a pennant race that St. Louis won on closing day. The A's were rooting for Detroit, but in their last start in St. Louis they butchered a game which they should have won easily, enabling the Browns to preserve their tie.

In Detroit the next day, the Athletics were literally ashamed to face the Detroit players whom they had let down. Christopher felt the disgrace as deeply as anybody, though he had had no part in it. Now it was his turn to pitch, and he mowed the Tigers down, compounding the injury with a four-hitter.

"Gee, I hated to beat those guys," he confessed to Brucker, "but I couldn't let up, could I?"

The mere thought left Brucker aghast. "Don't ever let me hear you say a thing like that again!" he said. "There's only one way to play this game, Christy, and you know it."

Of course Russ knew it, but he was the gentlest of guys. He was shy and quiet, with unsuspected laughter beneath the surface. In his quiet way, he could clown a bit. Coming out to warm up for the second game of a doubleheader in Washington one day, he brought flabbergasted howls from the stands. There was a hard straw hat on his head; a loud cravat with a huge knot was looped about his bare neck; his pants legs reached down to two-toned shoes, making him appear taller and gaunter than he was; a three-foot watch chain was looped from belt to hip pocket.

Seemed he and Eddie Mayo, the infielder, had worked out a zoot suit for ball players and Russ was trying it out for effect. The effect of this apparition practically put Connie Mack in a swoon.

Russ married a sweet girl in Philadelphia who ultimately induced him to retire for his health's sake. Before he quit, the Athletics sent him to Cleveland where he made one brief appearance in the 1948 World Series.

Memory retains a small tableau. An hour or so after a game in St. Louis, the last group to leave Sportsman's Park caught a cab at the press gate and, crossing Dodier Street, noticed a mob of at least fifty kids on the sidewalk. They had a tall young man pinned against the wall.

By this time, healthy ball players were back in the Chase Hotel, complaining because the steak was overdone. Russ Christopher was patiently scribbling autographs.

JIMMY AND BOBBY WILSON

THERE IS so much to write about Jimmy Wilson it was necessary to take back and wait a day in an effort to write it straight, as though this were just another great ball player who had died and not a great ball player who was a great friend.

Jimmy was only forty-six years old and he had been out of baseball less than a year. He turned up with Mrs. Wilson at Sunshine Park, the little racetrack near Tampa, one day this spring looking exactly as he looked when he succeeded Bob O'Farrell as catcher for the Cardinals eighteen years ago. His black hair was as black as ever, he had the same dark, healthy tan, and if he had added a pound since quitting baseball to become a big Florida landowner and orange grower it didn't show on his naturally stocky figure.

You'd have said he could go out and catch a doubleheader that afternoon. But death came to him almost as swiftly as it had come to his son, Bobby, in the China-Burma theater.

Bobby had been a well-behaved kid around the training camps ever so long ago, and then he was a leggy, rangy boy growing up swiftly in prep school, and then he was getting ready to finish Princeton, a handsome youngster as fine and decent as any you ever met, an all-around athlete like his father, a catcher on the ball team.

They were tremendously good friends and Jimmy's pride in the boy was something to see. Jimmy insisted on the best of schools and the best of everything else that he himself hadn't had a chance for, but indulgence never spoiled Bobby. Jimmy was confident that a couple of years of seasoning and Bobby would be in the majors, but Jimmy's problem was not how to get the kid started in baseball but how to persuade him to finish his education before joining the Air Corps.

Next thing, there came the word that Bobby had volunteered to fly a special mission over enemy territory and had flown out, and wouldn't be flying back. You couldn't say the news changed Jimmy outwardly. But afterward he seldom talked about the boy, and when a trophy was presented in Bobby's memory at a banquet one night Jimmy had to excuse himself and ask an old friend to accept it for him.

Chances are there never was a finer all-around athlete in baseball than Jimmy Wilson. He could have excelled at any game. He happened to excel first in soccer, because he was born in northeast Philadelphia, a section where no boy child dare hold up his head if he hasn't kicked goals from forty yards out before cutting his first tooth.

For years afterward when a foul tip dropped near the plate, the reformed soccer player rarely bothered to stoop for it. It pleased him— and the trick never failed to delight the fans—to kick the baseball back to the pitcher, lifting it smack into the pitcher's glove at shoulder height.

Before Bill Dickey reached his peak, the fiery Mickey Cochrane and the marvelously dexterous Jimmy Wilson were all by themselves as big-league catchers. When Gabby Street was let out as manager of the Cardinals the choice of a successor lay between Wilson and Frank Frisch. Sam Breadon picked Frisch, and Jimmy went East to manage the Phillies. Before that, however, there was an incident altogether characteristic of Wilson.

There was a good, ambitious young catcher in the Cardinals' training camp and word got around that he had declared his intention of running that old gaffer, Wilson, off the first-string job. When Jimmy heard of it he grinned and sought the young man out.

"You're going to be a great catcher," Jim told him, "and no club ever had too many great ball players. Will you work with me and let me show you what I've learned?"

The young guy's name was Gus Mancuso.

Wilson's skill with young ball players is a thrice-told tale. Every one has recalled how he succeeded with pitchers like Bill Hallahan, who'd never been able to stick it with another battery mate, how he scored with guys like Hugh Mulcahy and Clause Passeau and Curt Davis and Dolph Camilli, how he moved Bucky Walters from third base to the mound.

It has been recalled, also, how at the age of forty he quit the coaching lines to catch the 1940 World Series for the Reds; how he was the star of that Cincinnati victory behind the plate with his bat, and even made off with the only stolen base of the Series. And how Phil Wrigley, owner of the Cubs, was so impressed with the old guy's inspirational play that he hired him to manage Chicago.

Hardly anyone today remembers the famous Wilson "boner" of the 1931 World Series, yet the way he handled that incident reflected as much credit on him as any of his countless heroics. He was catching Hallahan, who had the Athletics shut out with three hits, 2–0, with two out in the ninth inning of the second game. Jimmy Foxx was on second base and Jimmy Dykes on first.

Foxx dashed for third as Jimmy Moore, a pinch-hitter, swung and missed a third strike. Wilson, responding instinctively to Foxx's move, whipped the ball to Jake Flowers at third base. Moore flung away his bat and started off the field, but Eddie Collins ran in from the third-base coaching line and literally strong-armed Moore to first base. Collins had realized that Hallahan's last pitch had hit the dirt ahead of the plate, so Wilson had trapped the ball instead of making a legal catch of the third strike.

A throw to first instead of third would have retired Moore and ended the game. Instead, the bases were filled. Afterward Wilson made only one comment, a candid "I pulled a rock." But now he went out and apologized to Hallahan.

"Forget it," Bill said. "You've pulled me out of enough jams. I'll take care of this one."

Meanwhile in New York, a young fellow named Tom O'Reilly, out of Lancaster, Pennsylvania, was making up the World Series extra for the *World-Telegram*. When Moore struck out he locked up his page and sent it away with the news of a Cardinal victory. A few minutes later word came that the game wasn't over. Mr. O'Reilly clapped on his hat and reached for his coat.

Out in St. Louis Jim Bottomley leaned far into a box behind first base and caught a twisting foul. So the game ended and the Cards won after all. In New York O'Reilly was asked why he'd grabbed his hat.

"If the next guy had hit," he said, "I was on my way back to Lancaster."

GUS DORAIS AND THE FORWARD PASS

OBITUARIES ON Gus Dorais retold for the thousandth time the tale of the first football game between Notre Dame and Army on the Plain at West Point, November 1, 1913. Chances are they set some readers to musing on the changes that forty years have wrought in the game of football. Perhaps others read the same stories and thought with surprise, "Why, this game could have been played last week. Fundamentally, there's been no change at all."

With Dorais, the quarterback, throwing forward passes to his ends, Knute Rockne and Fred Gushurst, and to his halfbacks, Joe Piska and Sam Finegan, Notre Dame won, 35–13. Two of the five touchdowns were scored on passes.

In the matter of figures, contemporary accounts vary, for in those days a football writer followed the play along the sidelines, made his own estimates as to yardage and kept such statistics as he was able. According to one reporter, Dorais attempted fourteen passes and twelve were completed; according to another, he threw seventeen and missed with four, getting thirteen completions for 243 yards.

Anyhow, modern football men talk about the development of the forward pass. The professionals, when they are caught with their modesty down, confess that they have perfected the tactic. Yet they do not do better today than Gus Dorais did forty autumns ago.

The obituaries described Gus Dorais as the "innovator of the modern forward pass," and repeated that it was his demonstration of the play's possibilities which altered coachly thinking and opened up offensive football. That is more or less correct, but it isn't entirely correct.

The pass was introduced in 1906. A year or two later an obscure team representing St. Louis University, coached by a man named Eddie Cochems, was employing the air game to murder its opposition. Army was using the pass before Gus Dorais visited West Point.

A pass from Vernon Prichard to John Jouett gave Army first down on Notre Dame's 15-yard line and set up the game's first touchdown. Enroute to Army's second score, the same combination connected on the 5-yard line. And with West Point bidding for a third touchdown Prichard threw into the end zone—where Louis Merillat was waiting, but Dorais intercepted.

Notre Dame has no copyright on the play, you see. It was only that these upstarts from the West—"from South Bend, Illinois" wrote a dreamy geographer on a New York paper—used it more skillfully than any team the East had seen.

Wrote Harry Cross, of beloved memory, covering the game, "The Eastern gridiron has not seen such a master of the forward pass as Charley Dorais. . . . Bill Roper, former head coach at Princeton, who was one of the officials of the game, said he had always believed that such playing was possible under the new rules but that he had never seen the forward pass developed to such a state of perfection."

In 1947, at the last meeting before the Notre Dame–Army series was interrupted, there was present the man who started the series, Jesse Harper, the Notre Dame coach in 1913. He was asked how the game came to be scheduled. "I wrote them a letter," he said.

Notre Dame received a $1,000 guaranty and, the obituary recalled, brought along sandwiches made on the campus to shave expenses. There were eighteen players on the squad but only twelve participated, one Larkin substituting for Finegan at right half. No further financial details are available for that trip, but there is preserved at Notre Dame Knute Rockne's handwritten expense account for the West Point visit of 1919. It reads:

"Receipts, $1,000. Railroad, $1,381.35; meals, $184; ferry $6.90; tip to porters, $6; tips to waiters [this was written first as $6, then changed to $12]; trip to Chicago to get shoes, $10.58; transfer of trunks, $3. Total expense, $1,603.83. Loss, $603.88."

After the first game, Harper recalled, he dropped in on Charley Daly, the Army coach, and some of the West Point brass.

"Off in the corner I saw an officer who was really giving his wife hell. Being a married man, I sidled over to get an earful. 'Well,' he was telling her, 'well, you've been hollering about why don't we play some decent opposition. Now, dammit, are you satisfied?'"

EDWARD GRANT BARROW

MILLER HUGGINS was the first to go, and then Colonel Jake Ruppert. Then Lou Gehrig died, then Tony Lazzeri, then Babe Ruth, and now Ed Barrow. Now the palace guard is disbanded. Now the old Yankees are dead.

In October of 1920, Ed Barrow had resigned as manager of the Red Sox and accepted the offer of Colonel Jacob Ruppert and Captain Tillinghast L'Hommedieu Huston to become general manager of the Yankees. He brought with him Paul Krichell, who had been a catcher for the Browns and was now a coach with the Red Sox.

"Do you know what you and I have got to do?" Barrow asked Krichell after they'd got settled in New York.

"No, what?"

"We've got to work like hell," Ed Barrow said, "to make good in this town."

Before he was old enough to vote, Ed Barrow had been a sandlot player and a newspaper man, a salesman of oil pumps and soap, an associate of Harry M. Stevens in the catering business, a founder of the Interstate League and owner of the Wheeling, West Virginia, franchise, where he managed the team and won the pennant.

He had discovered Honus Wagner, a bowlegged kid in a derby hat throwing lumps of coal at targets along the railroad right-of-way near Carnegie, Pennsylvania. He had been a hotel man, president of the Atlantic League and the Eastern League, later the International. He had been a minor league club owner and manager and, in his first year in Boston, manager of the team that won the world championship.

He had the judgment and the guts to move the greatest left-handed pitcher of his time from the mound to the outfield, taking the ball out of his hand and putting a bat there instead. This was Babe Ruth, of course.

Baseball men always argue and probably always will about the identity of the greatest player of all time. Some say Ruth, some say Wagner, some say Ty Cobb. Nobody ever suggests anybody else. There are only those three, and Ed Barrow had a big hand in the making of two of them.

How he "made good" requires no retelling. There came a time when, if you were touring minor league towns on the route home from spring training, your attention might be caught by some busher in Valdosta, Georgia or Tulsa, Oklahoma, or even—on one occasion—San Quentin Penitentiary.

"Who," you would ask, "is that big, good-looking kid in right field?"

"Oh," you would be told, "the Yankees have him."

They used to say that Ed Barrow could press a button on his scarred oak desk in Yankee Stadium and know within five minutes what brand of cereal the shortstop in Hutchinson, Kansas, had eaten that morning.

That desk was the heart and the nerve center. The Yankees of Ed Barrow's day were the greatest baseball team in the world with the greatest organization in baseball, but they were still a baseball team. Their name had not yet become synonymous in the minds of the fans with United States Steel.

They were a baseball team directed from a baseball park by a baseball man whose religion was simple: "We have nothing to sell but baseball." The Yankees then had no need for a Fifth Avenue address with thick carpeting and chrome fittings. When that came in, Ed Barrow went out.

Now he has gone farther still, that great, burly, wonderful man with the soft chuckle and the extraordinary eyebrows. He worked like hell; he earned his rest.

DOC GREENE

DOC GREENE, whom Sam and Kitty named Edgar before he could resist, lived fifty years, an achievement considering that some of the keenest medical brains in our Armed Forces agreed that he'd never make twenty-five.

This was after Major General Vandegrift's Marines landed on Guadalcanal and Lieutenant Greene was carried off with something like thirty-five wounds, including one so close to the heart the doctors couldn't understand why the pump kept working.

As Doc told the story, a whole team of specialists gathered around his bed in Hawaii trying to discover why he wasn't dead. Also present was a nurse who had given the patient considerable attention. Doc never admitted that he had, as the saying used to go, toyed with her affections, but he was a free agent in those days. At any rate, she listened while the doctors reviewed the case history, conjectured, theorized, and marveled. At length she spoke up.

"I'll tell you the answer, gentlemen. He's meant to hang."

Doc Greene was a genius in a freestyle, catch-as-catch-can sort of way. For greater or lesser periods of his life he was an apprentice matador, a newspaper columnist, a racetrack president, a croupier and a man-about-the-world who was at home anywhere on the globe provided the telegraph office there stayed open all night.

(Strictly a night person, he customarily showed up at Western Union to file his copy when the sun was climbing and suckers were going to work. Though this was the end of his day, his dark suit would still be impeccably pressed, his ruffled or pleated shirt immaculate. He had a shocking experience during the 1964 Winter Olympics in Innsbruck. For a week or more he drove himself to get the column off by midnight before he learned that he had been calculating the time difference backwards and could have filed as late as 2:00 P.M. the next day and still made deadline.)

In those days he was sports editor of the *Detroit News*. Later he wrote a column of general comment, and a few weeks ago he left the newspaper business by request and moved into boxing promotion. Just two or three days before his death he signed Joe Frazier and Bob Foster for a heavyweight championship fight in Detroit next October.

He had got into fight promotion because the *News* fired him for trying to help a Detroit group match Frazier and Cassius Clay, a project that fell through. Doc was such a figure in Detroit journalism that the *Free Press* played the news of his discharge under an eight-column banner on Page One and readers organized a protest march on the *News*.

I wish I could tell what my friend was like. Sometimes his life-style seemed flamboyant, but he was a quiet man who spoke barely above a whisper. He loved the unexpected, the unconventional.

When Ingemar Johansson was heavyweight champion, he went trout fishing in Swedish Lapland. At the end of a day he came out of the stream and made his way to a road just as a convertible with the top down pulled to a stop. Doc Greene stepped out. "Hello, Ingo," he said, flicking a speck of lint from his sleeve.

For a time Doc and his wonderful Mickey had a double apartment in Detroit with two picture windows. At Christmas when holiday lights festooned every other apartment, the Greene windows bore a legend painted by the Dickens scholar in residence: "Bah! Humbug!"

Still, he wasn't against the Christmas custom of giving. When Mickey needed binoculars for their occasional visits to the races, he had a pair covered with mink for her.

The late George Preston Marshall, then owner of the Washington Redskins, introduced Doc to Mickey, who had been Miss Florida. They were married on the isle of Elba en route to the 1960 Olympics in Rome.

Doc insisted on Elba. A year or two earlier he had found himself on the Tuscany coast within sight of the island and had decided he'd better get over there and see why Napoleon was in such a sweat to get away. He found it enchanting, the only place he knew that would do justice to Mickey as a bride.

One evening during those Rome Olympics, some of us were dining at an outdoor restaurant when Doc and Mickey arrived with another considerable group. Along came a hawker with colored balloons tugging at their strings. Doc had him tie one to every chair at each of the long tables.

You meet a lot of guys who'll stand you drinks. Doc Greene, God rest him, may have been the only one who ever bought balloons for the house.

ROCKY

STANLEY KETCHEL, the middleweight champion whom they called the Michigan Assassin, was shot and killed in Conway, Missouri, sixty years ago. When Wilson Mizner, the writer, heard about it, he said, "Start counting ten over him. He'll get up."

Mizner's words come back now because of an anniversary that has just passed. It was a year ago that Rocky Marciano went down with a private plane in Iowa. It is still hard to believe that he didn't get up.

Rocky was by no means the most skillful of boxers and may, indeed, have been the crudest operator ever to win the heavyweight championship. Primo Carnera would crowd him for that distinction, though, and it would be difficult for anybody who saw Joe Louis to regard Rocky as the greatest fighter of our time, no matter what the records say.

The records make Rocky the best. In forty-nine fights, nobody ever held him to a draw and only six opponents finished on their feet. Only one other heavyweight champion could show comparable figures: Gene Tunney, the most grievously underrated fighter of them all, lost once in seventy-six bouts.

Rocky Marciano couldn't box like Tunney and probably couldn't hit like Louis, but in one respect he had no challenger. He was the toughest, strongest, most completely dedicated fighter who ever wore gloves.

Fear wasn't in his vocabulary and pain had no meaning. Sixteen years ago this month he defended his title against the former champion, Ezzard Charles, for the second time. In their first match Charles had stood up to a frightful beating for fifteen rounds and walked out of the ring, unrecognizable but upright.

In the seventh round of their second bout a punch split Rocky's nose like a walnut. In the eighth blood poured from this wound and a cut opened above the left eye. One good punch would have spread the nose all over his face and the doctor would have been forced to order a halt, but Rocky wouldn't let Ezzard throw one punch.

Boring in through a crimson haze, he clubbed Ezzard to the floor twice. In five years, only Ezzard Charles was good enough to walk into the ring against Rocky and walk out. Now here he was just one stiff jab away from the title and the jab wasn't there. He took the count on his knees.

Any decent boxer could outpoint Rocky for a few rounds. A marksman could cut him up. Gladiators like J. J. Walcott and Archie Moore could and did knock him flat. But whenever a man started counting over him, Rocky got up.

On his word, no punch ever stunned or dazed him, though some wounded him and some knocked him down. He said that when he went down he was perfectly aware of going down, could see and recognize faces at ringside, could follow the referee's count.

"What did you think," Bill Heinz asked him, "when Walcott dropped you?"

Walcott was the champion and favorite, Rocky the crude young challenger, and this was only the first round.

"Funny thing," Rock said. "I didn't think anything when I was on the floor, but going to my corner after the bell I thought, 'Hey, this old man knocked you down. He might knock you down three, four times more tonight. This could be a tough fight.'"

He wouldn't stay down and he wouldn't lose. That was unthinkable. But it might be a tough fight.

His extraordinary fortitude was part courage and part physical condition. "Marciano," Frank Graham wrote, "is addicted to exercise as some men are addicted to the bottle."

Even in the months when he had no fight in sight, Rocky would train, living in the airport cottage above Grossinger's in the Catskills, jogging, hiking, sparring, punching the bag, skipping rope, doing calisthenics.

He even had an eye exerciser, a doodad he would set in motion and then follow with his eyes as he lay motionless. It used to make his trainer, little Charley Goldman, snicker.

"He wants stronger muscles in his eyeballs," Charley would say, shaking his head.

Once Rocky was asked when he had discovered that his physical equipment was out of the ordinary. He told about playing "king of the hill" one winter day when he was just a nipper in Brockton, Massachusetts. For hours he struggled to gain and hold a snowy summit against bigger boys. Making his way home at supper time, he passed two of the larger kids in the early dark. "Gee," one was saying, "that Rocky's tough, isn't he?"

"I knew then that everything was going to be all right," Rock said. It was, until a year ago.

JOE LAPCHICK

JOE LAPCHICK devoted most of his seventy years to a boys' game called basketball. Not many clergymen or doctors or scientists or policemen or philosophers did greater good.

"I saw the original Celtics in Green Bay, Wisconsin," a friend said one day. "You played the Northern Paper Mill team in Battery B Armory."

"What did we win by?" Joe asked. "One or two?"

"Joe," his friend said, "when you were holding a one-point lead in the last minute, weren't you afraid somebody would dump in a two-pointer and beat you?"

Joe shook his head. "We could always control the ball," he said.

A principal reason why they could was their center, a gravely smiling octopus of six-foot-five who dwarfed most athletes of his day.

If his height was unusual, his stature in his world was unique. When Joe was a kid in Yonkers, Dr. James Naismith's peach-basket game was just beginning to catch on in YMCA gyms and church halls. By the time Joe was twelve—and already over six feet tall—he was a member of several club teams, so he couldn't have been more than ten when he played his first game. When he retired fifty-five years later, he was the most widely respected and best-loved figure the game has ever known.

It has never been any secret to readers of this column that roundball was not my bag. It was never any secret to my friend, Joe Lapchick. Yet five years ago when St. John's University played its last game with Joe as coach, I sat transfixed by television in a crummy Florida motel room.

It was the final match of the National Invitational Tournament in Madison Square Garden and Joe's last because St. John's made retirement mandatory at sixty-five. When St. John's beat Villanova, 55–51, and the players swung Joe up on their shoulders, tears stood in all four of these eyes.

This was St. John's fourth NIT championship and it wrapped up Joe's second hitch as coach. His first term ran from 1936 through 1947; after eight professional seasons with the New York Knicks he returned to the campus in 1956.

His record over nineteen seasons at St. John's was an extraordinary 335 victories and 118 defeats. In the whole history of the National Basketball Association, the Knicks never won a championship until this year (1970), but under Joe they made the finals three times in a row and twice they carried the play-off to the limit of seven games.

He was a great coach and a greater man. The Czech immigrant's son who never went to high school lectured the kids at St. John's on the importance of education and breathed down their necks to make sure they kept up academically.

It was not an accident that when dumping games and shaving points was epidemic in New York, Joe Lapchick's kids were not involved. He taught kids more than they learned in school.

It's a debatable point, but perhaps basketball, which has so many close games, is harder on the coach's nerves and digestion than any other sport. Memory treasures an evening when two of the finest men in the world sat writhing on opposite sides of the court in Philadelphia —Joe Lapchick of St. John's and Billy Ferguson of St. Joseph's.

In the middle was a referee both coaches liked and respected, Lou Sugarman. As the evening unwound, you could tell how much they respected him. Billy Ferguson threw pennies at him. Joe Lapchick kicked over the water bucket and flooded half the court.

Still, his suffering on the bench never diminished the inner warmth, never wore out the gentle patience. Joe Lapchick remained always the best of companions, a delightful guy to be with whether he was telling about his efforts as the Knicks' coach trying to fan bland Sweetwater Clifton to wrath, or spinning yarns of adventure with the New York Celtics.

Joe was a star with the Celts when they won 109 of 120 games and were ruled out of the American Basketball League as "too good." When the league folded following the financial crash of 1929, Joe got the old gang back together and they barnstormed with the financial backing of Kate Smith, the singer, and her manager, Ted Collins.

He had a million tales of those days, like the one about touring the Georgia canebrakes in a private plane flown by Young Stribling, the prize fighter. Stribling might have been heavyweight champion of the world but wasn't, partly because he really wanted to be a basketball player instead. He flew the Celts around so they'd let him play a few moments in the boondocks.

In a way, the Celts were the most fortunate of men. Not only did they win ungrudging recognition as the best of their era, but their fame rang down the decades to make them a legend in their own lifetime. For a humble man like Joe Lapchick, this must have been riches.

PEAHEAD

WHEN GREASY NEALE was football coach at Yale, that fountainhead of refinement made a good game effort to persuade press and public to call him Earle, but it was like trying to make sex unpopular with the masses. Defeated on that score, the Yales were utterly routed a few years later when Herman Hickman, as head coach, hired Peahead Walker to be chief assistant.

Herman and Peahead were together in New Haven for one year, and college football has never been so much fun before or since.

Peahead was short and stocky, Herman short and vast. They were kindred spirits, gourmands, raconteurs, witty and gifted public speakers, pure of heart and great with cornpone laughter. *Collier's* magazine ran a piece about them whose title suggested the quality of their collaboration: "The Mountain Boys at Yale; or Frank Merriwell Never Had It So Good."

Herman's laughter was stilled first. The poet-laureate of the Little Smokies, as Grantland Rice called him, was still comparatively young when he suffered a fatal stomach disorder. Peahead was seventy-one when he died in Charlotte, North Carolina.

Tarheel country was home to Peahead, although he was born in Birmingham, Alabama. A minor league baseball player, he managed Snow Hill, North Carolina, in the Coastal Plain League and coached football at Atlantic Christian College in Wilson, then did ten years at Elon College before moving up to Wake Forest.

While he was at Elon, two New York sportswriters bound for the baseball training camps in Florida—Tom Meany and Garry Schumacher—drove two hundred miles out of their way just to meet a football coach named Peahead.

He developed outstanding teams at Wake Forest, and as the scores mounted his reputation spread. So did stories about him, not all of them guaranteed for veracity. For example, a sideline colloquy:

"Peahead, this boy is hurt bad. He cain't breathe."

"Dammit! you're the doctor. MAKE him breathe!"

When Peahead arrived in New Haven, he had served twenty-five seasons at Carolina colleges—one at Atlantic Christian, ten at Elon and fourteen at Wake Forest. It was Charley Loftus's job as Yale's director of sports information to fill out a dossier on the new member of the staff.

Charley is a New Haven townie with a store of information on many topics, but his Dixieland lore was learned as a boy from Al Jolson recordings. He was interested to discover that Wake Forest was founded in 1834 as a Baptist school.

"Are there a lot of Baptists in North Carolina?" he asked.

"Son," Peahead told him, "the only thing that outnumbers Baptists in No'th Ca'lina is the English sparrow."

Having survived one Yankee winter, Peahead mushed on over to Montreal, where for eight years he coached the professional Alouettes in the Canadian Football League. Montreal is second only to Paris in the number of French-speaking inhabitants, and Peahead found his stay there linguistically beneficial.

On his first evening in town he dined with the football team's owner and his wife. "By the way," he asked between the escargots and boeuf fondue bourguignon, "what's an alouette?"

"A bird," the owner's wife told him. "The most ferocious of birds, king of the skies. It attacks and drives off hawks, shrikes, the eagle, anything that flies."

It was two years, Peahead confessed later, before he learned the truth. When he did, he thought back to his dressing-room orations when he wanted to stir his warriors to a peak of savage ferocity. "Remember," he would cry, appealing to their pride, "remember—you're alouettes!"

CLARK DANIEL SHAUGHNESSY

THE OBITUARIES identified Clark Daniel Shaughnessy as the coach who revived the T-formation in football, and that's more-or-less accurate. He was the man whose example taught college coaches the possibilities of the T, and he played a part in the explosive events of December 8, 1940, the day professional football entered a new era that has not yet passed.

The one true prophet of the T-formation is George Halas, owner of the Chicago Bears. In 1920 when Halas organized the Decatur Staleys as the prototype of the Bears, he put in the T-formation because that was what he knew; they had used it during World War I at Great Lakes where he and Jimmy Conzelman, Paddy Driscoll, Hugh Black-lock, and other gobs made up a team that won the Rose Bowl game of 1919.

Though he flirted briefly with the single-wing in the early years, Halas never abandoned the T. His Bears were employing it during the 1930s when Shaughnessy was coaching the University of Chicago, and Halas says Shaughnessy was the first college coach to recognize its possibilities.

At any rate, when Chicago abandoned football after the 1939 season and Shaughnessy was hired by Stanford, he installed the T-formation at Palo Alto. He knew what he was doing: Stanford had a mediocre tailback named Frankie Albert who became a great left-handed quarterback, a beast at fullback named Norm Standlee, and a pair of running fools named Hugh Gallerneau and Pete Kmetovic.

Running from the T, the Stanfords blew through Shaughnessy's first session without defeat and whipped Nebraska in the Rose Bowl. Suddenly Clark Shaughnessy was in demand as an afterdinner speaker. On the banquet circuit he explained that where the single-wing formation stressed power, the T relied on speed and deception. He said that kids who had got lumps on their heads running the single-wing power plays really enjoyed fooling the opposition.

"And the secret of the T-formation's success," Clark Shaughnessy would say, "is simple: get a quarterback like Albert, a fullback like Standlee, and halfbacks like Gallerneau and Kmetovic."

Shaughnessy was no green hand at this stage. After graduation from Minnesota in 1914, he had been head coach at Tulane, at Loyola of the South, and at Chicago. He had been teaching football more than a quarter of a century when he hit the jackpot at Stanford.

It is inconceivable today that a coach whose team was going into the Rose Bowl could leave the campus a month before that game, but Shaughnessy did. At the start of December in 1940 he returned to Chicago as a specialist to polish the Bears' offense. Halas had clung to the T-formation over the years but it was Shaughnessy and Ralph Jones, a bald little man who had been with Halas since the 1920s, who introduced refinements like shuttling linemen and the back-in-motion.

The Bears had finished first in the Western Division of the National Football League and were about to play the Washington Redskins for the world championship. Just a few weeks earlier, they had lost to the Redskins, 7–3. In Howie Roberts's book, *The Story of Pro Football*, a Chicago demigod named Bulldog Taylor tells how it was:

"We were a pretty tense bunch: It was Shaughnessy who relieved the tension. He made the pregame talk and you've never seen anyone so calm. 'You can beat these Redskins,' he said, 'and here's how.' He outlined a play we had charted as our second of the game. 'It might go for a touchdown the first time,' he said. Somehow, we believed him."

The Bears' second play from scrimmage was the one Shaughnessy had diagramed. It didn't work exactly as it had worked on the blackboard.

Bill Osmanski slanted to his left on a dive-tackle plunge, saw his way blocked and swung wide around end. Straightening out, he found Ed Justice and Jimmy Johnston in his way, but all of a sudden here came George Wilson, the Bears' right end, galumphing across the field in search of trouble.

A horse player would say George Wilson put over a parlay. He hit Johnston with a block that flung the victim bodily into Justice and as both defenders went down Osmanski raced on alone for a 68-yard touchdown.

As Shaughnessy had promised, the play worked. It produced the first touchdown in a game the Bears won, 73–0. That game converted virtually every football coach in creation to the T-formation faith. It set off a boom in pro football that still shows no sign of leveling off. Clark Shaughnessy was considered something of a visionary, but not even he could have foreseen it all.

A HORSE YOU HAD TO LIKE

IF THIS bureau had a prayer for use around horse parks, it would go something like this: Lead us not among bleeding hearts to whom horses are cute or sweet or adorable, and deliver us from horse lovers. Amen.

In this case issue is not taken on the rhetorical grounds adopted by James Thurber when he observed that to him the expression "dog lover" meant one dog that was in love with another dog. Rather, the idea here is merely to get on record with an opinion that horses are animals which a guy can like and admire and have fun betting on or just watching. This is no knock at love, either.

With that established, let's talk about the death of Seabiscuit. It isn't mawkish to say there was a racehorse, a horse that gave race fans as much pleasure as any that ever lived, and one that will be remembered as long and as warmly. If someone asked you to list horses that had, apart from speed or endurance, some quality that fired the imagination and captured the regard of more people than ever saw them run, you'd have to mention Man O' War and Equipoise and Exterminator and Whirlaway and Seabiscuit. And the honest son of Hard Tack wouldn't be last.

It wasn't primarily his rags-to-riches history that won Seabiscuit his following, although reaching success from humble beginnings never dims a public figure's popularity. It wasn't the fact that he won more money than any other horse up to his time, although that hurt neither his reputation nor his owner. He wasn't a particularly handsome horse, nor especially big or graceful, and he never was altogether sound. Up to now, his get have not made him famous as a sire.

The quality he had was expressed one day by a man in the press box who said, "Look at his record. He's the Canzoneri of horses."

Look at his record and you see what the man meant. Just as Tony Canzoneri barnstormed through the fight clubs of the land taking on everyone they tossed at his head, so Seabiscuit made the rounds of most of the mile tracks between the oceans, and left track records at more than a few. Hialeah Park (his record reads), Bowie, Havre de Grace, Jamaica, Rockingham, Narragansett, Suffolk, Saratoga, Aqueduct, Agawam, Empire City, Pimlico, Belmont, Detroit, River Downs, Bay Meadows, Santa Anita, Tanforan, Laurel, Agua Caliente, Arlington, Del Mar, Hollywood.

He didn't always win, of course. Indeed, he was whipped seventeen times hand running in allowance purses and maiden races and claimers before he won one, and that one was worth $750. Those were the days when he went unclaimed for $2,500.

It has often been written how his first owner, Ogden Phipps, tossed him away for $8,500 in a private sale to Charles S. Howard. Actually, Phipps did all right with him. Seabiscuit ran forty-seven times and won nine races for his breeder: his winnings and sale price brought Phipps $26,965. No one could have guessed he would earn $419,265 racing for Howard.

In these days when a Shetland pony won't break out of a walk for less than $50,000, earnings are an incomplete measure of a horse's class. Seabiscuit's record of $437,730 has been surpassed by many horses. But he had to work for most of his. He often came out of a race with $25 or $50 in third or fourth money, and he had to make three runs at the Santa Anita Handicap, losing twice by a nose, before he grabbed his biggest prize of $86,650.

With the news story of his death was a photograph of Seabiscuit with Red Pollard, his regular jockey. It brought to mind several names that were associated with the horse. There was his owner, who was known as "Lucky Charley" Howard when his stable, led by Seabiscuit, was polishing off stakes like mad, making him first among money-winning owners. They haven't started running benefits for Howard yet —he was nineteenth among owners, with purses of $182,885 last year— but you don't see those red and white silks out front as often as you did, and they don't call him "Lucky Charley" any more.

There was Pollard, who certainly wasn't ever called lucky. The little redhead rode to fame on Seabiscuit but he missed the ones he wanted most. He'd been second, beaten a nose by Rosemont, in the Santa Anita Handicap of 1937 and he was getting ready for a second shot the following year when he got busted up in a spill. Had to sit back and look on while his horse lost the same race by the same margin, this time to Stagehand.

He was just about recovered from that injury when he came East to ride Seabiscuit in New England. A gypsy horseman, a friend, asked him to work a two-year-old for him. The colt bolted and smashed Pollard's left leg. He was still laid up when Seabiscuit ran the most memorable race of all, the match with War Admiral.

Seabiscuit broke down in his next start and Pollard went to the farm with him, put in a year helping to bring him around. They came back together in 1940, and together they finally won the $100,000 Handicap. One hasn't heard much of Red since, although he was still riding a fair share of winners last year.

There's Tom Smith, who trained Seabiscuit. He's changed jobs and things haven't been entirely smooth for him. Just got back this year after his suspension in that ephedrine case.

And then there was Georgie Woolf, who rode Seabiscuit in the match with War Admiral, the best horse race these eyes have seen. That was the race for which Sam Riddle, War Admiral's owner, dictated virtually all the conditions, including a walk-up start because his horse didn't like gates.

Ed Christmas was talking about Woolf recently, recalling how he used an old trick of quarter-horse racing to steal the start from Charley Kurtsinger, who didn't have his experience of racing on the Western plains. As they walked up to the line, Georgie kept Seabiscuit's head turned in toward War Admiral, determined that if he didn't get away alone he'd leave no room for War Admiral to dart past him. If ever a rider swiped a race, Woolf swiped that one at the start, leaping away ahead of a horse that was habitually first out of the gate.

Georgie Woolf? He's dead, too.

STANLEY WOODWARD

THE BEST and kindest man I ever knew died yesterday. His name was Rufus Stanley Woodward. He was my idol, twice my editor, and perhaps my truest friend. He was seventy-one and his health had been failing. A bronchial condition made breathing difficult. Early yesterday morning it became too difficult.

"Kindest" may not be the first word that would pop into the mind of a man who had drawn Stanley's wrath, and there were a lot of them over the years. But it popped into Joe Palmer's mind when Joe was asked to characterize his former boss. "Stanley is frequently disdainful of his superior officers," he said. "He tolerates his equals and he is unfailingly generous to his subordinates."

"Make no mistake," Stanley's friend Jack Martin of Bear Mountain told a crowd of newspapermen and sports guys gathered to salute Coach Woodward when he retired as sports editor of the *Herald Tribune*, "this man is a giant."

He was indeed—the finest of craftsmen, a leader who commanded loyalties almost as fierce as the loyalty he gave, a giant of integrity, dedication and honor, a brooder, a worrier, a fighter, and the dearest of friends.

He was also that rarest of phenomena, an honest wrestler. One winter we were scouting football players for the all-star game he used to run for the *Herald Tribune* Fresh Air Fund. It was his enthusiasm for football and his eminence as the game's best and most knowledgeable reporter that won him the title of respect, Coach Woodward.

Actually, Stanley was doing the scouting. He was just up after a bout with pneumonia and I was along as chauffeur and male nurse. In Pittsburgh we joined Jock Sutherland and his staff for dinner at the home of Frank Souchak, the All-American end who was an assistant to Jock with the Pittsburgh Steelers. As the party was breaking up, Dr. Sutherland casually dropped a gauntlet: "Stanley, would you care to wrestle?"

They stripped to the waist. The Doctor was about fifty-eight then, the Coach six years younger. Stanley removed his thick glasses, lunged blindly for a headlock and missed. A quarter-ton of beef smashed to the floor. The house trembled. Stanley was pinned. He lay gasping.

"Smith," he said weakly, "help me up." I handed him a Scotch and soda where he lay. He knew I went on newspapers because I disliked lifting things.

I realize that's no kind of story for a time like this, but some of us must laugh, lest we cry. Stanley, as all his friends knew, was helpless without his glasses. His sight failed when he was a boy in Worcester, Massachusetts, defeating his father's ambitions to bring him up to be a major league catcher. During his blindness he learned to play the fiddle.

A series of operations partially restored his sight. He had no peripheral vision, which made riding with him as a passenger a memorable adventure, yet with the throttle on the floor the old bird watcher could identify a Cooper's hawk darting across the highway.

Instead of a catcher, he became a pitcher, fast and wild, on the college and town team level, and a rough tackle at Amherst. "I once started a beautiful riot on that field," he remarked one day passing a New England pasture that still bore traces of a baseball diamond. "Beautiful." He didn't elaborate and it wasn't necessary. No doubt he had only intended to brush the hitter back.

As a fighter in print he was immense. For the fun of it, he picked a quarrel in his column with his friend Dan Parker of the *Mirror*. Friends warned Stanley that Dan at the typewriter was like Juan Marichal with a Louisville Slugger.

"Oh," he said mildly, "I know Dan's smarter than I am, but I fight dirtier."

Stanley Woodward could do any job on a newspaper and do it superbly. In spite of an educated and discerning taste, he had a blind spot where his own writing was concerned and never regarded it highly. Yet no one could write with more smashing impact. He could deflate the pompous, expose the ridiculous or explode a fallacy with one devastating line.

His great friend Red Blaik, coaching football at West Point, decided after studying the films of a horrendous defeat by Michigan that Army's weakness lay in the center's failure to give the ball a quarter-turn on delivering it to the T-formation quarterback.

"Attributing that catastrophe to such a cause," Stanley wrote, "is like blaming the Johnstown flood on a leaky toilet in Altoona, Pennsylvania."

One winter Jack Kramer, the tennis pro whose checkbook ended more amateur careers than old age, helped coach the United States Davis Cup team through the challenge round with Australia.

Putting the old pro in such a job, Stanley wrote, was "like electing Jean Lafitte commodore of the New Orleans Yacht Club."

One clings to the happy memories. The day Stanley's and Rice's younger daughter, Mary, was married, the bridal couple left the reception in a shower of rice and Stanley followed outside to see them drive away. When he returned, the guests fell silent, for Mary was the baby. For a moment they looked at Stanley and he looked at them.

Then he shrugged. "Oh, well," he said, "easy come, easy go."

LAST OF THE BLACK SOX

ON THE DAY the World Series moved from Boston to Cincinnati, a man named Charles August Risberg died in a convalescent home in Red Bluff, California. Death came on his eighty-first birthday, exactly fifty-six years and four days after the Cincinnati Reds won a World Series for the first time. Swede Risberg helped them win it. He was the shortstop on the Chicago White Sox, the losing team.

Risberg was the last survivor among the eight Chicago players—identified as "Black Sox" in all baseball literature composed since 1920 —who were ruled out of the game for life for selling out the 1919 Series. In the eight games he batted .080 and made four errors, contributing somewhat more to the dump than some of his accomplices, somewhat less than others. More than Fred McMullin, for example, who went to bat twice as a pinch-hitter and got one single. McMullin was a utility infielder nobody tried to bribe but he overheard Chick Gandil, the ringleader, propositioning Risberg, and he declared himself in.

Of the others, Buck Weaver, the third baseman, received no payoff and played superbly, hitting .324, and although Shoeless Joe Jackson did get $5,000, he hit a tidy .375. The rest were in to their ears—Gandil, the big, tough first baseman; Eddie Cicotte and Lefty Williams, pitchers; and Happy Felsch, the center fielder.

Risberg was a rangy six-footer out of San Francisco who had reached the big league at twenty-two. He could cover half an acre, had sure hands and a powerful arm, and enjoyed hitting line drives. When the World Series opened he was approaching his twenty-fifth birthday. After three seasons in the majors he was firmly established, and no stranger to chicanery.

At least, a Chicago gambler named Monte Tennes, whose bets were high enough to qualify him as a "sportsman" in newpaper accounts, indicated as much to Charles Comiskey, the White Sox owner. Tennes told Comiskey that a St. Louis gambler named Joe Pesch had boasted to him that he had Risberg, Gandil and Felsch on his payroll at $200 a week. All they had to do was throw a game or so a week.

In *Eight Men Out*, the definitive work on the scandal, Eliot Asinof reports that Tennes brought this information to Comiskey a few hours after Chicago's 9–1 defeat in the first game in Cincinnati. Asinof makes it clear that Comiskey preferred to see and hear no evil, and hoped the world would follow suit. The 1920 season was ending before he sent a telegram to eight players: "You and each of you are hereby notified of your indefinite suspension. . . ."

The 1920 season had been something special. Except for Gandil, who had made noises like a holdout and then quietly dropped out of baseball, the Sox had all the players who had tyrannized the American League a year earlier. They had four pitchers winning more than twenty games each—Red Faber, twenty-three; Williams, twenty-two; Cicotte, twenty-one, Dickie Kerr, twenty-one. Still, they managed to finish two games behind Cleveland, and that stands today as a record for a team with four 20-game winners.

Asinof mentions two occasions in 1920 when the results stirred suspicion. Early in the year the Sox lost to Cleveland in the ninth inning. A dreadful throw by Risberg opened the door. At the end of August Chicago dropped three games in Boston. Eddie Collins, the honest second baseman, told Comiskey the games had been thrown. Comiskey thanked him and did nothing.

In January of 1920, when clubs were sending out new contracts, a news dispatch from San Francisco reported that Swede Risberg, dissatisfied with the terms Chicago had offered, had announced he was retiring from baseball to open a restaurant. He signed two days before the season opened. That fall, when the dirt came out and one player after another was telling his story, Joe Jackson said Risberg had warned him, "I'll kill you if you squawk."

"Swede," Shoeless Joe said, "is a hard guy." Unlike Jackson and Weaver, the Swede never claimed innocence or sought to clear his name. For a while he worked a dairy farm in Minnesota, then he wandered to Northern California. He played a little semipro ball. He ran a tavern, and he died.

Risberg was a figure in history. A figure to be truly mourned was Leo Corcoran, a warm friend and the greatest bartender I ever knew. Leo, who was seventy-four and twice retired, died in his sleep last week. The Artist and Writers Restaurant in West Fortieth Street remains an agreeable watering hole, but it can never be the same without Leo behind the stick.

Bleeck's, as the joint is called even though Jack Bleeck (pronounced "Blake") sold out years ago, was as much a part of the *Herald Tribune* as the city room a few doors west. Printers drank with the publisher there, and all were under Leo's smile. The smile was genuine and almost perpetual. At the lunch and cocktail hours, when customers stood three deep, Leo would spot a new arrival without delay, hand him a drink across three or four shoulders—he knew each regular's preference without asking—and get the proper change back across those shoulders. He never seemed hurried, never out of sorts.

One regular sometimes brought his small, motherless son in, ignoring Jack Bleeck's frown. Leo would remove his apron, slip into a jacket and take the boy walking by the hour. The kid grew up knowing his way around New York better than most cops.

RECALLING CONN

THE FILLY was so fast, Conn McCreary couldn't understand why Steve Judge worked her openly in the mornings when everybody on the racetrack could clock her and spread the word. The result was that when she made her first start she was 4 to 5, not the sort of price to attract a bettor like Steve Judge. "Hold her," the trainer said when he hoisted McCreary into the saddle.

"Steve," Conn said, "I can't hold this mare. She's too strong for me."

"Hold her," Judge said, and he was the boss.

"Well," Conn thought during the post parade, "I'll get her left at the post, and I'll improvise from there."

He did get her left, but when she came out of the gate she came out flying, ready to eat up the field. Conn steered her up on another horse's heels, and she went to her knees, almost dumping her rider. Somehow she pulled herself erect and charged into contention. Conn took her as wide as he dared, giving away lengths of ground. Circling the whole field, she won by a head. Her backers cashed their tickets but Marshall Cassidy, the late, great steward, called McCreary upstairs, and he was not amused.

"Don't tell me you can cut it that fine," Cassidy said.

Conn McCreary had a hundred stories like that, and in company where he felt safe he could tell them with delight.

Conn was noted especially as a jockey who could wait with a horse and win with a powerful drive in the stretch, but he was also a keen judge of pace who could win "on the Bill Daly," as the saying goes. "They'll tell you to rate this horse," Jackie Westrope told him one day, "but pay no attention. The horse wants to be on the front end."

Unreliable memory suggests that the horse was Miss Grillo and the race the Pimlico Cup, an odyssey of two-and-a-quarter or two-and-a-half miles that is no longer run. Conn had the mount because Westrope, the regular rider, had broken a leg. Conn stole away at the start and kept increasing his lead to the tolerant amusement of the other riders, who knew Miss Grillo was strictly a come-from-behind horse that would soon be coming back to her field.

Conn won by fifty lengths, and all the way down the stretch he was standing up waving to Westrope, who sat with his plaster cast propped on the railing of the veranda outside the jockeys' quarters, grinning like a shark.

Racing was fun to McCreary, but his attitude toward the Kentucky Derby was close to reverence. Like his companions in the jockeys' room, he approved of the film patrol because that eye in the sky saves lives by policing riding tactics all round the track, but he was dismayed when he heard that Churchill Downs was putting the cameras in. "A kid should be able to take his shot in the Derby," he said.

"You know," he said on another occasion after watching the Derby crowds at their bourbon-scented devotions in Louisville, "I think the Derby has come to be a kind of religious thing in this country, like for people that don't have no Confession."

Still another time he said, "You know what the Derby means to me? I could get to be a bum in the park and I'd put the arm on some guy and maybe he'd slip me a buck. 'What do you do that for?' His companion might say. 'That bum's no good.' 'Why,' the guy would say, 'he win a Derby!' "

During the ten years that Conn rode for Woodvale Farm, Royce G. Martin, Woodvale's owner, withheld some or all of the jockey's share of purses to invest the money. Conn thought enough of his employer to name a son Royce. When Martin died, there was no money for Conn and no record of any such money.

Experiences like that never seemed to dampen Conn's spirit or diminish his gift of laughter. Merriment was his element and never more so than when he performed as star of the amateur theatricals that used to brighten the annual dinner of the Jockeys' Guild. As a thespian he had one stern rule that he laid down from the first rehearsal: "Nobody moves on my lines."

Conn had a man's body from the waist up but his legs were barely long enough to reach from his hips to the ground. This made it difficult to grip a mount between his knees, and until he mastered the art he had his share of spills leaving the gate.

"Aw dammit!" George Cassidy, the starter, heard him yell leaving the gate. "Here I go again!" He lit with a thud, whip flying over there, helmet landing here. One assistant starter retrieved his whip, another picked up the helmet but Conn hurled whip and helmet away in a fury. You wouldn't believe a man his size could contain so much rage.

When he was through riding and became a trainer he found older trainers unfailingly helpful. "For instance," he said, "I told Hirsch Jacobs how I was treating a horse that had been sore and he said, 'That's right. If it doesn't work, try something else and if that doesn't work, then try something else.'"

On a vacation in Puerto Rico Conn made friends with a veteran rider at El Comandante, San Juan's racetrack. "How are the stewards here?" Conn asked. "Tough?"

"Tough!" the jock said. "I've been ruled off for life eight times!"

THE ORCHID MAN PACKS IT IN

IT WAS June 17, 1970, the night Mac Foster, an attractive refugee from the Marine Corps with a professional record of twenty-four straight knockouts, was presented to the Eastern cognoscenti and to Jerry Quarry, who knocked him clear back to Fresno, California, in the sixth round.

Dempsey was about to turn seventy-five and Madison Square Garden seized the opportunity to gussie up the promotion with a birthday salute to the old mauler. Films of some of his fights were shown, and Jack was escorted into the ring to receive congratulations from his most celebrated opponents—Gene Tunney, Jack Sharkey, Georges Carpentier. Seated in the audience was Joe Frazier, then officially recognized as heavyweight champion of the world, although another nine months were to pass before he would clear the title by whipping Muhammad Ali. Joe's face was a caricature of slack-jawed incredulity as he stared at Carpentier and heard the announcer saying that this gaunt and grinning little old pappy guy had once fought the tigerish Dempsey for the heavyweight championship.

Frazier was twenty-six, and no great student of history. The Dempsey-Carpentier fight was over and done with almost twenty-three years before he was born. As he sat there in the Garden, forces were already at work making a match that would gross $20 million on closed-circuit and home television around the world and bring him half of a $5 million purse. If someone had told him that those men up in the ring—the tall one with the heavy brows lifted in laughter and that funnylooking Frenchman—had generated wilder excitement in one afternoon than he and Ali would rouse in three fierce fights, Joe would have been justified in walking out.

Yet of all the fist fights peddled over the years as the "Battle of the Century," the only one that justified the billing took place on July 2, 1921, in a wooden amphitheatre hammered together on a swatch of Jersey City tideland called Boyle's Thirty Acres. It lasted less than four rounds, and on Sunday, July 3, the *New York Times* gave over not only its sports section but most of Page One and the news pages to accounts of the event.

"Million-dollar gate," became part of the language that day, when slightly more than eighty thousand spectators—contemporary estimates ranged from ninety thousand to infinity—paid \$1,789,238 to sit on pine boards bubbling with pitch while the scowling champion methodically destroyed the 168-pound challenger they called the Orchid Man. As Irvin S. Cobb put it in a story that started on the *Times*'s front page and occupied most of Page Nine: "The arts, the sciences, the drama, commerce, politics, the bench, the bar, the great newly-risen bootlegging industry—all these have sent their pink, their pick and their perfection to grace this great occasion."

It was more than the Battle of the Century. It was the Mismatch of the Ages. Probably it couldn't have happened at any other moment in history. The War to End War was still a recent ordeal and the peace that followed still had the taste of champagne. French champagne, the stuff American doughboys had learned to associate with Mademoiselle from Armentieres. Here was a son of La Belle France, a certified hero who had won the Croix de Guerre and Medaille Militaire as an artillery spotter in the French Air Force, come to reach for the unreachable star.

"What's more, he was handsome and worldly—"a Greek athlete statue of Parian marble warmed to life," according to a lady on the *Morning Telegraph*. "A priestess of the white Attic times comes forth to some harmonious sacrifice," wrote James Hopper in the *Tribune*. The challenger was possessed, in the eyes of Heywood Broun, with "one of the most beautiful bodies the prize ring has known."

He could also punch.

To be sure, his reputation had been nurtured tenderly by a Gallic genius named François Descamps, who started him early fighting in saloons in the coal-mining country around Lens, took him to Paris to grow up on a diet of opponents named Young Snowball and Young Nipper, then let him feast on an assortment of English canvasbacks.

In 1913 he flattened a tall Briton named Bombardier Wells in the first round, and claimed the heavyweight championship of Europe. World War I limited his activity in the ring but after the Armistice he went to London and tagged Joe Beckett, the English heavyweight champion, with one right-hand shot, flattening him in a minute and fifteen seconds.

"I was startled by an amazing apparition," wrote a spectator named George Bernard Shaw. "Nothing less than Charles XII, 'The Madman of the North,' striding along in a Japanese dressing gown as gallantly as if he had not been killed almost exactly 201 years before."

Joe Beckett had hardly been restored to consciousness before Descamps was bawling for a match with Dempsey, who had demolished Jess Willard for the world championship five months earlier. The build-up that followed consumed a year and a half, but it was worth it. As the Dempsey fight approached, Frank Parker Stockbridge explained to *Times* readers why most fans wanted Carpentier to win: "We all share Rosalind's joy when Orlando overcomes Charles the Wrestler."

Neysa McMein, the illustrator, viewed the challenger from the side. "Michael Angelo," she wrote, "would have fainted for joy with the beauty of his profile." Neysa had a sure hand with a sketch pad, but her judgment of fighters faltered. It was Georges, not Michael, who fainted.

HOW BILL SWIACKI CAUGHT 'EM

FROM THE Navy game in November of 1943 to the Columbia game on October 26, 1947, the West Point football team went thirty-two games without defeat. Then with Gene Rossides completing twenty of thirty passes, eight of them caught by a gyrating genius named Bill Swiacki, Columbia upset Army, 21–20. The next week Army traveled to Notre Dame for the last game before that historic series was broken off. Bill Heinz, out to cover the game for the *New York Sun*, was dragooned to address a pep rally of the St. Joseph Valley Notre Dame Club. Notre Dame was undefeated and, Bill told his audience, Army might just as well be, too.

"It's true," he said, "that Army came up one point short last Saturday, but Columbia had a man named Swiacki who catches passes the way the rest of us catch the common cold: He knows where he gets some of them, and the rest he just picks up in a crowd."

Reading about Bill Swiacki's death in Sturbridge, Massachusetts, Gene Rossides, for one, was desolated. "He was just elected to the football Hall of Fame and was going to be installed in December," said Rossides, now practicing law in Washington.

"There never was a finer, more sincere man, or a harder worker. He was older than most of us, you know—he had been in the service three years—and very quiet, but very much a leader.

"The striking thing about that team was the total absence of internal bickering, and I think this was largely due to the leadership of Bill. We were an amalgam of service veterans and youngsters with Bill as the stabilizing influence and an example, because he played hurt a good deal. In the Navy game of '46 he played with a bad ankle, and he had shoulder trouble after that. Funny, but when he was coaching Toronto in the Canadian league after playing pro ball, he became garrulous, this quiet man."

Before entering the Air Force Swiacki was a student at Holy Cross, one of three outstanding players who left that university in that era to star on other campuses. The others were George Connor, who made All-America at Notre Dame, and Fritz Barzilauskas, who went from Yale to the pros.

"Bill wasn't graceful going for a pass," Rossides said, "but his speed was deceptive. Passing to him, you threw five yards farther than to other receivers. He was far ahead of his time in analyzing the defenders, anticipating what they would do in a certain circumstance. And work? Five yards and fake, five yards and fake, five yards and fake, he'd practice it for hours. His ability to get into the open wasn't just a knack.

"He was a fine college baseball player, you know. He was a .400 hitter and Mr. Little [Lou Little, the Columbia football coach] arranged for a tryout with the Red Sox. He had the tryout but decided to play football with the Giants. During spring practice in 1946, Bill would come out after baseball practice and run the down-and-out over and over.

"That was the pattern on the big play in the Army game. Army hadn't been scored on before our game and they got two quick touchdowns before we could score. Then Lou Kusserow went in to make it 14–7 but Rip Rowan came right back with an 83-yard run down the sideline and it was 20–7 at the half.

"For once, we never put a play on the board between halves. We just walked around that locker room and the reaction, mostly led by Bill was, 'We can get 'em.' We were burned up. Late in the second quarter we had the ball on Army's 4-yard line and Kusserow went to the 1 but the play was called back. The referee had gone to the Army bench to tell Red Blaik how much time was left, and he said he hadn't put the ball in play again. He wound up missing the field goal.

"We completely dominated the third quarter but didn't score. At the start of the fourth period I threw to Bill in the end zone and he made that diving catch where he was horizontal in the air. Army said he trapped the ball instead of catching it, but the films showed he had his hand underneath as the ball came to him.

"We went seventy-two yards for the third touchdown in six plays. Yabo [Ventan Yablonski] made seventeen. I ran a reverse around our left to the Army thirty-three and then we wasted a play to get to the right side of the field and isolate Bill. It was a handoff to Kusserow, I think, for five yards.

"Now came the most perfect pass of the day. It was on a broken play but it was a designed broken play. We had practiced: Where do we go if we're cornered? Why, we throw to Bill because one way or another he will be there. Army was dropping off the end so there was a man in front of Bill and another behind him as he broke down-field. Joe Steffy was in on me, and I threw over the safetyman's head, but soft, to give Bill a chance to get there.

"The pattern was down and out to the flagpole but the last thing I saw as I went down under Steffy was Bill turning his head in instead of out. Then I heard a roar and I knew he must have caught the ball anyhow. He told me later he was so close to the sidelines he thought I might throw inside but at the last instant he turned out and made the catch on his knees at the 3-yard line. I tried a sneak and made only a yard, and then Kusserow went in for the tie.

"Yabo converted and we were ahead with 7½ minutes to go. The way they tell about that game, we won in the last second on a lucky break, but we held a one-point lead for 7½ minutes. We controlled the ball more than five minutes, and Bill said we could have scored again."

GOOD THING FOR A HORSE

THERE WAS a wire service dispatch out of Glyndon, Maryland, the other day reporting the death of the thoroughbred gelding Find at the advanced age of twenty-nine. When he was racing, Find won $803,615, then and now the biggest bankroll ever earned by a horse foaled in Maryland.

Joe Palmer wrote about a quartet of pensioners known to the staff on Greentree Farm in Kentucky as the Gas House Gang. They had raced for Mrs. Payne Whitney, "which," Joe wrote, "was a good thing for a horse," because if he was sterile or a gelding he wasn't sold for dog food when his earning days were over. He went instead to the farm, where he had roomy paddocks and sweet green grass all the days of his life.

The Gas House Gang was composed of Twenty Grand, whose closing rush in the Kentucky Derby of 1931 had set a track record; Cherry Pie, one of Mrs. Whitney's best-loved horses; Jolly Roger, who held the money-winning record for steeplechasers at $143,240, and Easter Hero, who won undying fame by racking up the field at the Canal Turn in the 1928 Aintree Grand National so that, of forty-two starters, only Tipperary Tim and Bill Barton finished.

As the years rolled by, the old stagers lived it up on Greentree's mellow acres, but nothing is forever. Cherry Pie died in 1947 at the age of twenty-seven. The following February, Easter Hero departed. A month later, Twenty Grand shuffled off. That left Jolly Roger alone with his record that no jumper had ever matched. On July 2 of that year the grand ten-year-old Elkridge won $8,800 in the Indian River Steeplechase at Delaware Park and set a new record for earnings. The next day the Gas House Gang was disbanded. Jolly Roger died.

Well, Find raced for Alfred Gwynne Vanderbilt, and that was a good thing for a horse too. As long as he lived, he shared a paddock on Sagamore Farm outside Baltimore with a band of mares, who treated him like a favorite uncle. He was the last survivor of Sagamore's class of 1950.

That class was something special, for it included the incomparable gray, Native Dancer, along with such talented runners as Social Outcast and Crash Diver. By comparison with these, Find was considered junior-varsity material, but he won more races and more money than any of his twenty-four classmates. Native Dancer won twenty-one races in twenty-two starts. When Find was ten years old he scored his twenty-second victory. When he packed it in at eleven after 110 races, his bank account topped that of Social Outcast by $135,000 and Native Dancer's by $18,375.

When they were two years old Native Dancer swept through the season undefeated. Find never started, because he flatly refused to be trained. Even gelding him didn't cool his rambunctious temperament. When they were three and Native Dancer was the undefeated favorite for the Kentucky Derby—the only race he ever lost—Find managed to get loose while cross-tied in his stall.

Cross-tied, a horse is held by one shank attached to the left wall of the stall and the right side of his halter, and another to the left side of the halter and the right wall. Find simply ripped a board out of each wall and took off. He came back dragging two 10-foot boards and without a scratch on him, and everybody remembered the racetrack adage: "A bad horse never hurts himself; only the good ones do."

Everybody was wrong. Find got to the races at old Jamaica about the time Native Dancer was shipping to Louisville. He won first time out. He had won several more when he picked up his first trophy, a first edition of *The Hound of the Baskervilles*.

Provided by Thomas L. Stix of the Baker Street Irregulars, the book was a memento of the first running of the Silver Blaze Purse, which old Aqueduct put on for that band of Sherlock Holmes admirers. When Find won, a junior member of the Irregulars fidgeted in the winner's circle. He had been dragooned into presenting the trophy, and he wasn't familiar with the protocol. Was he supposed to make a spread-eagle speech? He stood chatting nervously with Vanderbilt.

When the "official" sign flashed, Alfred said, "Well, damn it, give me the book." The Irregular did. End of ceremony.

It was just the beginning for Find, though. He was to win thirteen more trophies and finish second or third in thirty-eight other stakes. In addition to the New York tracks, he raced at Hollywood Park, Pomona and Del Mar in California; Thistledown in Ohio; the Fair Grounds in

Louisiana; Hialeah and Gulfstream in Florida; Woodbine in Canada; Lincoln Downs in Rhode Island; Hawthorne and Washington Park in Illinois; Garden State, Monmouth and Atlantic City in New Jersey; Longacres in Washington; and Delaware.

Like his classmates—Native Dancer was by Polynesian–Geisha, and Social Outcast by Shut Out–Pansy—Find was thoughtfully named. He was by Discovery from Stellar Role. Alfred Vanderbilt worked hard at finding good names, but his friend Pat O'Brien hesitates to concede him a championship in this area. Pat's favorite is a guy out in Nebraska with a colt by the French stallion Compte de Grasse. He named the colt Mow de Lawn.

The name game still goes on at Sagamore. The class of '77, two-year-olds as of January 1, includes colts named Caught in a Jam, by Dundee Marmalade out of Squawk; Rum Ration, by North Sea from Tot; and Hernandos Hideaway, by Spanish Riddle out of Slink. Three young fillies are Bunkmate, by North Sea out of Captain's Joy; QE Two, by King's Emperor out of Second the Motion; and Sanctum Sanctorum, by Secretariat out of Ivory Tower.

William Woodward, banker, chairman of the Jockey Club and master of Belair Stud, looked like an artist's conception of a gentleman of substance—clipped white mustache, white piping on the waistcoat and so on. When Vanderbilt's Loser Weeper (Discovery–Outdone) won the Metropolitan Handicap, Woodward said, "Nice looking colt, Alfred, but that's an odd name. Where'd you ever get it?"

"You know the old expression," Vanderbilt said. " 'Finders keepers, losers weepers.' "

"Never heard of it," Woodward said.

"That puzzled me at first," Alfred said later, "but then I got thinking. I guess they don't use that expression much around banks."

MEMORIES OF ADMIRAL DAN

THE CARIBBEAN WORLD SERIES was on in San Juan, Puerto Rico, when an invitation arrived at the hotel to join the admiral for cocktails at his residence. It was a bleak prospect, making manners with the braid and maybe having to miss dinner before the evening ball game. Still, the invitation had the ring of an order to be obeyed. It turned out that Rear Admiral Daniel V. Gallery, commander of the Caribbean Sea Frontier, had quarters right on the water overlooking the pretty little fort of San Geronimo. He and his lady served a rum punch that comforted the soul, and the admiral, it developed, was the brother of Tom Gallery, an old friend.

Everybody who knew him was fond of Tom Gallery, and practically everybody knew him because Tom had done so many things. He had been an actor in the silent films. (He was the handsome trooper in the Royal Northwest Mounted in pictures starring Rin Tin Tin, a dog.) As West Coast representative of Mike Jacobs, Tom promoted fights in California, including a middleweight championship bout between Henry Armstrong and Ceferino Garcia. And through the early years of television he was director of sports for the National Broadcasting Company.

Tom's brother was a wit, a warrior, a raconteur, an aviator, and as the most dedicated baseball fan in the Caribbean, president of Little League in Puerto Rico. In Trinidad he had been charmed by steel bands, those groups that beat music out of sawed-off oil drums, and he had introduced this art form to the Navy. In their time, Dan Gallery's Pandemoniacs became at least as famous as the Philadelphia Symphony.

We went to ball games together, watched warm-blooded fans protest an umpire's decision by throwing folding chairs and formed a friendship that was sustained by the exchange of occasional letters year after year until Admiral Dan's obituary appeared in a recent edition.

In the last line of his last letter he had reported, "I am in the last stages of an incurable ailment—old age and senility."

During World War II, Dan Gallery brought off an exploit unmatched in a century and a half. He hunted down and captured a German submarine, *U-505*, the only time in history that a sub was captured in combat and the only time since the War of 1812 that a warship of any kind was taken in the open sea.

The boarding party he put into the sub to close the scuttle valves and defuse demolition charges brought back an incredible prize—the German naval code books, the cipher machine and hundreds of coded messages with the German translation on the reverse side.

"Some people," Dan wrote, "in their enthusiasm over this capture, say that the ability to read the German naval codes from then on shortened the war by several months. I doubt this."

He did concede, however, that "we read the operational traffic between U-boat headquarters and the submarines at sea for the rest of the war. Reception committees we were able to arrange as a result of this eavesdropping may have had something to do with the sinking of nearly 300 U-boats in the next 11 months."

The extraordinary thing was that Dan Gallery's eloquence so impressed three thousand kids in his task group with the importance of keeping the whole adventure secret that not one opened his mouth, even in a saloon. Until the war was over, the German command never suspected that *U-505* and its secrets had not gone to the bottom of the sea.

Another thing about Dan Gallery. After the war he wrote a book titled *We Captured a U-Boat,* and this is the credit he took for himself: "It was my great fortune and high honor to command the task group that did this job."

Actually, Dan had been planning such a capture for about two years. The question "Why couldn't we?" had come up in the officers' club in Iceland in 1942 when Dan commanded the United States Navy Fleet Air Base at Reykjavik, from which American and British planes helped escort convoys past U-Boat wolfpacks. In 1944 Dan commanded a hunter-killer task group, and before shoving off from Norfolk he told his skippers of his plan.

"I want each ship to organize a boarding party," he said, "and keep a whaleboat ready to lower throughout the next cruise. Also, keep your tow line where you can get at it in case we need it. Any questions?"

Still, when the deed was done and he could have taken bows, he put it this way: "I could, I suppose, make out quite a case showing how shrewdly I anticipated every move *U-505* made during the last week before we captured her, and took proper action to counter it. I would only have to lay her tracks alongside mine on a chart without comment and let the reader draw his own conclusion from the way they converged to a point at 11:20 A.M. on June 4, 1944.

"But I don't intend to do this. The German skipper and I had what we thought were sound reasons for every move we made that last week. Looking back now, our reasons were wrong in almost every case. It was a combination of errors on both sides in which his mistakes counteracted mine and produced a fantastically improbable result."

Early in the war the Iceland-based pilots were overeager, and when they had fumbled three opportunities to sink subs, Dan ordered the officers' club closed until they should score a kill. Soon a message arrived from one Lieutenant Hopgood: "Sank sub, open club." Before the club closed that night, it was agreed that the U-boat skipper's pants should be displayed in the lounge as a victory trophy.

Dan was Irish enough to address an official letter to the First Lord of the Admiralty in London explaining the American saying "Caught with his pants down" and requesting that when the prisoners arrived in England on a British destroyer, the skipper's pants be forwarded to Iceland. He sent along a pair of his own pants in exchange.

In time there came a stern letter from the Director of Naval Intelligence citing the Geneva Convention rules about humiliating prisoners. The Geneva Convention didn't worry Dan, but the English never sent his pants back. That did burn him up.

JOE McCARTHY

WHEN TOMMY HENRICH was a rookie with the Yankees, Joe McCarthy told him, "They're making a sucker out of you with that outside curve. I want you to lay off it." A week or ten days later, McCarthy said, "Tommy, I told you to lay off that pitch. Now, either you lay off it, or you'll learn to hit it in Newark."

"When he put it that way," Henrich said later, "you listened."

The sports world in general had its attention fixed on New Orleans and Super Bowl XII when Joseph Vincent McCarthy stepped quietly off this mortal coil. He was ninety and, by all accounts, still the same square-jawed intelligent Irishman who, as a manager in both major leagues, was able to bring out the best in such disparate individuals as Hack Wilson, Rogers Hornsby, Babe Ruth, Lou Gehrig, Joe DiMaggio and Ted Williams.

"Williams was no problem," McCarthy told Don Honig last year when Honig interviewed him for *The Man in the Dugout,* wherein fifteen present or former managers have their say. "He was in the ball game every day. He played. He hustled. Followed orders. Of course I only gave him one order—hit. No insubordination there. He hit."

Drunks can argue till they're sober about who was the greatest of all managers—John McGraw, who had ten pennant winners; Casey Stengel, who had ten with five in a row; Connie Mack, who built eight championship clubs on his way to sainthood; or men with special credentials like Billy Southworth, Bill McKechnie, Miller Huggins, Al Lopez, Fred Hutchinson. For all Yankees like Henrich, Phil Rizzuto or DiMaggio it is no contest. There never was another like Joe McCarthy, who steered them to seven championships in eight years.

Yankee-haters called him a push-button manager, implying that the batboy could have won with those players, but it has been shown that

not even managers as brilliant as Charlie Finley or George Steinbrenner can win with bad ball players. Remembering the richness of
his Yankee talent, it is easy to forget McCarthy's first job in the majors.
In 1926 he took over the Chicago Cubs, a last-place club the coroner
had pronounced dead and partly decomposed. In Joe's four years in
Wrigley Field, the Cubs finished fourth, fourth, third and first.

The Athletics creamed the Cubs in the World Series, putting on a
ten-run inning in the fourth game when Chicago was leading, 7–0.
McCarthy got fired. A year later he was back in Philadelphia, a spec-
tator at the World Series this time, when the Yankees came after him.
There had been feelers from other clubs, so Joe called Kenesaw M.
Landis to ask the commissioner's advice.

"I want you to get the best job in baseball," Judge Landis said. "I
can't," Joe said.

"Why not?"

"Because you have it."

"Then get the next best," the Judge said, and Joe did.

One Yankee who was happy to see him in New York was Earle
Combs, the center fielder, who had not forgotten his own experience
in Louisville, where McCarthy was manager when Combs joined the
Colonels as a scared country schoolteacher. In his first game for Louisville, Combs dropped the first ball hit to him. McCarthy said nothing.
Combs misplayed a single into extra bases. McCarthy was silent. In the
eighth inning with the score tied and two runners on base, the hitter
drove a single to center. The ball hopped between Combs's knees and
rolled to the fence.

In the clubhouse, McCarthy strolled over to the rookie's locker.
"Forget it," he said. "I told you today you were my center fielder.
You still are." Then Joe laughed. "Listen," he said, "if I can stand it, I
guess you can."

The year before McCarthy took over, the Yankees ran third. "I will
stand for you finishing second this year," said Colonel Jacob Ruppert,
the owner, "because you are new in this league. But I warn you,
McCarddy, I don't like to finish second."

Joe looked him in the eye. "Colonel," he said, "neither do I."

The Yankees did finish second. Then they finished first, again and
again. After one World Series, Joe went to call on the Colonel, who
was sick in bed. "Colonel," he said, "you're the champion again."

"Fine, fine, McCarddy," Ruppert said. "Do it again next year."

McCarthy's favorite story about the Yankees concerned a game with
the Red Sox. Johnny Broaca, a student-athlete from Yale, was the New
York pitcher. He had a 1–0 lead in the top of the ninth with two out,

the tying run on first base, and Joe Cronin coming up. On deck behind Cronin was Jimmy Foxx.

"Broaca starts pitching to Cronin," Joe told Honig, "and he's not coming close to the plate. I couldn't believe it—he's walking Cronin to get to Foxx. I yelled out to Bill Dickey, "What the hell's going on?" Bill just shrugged. There wasn't anything he could do about it. And Broaca was pitching such a good game I couldn't take him out.

"So Foxx comes up and now the tying run is on second. And Jimmy laid into one. He hit it into deep center field, as far as any ball I ever saw hit in Yankee Stadium that wasn't a home run. DiMaggio went out there and caught it. It didn't miss by much from going into the bleachers in dead center. But Joe got it and the game was over.

"In the clubhouse I went over to shake hands with Broaca. 'Johnny,' I said, 'that was quite a game. But will you tell me why you didn't pitch to Cronin?'

" 'I was afraid of Cronin,' he said, 'but I knew I could get Foxx.'

" 'You did, eh?' I said. I looked around. DiMaggio still hadn't come in with the ball."

JUDGE LEIBOWITZ'S PICKPOCKET

THE RECENT death of Judge Samuel Leibowitz recalled a story of his that should not go to the grave. The judge was a fan of the Brooklyn Dodgers and, like all Dodger fans of the 1940s and 1950s, he remembered how excitement boiled over in Ebbets Field the day a customer, infuriated by a decision, sprang out of the stands, leaped upon George Magerkurth, the umpire, and struck him repeated blows.

It was a humiliating experience for Maje, for he was the tallest and burliest umpire in the business, he had boxed in his youth, and his assailant, though stockily constructed, didn't come up above George's wishbone. Yet his impetuous attack caught Maje by surprise and carried him to earth. Newspapers all over the country published a photograph of the massive umpire flat on his back with a guy in a polo shirt astride his abdomen, punching down.

Maje was a big man in every sense. Painfully embarrassed though he was, he refused to press charges after the law dropped a net over his adversary. "I have a boy of my own," he said, spicing magnanimity with non sequitur. However, it turned out that the guy was a parole-breaker, so he did time anyway.

Several years later, a pickpocket appeared before Judge Leibowitz for sentencing. There was no question of guilt or innocence. The dip was no special credit to his profession. His level of skill was approximately that of the pickpocket acquaintance of the late Wilson Mizner, of whom Mizner said, "He couldn't dip his hand in the Hudson without knocking over the Palisades."

The man in Judge Leibowitz's court had a police record that testified to the stone-fingered character of his work. He had made the mistake of trying to operate alone, which should be attempted only by polished professionals who take pride in their craft. As a result, he had been grabbed with his hand still deep in a pocket.

He should have realized that he needed a confederate to create a diversion. Only once in a long time do circumstances make the game easy for a loner. Joe Palmer wrote that the racetrack was an ideal training ground for pickpockets because if you came upon a horse player studying the past performances with ten minutes to post, it was possible to remove his coat and vest without attracting his attention. Usually, though, you need a partner to jostle the mark and distract him.

As Judge Leibowitz regarded the prisoner, he felt a vague stirring of memory. The man had never been in his court before, and yet. . . . He took a shot in the dark.

"Are you a baseball fan?" he asked.

The prisoner brightened, nodding vigorously.

"A Dodger fan?" the judge suggested.

The prisoner was grinning now. "One of the best," he said.

"You," the judge said, "are the fellow who jumped George Magerkurth that day! I thought I recognized you."

"That was me." The guy was beaming, reliving his hour of glory.

"Well," Judge Leibowitz said, "I'm giving you three years. You won't find it so bad. They've got a ball team up there, a pretty good one, I'm told.

"But tell me something," the judge said. "I'm a Dodger fan, myself, and I know what the umpires can do to us. But to jump out on the field and slug one of them! Are you really as hot a fan as that? Did that decision—I forgot what it was—did it make you lose your head altogether?"

The pickpocket smiled tolerantly.

"I'm a good fan," he said. "I can get excited. And I was sore that day. I was sore as hell. It was a lousy decision and it burned me up.

"But to tell you the truth, Judge, I had a partner working in the stands that day."

CLASS ALL OVER HIM

AT BELMONT PARK a man said to Elliott Burch, "I read about your father's death in the *Blood-Horse*. He was one of the nicest men I ever knew." Quietly, Elliott agreed. Preston M. Burch saddled his first winner at Gravesend in 1903 and—except when he was an ambulance driver in France before we got into World War I—never was far away from horses until he died at ninety-three. His book *Training Thoroughbred Horses* probably is the most widely read work on the subject.

Both Preston Burch and his father, William P. Burch, are in racing's Hall of Fame. Preston's uncle, Green B. Morris, and brother, Selby Burch, were successful trainers. So it probably figured on breeding alone that Elliott Burch would wind up training for Alfred Vanderbilt and Sonny Whitney in spite of his father's efforts to steer him away from the racetrack.

"In the 1920s," Phil Bieber writes, "Preston was training for George Wingfield's Nevada Stock Farm, then racing in Hot Springs, Arkansas. Purses were only $400 but the weather was exquisite and accommodations pleasant. Most beautiful mornings after training hours, Preston Burch, Hollie Hughes and my brother Isador would hike the four miles back to the hotel. They found it so exhilarating they determined to come back every year; not one ever returned.

"One evening they gathered for dinner with an added starter named Chris Blodgett, a fine-looking fellow who spoke with a soft Southern drawl. He was an unbelievably good golfer who specialized in setting up wealthy marks, playing dismally and losing moderate bets. Then when his handicap and the bets had soared, he would still play like a dub but contrive to squeeze through by a stroke, saving the marks for future plucking.

"The day this con merchant joined the horsemen for dinner they had, unknown to one another, one thing in common: they were all flat broke and all confident that somebody else would grab the check.

"The dinner was excellent and everyone was enjoying the story of Blodgett's latest adventure on the golf course. While he was telling it, the waiter showed up behind him with the check. At my brother's surreptitious signal, he laid the bill on Blodgett's plate. Blodgett went right on with his tale.

"'It was the last hole and I had a putt only this long to win. As I started my stroke, a bee lit on my cheek. I jerked my head, just skinned the ball and it bounded from here—' he plucked the check off his plate '—to there.' The tab dropped in front of Preston.

"Everybody howled. 'I'll take care of this,' Preston said when the laughter subsided. 'Chris must have kept that bee to put the sting on us. It was worth every penny.' With that magical laugh of his, he called the manager and arranged to have payment postponed.

"In those days bookmaking was permitted at the New York tracks. For betting purposes, a horse was considered a starter when he left paddock, even if he was injured on the way to the post. Sometimes a player might decide that a short-priced horse wasn't going to win. By offering better odds, he could attract bets from the bookmakers who, having booked the horse at a lower price, were glad to hedge.

"One day Pres Burch saddled a 2-to-5 shot named Rose Tree. As she left the paddock I noticed that she was sweating quite a bit and taking short steps. This convinced me that she was hurting. Knowing Preston for a top trainer, I told him what I had seen. 'I saw it too, Phil,' he said. 'She was okay when she came into the paddock. When she started out I saw she wasn't right but it was too late to do anything.'

"In the betting ring I started laying Rose Tree with the books, giving 3 to 5, 4 to 5, 9 to 10. Harry Fink, a player, price-maker and sometimes layer, called to me: 'Phil, what the hell are you doing? This mare is a cinch.' I explained, and he strode through the ring making some large transactions.

"Rose Tree finished last. Next morning Pres told me a pebble had lodged in the frog of a foot, causing pain. That afternoon the stewards called me up to ask about the commotion in the betting ring. I told what had happened. They talked to Pres Burch, his jockey, Buddy Hanford, and Harry Fink. They didn't like Fink and told him they'd be pleased if he left New York but they were satisfied with the explanations of Hanford and Pres Burch.

"I could tell you a lot more about Preston Burch, who Hollie Hughes called a guy with class all over."

More than twenty-five years ago, Joe Palmer described Preston Burch as "a spare, slightly graying man, soft in speech, easy in manner, quiet in humor." One can hear him still:

"Like my daddy used to say. Somebody'd ask, 'Kin your horse go a mile and a half, Mr. Burch?' 'He kin if you give him time enough,' my daddy would say."

THE IMPOSTER

DAY WAS treading timidly on the heels of night when the telephone rang in a room in the Kenmore Hotel in Boston. Through the fog of sleep, the caller's brassy voice sounded familiar but only vaguely so. The conversation, if you could call it that, went like this:

"Red? This is Leo."

"Who?"

"Leo."

"Oh, Leo."

"I've been talking to Bob."

"Who?"

"Bob Hannegan. Horace is drinking again."

"Oh?"

"You coming up to see me?"

"Yes, I'll be up. Goodbye."

Slowly the facts assembled themselves. The 1948 World Series was on and the baseball hierarchy was in Boston to see the Braves play the Cleveland Indians. The brassy voice belonged to Leo Durocher, who had moved from Brooklyn to Harlem that summer to become manager of Horace Stoneham's Giants. In 1948 Robert E. Hannegan was president of the St. Louis Cardinals and Richard P. Smith, called Red, was a coach with the Chicago Cubs who doubled as the team's ambassador-at-large.

Red Smith, The Imposter, was large and round and companionable and patient. Because he was less explosive temperamentally than Jim Gallagher, the Cubs' general manager, and could consume even more beer than Charlie Grimm, the manager, he was assigned to sit up nights with executives of other clubs in the hope that they might grow mellow enough to trade him a twenty-game winner or .325 hitter for a round of drinks and a player to be named later. It seemed likely from Durocher's remarks on the phone that Leo and The Imposter and Bob Hannegan had been cooking up a three-way deal. A return call was made.

"Hello, Leo? Listen, you called the wrong Red Smith."

"Oh, migod! Wow! Hey, uh, listen, uh—"

"Don't worry about it, but next time, check the room number. I don't want to wind up with one of your pitchers to feed."

What brought this back to mind was a dispatch out of Toledo reporting, "Richard P. (Red) Smith, a former professional football and baseball player and a brewing industry executive, died yesterday at 73." We turn down an empty glass, and another memory comes back across thirty years.

In 1948 a special train hauled the press and assorted members of the baseball community from one World Series city to the other. On the noisy club car bound from Boston to Cleveland, Joe Reardon, head of the Phillies' farm system, kept trying to make himself heard. He seemed to be saying something about Bill Nicholson, the brawny outfielder whom the Cubs had just traded to the Phillies for Harry Walker. Joe had to say it two or three times before his words came through: "I know you made that Nicholson deal. I was listening on another extension."

Joe hadn't been aware of The Imposter's special duties with the Cubs. When the confusion was explained, a wave of understanding crossed his features.

"I see. When I asked Bob Carpenter who he was dealing with he said, 'Red Smith.' I thought. 'How far can they trust him? He'll put it in the paper.'"

When he wasn't busy as coach and flesh peddler for the Cubs, Red rounded out the year as line coach of the New York Giants under Steve Owen. Fortunately, his football duties did not include swapping players; no 300-pound defensive tackles were mailed by mistake to the wrong address.

Red was the last survivor of a jocund company that doubled the flavor and doubled the fun on the sports beat in his time. Owlish Steve Owen, his burly boss; Jack Lavelle, the incomparable raconteur who scouted pro teams for the Giants and undergraduates for Notre Dame; Herman Hickman, waggish and scholarly, who was Red Blaik's assistant at West Point before he became head coach at Yale; and Toots Shor, host to all of them—they were immense and mirthful and almost inseparable, and together they had the weight to stop an express train.

Sport was the magnet that brought them together, for Owen was a frontiersman from Oklahoma's Cherokee Strip, Lavelle was from the sidewalks of New York, Hickman came out of the mountains of eastern Tennessee and Toots Shor the wilds of South Philadelphia. The Imposter was born in Brokaw, Wisconsin, which is up in the woods outside Wausau, but he grew up in Combined Locks, a paper mill on the Fox River near Kaukauna. That's about twenty miles from my hometown but we never met until we were classmates at Notre Dame.

There Red was a guard in football and a catcher in baseball. After graduation he played with the Green Bay Packers, New York Yankees and the Giants. He coached the Packers' line before joining Owen's staff, and even got into a major league game as catcher for the baseball Giants.

His plagiaristic name gave him one uncomfortable moment. The day before the Cubs and Tigers opened the 1945 World Series, a telegram arrived in the Detroit clubhouse in Briggs Stadium addressed to Red Smith. It read, "Okay on Thompson and Patulski," and was signed, "Well." (Thompson and Patulski are fictional, the real names having been forgotten long ago.)

It was obvious at a glance that the message was intended for The Imposter, so it was handed over. He read it and blushed. Thompson and Patulski, he confessed, were senior linemen at Iowa and this was authorization from Wellington Mara to go sign them up.

Some years later when the All-America Conference was clawing for a foothold, the Giants and their colleagues in the National Football League were scandalized at the sneaky tactics of the newcomers, who held a secret draft as early as December so they could get to college players first. In October of 1945 there was no rival league and the Giants had nobody to cheat on except their own lodge brothers.

HE WASN'T A HOUSE DICK

FORD FRICK's finest hour came when he was president of the National League, before he became baseball commissioner. It was early in the 1947 season, the year Jackie Robinson crossed the color line in the major leagues. Sam Breadon, owner of the St. Louis Cardinals, advised the league office that some of his players were talking about going out on strike on their first visit to Brooklyn as a protest against the black man's presence. Ford sent the ringleaders a message through their employer: "If you do this you are through, and I don't care if it wrecks the league for ten years. You cannot do this, because this is America."

That warning, plus the publicity that ensued when Stanley Woodward broke the story in the *New York Herald Tribune,* averted the strike and silenced all who might have spoken up for Jim Crow. (There were more of these than one would suspect, and not all were players with scanty education; some of the saintliest club owners who ever ornamented the game were secretly furious at Branch Rickey for hiring Robinson.)

Ford's response to the strike threat was instinctive and immediate. In his seventeen years as league president and fourteen as commissioner, Ford encountered many other issues. Usually his instincts were good, but rarely did he act with the force and vigor he displayed the time he came face-to-face with bigotry. At least, he hardly ever did so publicly.

He was a good man but he will be remembered chiefly as a reluctant leader. As league president he tended to say, "That's not in my jurisdiction." As commissioner he said, "It's a league matter."

This was due not so much to irresolution as to the way he viewed his job. He didn't think baseball needed a house dick and didn't consider himself one. He regarded his employers as honest men capable of making their own rules and felt that he was there only to administer the rules. When he did take firm action, it was not announced in a press release from the commissioner's office. Though the press found him always accessible, this reformed member of the press shrank from personal publicity.

In retrospect, the low-keyed tone of his administration and his concept of the commissioner's role offer sharp contrast with the administration immediately preceding his, and with the current one. Ford's natural distaste for the spotlight was reinforced by his dislike for the strutting and posturing of his predecessor, Harry Chandler. His conduct of the office was as different as can be from the reign of today's incumbent, Bowie Kuhn.

Bowie makes up rules out of his own cleanly head and promulgates them as revealed truth. (No more than $400,000 may change hands in any player transaction.) He rejects rules he doesn't want to enforce. (When the Mets made a bonus agreement with Jon Matlack that fractured Major League Rule 3(a) in three places, Bowie threw out the rule and let the illegal arrangement stand.) Bowie trespasses on the league president's domain by canceling legitimate deals between Oakland and the Yankees, Oakland and the Red Sox, Oakland and Texas.

Then Bowie lifts up his hand like Moses, and press releases gush from his office as water gushed from the rock that Moses smote.

America was still wallowing in the Great Depression in 1934 when Ford Frick became president of the National League. In Cincinnati, Sid Weil had gone broke in the stock market and control of the Reds was passing to Powel Crosley. The Boston Braves were virtually penniless. The Brooklyn Dodgers were in hock to the Brooklyn Trust Company. Gerry Nugent kept the Phillies together by saving string and selling players. During Ford's administration the sick clubs got well, thought not always in the way he expected.

"I'm not sure about the Phillies' future," he told a Philadelphia newspaperman, "but anytime you hear a rumor that involves moving the club, forget it. Baseball franchises don't move."

He lived to see franchises fly around like rice at a wedding while sixteen major league clubs begat ten offspring and the majors spread south to Georgia and Texas, west to the Pacific and north into Canada.

Depression, World War II, defectors jumping to the Mexican League, the era of the bonus player who couldn't play and who couldn't be farmed out, shifting franchises, expansion in the majors and atrophy in the minors—as league president and commissioner, Ford was there through it all. He was still there when the owners adopted a draft of high school and college kids but he had retired before the advent of ten-man baseball and before Andy Messersmith and Dave McNally shot the reserve system full of holes.

It would have been interesting to hear Ford's thoughts about the multimillion-dollar market in free agents, for as long as twenty years ago he considered the reserve system a repugnant necessity. However, his health had deteriorated in recent years and he didn't make the baseball scene often.

As a matter of fact, there were times during his most active years when he was almost a stranger in the ball park unless the World Series or All-Star game was on. In 1953 Jack Orr interviewed the commissioner for the *Sporting News*. They chatted of many things and at one point Ford said, "You know, Jack, I haven't been to a regular game in four years. I can sit up home in Bronxville and see them on TV."

Surreptitiously wiping the canary feathers from his lips, Jack gathered up his notes, made his manners and started out of the office to tell the world about a baseball commissioner who didn't go to ball games. He had a hand on the doorknob when Ford spoke.

"By the way, Jack, that stuff about me not going to games—that's off the record."

JOE ONLY BEAT YOU

EIGHT MORNINGS AGO Joe Gordon got up to keep a golf date in Marysville, California. At sixty-three, the finest of Yankee second basemen was living the good life in Sacramento, golfing, fishing, shooting, selling a little real estate when he felt like it. Still in pajamas and robe, he was having orange juice when he told his wife, Dorothy, "I don't understand it but my shoulder is sore. Maybe a hot shower will take care of it." He came out of the shower white as a ghost, and Dorothy got him to the hospital.

It was a heart attack but he came through fine. In a day or so he was complaining about the cuisine in intensive care, teasing the nurses, laughing with visitors. Last Friday Dorothy brought homemade soup for lunch. Joe got out of bed, walked into the bathroom, and a second seizure hit him. Next day the obituaries described his baseball career as best they could but, truly, the way Flash Gordon played ball defied adequate description.

He was 175 pounds of rawhide and whalebone, and an acrobat to boot. An all-round athlete with uncommon agility, he had trained as a gymnast and tumbler and he could make plays that were beyond any other second baseman I ever saw. He could also hit big-league pitching for an average as high as .322, make as many as thirty home runs in a season and drive in 111 runs. In his second year out of the University of Oregon he was playing for the Yankees' Newark farm and one day his manager, Oscar Vitt, told Joe McCarthy, the Yankee manager, "Gordon is going to be the greatest second baseman you ever saw."

"Take it easy, Oscar," said one of the newspapermen sitting in McCarthy's office in Yankee Stadium. "I've seen some pretty good second basemen, myself."

"So have I," Vitt said. "I've seen Lajoie, Collins, Evers, Hornsby, Frisch, Lazzeri and Gehringer, among others. I don't say this kid is better than them. All I'm saying is that some day he will be. He's better than anybody in the big leagues now, with the exception of Gehringer—and he'll catch him in a year."

"Wow!" Tommy Henrich said yesterday. "What a compliment!"

Henrich was on the phone in his home in Prescott, Arizona. When he played the outfield and first base for the Yankees, he and Gordon were special friends. "It didn't take us long," Tommy said, "to discover we thought the same way. We both thought baseball was fun. We traveled by train then, and Joe and I would memorize those dumb gags out of Joe Miller's *Joke Book* and work up routines. The other players would throw pillows at us and sometimes other things but they enjoyed it.

"When I joined the Yankees, Joe was with that great 1937 team in Newark, the one that had six outfielders that went to the majors, including Charlie Keller, Bob Seeds and Jimmy Gleeson. Buddy Rosar and Willard Hershberger were the catchers, Babe Dahlgren and George McQuinn on first base, Merrill May at third and there were pitchers like Spud Chandler, Atley Donald, Marius Russo, Joe Beggs, Steve Sundra."

"I hung around Yankee Stadium a couple of weeks and never got in a game and they sent me to Newark," Henrich said. "Ten days later I was back in New York. Somebody wondered why McCarthy called me up after only ten days and Gordon said, 'Because he couldn't make it here.'

"Newark won the International League pennant by 27½ games, and you know what Vitt did to Gordon? On the day they clinched, Vitt pinch-hit for him with two strikes against him. A 27-game lead and Joe had twenty-six home runs that year to twenty-two for Keller!

"Joe came up the next year and he was always a special favorite of McCarthy's, more than the usual deal. One day McCarthy was talking to some newspaper guys on the bench and he said, 'I'll take Gordon's kind of baseball, and I'll show you why.' He called: 'Hey, Joe, what are you hitting now?' 'I don't know,' Joe said. 'What's your fielding average?' McCarthy said. 'How the hell would I know?' Joe said, 'See what I mean?' McCarthy said, 'All he does is try to beat you.'"

"Joe was the second baseman when I came up in forty-one," said Phil Rizzuto, "and he kind of took me under his wing. At the same time, he was always playing practical jokes on me—tying my shoelaces together under the table, giving me a hot foot, that sort of thing. A happy-go-lucky guy, and the most acrobatic fielder I ever played with.

The plays he could make off balance, throwing in midair or off one foot or lying down, unbelievable!"

Joe Gordon was the outstanding player in the 1941 World Series, in which he batted .500. The next season he won the Most Valuable Player award in the American League.

"He had the guts of a burglar," Henrich said. "I think it was after the '41 World Series that he hailed Ed Barrow at our victory dinner. [Barrow, the general manager, was a crusty old Roman whose black-browed visage wore a beetling scowl in repose.] Joe said to him, 'I need to make a phone call. Lend me a dime on next year's salary.' Even Barrow laughed that time.

"Afterwards we went to Leon and Eddie's. Eileen was with me and there were Vi and Bill Dickey and Joe and Dorothy, about a dozen of us. We were all introduced and we danced with the pretty girls and then Joe told Eddie Davis, 'I want to sing a song.' Eddie said, 'Ladies and gentlemen, a special treat. Joe Gordon is going to sing.' I thought, 'What is that meathead up to now?'

"Joe said, 'I'd like to sing a song entitled 'Let Me Call You Sweetheart,' and he turned to the band. 'Do you know it?' Then he gave it the grand-opera treatment—'Lait me call yooooo sweeeeethot. . . .' He was pulling the leg of the whole audience and they held still for it.

"I enjoyed the guy's company so very much. I always felt good when I was with him."

"Me, too," said Dario Lodigiani from a motel in Sacramento. Lodi, an infielder with the Philadelphia Athletics and Chicago White Sox, had driven over from San Francisco when he heard of his friend's death. They had been pals since 1936, when they were rookies in Oakland, Lodi at second base and Joe Gordon at shortstop. Later, when Joe managed in Cleveland and Kansas City, Lodi was his coach.

The general manager in Cleveland was Frank Lane, the demon dealer whose standing advice to his players was "don't send out your laundry." In 1960 Lane and Bill DeWitt, in Detroit, brought off baseball's only man-for-man swap of managers, Joe Gordon for Jimmy Dykes. In Kansas City, Joe was fired by Charlie Finley, a record shared by many.

"Funny thing," Lodi said, "Joe and Lane were real close friends to the end. And Joe got along with Charlie, too. That's got to tell you something about him."

NICEST TOUGH GUY

WHEN KNUTE K. ROCKNE was winning renown as a football coach, the Notre Dame varsity was only one of his responsibilities. He also coached track and field, administered all sports as athletic director, turned out a syndicated column two or three times a week, had several books published under his name and toured the country as an after-dinner speaker.

During spring practice, runners would be working on the cinder track encircling Cartier Field—the predecessor of today's stadium—while the padded gladiators butted heads on the infield, and somehow Rock seemed able to watch a half-miler and a left end simultaneously. In those days his only assistant was Hunk Anderson, who would finish his job at the Edwards Iron Works in South Bend and hustle out to the campus to serve as unpaid line coach. Most practice sessions started with Rock giving preliminary instruction to the backs and ends while Hunk got the interior linemen warmed up. At length, Rock would call, "Ah, Heartley, would you be good enough to bring the behemoths over here?"

"Hell, Rock," Hunk would say, "they ain't even bleeding yet."

Starting in 1925, after Notre Dame defeated Stanford in the Rose Bowl, Rock got Hunk on the payroll, at $500 a season. Not that Hunk needed the money. Besides drawing a salary at the iron works, he would catch a train on Saturday, put in most of the night studying the game plan of the Chicago Bears and on Sunday play sixty minutes at guard with the pros. What he liked best about George Halas was that Papa Bear paid his players, though not much.

Rockne is a legend today, for it was forty-seven years ago that he died in a plane crash. Hunk Anderson remained in football until about twelve years ago, when he retired to Palm Beach. He died there on

April 24. Charley Callahan, who handled athletic publicity for Notre Dame before going to the Miami Dolphins, saw Hunk about two weeks before that. "He hadn't changed," Charley reports. "He told me Don Shula was a *profanity* good coach and Joe Robbie an *obscenity* good owner."

Hunk Anderson was the toughest nice guy or the nicest tough guy I ever knew. He had to get tough early because he grew up on the Copper Peninsula in northern Michigan and his parents stuck him with the given name of Heartley. The Copper Peninsula is a rocky spur thrust into the icy waters of Lake Superior. Villages bear names like Franklin Mine, South Range, Trimountain, Atlantic Mine and Copper Harbor, but there is also the town of Laurium, birthplace of George Gipp.

Of all the names on the roll of Notre Dame sports, Gipp is the holiest. Growing up a few miles apart, he and Hunk knew each other as high school players, and Gipp brought Hunk to Notre Dame. Even for those days, Hunk was small for a lineman, but he was ferocious. He was a regular on the first four teams Rockne directed as head coach (1918–21).

Hunk took his degree in engineering, but in those first postgraduate years he was really a football player and coach moonlighting at the iron works. In the late 1920s he signed a two-year contract as head coach at St. Louis University. The agreement provided for a substantial wage increase if he "improved football" at the university. Never one for half-way measures, he combed the Ozarks for swift young scholars with sloping necks and pointed ears, quartered them in a decrepit residence called the S.L. House, saw that they were shod and fed and permitted to attend classes if they wished.

The football program prospered, but after two years, some of the Jesuits in the administration had reservations about the contributions Hunk and his muscular recruits were making to the university's academic reputation. When it became clear that he wasn't going to get the promised raise, Hunk—whose speech was always direct and colorful—told the authorities what they could do with the job and returned to Notre Dame as Rock's assistant.

When Rock was killed in the spring of 1931, Hunk succeeded him as head coach. Rock's last two teams had been undefeated and the only flyspeck on the record of the 1931 squad was a tie with Northwestern, until the last game. Southern California sent a strong team east but Notre Dame hadn't lost in twenty-six games and had been beaten at home only once in twenty-seven years.

In 1931 a player taken out of the game could not return until the next quarter. After three periods, Notre Dame had the game in hand, 14–0. Hunk pulled out his regulars. Against the second string, Southern Cal marched for two touchdowns. Only one extra point was converted, but in the last minute Johnny Baker, a guard, kicked a field goal that won for USC, 16–14.

In later years it was said that this defeat broke Hunk's pick at Notre Dame, but the fact is that he coached two more years and quit voluntarily. He was unhappy with a policy that limited him to twenty one-year football scholarships, renewable by the administration. The story goes that when he was leaving for a job at North Carolina State he made one of his most trenchant speeches on behalf of his successor, Elmer Layden.

After North Carolina State, Hunk joined the Bears' coaching staff. He is credited with introducing the reverse body block, the red dog blitz by linebackers and the safety blitz. Halas, who had been in the Navy in World War I, reenlisted in 1942. Though many of Chicago's top players were in service, the Bears went through that season undefeated with Hunk and Luke Johnson as cocoaches. The Redskins beat them in the championship play-off.

The manpower squeeze grew tighter. For 1943, Bronko Nagurski was wheedled out of retirement. He played tackle until the Bears came to the last game needing victory over the Chicago Cardinals to make the play-off. Hunk asked the Bronk if he'd like to "play a little fullback." That was something he hadn't tried in six years, but the Bronk loved to run over people.

Late in the game, with the Cardinals leading 24–14, the Bronk went in and bulled through to a touchdown. The Bears got another drive going but seemed stalled on fourth down with four yards to go. The Bronk came back and got the first down. Then Sid Luckman passed for the winning touchdown, the Bears went on to whip the Redskins and the Anderson-Johnson team had the championship.

"The greatest line coach in college football," Rock said of Hunk. "The best line coach in pro football," Halas said.

LONG TOM SHAW

DURING THE administration of Mayor William O'Dwyer, New York slapped a surtax on mutuel betting that was known as the "O'Dwyer bite." A reporter who excelled at neither mathematics nor gambling dropped into the office of Tim Mara, the former bookmaker who owned the New York Giants football team. The reporter wanted to ask an expert what the increased takeout would do to a horse player's chance of breaking even. With Tim was a tall man whose erect carriage lent a kind of formality to his appearance.

Tim introduced him as "Mr. Shore."

In the conversation that ensued, it became clear that Mr. Shore was as well versed in the mathematics of gambling as his host. Both cited figures showing that a player could get a fairer shake at craps or roulette than at the racetrack under the O'Dwyer bite. They told stories of the days before the mutuels when bookmakers operated at the New York cavalry posts and sometimes backed their own judgment with their own money.

Mr. Shore remembered a horse named Coventry that had come up from Kentucky backed by more than just the admiration of his neighbors. Having hocked all visible heirlooms to bet on the steed, citizens of the Blue Grass country were digging in the backyards for forgotten treasures buried in 1861 to keep them out of Yankee hands. For reasons of his own, Mr. Shore did not share the popular notion that Coventry was a good thing. He took every dollar clients wanted to bet on the horse.

"I stood to lose . . ." he said, telling the story in Tim Mara's office. "Well, I won't tell you what I stood to lose."

"He won't tell you," Tim said, "because you would fall off that there chair."

Anyway, Mr. Shore said, it turned out that his judgment was sound. Coventry lost and Mr. Shore made a nice score. Concluding the story, he rose to say goodbye to Tim, bowed, and departed.

"Does he spell his name with an *e*," the reporter asked, "or just S-*h*-*o*-*r*?"

"S-*h*-*a*-*w*," Tim said. "Tom Shawr."

The reporter knew that name well enough. Anybody who read the sports pages then recognized the name of Long Tom Shaw, dean of New York books.

"That story he was telling you about Coventry," Tim said. "He stood to lose one million dollars and he had it to pay off."

Tim paused. "He," Tim said, "is what you call a real high guy."

Tom Shaw lived to be 102. Like men who saw Man O' War or men who knew Christy Mathewson or men who were with Ketchel, men who knew Tom Shaw are dwindling in number, but the racetrack abounds with tales about him. Like the one about the time Commander J. K. L. Ross wanted to get down for $100,000 on his Sir Barton, first winner of the American Triple Crown. Long Tom nodded, and the Commander had a bet.

Tom Shaw first won prominence as a bicycle racer. One of his chief rivals was Charles S. Howard, who opened a bike repair shop in San Francisco in 1905, became an automobile dealer, made millions and owned, among other horses, the gallant Seabiscuit, who beat War Admiral in a memorable match race at Pimlico and took the Santa Anita Handicap the year after his stablemate, Kayak II, had won it. Howard imported Noor, the conqueror of Citation.

Shaw, meanwhile, went from bikes to the gambling room of Parson Davies in New Orleans, then moved west to make book at Santa Anita. He teamed up with another bookmaker, Barney Schreiber, who owned a horse named Jack Atkin. A brilliant sprinter, Jack Atkin was usually odds-on at six furlongs, but the books in New Orleans laid 5 to 1 against him when Shaw and Schreiber put him in the Rex Handicap there at a mile and an eighth.

With the winner's purse and the bookies' money, the trio proceeded to New York, where Jack Atkin was assigned 128 pounds in the Metropolitan Handicap. Shaw wiped out the books that gave him 8 to 1. He and Schreiber were said to have cleaned up $100,000 when their sprinter went a mile and a quarter to win something called the Dominion Handicap.

Tom Shaw's daughter married Bill Shea, for whom Shea Stadium is named. The form on Bill Shea's father-in-law read, "Never refuse a bet, any amount, any price." His predecessor as dean of the clubhouse betting ring was Johnny Walters, another fearless operator. The tale is told of the time Johnny Walters sailed for a holiday in Europe, occupying the most expensive quarters on the ship, receiving and paying for the most attentive service. Another passenger—a Morgan or Rockefeller or Carnegie—asked how he was able to afford such luxury.

"Odds-on favorites," Mr. Walters told him.

Tom Shaw booked odds-on favorites and the longest of long shots without the flicker of an eyelid. In 1930 Saratoga witnessed an upset still celebrated as a classic when Jim Dandy dropped down out of nowhere to win the Travers Stakes from the Triple Crown winner, Gallant Fox, and the brilliant Whichone.

Most bookmakers had made Jim Dandy 100 to 1. As the race ended, they heard wild animal cries from Subway Sam Rosoff, who crowed that he had bet $100 with Shaw at 150 to 1. So Tom paid him the $15,000. What the hell, it was only money.

THE MAN WHO CAME TO DINNER

THE NAME of the man who came to dinner was Tommy Brophy, and in all their lives Bill and Mildred O'Brien never had a more agreeable guest. In 1946 on his way home to Elmhurst, Queens, from World War II, Tom stopped to say hello to the O'Briens in their apartment on West 116th Street. They persuaded him to stay for the weekend. He stayed fourteen years.

Bill O'Brien worked for Metro-Goldwyn-Mayer in New York and drank in the Artists and Writers on West Fortieth Street, which was called Bleeck's then and, in a diminishing circle, still is. He also favored a spa on the upper West Side known affectionately to Columbia students as the Armpit, but that's incidental. Bill bred, owned, raced and bet horses without spectacular success in any department.

Tom Brophy's siblings were in show business. One brother, Eddie, was a movie actor who played cops' roles mostly and another, Jeff, sang in nightclubs. It could have been through the showbiz connection that Tom and Bill got to be friends, but it wasn't.

"Brophy was sheet writer for my father's bookmaker," said Bill O'Brien's son Pat.

After the war Tom worked as outside man for a race book, taking bets from players and relaying them to the bookie. One day he got off a Fifth Avenue bus at Seventieth Street and wandered into the Frick Collection to admire portraits of Sir Thomas More and Thomas Cromwell by Hans Holbein the Younger. On the third floor he noticed a public telephone.

About that time Mayor Fiorello La Guardia came down on "tinhorn gamblers," smashing pinball machines and raiding handbooks. "Thoroughbred racing," the Little Flower shouted, "has the same relation to improvement of the breed as prostitution to the science of eugenics."

Most bookies took it on the lam to Jersey, but Tom Brophy stayed in Manhattan, operating quietly on the phone up above the saint and lord chancellor.

One night Brophy came home to the O'Briens and announced that he was turning square. Somehow he had come upon a newly developed food grater, and he had a job demonstrating the device in Macy's basement. The job challenged his powers of persuasion and charm, and he loved it.

He smiled and talked and grated cheese and stuff, and each night reported to 116th Street with Band-Aids on every finger. Pat O'Brien painted the cuts with his sister's nail polish to stop the bleeding. While still a boy, Pat got to be one of the best cutmen in New York, perhaps on a par with Whitey Bimstein.

For a long time Brophy handled sports publicity for New York University. At the same time, he and Walt Kelly, creator of the comic strip "Pogo" did a news commentary on radio, and in the early days of television Tom was the star of what must have been one of the first TV commercials. He demonstrated the versatility of a toilet soap called La Toja by lathering his round face and shaving.

Tom was quietly proud of his connection with NYU, partly, perhaps, because he hadn't got around to finishing high school. His radio experience, his taste of television and his labors in Academe combined in his fertile mind and became an innovation in continuing education.

On the NYU faculty was one Dr. Zuli, a brilliant lecturer. Brophy got him on TV conducting a class at 6:00 A.M. that was called Sunrise Semester. It was immensely popular.

When the show was new, Tom took Dr. Zuli and another member of the NYU faculty to Bleeck's bar. It seems improbable that the educators knew much about the back side of a racetrack with its population of trainers, exercise boys, swipes and hot walkers, who lead horses around and around the barn to cool the animals out after they have worked or raced. No matter. Every little while Brophy and Dr. Zuli left the bar for a stroll on Fortieth Street.

"What's going on, anyway?" their companion asked after the third or fourth stroll.

"I'm walking an intellectual hot," Brophy said.

Doing sports publicity, Tom wasn't a pushy press agent. He knew what made a story or column, and he knew which sportswriters could make the best use of it. There was one column about an NYU student from South America who owned a race horse that was paying the kid's way through school.

Another concerned Johnny Law, a former Notre Dame football

player who coached a team of inmates at Sing Sing. To have a guy named John Law coaching the lawless was pretty good copy by itself, but Brophy came up with an additional angle.

It seemed that a pickpocket working the crowd at an Army–Notre Dame game got Johnny Law's watch. A day or two later the watch was returned to the police. Johnny was relieved, because the watch had been a gift he treasured. It was engraved: "To John Law from the Sing Sing Inmates." Could be the pickpocket had been one of the donors.

JOE LOUIS: A SENSE OF DIGNITY

WHEN JOE LOUIS's tax troubles were still making headlines, a man told him, "You were fifteen years ahead of your time. You should have been around today to cut in on these multimillion-dollar closed-circuit shows."

"No," Joe said, "when I was boxing I made five million dollars and wound up broke, owing the Government a million. If I was boxing today I'd make ten million and wind up broke, owing the Government two million."

Joe Louis Barrow lived a month less than sixty-seven years. He was heavyweight champion of the world in an era when the heavyweight champion was, in the view of many, the greatest man in the world. He held the title for twelve years, defended it twenty-five times and retired undefeated as a champion.

Not once in sixty-six years was he known to utter a word of complaint or bitterness or offer an excuse for anything. To be sure, he had nothing to make excuses about. In seventy-one recorded fights he lost three times, on a knockout by Max Schmeling before he won the championship, on a decision to Ezzard Charles when he tried to regain the title, and finally on a knockout by Rocky Marciano when that young man was on his way to the top.

Joe had just celebrated his twenty-first birthday when he came to New York the first time. This was 1935, not a long time ago, yet some people still saw any black man as the stereotype darky, who loved dancing and watermelon. Some news photographers bought a watermelon and asked Joe to pose eating a slice. He refused, saying he didn't like watermelon.

"And the funny thing is," said Harry Markson, telling the story, "Joe loves watermelon."

At twenty-one, this unlettered son of Alabama sharecroppers had the perception to realize what the pictures would imply and the quiet dignity to have no part of the charade. Dignity was always a word that applied to him. Dignity and candor.

Early in Muhammad Ali's splendacious reign as heavyweight champion, he hired Joe as an "adviser" and they appeared on television together.

"Joe, you really think you coulda whupped me?" Ali said.

"When I had the title," Joe said, "I went on what they called a bum-of-the-month tour."

Ali's voice rose three octaves. "You mean I'm a bum?"

"You woulda been on the tour," Joe told his new employer.

During World War II, Joe defended his championship against Buddy Baer for the benefit of the Naval Relief Fund. Wendell Willkie, defeated candidate for president of the United States, made a resounding speech in the ring. "And you, Max Baer," he said, "and you, Joe Louee . . ." Earlier that day Harry Markson, then doing publicity on Mike Jacobs's promotions in Madison Square Garden, offered to write a few words for Joe in case he was called on to speak. Joe said no, thanks, he wouldn't be invited.

To his surprise, he was asked to address the crowd. Unprepared though he was, he said a few altogether appropriate words, assuring listeners that we would win the war "because we're on God's side." Dignity. If memory serves Buddy Baer wasn't called on. Before the first round ended, he couldn't speak, being unconscious.

This story has been told here before but perhaps it will bear repeating. Before Floyd Patterson's second match with Sonny Liston, the one in Las Vegas, a visitor remarked to Joe that every time Floyd talked with the press he spoke of losing. "If I lose, if I lose bad, if I'm humiliated," he would start over again at the bottom and work his way back to main events.

"A fighter can't think that way," Joe said, "and he can't talk that way."

"It seems to me," his companion said, "that any time a man of intelligence goes into an athletic contest, he realizes that he stands a chance of losing."

"Oh, I think I reckanized it," Joe said. "Especially when I was just starting out and scared. After I won the title I didn't think about it no more. Oh, I knew that if I kept on fighting, some guy would come along and take the title away from me, but not this guy, never tonight."

Joe Louis may very well have been the greatest fighter who ever lived. Comparisons with Jack Dempsey and Gene Tunney and others are foolish, though there is no shadow of doubt here that he would have caught and destroyed Muhammad Ali as he caught Billy Conn and other skillful boxers.

At the top of his game he would have outboxed Rocky Marciano and perhaps have taken him out, though after forty-nine fights without a defeat or draw, Rocky said he had never been dazed by a punch, even the punches that floored him. Joe's aging legs betrayed him when he finally fought Marciano.

That was his last competitive match, though he boxed a few exhibitions afterward. Marciano knocked him out of the ring in the eighth round, and afterward Joe lay on his stomach on a rubbing table with his right ear pillowed on a towel. He wore his faded dressing gown of blue and red, with a raincoat spread over it. His left hand was in a bucket of ice on the floor and a handler massaged his left ear with ice. With his face squashed against the padding of the table, newspapermen had to kneel with their heads close to his lips to hear his words.

He said the best man had won. Asked whether Marciano could hit harder than Schmeling, who had knocked him out fifteen years earlier, Joe said, "This kid knocked me out with what? Two punches. Schmeling knocked me out with—musta been a hunderd punches. But I was twenty-two years old then. You can take more then than later on."

"Did age count tonight, Joe?"

"Ugh," Joe said, and bobbed his head.

HIRSCH JACOBS

EVEN THE man from *Izvestia* was talking about the fight, which was no more than proper because this was in the offices of Madison Square Garden's boxing department, and unless you've got a live horse to mention you'd better talk fight around there, or keep quiet.

Somebody was saying that he thought he'd heard more talk of this fight around town than he'd heard about any match in . . . hell, he couldn't remember how long, and somebody else said naturally, this was for the heavyweight championship of the world and there hadn't been a real heavyweight title bout in New York since Cassius Clay defended against Zora Folley in 1967, and before that you had to go back ten years to the second Patterson-Johansson.

To be sure, the boxing commission had called it a match for the heavyweight championship when Joe Frazier beat Buster Mathis, and since then Frazier had twice defended his share of the title in New York, but at the same time Jimmy Ellis had been taking bows as the World Boxing Association's notion of a world champion.

"Which reminds me, Angie," a guy said to Angelo Dundee, the manager of Ellis, "that it was on the Clay-Folley card that your boy showed here last. He stopped Johnny Persol, but it was in a preliminary and nobody ever sees anybody underneath a heavyweight championship. And three years had gone by then since Ellis last showed here, when he was a middleweight and lost to Hurricane Carter in a bad fight. So that's why they're betting six to one against your boy this time."

"That's right," Dundee said calmly. "This is the one where he wins recognition in New York."

A guy chuckled. "That's funny, in a way. He hasn't won recognition and here he is fighting for the heavyweight championship of the world."

Angelo corrected him firmly. "For the championship of New York State. He's been world champion for two years."

The argument could have got lively, but just then word came that Hirsch Jacobs had died.

"Oh, hell," a guy said. "Talk about your champions!"

Talk about champions, indeed. In no sport from archery to volleyball has there ever been a truer champion than the pudgy, smiling little redhead from Brooklyn, who led the ranks of American horse trainers oftener than any other man from Sam Hildreth to Eddie Neloy.

It's an old story but a wonderful one, how Hirsch Jacobs started as a trainer of racing pigeons, went from birds to horses, and, racing the cheapest kind of stock against such giants as Ben Jones, Preston Burch, and Jim Fitzsimmons, was America's leading trainer in eleven of twelve consecutive seasons. (The year he missed he was beaten out by Dave Womeldorff, who saddled just ten more winners.)

That was in the period from 1933 through 1944 when Hirsch Jacobs couldn't afford fashionably bred horses. He claimed animals that couldn't win for other people and he did something to them that made them win for him. In that stretch of a dozen years when he saddled more winners than anybody else in the world, he never once topped the trainers' list in money won, because the kind of horses he had didn't qualify for many $100,000 stakes.

After 1944, he won fewer races but more money. In 1946, 1960 and 1965, horses saddled by him topped the country in earnings. He was just as skillful with good horses as with bad, and vice versa. Strangely, this is a rather unusual trait. In the case of Hirsch Jacobs, the secret probably was that he treated all horses alike.

Some said he used his horses hard, but what they really meant was that when he had an animal fit to run, he did not believe in keeping it in the barn. Once, many years ago, he had a two-year-old he thought would be a champion, and he resolved to bring the little fellow along cautiously, saving it for the big chance.

One night the horse got cast in the stall, suffered irreparable damage, and never raced. From that time on, when Hirsch Jacobs had a horse ready for a race, he started him.

Starting with selling platers, Hirsch Jacobs came to have horses as royally bred as any that carried the silks of the Jockey Club's loftiest. Yet the horse for which he'll be remembered best—and he would surely approve it that way—was common folks.

The horse was Stymie, the son of a sire that won two ordinary races and a mare that won none at all. Stymie began life as a $1,500 plater and he was overpriced at that figure. Before he found himself, he ran in seventeen claiming or maiden races, and finished first only once.

Hirsch Jacobs claimed the colt out of the third race of his life, started him 128 times, and retired him with a bankroll of $918,485, the biggest in history up to that time. Just by way of comparison: Man O' War raced 19⅝ miles in his lifetime; Stymie went slightly more than 142 miles.

He was, as Joe Palmer wrote, one of those who "do it the hard way in the handicaps, pounding out mile after bitter mile, giving weight and taking their tracks wet or dry, running for any jockey, and trying with what they've got, even when they haven't got enough."

This was a bright red horse, a showy chestnut with a crooked blaze that gave him an almost comic, devil-may-care look. He held his red head high, and the faster he ran the higher he held it. Sort of like the redhead he worked for.

PART INDIAN, PART FIRST BASEMAN

RUDOLPH PRESTON YORK, the muscular house painter of Cartersville, Georgia, was a large, copper-colored man with about three fingers of Cherokee blood in his veins. "Rudy York," wrote the late Tom Meany, "part-Indian and part first baseman . . ."

The record book shows that, at one time or another during his thirteen seasons of big league baseball, Rudy York was an outfielder, a third baseman, and a catcher as well as a first baseman. If this suggests the adjective "versatile," it is misleading. No matter where he was stationed in the field, Rudy York always played the same position.

He played bat.

He was slow, unskilled, awkward, sincere, tireless, and stronger than dirt. There were many things he couldn't do well on a playground and some he couldn't do at all, but when he swung a bolt of mountain ash, the baseball left the neighborhood.

As an outfielder Rudy had only one important flaw. He could not be trusted to get there before the ball did, though it wasn't for want of trying.

As a third baseman he had the toughest chest in the American League, and needed it. Mickey Cochrane, who may have been the greatest of all-around ball player who ever made a living as a catcher, disguised Rudy in mask and pad and tried to hide him behind the plate between his turns at bat. This was in 1937 when Rudy was a rookie with the Tigers, managed by Cochrane.

The success of the experiment can be measured by what followed. What followed was that the Detroit club gave Hank Greenberg a $10,000 bonus to move to left field and let Rudy play first base. At the time Greenberg was the best first baseman in the business, a mighty swatter who had hit as many as fifty-eight home runs in a season. Even so, the Tigers deemed it worth $10,000 to ransom Rudy York out from behind the plate.

As a first baseman, Rudy got by, though he was only half-taught. Every ball he caught was caught with the glove alone, unassisted by the other paw. "He has a great pair of hand," wrote Warren Brown of Chicago.

A kid out of Ragland, Alabama, Rudy was working as a painter for a rubber company and playing on the company ball team when a Detroit scout signed him to a contract in 1933. It meant a financial sacrifice because he'd been earning $25 a week as a painter–ball player. As a Detroit farmhand his pay was $95 a month.

Neither the Tigers nor any other employer ever lost money on him. As a rookie catcher in 1937 he hit thirty-five home runs in 104 games, swatting eighteen in 29 games that August. In all the years since Doubleday, nobody else ever hit so many balls out of sight in one calendar month. Ted Williams hit thirteen in his biggest month, Mickey Mantle sixteen in his, and Babe Ruth seventeen.

In those days the Yankees always won the pennant. By August the only excitement left in Detroit revolved around the rookie's pursuit of Ruth's one-month record. Going into the last game, Rudy had sixteen August home runs, needed one to tie the record and two to break it. He got 'em both off Pete Appleton.

Rudy played in two World Series with Detroit, 1940 and 1945, and he was chosen on four American League All-Star teams—an honor that eluded Nijinsky. Traded to the Red Sox in 1946, he helped them win their first pennant in twenty-eight years. (One day he knocked in eight runs with two homers.) His bat won two of Boston's three World Series victories, with a home run in the tenth inning of the first game and a three-run smash in the third game. Playing an overshifted defense against Williams, the Cardinals reduced Ted to the role of spectator in that Series, but they couldn't cool Rudy York.

During World War II there was an All-Star game at night in the Polo Grounds. The start was delayed by a cloudburst and at the end a wartime blackout plunged the park into darkness. In between, Rudy York dodged an inside pitch and, falling away, hit the ball into the right-field seats. The scorers ruled self-defense.

There is a bitter irony in the cause of Rudy's death. Lung cancer. In 1947 he set fire to his hotel room smoking in bed and narrowly escaped death. Thirteen years before he died, a cigaret almost killed him.

JOHN JOSEPH MURPHY

FOR THIRTY-SEVEN YEARS, John Joseph Murphy and Elizabeth Havern Murphy had a double celebration on New Year's Eve, for December 31 was also their wedding anniversary. The one just past, their thirty-eighth, should have been extra special, an occasion for the biggest celebration of all. Instead, the end of Johnny Murphy's greatest year found him in a hospital. He had suffered a heart attack one day earlier, but it wasn't bad, it wasn't anything he couldn't handle.

Last weekend there was a requiem mass for Johnny Murphy in St. Joseph's Church in Bronxville. It was four months to the day after Cleon Jones made the final putout in the World Series.

The putout had set the official seal on an extraordinary achievement. Johnny Murphy would be the last to claim the achievement as his own, yet it was he and nobody else who brought it to its implausibly successful conclusion.

When historians in some distant tomorrow look back on the last year of Johnny Murphy's life, they will recognize it as the year of improbable wonders and wondrous improbabilities—the year man walked on the moon, the year Joe Namath and his Jets thumbed their noses at the pro football Establishment, the year Johnny Murphy's New York Mets realized their impossible dream.

George Martin Weiss was in St. Joseph's. He had flown up from Phoenix. The very first thing George Weiss did as president of the foundling Mets in 1961 was to hire Johnny Murphy away from the Boston Red Sox. He wasn't buying a pig in a poke.

When Colonel Jake Ruppert bought the Newark club as the Yankees' first farm team and hired Weiss to run it, John Murphy was one of Newark's pitchers. He was a big, strong young guy out of Fordham who could throw all day, every day. After two years, Weiss sent him across the river to the Bronx, and for the next fourteen years George looked on while Johnny Murphy held the pass as one of the great relief pitchers of any era.

Those were the days of beer and laughter, and nobody laughed it up like the incomparable Lefty Gomez. To hear Lefty tell it, he couldn't have crossed Fifth Avenue without Murphy to hold him up. Actually, there isn't a pitcher working today who wouldn't envy Gomez's record for throwing complete games, but when Lefty did falter it was almost always Murphy who picked him up. To Gomez, Murphy was the beloved St. Bernard plowing through the Alpine blizzards with a case of rum and lemon peel on the side.

"Murph and I were in the elevator after breakfast," Gomez would say. "I got off at six but Johnny went on up to nine."

George Weiss knew all about Johnny Murphy. The last year before Weiss became manager of the Yankees, Murphy was turned loose. John finished that season in Boston, then got into scouting and personnel. George Weiss knew exactly what he was getting when he hired Johnny Murphy for the Mets.

John's original title was chief scout. Pretty soon he was a vice-president. On Weiss' retirement three years ago, Bing Devine moved up to be general manager. When he left after one year, Johnny succeeded him.

After the Mets won everything, a guy dug into the question of who was responsible. Who had put this winning team together? With Murphy, he went through the roster. "Wid Mathews hired the scout who found that fellow," Johnny would say, "and of course Wid was one of George's original men."

Mostly Johnny Murphy wouldn't take credit. About the most he would say was, "Bing started that deal. After he left, I just kind of tied up the loose ends."

What it came down to was, of course, that no one man fashioned the team that won everything. George Weiss started it, Bing Devine carried the job on, and Johnny Murphy finished it. Scores of other guys helped.

Only one who was there at the beginning was still left at the finish. Johnny Murphy watched it all developing, and in the end he put it all together. They gave him a pitching staff and he gave them the champions of the world. He did a wonderful job for management without forgetting that he had been a player too.

"When you think of Johnny Murphy," a man asked Bob Fishel of the Yankees, "what word comes to you first?"

"Warmth," Bob Fishel said.

LEFTY

WHEN LEFTY FRANK O'DOUL was manager of the San Francisco Seals in the Pacific Coast League, he took the team barnstorming through Japan so often that the baseball buffs of Nippon came to regard him with the reverence they ordinarily reserved for the emperor. He was truly the father of baseball in Japan.

In a Catholic mission in Tokyo, the kids were preparing for Confirmation. They were told they had the privilege of adding a new name to that received at baptism, but little Toshi couldn't think of a saint's name he wanted to adopt.

"Why don't you choose Francis?" suggested the nun who was his teacher. "For St. Francis de Sales."

"Ah, so," Toshi said.

A few days later the bishop was about to administer the sacrament. "And what is your Confirmation name?" he asked.

Toshi's face lit up.

"San Francisco Seals," he said.

Lefty O'Doul was seventy-two years old when he died in San Francisco, his hometown, where he was bigger than cable cars and more fun. About three weeks earlier a mild stroke had impaired the use of his left arm, but by itself that wouldn't have bothered him. It had been forty-five years since the arm was good for much besides drawing a beer.

He had set out as a left-handed pitcher in the years immediately following World War I. Failing to distinguish himself in three seasons with the Yankees, he was waived to Boston, where his arm went dead. Moving to the outfield, he became one of the finest hitters in an age of hitters.

He batted .398 to lead the National League in 1929, a year when just leading the Phillies was a distinction beyond ordinary mortals. With Lefty on the Philadelphia team that season were Chuck Klein, batting .356; Spud Davis, .342; Pinky Whitney, .327; Tommy Thevenow, .327; Fresco Thompson, .324; Denny Souther, .306; Don Hurst, .304; and Barney Friberg, .301.

With nine regulars—Friberg played first, second, third, shortstop, and the outfield—batting over .300, the Phillies finished fifth. The next year, some improved—Klein hit .386, Whitney .342, Friberg .341, and Hurst .327—and they finished last. Which tells something about their pitching.

In a menagerie feared for brute strength, O'Doul was a craftsman, perhaps the keenest and most dedicated student of hitting in his day. In his years as manager in the minors, he was celebrated for his ability to impart his knowledge to kids.

Joe DiMaggio played for him in San Francisco. Lefty would have been the last to claim credit that belonged to Joe's maker, but in all probability his advice helped refine the classic stance and lovely, level swing that Joe brought to Yankee Stadium.

Lefty had a rope trick for overanxious young players who tended to lunge at the pitch. He would loop a rope around the kid's waist and stand back holding the loose end. If the kid lunged, the rope brought him up with a jerk. It was an effective remedy, and Lefty's good-humored flow of reassurance eased the pupil's embarrassment.

A player didn't have to be on Lefty's side to get the benefit of his teaching. Memory recaptures a picture of him using his rope trick on a boy named Jack Wallaesa, a rookie shortstop with the Philadelphia Athletics in 1942.

Wallaesa was a gangling six-foot-three, eager as a puppy and twice as awkward. He could trip over his own feet in the field, and sometimes at the plate he looked as though a fastball would knock the bat out of his hands, but there was a flair about him that caught the professional eye. Al Simmons, then a coach with the Athletics, spent a lot of time with him in camp in Anaheim, California.

"Who's that big kid at shortstop?" Babe Ruth asked, watching infield practice before an exhibition in the Hollywood Stars' park. Ruth was in Hollywood working in the film *Pride of the Yankees*. Before the game started, the Babe was in the dugout with a bat in his hands.

"Look, kid," he was saying, "you're not following through. You want to step into the ball and then come clear around, like this."

"I like your big shortstop," Lefty O'Doul said when the Athletics got to San Francisco. Next morning he had his rope around Wallaesa's middle.

Touring home, the Athletics stopped in Oklahoma City, where Rogers Hornsby was manager. "Let me work with that kid," Rogers said to Connie Mack. "I want him to smooth out that swing."

When Jack Wallaesa got back to Philadelphia he had a little bit of Simmons in him, a little bit of Ruth, a little bit of O'Doul, and a little bit of Hornsby. He should have become the greatest hitter of all times, but soon after the season opened he received a letter beginning, "Greetings—"

He was gone four years, and he left it all in the service.

PEG

CHANCES ARE almost everybody who read of the death of Westbrook Pegler reacted to the news in his own separate way, depending on what the man had meant to him. The reactionaries whose spokesman Pegler often was, the racket guys he sent to prison, the individuals he excoriated in unmerciful prose, the readers who were delighted or outraged or repelled or entertained by his columns—for each of these the news must have had a different impact.

Curiously, one guy was left with an odd sense of loneliness. He realized that for the rest of his working life he might as well be resigned to being the last newspaperman out of any press box. Once he could rely on having company in his misery, for Pegler, a bleeder at the typewriter, would be just as slow as he to get the words on paper after a ball game, a prize fight, or a horse race. A difference between the two was that Pegler's words usually were the best words written on the event.

Most of the obituaries made only passing mention of the years when Pegler was a sportswriter. That was proper enough, for when he appeared on the sports page Peg never exerted any such influence as he did later as a crusading columnist exposing the criminal activities of hoods like George Scalise and Willie Bioff.

Just the same, it was during his hitch in sports that he refined his exceptional gifts as a writer, reached his peak as a light essayist, and brought more pure delight to his readers than he ever did again. Whatever else James Westbrook Pegler may have been, he will be remembered here warmly as one of the finest sportswriters who ever lived.

Not that he was the best-informed sportswriter. To Peg, a little knowledge was a useful thing but too many facts could get in the way. One day, for example, he telephoned Grantland Rice to ask why Johnny Goodman had not been chosen for the year's Walker Cup team.

"Johnny Goodman?" Granny said. "What for?"

"Isn't he the champion or something?" Peg asked. "I've been getting letters from Nebraska or wherever he plays complaining because he isn't on the team."

"Johnny was the amateur champion one year," Granny said, "and he's a nice fellow. But he hasn't licked anybody lately."

"Thanks," Pegler said, and proceeded to write a savage attack on the cartel of Nebraska hicks who were trying to foist a monstrous fraud named Goodman onto the leaders of amateur golf.

Wit and irreverence were the chief ingredients of Pegler's sports pieces. When the "gee whiz" approach was fashionable, he was a prophet of the "ah, nuts" school. He wrote of games during the 1920s and early 1930s, a period celebrated by some as the Golden Age of Sports; to Peg it was the Era of Wonderful Nonsense.

Yet he had his mellow moments. One of the most memorable found him captivated by the eloquence of Knute Rockne, the great Notre Dame football coach. Rock was a stocky man of slightly less than medium height who gave the impression that instead of dressing he just stood in a room and let clothes drop on him. The most noteworthy feature of a flat Norwegian face was a nose that appeared to have been hammered into place with a bung starter.

And yet, Pegler wrote, the honeyed words that poured forth from this face were like rare wine foaming out of a battered oil can. Rock read the panegyric and cried aloud that if his place in the public eye required him to endure such abuse he was going to quit. Peg promised himself that in the future he would keep his softer side concealed.

Thereafter he saved his literary talents for subjects like Old Paddlefoot, a beat-up horse player whom he described during a race meeting at Saratoga. In younger and more prosperous days, Peg reported, Paddlefoot had owned a string of horses and had colors registered with the Jockey Club. The silks were "a dirty shirt with a louse in it."

When Pegler forsook sports to disembowel liberals and others whom he disliked, he and Heywood Broun conducted a running battle in their columns. Taking a train to Saratoga to join his father, Heywood Hale Broun found himself sharing a coach with Pegler, and loyally cut him dead. Next morning, young Woody awoke about the time his sire rolled in, jovial from a night on the town with his old buddy Peg.

Up to Heywood Broun's death, he and Pegler were Connecticut

neighbors. In what may have been his last column, Broun expressed a wistful notion that things were looking up in the world. "Even a former sportswriter who lives down the lane gave me a crooked smile this morning," he wrote.

Yet later Pegler included Broun in a savage column that resulted in a $175,001 libel judgment in favor of Quentin Reynolds. He was a strange guy who often seemed to be viewing the world through the haze of a hangover. Sometimes he was.

"The column submitted for publication this morning," announced the *Philadelphia Inquirer* one New Year's Day, "consisted of the words, 'I must not mix wine, whisky, and gin,' repeated fifty times. The *Inquirer* does not care to waste its own space or its readers' time in needless repetition."

RED ROLFE

THE UNWELCOME word is that Red Rolfe, the quiet tiger of the Yankees' infield during the glory days leading up to World War II, is ill in Hanover, New Hampshire. Not that illness is anything new to Robert Rolfe, the indomitable invalid. Even when he was the best third baseman in the business, he was a sick man. Nobody will ever know how great he might have been if he had had his health.

Red is a Hampshireman all the way. He was born in Penacook just up the Merrimack from Concord, and he went to school at Dartmouth, where the Yankees found and signed him as an undergraduate. When he was through with baseball, he went back to Hanover to be Dartmouth's director of athletics, a job he resigned a couple of years ago.

The book says Red was born October 17, 1908. That would make him sixty years old going on sixty-one, and stubborn memory balks at the figures. In memory he's about twenty-nine or thirty, a pale and slender man growing thinner as the summer wears on until he seems almost spectral.

October comes and there he is, gaunt and silent and faultless, the almost perfect third baseman in six World Series over a span of seven years. Only once in that time do the Yankees lose a World Series, and that year, 1942, Red Rolfe bats .353.

That was his last time around, the World Series of 1942. He was only thirty-four and there was a war on. There wasn't a team in baseball that wouldn't have welcomed his services, but the long struggle against ulcers and other ailments had left him feeling a good deal older than thirty-four. Unwilling to overstay his time, he departed as quietly as he had come, going up to New Haven to coach baseball and basketball at Yale.

He left behind a record unmatched by any other Yankee third baseman, though this is a fact not widely recognized. When polls are con-

ducted today to pick an all-time Yankee team, most voters go for
Clete Boyer. Most voters are young, and when they saw Boyer they
saw a third baseman who never had an equal on defense unless it was
Billy Cox of the old Brooklyn Dodgers.

Some of the older voters go for Joe Dugan, and a few antiquarians
may take a flyer on Home Run Baker. Not many give Red Rolfe the
call, though he was almost surely the best who ever played the position
for the Yankees.

Dugan and Baker spent some of their best years with other teams.
Rolfe's lifetime average was a shade better than the figures those two
compiled as Yankees, and about seventy-five points above Boyer's.

Red came up as a rookie in 1934. In four of the next five years he
hit .300 or better. He was a left-handed hitter and Joe McCarthy
placed him second in the batting order because of his ability to pull
the ball into right field, sending a runner from first to third. The second
batter in the lineup doesn't get many chances to drive in runs, but in
his good years Red knocked in about eighty.

Rolfe never was close to being the big man on the club. He played
with Babe Ruth and Lou Gehrig and Tony Lazzeri and Joe DiMaggio
and Bill Dickey and Tommy Henrich, all of whom attracted more
attention than he.

Yet there was one guy he kept beating who recognized his worth.
Connie Mack's Philadelphia Athletics were a bad team that kept
attacking the Yankees with frantic charges that were almost always
flung back.

"You know," Connie used to say after those experiences, "they talk
about all the other fellas on that team, but I notice the man who hurts
us when it counts is that third baseman."

"There," Connie used to say, "is a real team player. You might get
him out three times but then he'll come up where it means the ball
game, and sure as anything, he's going to knock those runs in. Or if
the Yankees need that one big play in the field, they usually get it at
third base."

After his hitch at Yale, Rolfe managed Detroit for several seasons,
and in the winter of 1949 when the Yankees reluctantly turned Charley
Keller loose because of a crippled back, Red talked him into giving it
one more try with the Tigers.

"I didn't hire Charley because he was a Yankee," Red said, "or because we're friends or because I wanted to do him a favor. I hired him
to give my ball club a touch of class."

Class was something Red had no trouble recognizing. He saw it
every morning when he shaved.

LEW BURSTON

THE PLAN was to drive up to Grossinger's and see Jerry Quarry train for his match with Buster Mathis, but death, as the saying goes, intervened. Lew Burston's death.

They were giving Lew a send-off in the Riverside Memorial Chapel and all the right people were there—Jack Dempsey and Ned Brown and Harry Markson and Sam Taub and Barney Nagler and Gus Steiger and Murray Goodman and, in fact, just about all the good guys who still walk the fight beat in the Big Town.

Chris Dundee had flown up from Miami Beach and out of the past came Oliver Cromwell, who used to tend bar in the Long Pond Inn when fighters of distinction used that pub on the shore of Greenwood Lake as a training camp. Oliver Cromwell, whose singing dog was enough to set Cavaliers and Roundheads at one another's throats all over again.

Lew Burston would have been pleased to see them all, for all were his friends. Nobody ever got more genuine pleasure from the company of friends than Lew did, or gave back more pleasure.

"A boxing manager and promoter for more than forty years," is the way the obituary identified Lew.

He was that. He was also guide and counselor and friend to fighters and managers and promoters and newspapermen on a variety of continents, an internationalist who was equally at home in London, Paris and New York.

"How did you, a fishmonger, get into boxing?" a man asked Jack Solomons at first meeting.

"Ho!" said London's dominant promoter. "Arsk Lew Burston."

"What kind of fighter is Brian London?" a fellow asked when Cus

D'Amato was importing that brave and inoffensive Limey to challenge Floyd Patterson for the heavyweight championship.

"The copybook type of stand-up boxer," Lew said, "with that long, inviting chin that you love to tag."

On matters international and pugilistic, Lew was the authority. For years he lived mostly in Paris and London and was active in promotions there. In more recent days he was Madison Square Garden's ambassador-at-large, and through both eras he was American advisor to a long list of foreign boxers from Marcel Thil to Dick Tiger.

Jack Solomons wasn't the only one Lew started toward prominence in the industry. Back in the 1930s a kid named Jo Longman was cabin boy on the ship that brought the Belgian middleweight, Rene deVos, to this country under Lew's guidance. Smitten with hero-worship, the cabin boy jumped ship to stay here with the fighter, and Lew had a case of illegal entry on his hands.

That was the start of a friendship that endured until 1949 when a plane carrying Longman and his fighter, Marcel Cerdan, hit a mountain peak in the Azores. The crash ended a career that Lew described in detail to only a few.

During World War II Jo Longman was an underground fighter in France. He and four buddies—they called themselves the Club de Cinque—kept a little list of collaborators who were doing well financially under the Nazi occupation. After the liberation there was a rash of suicides in high places after which members of the Club de Cinque turned up in commanding positions in various fields such as the dress goods industry.

Jo Longman, for whom boxing had never lost its fascination, blossomed as the top promoter in Paris and a wheel in the nightclub world. "You've noticed that he hardly ever smiles," Lew Burston said sadly. "I don't know how many members of his family went into Nazi ovens."

In 1948 when Lew was scheming and struggling to get Marcel Cerdan a shot at the middleweight championship of the world, Cerdan carelessly blew his European title to Cyrille Delannoit, a redheaded Belgian. Now all Lew's plans depended on Cerdan's regaining the title in a return match in Brussels.

The show was a total sellout. Characteristically, Lew gave his ticket to an American newspaperman. Then, although he wasn't scheduled to work in Cerdan's corner, he tucked his second's kit into his pocket and made his way into the hall as a member of the fighter's official party.

Early in the fight, Delannoit broke Cerdan's face apart. It was a cut that could, unattended, have forced the referee to stop the fight. Now it came out that in the prefight excitement Lucien Roupp, Cerdan's manager-of-record, had forgotten to bring along as much as a styptic pencil.

Lew Burston scrambled up the steps, pushed the others aside, and went to work staunching the blood and closing the cut. Cerdan gave the gallant Delannoit a stylish licking, qualified for a match with Tony Zale for the world championship, and won it. Sometimes fate goes for the good guys.

CULTURAL COLLISION

THE CONGENIAL cultures of scholarship and pugilism collided head-on one afternoon in 1946 on the campus of Seton Hall College, in South Orange, New Jersey. Seton Hall has won a lot of basketball games and become a university since then without ever regaining the intellectual heights it touched on the day savants like Dr. Tony Galento and Dr. Gus Lesnevich snapped watercress sandwiches there and Dr. Willie (The Beard) Gilzenberg prowled the halls in full academic regalia—baggy corduroy pants, a shirt of lipstick red, leather windbreaker, and a hunter's cap.

The occasion was Schoolboy Red Cochrane's last training session preparatory to defending the welterweight championship of the world against Marty Servo.

Boxing titles had been frozen during World War II, and Red Freddy Cochrane was the first champion to risk his crown after V-J Day. In 1946 he was a thirty-year-old Seton Hall freshman under the GI Bill of Rights, having kept his title in mothballs for four-and-a-half years while he served in the Navy.

In those days Sugar Ray Robinson was widely regarded as the uncrowned champion of the welters, and Freddy resented the implication that he was a cheese champion. He said his manager, Dr. Gilzenberg, was the only man who had faith in him and that he was determined to justify The Beard's faith. "Friday night," the Schoolboy predicted, "will be Gilzenberg Night."

The campus scene is only one of many dredged out of the past by news that Marty Servo had died of cancer at the age of forty-nine.

Two others come back with special clarity.

In one, Servo is bringing a left hook up from Battery Park to the southernmost tip of Cochrane's profile. Ten seconds later class was dismissed for the Schoolboy, Gilzenberg Night was over, and Marty Servo was welterweight champion of the world.

In another scene, Marty has his back to the ropes on the Eighth Avenue side of Madison Square Garden, a maniacal Rocky Graziano is holding him by the throat with a gloved left hand and smashing Servo's blank face again and again with dreadful rights.

Marty had been champion for fifty-six days. When he woke up he was still champion, for Graziano was a middleweight and couldn't qualify for the 147-pound title, but he was through as a fighter. Rocky had hammered his nose permanently askew—"a deviated septum," doctors called it—and Servo never again would breathe without difficulty. He had to relinquish the championship without a defense.

That's why Marty is seldom mentioned among the welterweight champions of the first rank, and it is the reason why benefits had to be conducted for him during his six-year battle with cancer. He deserved better on both counts.

Marty never made a dollar out of his championship. In fact, the title may have cost him money. To get the match with Cochrane, Al Weill, Servo's manager, guaranteed the champion $50,000. The purse didn't come to that, and Weill took the Graziano bout to recoup the loss before agreeing to risk the title against Robinson.

Al Weill bowed to no man in his admiration for a dollar, yet in his fashion he occasionally revealed something suspiciously like principles. When he realized that his champion could not fight again without risking grave permanent damage, Al took it on himself to retire Marty just as he had retired Marty's cousin, Lou Ambers, five years earlier.

While he was physically able, Marty supported himself at various jobs. (Chances are he never knew how many friends Graziano chivvied across town to bring business into one restaurant where Marty was tending bar.) At best, Marty only got by financially. After he fell sick, his hometown paper, the *Schenectady Union-Star,* raised $13,000 through the efforts of Al DiSantis, the sports editor.

When Weill announced Marty's retirement, pronouncing "deviated septum" with visible effort, some skeptics hinted that it was a trumped-up excuse to avoid a match with Ray Robinson. This was cruelly unfair.

Marty had already met Robinson twice, losing both ten-rounders by narrow margins. He was the only welterweight who had ever held Sugar Ray to a split decision—one of the Philadelphia officials thought he won their first match—and these were Marty's only defeats in forty-nine professional fights over five years. Before that he had won ninety-one times in ninety-five amateur starts.

Cool, confident, and polished, with a swift and accurate hook, Marty was an excellent fighter who believed with all his heart that he could whip any man his size in the world. The only time he ever went in knowing he couldn't win, his opponent was cancer. And he fought that one off for six years.

BRED TO BUCK

C. E. FEEKE TOOKE, born in Redfield, South Dakota, fifty-nine years ago but dragged up on a homestead outside Ekalaka, Montana, was having the very hell of a time with the showy palomino between his knees, but he wore a grin that lit up the corners of Oklahoma City's Fairgrounds Arena. It was the next-to-last night of the recent National Finals Rodeo and Feeke had two armfuls of honors.

Under one arm was a plaque saluting him as breeder of Sheep Mountain, the outlaw voted best saddle bronc of the 1967 National Finals, and the other arm embraced a glob of hardware designating his Bay Meggs as runner-up among the bareback horses.

Getting the palomino to strike a pose while Feeke faced the camera with the inscriptions showing on both plaques was a lot like carrying three watermelons, but nothing could wipe off that grin. Never before had a producer of livestock scored a first and second in the same year.

They got the pictures made at last and Feeke rode off with the other stock contractors who had received awards. Ogden Phipps never knew a prouder moment with Buckpasser, Kelso never made Allaire du Pont happier than little Feeke was about the ornery hides that he had taught to pitch cowboys across the county line.

In the view of most of us, there is nothing especially cuddly about a brute with the disposition of Sonny Liston and a yen to spatter riders against the outfield walls. Yet the men who get hooked on bucking stock really fall in love with the critters. Chances are every saddle bronc and bareback rider at the Finals was a friend of Feeke's, but every one of them knew that if the little guy's mother got up on one of his animals Feeke would be rooting to see her flattened.

Funny thing about the four-legged outlaws, too. Like prize fighters, many of them are so gentle a child could ride with a silk string, out-

side of business hours. They're fat and sassy and they seem to live forever, the average age of bucking horses at the Finals being about
eighteen.

You can subscribe to bleeding-heart literature that sobs about
these beasts being goaded into frenzy by "bucking straps pulled cruelly
around their loins," but the fact is that a horse flanked too tightly
would stop bucking. Contractors who pay up to $4,350 for a bucking
horse—that's what a star named Trial's End brought—don't want him
hurt.

Four years ago three young fellows decided to set up as stock
contractors. There was Mel Potter, a calf roper out of the University
of Arizona who had begun life in Wisconsin Rapids, Wisconsin, on his
father's cranberry bog and mink ranch. There was John Snow, a
psychology teacher turned bronc rider and steer wrestler. And there
was Jack Brainard from Iowa State U., who raises rodeo and show
horses on his Diamond B Ranch at Rochester, Minnesota.

They had, of course, heard of Feeke Tooke, who had been breeding
horses since the 1930s and had built the family homestead up to a
spread of twenty-five thousand acres. Mel and Jack flew to Elkalaka.
On the ranch was some of the most impressive stock they had ever
seen. "Boy, I wish I had brought my bronc saddle!" Brainard said.
"I'd sure like to spur that bunch out one by one."

He was being facetious, but his host didn't smile. "Son," Feeke said,
"if you think you can, you can own this ranch."

Jack declined the challenge. Talking business instead, the partners
told Feeke they could use more of his horses than they could afford
to buy. Feeke said they could make money with his stock. "People
will come to see 'em buck," he said, "because they got the courage of
their convictions."

With a handshake for a contract, the partners began using Tooke
horses and paying for them at the end of the season. "Hell," Mel said,
"there were times we owed the old man ten thousand dollars, and not
a peep out of him. When we'd get far enough ahead we'd pay up."

Early this year Mel and Jack showed up at a small rodeo where
Feeke was trying some new horses. A four-year-old named Major
Reno stuck his rider's head in the ground and then bucked clean over
a six-foot cyclone fence without ticking the wire. Feeke had had a lot
with the courage of their convictions, like Indian Sign, Bald Hornet,
77 Sunset Strip, Sheep Mountain, and Bay Meggs, but none had
been ranker than this one as a colt. When this colt got to the Finals
this month, the score for his short working life was Major Reno 7,
Cowboys 0.

In Oklahoma City, Larry Mahan drew Major Reno for the last round. Larry Mahan, the perennial all-around champion whom the cowboys call Goldfinger because he is the only rodeo hand who ever won $50,000 in a year, needed only to stay aboard his last horse to top fifty grand for the second straight season. Major Reno whomped him quick, and Larry settled for $49,105.

Feeke Tooke would have cheered, but he didn't see it. After receiving his awards the night before, he had ridden off the arena floor and dismounted behind the bucking chutes. There, leaning against a post, he had crumpled silently and died. They found him still clutching the two plaques.

CHARLIE'S IRON HAT

CHARLIE GOLDMAN weighed about as much as thirty-five cents' worth of liver. He had a flat nose, a pair of outsize walnuts for ears, a stripe of scar tissue over each eyebrow, and a rather battered look around the mouth. He had earned these badges honorably in something like four hundred fights.

Charlie died the other day. He was eighty years old and spry, but he had a heart attack. It is easy to picture him shaping up at those glistening gates with a bouncy stride, wearing his rusty bowler cockily over one eye, and yet curiously diffident in manner.

The iron hat was Charlie's trademark and perhaps his symbol of success. He was a kid out of Beecher's Gym in the Brownsville section of Brooklyn, a neighborhood that has produced judges and humanitarians as well as the fraternity called Murder, Inc., and the derby marked him as one who could afford the tastes of a toff.

Like many professional fist-fighters, Charlie was the gentlest of men, and perhaps the most patient. It was the latter quality that distinguished him professionally when he became a trainer and instructor of fighters. It may not be unfair to say that Rocky Marciano, for all his physical gifts, might never have risen above the four-round preliminary class if Charlie hadn't been so uncommonly patient.

When Rocky decided he wasn't going to make it as a major league catcher, he and his pal Allie Columbo came down to New York from Brockton, Massachusetts to make a start in the fight game. They'd been advised to seek Al Weill's services as manager, and Weill turned them over to Charlie Goldman, who trained all his fighters.

Charlie put Rocky in the ring with a sparring partner, and as Marciano flailed and floundered tirelessly, an invisible burden settled on the little man. "Lord," he thought, "how I hate to start all over with this crude kid at my age."

He telephoned his report to Weill. The new boy was exceptionally strong, he was game and willing and looked as though he could generate some power, and he was so green it made a guy sick to watch him.

"Can we get him for nothing?" Weill asked, putting first things first.

"Yes."

"Good. We got us a heavyweight."

Al Weill had all the useful connections and nobody knew better than he how to "move" a fighter, as they say. Nobody in the world excelled Charlie Goldman as a teacher. Give him a boy with courage and strength, and Charlie could be trusted to get out of him just about everything heredity and environment had put in.

He was never able to make a dancing master out of the thick-bodied, short-armed Marciano, but his patience and Rocky's dedication produced a fighting machine that went through forty-nine professional battles without a defeat or a draw.

Watching Rocky come up, win the championship of the world, and whip every challenger in sight before retiring, ringsiders learned what Charlie had known for many years—that it doesn't take a Nijinsky to outbox an opponent; an awkward slugger who simply bats the whey out of the other guy can win on points, too.

Next to his patience as a teacher, Charlie was celebrated for his coolness in the corner. "Okay," he would say between rounds if a bout was going badly, "so let's try this instead," and he would recommend a small change of strategy. More than one kid, convinced that Charlie would find a way, fought better than he knew how.

Over more than half a century—he started training fighters in 1914—Charlie handled hundreds of kids. When Weill came along as proprietor of a large stable, Charlie carried a heavier workload than the entire coaching staff of the New York Giants or Green Bay Packers. In addition to his chores as trainer and teacher, he lived with the boys, doubling as house-mother and father-confessor.

He helped guide five of them to world championships—Joey Archibald, Lou Ambers, Marty Servo, Al McCoy and Marciano. It says here that Rocky was his masterpiece because he went into the ring at an age when most boxers have already laid in a backlog of experience, and he required more polishing than most.

They made a fine team. Rocky's addiction to exercise amused Charlie as much as it helped him, and Rocky enjoyed joshing the gnome who never lost his temper. "Charlie loved it in the Philippines," Rocky reported after a Pacific tour. "Out there he was just as big as anybody else."

LUIGI PICCOLO

IN THE football game Lou Little loved to tell about, he played tackle for a Pennsylvania team that lost to Dartmouth, 20–19, in the Polo Grounds in New York in 1919. Like Lou, who had been a captain of infantry in World War I, the top players on both sides were several years older and many degrees tougher than the average undergraduate.

"Dartmouth," Lou recalled, "had Jim Robertson, who got a broken leg; Laddy Meyers, whose collarbone was broken; Swede Youngstrom; Jack Cannell; Cuddy Murphy; Bill Cunningham, later a newspaper columnist in Boston; and Gus Sonnenberg, who went into professional wrestling and was heavyweight champion of the world. Our captain was Bert Bell, who became commissioner of the National Football League.

"Our tackle playing opposite Cuddy Murphy was John Titzel, a real man and a real gentleman. Between plays he spoke to me about the way Murphy was behaving, so we exchanged positions for one play. I said to Murphy, 'Why don't you just play football? Why don't you leave this man alone?' He said nothing at all. He just shot a stream of tobacco juice past my nose.

"'Look, John,' I said to Titzel, 'I've got all I can take care of over on my side with Sonnenberg. You take care of it over here.'

"I started that game without a headgear or thigh pads. After the first play, I got the headgear on in a hurry. Between halves I could hardly pull the pads on, my thighs were so swollen. Tiny Maxwell, who was one of the officials, and Doc Spears, the Dartmouth coach, got into a fist fight. Dartmouth lost six men. We lost one with an injury and one put out by the referee."

Perhaps the most striking part of that story, to those who knew Lou Little, was that Murphy was able to get his quid past Lou's nose. Born

Luigi Piccolo, Lou had the noblest of Roman features. "Big-Nose Louie" was Toots Shor's pet name for him.

Gene Rossides, now an attorney in Washington, was at Columbia for a class reunion on the weekend. Gene and those who played with him at Columbia in the late 1940s had read of their old coach's death a few days earlier in Delray Beach, Florida. It isn't hard to guess what they talked about when they got together on Morningside Heights.

It goes without saying that somebody mentioned the Army game of 1947. That was the year Rossides and Lou Kusserow were living it up in the Columbia backfield, as gifted and versatile as any two backs in the land. Their captain and leader was end Bill Swiacki.

Army had gone through three seasons without defeat. Now stars like Glenn Davis, Doc Blanchard and Arnold Tucker were gone, but the 1947 team won its first four games, carrying the streak through thirty-two games without defeat. As expected, Army scored first. Rip Rowan, the fullback, ran eighty-four yards for one touchdown, and the half ended with West Point in front, 20–7. The third period ended and the fourth began with the score unchanged.

Then with the ball on the Army 28-yard line, Rossides threw a pass into the end zone. The ball was falling incomplete when Swiacki materialized in midair and fell with it. The field judge said he caught it. Leading by six points now, 20–14, Army pulled a lineman back to help cover on passes. Mixing runs and passes, Rossides moved Columbia sixty-six yards in six plays. Kusserow carried the ball over and when Ventan Yablonski kicked the extra point, Army's streak ended, 21–20.

As a coach, Lou Little was a screamer until surgery on his throat reduced his voice to a rasp. After that he used a bull horn at practice. Yet for all his shouting, he was genuinely interested in the under-graduates who played for him, and the interest carried over to post-graduate days. In the Columbia locker room after the last game of a season, seniors would come up to the coach one by one to shake hands and thank him for letting them play on the squad.

Tall and square-shouldered, with pince-néz glasses straddling the bridge of his nose, Lou was a commanding figure and a polished dip-lomat. He was popular with his fellow coaches, with university ad-ministrators and with the press, and if his teams consistently lost as often as they won, newspaper readers were advised that skimpy ma-terial was to blame, not the coaching.

At least once during his twenty-six years on Morningside Heights he was greatly tempted to leave. In 1947 Yale invited him to move to New Haven as athletic director. At the urgent request of Columbia alumni, General Dwight D. Eisenhower, then Columbia's president-designate, talked him into staying. Then somebody talked General Eisenhower into becoming president of the United States, and Lou was stuck with his young engineers and doctors and architects.

He remained, nevertheless, the most cheerful and companionable of men, and one who favored life. He was a formidable trencherman who could hold his own at table with world-class feeders like Steve Owen, then coach of the football Giants; Herman Hickman, the Yale coach; and Jack Lavelle, football scout and raconteur. The four of them could lay waste to a forty-acre field.

One unflagging admirer of Lou's was Bo McMillin, legendary hero of little Centre College's upset of Harvard in 1919. When Bo was coaching Indiana, Little telephoned to ask, "How would you like the best schoolboy passer in New York?"

"It'll be mighty tough getting him here," Bo said, "but get him on the next train." Lou sent Ben Raimondi west to play quarterback on the team that won the Western Conference championship and election as coach-of-the-year for McMillin.

Back in Bloomington after a visit to New York, Bo said to his assistant coach, "You know something? That Lou Little's got him maybe forty different suits, all kinds of hats and coats and shoes, probably hundreds of shirts and maybe five hundred neckties."

"So?" said the assistant.

"So," Bo said, "gotta get me some suits and hats and coats and shoes."

MR. FITZ

IT MUST have been seven or eight years ago that Kathleen Fitzsimmons, granddaughter of the great trainer, James E. Fitzsimmons, organized the first annual corn roast and sangerfest at Fitzsimmonsville, the family community on the shore of Lake Desolation near Saratoga where Mr. Fitz and his countless siblings lived every August while the horses were running at the Spa.

"Who'd want to come?" Mr. Fitz had protested, for although he knew a great deal about many things, he knew nothing at all about the stature of James E. Fitzsimmons and the deep and abiding affection he inspired in everybody touched by his sweetness.

Kathy insisted and sent out invitations by the gross. As the appointed Sunday drew near, Mr. Fitz was like a bride cooking her first dinner for "his folks." On Sunday morning after Mass he sat wrapping ears of corn in aluminum foil, still convinced it was all a waste of time.

It was a howling success. Everybody lent a hand. The bartenders were Walter Salmon and Raymond Guest, our ambassador to Ireland today. Everybody came, everybody had a whale of a time, and the host was delighted. It probably was the first big party he'd ever known.

"Kathy," he told his granddaughter, "if the good Lord spares you, we'll do it again next year."

He was in his eighties then and it didn't occur to him that the Lord might call him first. He was such a quiet little man, who'd ever notice him? But the night came when Mr. Fitz slipped quietly away in his sleep. He was ninety-one and he just wore out.

Little Jim Fitzsimmons was born within walking distance of the Sheepshead Bay racetrack. When he retired on June 15, 1963, he had spent seventy-eight years in racing as exercise boy and stable hand, as a jockey and as trainer of many of the greatest horses on the American turf.

Sheepshead Bay, the race course, is long gone but its name is still remembered. There were dozens of others where Mr. Fitz raced whose very names have been lost to history, like the bush track in a tomato patch beside the Patapsco River outside Baltimore.

A small boy, he never grew tall, though he did put on enough size to end his career as a jockey. (He always suspected that he softened the marrow of his spine sitting wrapped in blankets in a brick kiln one day trying to make weight for a riding assignment he needed desperately, and that this started the progressive curvature that ultimately bent him almost double.)

Yet if he was not big physically, make no mistake, this was a giant.

One of the greatest privileges was to be with him around the barns in the morning, having coffee and Danish in his stable office or riding with him to the track to watch a string work. Until the last few years he drove his own car and Kathy said it was pretty exciting when he'd set out with Jonesy beside him.

Jonesy was an old crony, deaf as a stone. Mr. Fitz would come tooling along to an intersection, hunched over and peering through the steering wheel out of the tops of his twinkling blue eyes.

"Anything coming, Jonesy?" he'd ask.

"Hah?" Jonesy would shout. "Hey, how's that again?"

And they would pour safely through the intersection.

Usually, though, somebody else drove him from the barn to trackside, where he'd take up his position on the rail at the clubhouse turn, stopwatch in hand. It was always the same as the other trainers went by on their ponies and the jocks and apprentices and exercise boys passed within range.

"Mornin', Mr. Fitz."

"Hello, son."

"Hi, Mr. Fitz. Nice morning."

"How are you, Mr. Fitz? You look wonderful."

He was always wonderful—kindly, spritely, gentle, generous, gracious, humble, wise and brimming with life. It was always a nice morning, even when it rained.

All retirement meant to Mr. Fitz was a chance to sleep past 6:00 A.M. when he felt like it. At ninety he was still going, still making pancake batter every Saturday night and cooking breakfast for the family on Sunday, still going to the races and holding court back in the paddock area, with his friends squatting on the grass in front of his chair so he wouldn't have to cock his head back to see them.

The horses of Wheatley Stable and Ogden Phipps must have made him very happy this winter. He had those barns in high gear when he retired. Bill Winfrey won with them for two years and now Eddie Neloy is loaded in every division with three-years-olds like Buckpasser, Impressive, Stupendous, Brave and Bold, and Poker and a whole raft of fillies and mares and two-year-old colts.

Bill Winfrey and Eddie Neloy are trainers who can move a horse up several lengths but neither would claim credit for the mighty string of Phipps horses today. They know these stables are as powerful as they are because of the set of broodmares Mr. Fitz developed and left behind him.

Mr. Fitz, of course, would never make that claim. This man was so modest that for eighty-odd years nobody ever got him to pose for a formal photograph until the family harried him to a studio just a few years ago. What came out was a beautiful portrait with the old gentleman wearing his Sunday suit, a hard-collar and bow tie, smiling his sweet smile up into the camera.

"Oh, golly, Mr. Fitz," said a friend who got an autographed print, "that's just great! Gee, thank you."

Mr. Fitz was so pleased he talked like an old jockey.

"I was really trying that time," he said.

THE TERRIBLE-TEMPERED MR. GROVE

LEFTY GROVE was a pitcher who, in the classic words of Bugs Baer, "could throw a lamb chop past a wolf." One day in Yankee Stadium he threw them past three wolves named Babe Ruth, Lou Gehrig and Bob Meusel. The Philadelphia Athletics were leading, 1–0, when Mark Koenig led off the Yankees' ninth inning with a triple. Grove threw three pitches to Ruth, three to Gehrig, and three to Meusel, all strikes. Meusel hit one of them foul. Another time Grove relieved Jack Quinn with the bases full of Yankees. That day it required ten pitches to strike out Ruth, Gehrig and Tony Lazzeri, who hit two fouls. In still another game he relieved Roy Mahaffey in Chicago with runners on second and third and nobody out. Again he struck out the side on ten pitches. When Don Honig's book *Baseball When the Grass Was Real,* comes out, it will include George Pipgras's account of batting against Walter Johnson for the first time. He took two strikes, stepped out of the box and said to Muddy Ruel, Johnson's catcher, "Muddy, I never saw those pitches."

"Don't let it worry you," Muddy said. "He's thrown a few that Cobb and Speaker are still looking for."

Grove's fastball was like that, but he didn't have Johnson's comforting control. (One season when Johnson won thirty-four games he gave up only thirty-eight bases on balls; batters could oppose this gentleman confident that they wouldn't be hit in the head by accident or design.) Along with his blinding swift, Grove had the quality that Uncle Wilbert Robinson described as "pleasingly wild."

"But Groves wasn't a pitcher in those days," Connie Mack once said. "He was a thrower until after we sold him to Boston and he hurt his arm. Then he learned to pitch, and he got so he just knew, somehow, when the batter was going to swing."

It was typical of Connie Mack that he could pay an all-time record of $100,600 for a man—$600 more than the Yankees gave the Red Sox for Ruth—manage the guy for nine years, win three pennants and two world championships with him, and never learn to pronounce his name. To Connie, Lefty was always "Groves," Lou Boudreau was "Mr. Bordeer," and Zeke Bonura and Babe Barna were both "Bernair."

Robert Moses Grove was a tall, genial gentleman of seventy-five with a head of lustrous white hair who loved to sit around at baseball gatherings cutting up old touches. Lefty Grove, who threw bullets past Ruth and Gehrig and the rest, stood six-foot-three and wore an expression of sulky anger stuck on top of a long, thin neck.

He was a fierce competitor who made little effort to subdue a hair-trigger temper. His natural speed had dazzled and overpowered minor league hitters, and he wasn't accustomed to adversity when he got to the American League. When things went bad he raged blindly, blaming anybody who was handy.

One team that drove him wild was the Washington Senators. Before reaching the majors he had worked against them in an exhibition game. He was wild and they combed him over without mercy. When Clark Griffith heard about his old friend Connie paying all that money for Grove he said it would be a cold day in August before that busher ever beat his club, or words to that effect. Chances are some thoughtful soul relayed the remark to Grove. At any rate, the Senators whipped him the first seventeen times he worked against them.

Lefty threw his most memorable tantrum in St. Louis on August 23, 1931. He had won sixteen straight, tying the American League record shared by Smoky Joe Wood and Walter Johnson, and was going for his seventeenth against the tractable St. Louis Browns. While Dick Coffman was pitching a shutout, Goose Goslin got a bloop single off Grove and ran home when Jimmy Moore, a substitute for the injured Al Simmons in left field, misjudged an ordinary liner by Jack Burns. Beaten, 1–0, Grove took the visitors' clubhouse apart locker by locker, cursing Moore, Coffman, Goslin, Burns and especially Simmons, who was home in Milwaukee consulting his doctor.

The press found Grove surly and laconic and put him away as a grouch, although it wouldn't have been hard to discover what made him the way he was. A product of the bituminous fields of the western Maryland mountains, he had little experience with strangers and no exposure to social graces. People who had more schooling than he or had traveled more widely made him uneasy. Retreating into a shell, he became one of the great lobby-sitters of his time, a graven image shrouded in cigar smoke.

On the mound he was poetry. He would rock back until the knuckles of his left hand almost brushed the earth behind him, then come up and over with the perfect follow-through. He was the only 300-game winner between Grover Alexander and Warren Spahn, a span of thirty-seven years. He had the lowest earned-run average in the league nine different years, and nobody else ever did that more than five times. If the old records can be trusted, Alexander, Christy Mathewson, Johnson and Sandy Koufax each won five ERA titles. Some men would say these were the best pitchers that ever lived. Are the records trying to tell us Old Man Mose was twice as good as any of them?

Grove held at least one record that doesn't appear in the books. In 1920 Martinsburg, West Virginia, got a franchise in the Blue Ridge League and hired Grove at $125 a month. Martinsburg had no ball parks but the team opened on the road and a little jerrybuilt grandstand was flung up before the first home game. There was no money for a fence, however, so Grove was sold to Jack Dunn's Baltimore team for $3,000. That makes Old Mose the only player ever traded for an outfield fence.

CHARLEY LOFTUS LEAVES NEW HAVEN

FOR THE first time in many years, Charley Loftus was absent from New Haven last weekend. He left town Saturday by the only route still open to him. Charley died, apparently of a heart attack. He was fifty-five years old.

Charley was a prisoner of the mind, and the city limits of New Haven were his walls. During his latter years as director of sports information at Yale and in the poor times that followed, he was psychologically unable to leave the city where he had grown up. It had not always been that way, for he attended Ohio University in Athens, Ohio, and when he took the Yale job as a young man in his middle twenties there were no outward signs of the phobia that would ultimately confine him. Probably the condition slipped up on him. Certainly it caught his friends unaware. Herman Hickman, who coached Yale football from 1948 through 1951, was nearing the end of his term there when he discovered that it made Charley acutely nervous to venture beyond the Wilbur Cross Parkway to the house Herman and Helen had built in suburban Woodbridge.

Charley never mentioned his problem. Indeed, he employed elaborate fictions to conceal it. "You know those red banquettes up front in Shor's where the celebrities sit," he might say, implying that he had been in Toots's place just the other day. He would make out-of-town engagements in good faith. Then as the appointed date drew near, he would make excuses. As a last resort, if the excuses failed, he would sign himself into hospital.

The last time anybody remembered his leaving town was years ago when he attended a sports dinner in Cheshire, Connecticut, maybe a dozen miles from New Haven. He made it, but he had to recruit a police escort to lead him and a doctor to accompany him.

When it came to making friends for Yale, informing and assisting the press, beating the publicity drums and selling tickets, no college ever had a better press agent than Charles Randall Loftus. Hard work and easy laughter filled his good days. His seven-day work week, whose working days sometimes were eighteen hours long, amazed Herman Hickman, who wasted precious few hours in his own short life.

They made a colorful team—the fat, jocular, scholarly wit who coached football and the blithe spirit who complemented him with his lively interest in everything, his fertile imagination, his capacity for friendship. Charley stayed on at Yale some fifteen years after Herman resigned but never again had it so good as in the days of Hickman and his top assistant, Peahead Walker. The saga of the Mountain Boys at Yale was right up Charley's alley.

Last to bring out the best in Charley, and to profit from it, was Brian Dowling, whose many-splendored career as Yale quarterback ended in 1968. Dowling was an insouciant undergraduate with reckless self-assurance and a talent for bringing off the unexpected. With his theatrical flair, he struck Charley as the embodiment of Yale's . Frank Merriwell legend. "Merry lives again!" Charley sang, until the whole Ivy League believed him. Then he packed it in.

Charles Loftus Associates, a public relations firm, didn't last long. After that came a succession of jobs. They weren't much account, but they were in New Haven.

Charley was a charter member and probably the founding father of one of the most exclusive clubs in the world. In Hickman's first year as coach, half a dozen friends drove up to New Haven to drink his health. It was such fun they made a compact to meet again in six months or so. Thereafter they made a point of assembling once or twice a year for sustenance physical and spiritual.

By the second or third meeting the group had a name and a club uniform, both provided by Charley. The uniform was a red cap with a patch depicting a Tennessee-type mountaineer with squirrel rifle and jug, and a white sweat shirt bearing the words "Village Green Reading Society" over a cracker barrel on which lay an open book and a pair of spectacles.

We were eight—the late, great sportswriters Grantland Rice and Frank Graham; the gifted cartoonist Willard Mullin; Tim Cohane, then sports editor of *Look* magazine; and the late Joe Stevens of the catering clan, in addition to Charley and Herman. There were no new members admitted, no resignations, no officers, no constitution and only one by-law: "No Yalies need apply." (Joe Stevens, who had

captained the Yale baseball team, was a lifetime pledge never admitted
to full membership.)

For one meeting, Granny Rice brought two watermelons to go with
the Stevens steaks that Herman would grill, the salad Willard would
toss and the potables everybody would mix. That reminded Herman
of a recipe he had learned from General Bob Neyland, the coach at
Tennessee: Cut a plug out of the melon, up-end a bottle of rum in the
opening and chill. Before the last words were out of his mouth, Loftus
and Mullin were out of the room headed for the nearest liquor store.
There they gazed in perplexity at the shelves of rum, a drink neither
favored. Should they choose one pale or dark, light or heavy, from
Cuba, Jamaica, Barbados?

"If you'll tell me what you want it for," said the woman behind the
counter, "maybe I can suggest something."

"We want to plug a watermelon," Charley said.

The lady was not amused. "I was only trying to be helpful!" she said.

THE NOBLEST BADGER

AMBROSE BIERCE defines *epitaph* as an inscription on a tomb showing that virtues acquired by death have a retroactive effect. And Dr. Samuel Johnson, musing on the discrepancies that sometimes occur between a person's standing with his fellows and the sentiments graven on his tombstone, observed that "in papidary inscriptions a man is not upon oath." Perhaps it is not impertinent to suggest a line for Avery Brundage's headstone: "For once, he gave in."

It is difficult to believe he went meekly, though, even at eighty-seven. One pictures him still haughtily erect at the end, shoulders squared, staring coldly down his nose at an apologetic angel of death. "So he passed over and all the trumpets sounded for him on the other side." As president of the Amateur Athletic Union, president of the United States Olympic Committee and for twenty years president of the International Olympic Committee, Avery Brundage stood as a monument to Avery Brundage's concept of sport. It did not trouble him that what he stood for existed mainly in his own mind.

To him there was no sport except amateur sport, though the fact is there is hardly a real amateur competing today above the high school or yacht club level. Excluding professional games from his definition of sport, he was able to shut his eyes to the fact that in the international circles where he presided not one athlete in a thousand could meet his standards. In this respect he was a vestigial remnant like the vermiform appendix, a throwback to a day when there was a leisure class that could afford to give full time to games for pleasure alone.

Avery himself was no product of a leisure class. He was a working stiff whose strength of character and love of competition enabled him to excel at athletics in his spare time while making a fortune in business. Characteristically, he took the attitude forever after that if he could do it, so could anybody else.

"The noblest badger of them all," John Lardner called him. He was sincere and honest and inflexible and intransigent, with an integrity equaled only by his insensitivity. Before the 1948 Olympics he attended a luncheon in his honor given by American news correspondents stationed in London. Instead of saying, "Thanks, it's nice to be here," he lectured his hosts on the newspaper business, instructing them to expunge baseball, football, boxing, racing and other commercial activities from the sports pages.

When there was opposition to holding the 1936 Olympics in Nazi Germany, he rode the protests down. "Certain Jews," he said, "must understand that they cannot use these games as a weapon in their boycott against the Nazis."

No matter how these words sound today, Avery wasn't an evil man, only blind with righteousness. When black African nations threatened to boycott the 1972 Olympics if Rhodesia were admitted, he denounced their actions as "naked political blackmail," although it was only through a transparent political expedient that Rhodesia had been invited in the first place. Later, after the massacre of eleven Israelis in Olympic Village in Munich, he bracketed the mass murders and the Rhodesian argument together.

At a memorial service for the dead Israelis, he spoke as though these events were equally disagreeable incidents staged to disrupt the games. With the cry, "The Games must go on!" he turned a ceremony of mourning into a pep rally.

It is not easy to comprehend a mind like that, but it helps if one remembers that Avery was a member of the America First Committee and a self-described "110 percent American"—the Ku Klux Klan only claimed 100 percent—who once admitted, "People like me haven't had anybody to vote for since Hoover and Coolidge."

Although Avery was frequently wrong-headed, he could also be arrogant and condescending. In the informal climate of sports, he addressed people by surname as though they were servants. Having him call people "Walsh" and "Spelvin" did little to warm up a gathering.

Once he wrote a surprisingly warm note of acknowledgement for a column defending his position on some issue. (Opportunities to write in that vein were a special pleasure because they were so rare.) In the column a nickname had appeared which was then popular with English Olympians—Slavery Avery. The note of acknowledgement ended with a postscript that had a harrumphing tone: "Don't care much for that 'Slavery Avery.'"

That, of course, was only one of many nicknames pinned on him by the young people he encountered around the world. His imperious mien, his starchy manners and his unyielding attitudes made him irresistibly attractive as a target for the young. It was not by accident that the first big boulder encountered in the canoe slalom course at the 1972 Olympics came to be known as Avery's Nose. It was the hardest rock in the stream.

De mortuis nil nisi bonum and all that, but it is a fact that with the news of Avery's passing, there came to mind Dorothy Parker's epitaph for another rich man:

"He lies below, correct in cypress wood, and entertains the most exclusive worms."

GAYLORD RAVENAL'S YARNS

GAYLORD RAVENAL stepped out of here over the weekend, though that isn't how the obituaries identified him. They used his square name, Lloyd Mangrum. Ravenal was what his companions on the professional golf circuit called him because his rakish good looks and meticulously trimmed mustache gave him a debonair jauntiness that they associated with the riverboat gambler in Edna Ferber's *Show Boat*.

"Any man's death diminishes me," John Donne wrote, "because I am involved in Mankind." Of course, and some men leave a bigger gap than others. Never again can any of us sit on the veranda at the Augusta National Club—where, incidentally, Lloyd held the course record of 64—while those easy Texas accents weave inexhaustible yarns. Such as:

"It was a tournament in Fort Worth and I was playing the last round with Jimmy Demaret. It was a Sunday. When I called him for a lift to the club he said, 'Fine, we're going to church first.' 'Oh, no,' I told him, 'I've graduated.' But he said, 'Come along, it'll do you good.' Well, the way I was playing—anyhow, I went along.

"I don't know the rules and I didn't dig everything that went on but there was a priest up there talking Latin and kids carrying candles and I just watched and did whatever Jimmy did. We'd stand or sit or hit that kneeling bench. I caught some shrapnel in a knee when I was with the Third Army and I could feel it when I hit that bench.

"After a while here comes a guy around with a basket on a stick and I took a look at Jimmy. He gives me the okay so I reach in my pants and drop a hawg in the basket.

"We stand and sit and hit the bench, and then here comes the guy with the basket again. I take a long look down the pew at Demaret. He nods, so I come up with another hawg and drop it in. So does

Jimmy, of course, both times. Finally the guy comes around for the third time. Figured he'd caught a couple of lives ones, I guess.

"This time I took a real long look at Demaret. Finally he shrugs and reaches, so I shrug and get it up once more. That makes three bucks apiece and services are over but I can't get up. That bum knee of mine had stiffened up so bad Jimmy had to help me out of church.

"We went out to the club and I got loosened up a little and we teed off. You can drive the first green on this course, but Jimmy took a 5. You can drive the second but he took another 5. The third is called a par five; it's about a drive and a seven-iron.

" 'If I bogey this one,' Jimmy says, 'I'm going back to St. Peter's and get my three dollars back.' But he birdied the hole, and in spite of his terrible start he wound up with a 64 or 65. Which proved something about St. Peter's or about the course, I'm not sure which.

"We were both hopelessly out of contention but I think that last round moved Jimmy up to where he collected something like $225. Me, I was just along for the exercise.

"On one hole I hit into a plowed field. 'What's this?' I asked Demaret. 'What's the ruling here?' 'That's gopher dust,' he said. 'You get a free lift. Just drop it over here.'

"Farther on there was a little clump of cedars about as high as your knees and my ball was plumb in the middle, down deep. 'What's this?' I said.

" 'Casual trees,' Jimmy said. 'Drop it over here.'

"We had a little gal along as scorer, a nice lady. After I putted out she said, 'What did you take on that hole?' Before I could answer, Jimmy said, 'Three.' She said, 'Three?' I said, 'I only hit it three times,' and she said, 'Oh,' and put down a three.

"Finally I wound up behind a barn, a great big barn. 'What's this?' I asked Demaret.

" 'Artificial obstruction,' he said. 'Carry it around the corner there and drop it.' Say what you like about old Jimmy, but there's a man who really knows the rules of golf."

JIMMY WROTE TO END WRITING

"WHAT DO YOU think of my stuff?" Jimmy Cannon asked Frank Graham back in the days when Jimmy's column in the *New York Post* was a comet in the sports-page firmament and Frank was the bright particular star of the *Journal-American*. Through all his life, Frank Graham managed to combine two qualities that are not always compatible—absolute honesty and unfailing gentleness. His answer was gentle and honest: "Jimmy, you remind me of a young left-handed pitcher with all the speed in the world and no control."

Coming from somebody else, the comment might have affronted Jimmy, for he was not a secure person and needed frequent assurance that he was one of the very best. He took it with good grace from Frank, however. "Overwriting," he said. "Yes, that's my greatest fault."

Ernest Hemingway phrased it a little differently. "It's like when Jimmy Cannon sets out to write a piece to end writing," he said. "He's going to leave writing dead on the floor."

The point is, there were times when Jimmy very nearly brought it off, and nobody accepted that more readily than Hemingway. The mother tongue behaved for Jimmy as it behaved for hardly anyone else. At his best, he could make any writer wonder what was the use.

I can speak only for myself, but I doubt that many of Jim's friends and admirers were saddened when he died. After the stroke that knocked him out a couple of years ago, we were saddened when we saw him alive. He didn't stay down, though. He made it far enough back to resume his column, dictating instead of typing it, sometimes with the old perception and pungency: "If Howard Cosell were a sport, he'd be roller derby."

There used to be an advertising slogan, "When you've got it, flaunt it." Jimmy had and did. He could begin a column about a boxing match: "Once, dreaming with morphine after an operation, I believed the night climbed through the window and into my room like a second-story worker. . . . The night had the dirty color of sickness and had no face at all as it strolled in my brain. . . ."

In Korea, gray smoke from a bursting bomb reminded him of "the color of cataracts on blind men's eyes."

He might devote half a dozen paragraphs to a description of cellar-door dancers he had seen as a boy in Greenwich Village, and only then get into the splendid meat of a column. "What Jimmy doesn't understand," Hemingway said, "is that stuff up top is just the warm-up. You write it all, then you throw away those first paragraphs."

Jimmy's spoken lines were as swift and pointed as the ones he wrote. At a World Series he was scolding about Baltimore fans—he was capable of throwing a hate on a whole city—and a press box companion demurred: "Oh, Jimmy, people are alike everywhere." "Like Francis of Assisi and Adolf Eichmann?" he shot back. Another time Bill Heinz remarked on Ben Hecht's predilection for referring to Germans as "those people with short necks, thick ankles and watery blue eyes." "Means Marlene Dietrich," Jimmy said.

It is no disrespect to Jim to mention that hours before his death another champion died. Count Fleet, the only surviving Triple Crown winner before Secretariat and as preeminent in his time as Secretariat was in his, failed by a few weeks of reaching his thirty-fourth official birthday. Under the weight of his years his front legs gave out; he tried for a day or two to get up and, failing, slipped quietly away on Stoner Creek Farm, Paris, Kentucky, his birthplace, where Norman Woolworth and David Johnston made him a welcome pensioner.

One of the wisest racing men, Walter S. Vosburgh, advised long ago that in comparing stars of different eras it was safest to rank the newest idol as the greatest, for that way one would always be assured of voting with the majority. Well, when Secretariat retired this fall as "Horse of the Century" he had won sixteen of twenty-one races, been unplaced once, had earned $1,316,808 and had been syndicated for $6,080,000. Some who had seen him win the Belmont Stakes by thirty-one lengths felt they would never witness a performance to match it.

Count Fleet also won sixteen of twenty-one races, he finished as far back as third only once and earned $250,300. In the Triple Crown series, the Kentucky Derby, Preakness and Belmont, no horse ever got a head in front of Count Fleet. He won his last nine races by an average of ten lengths, taking the Walden Stakes at Pimlico by thirty and the Belmont by twenty-five in spite of an injury that ended his career. On three sound legs, he broke the Belmont record.

In terms of man's lifespan, how old is a horse at thirty-three? "People ask me," said Charles Kenney, Stoner Creek's manager, "and I don't know. Somewhere in the nineties, would you say?"

It was suggested that men reach ninety oftener than thoroughbreds live to thirty-three.

"Like the man whose doctor told him he had to quit drinking," Charlie said. " 'Maybe so, Doc,' he said, 'but I see a lot more old drunks around than old doctors.' "

CONSTANT READER

SONNY LISTON's death brings memories, some rather personal in character. One has to do with a breakfast among the slot machines and blackjack games in Las Vegas before Liston's second match with Floyd Patterson.

Not many heavyweight champions have been distinguished for their scholarly attainments, as Gene Tunney was, but Liston was the only real illiterate among them, unable to read or write. His wife Geraldine often read from the sports pages aloud and Sonny listened. He was generally uncommunicative, though, so it was difficult to guess how much he retained and whether he associated the writer's name with what was written.

The Las Vegas match was his first defense of the championship that he had won from Patterson with a first-round knockout in Chicago. When Patterson agreed to fight him, some of the Eagle Scouts in and around sports had been scandalized. They insisted that a labor goon and head-breaker who had done time for armed robbery should not have a chance to win the heavyweight championship of the world and so qualify as a model for hero-worshipping youth. Their attitude inspired a column in this space asking what was wrong with having jailbirds in boxing all of a sudden.

The breakfast engagement in Vegas was the idea of Benny Bentley, the publicity man in Liston's camp. Setting up the date, he started to brief the fighter about the party of the second part. "Now, Red Smith . . ." he began, but an uplifted palm silenced him.

"He's the one," Sonny said, "wrote there ain't hardly no archbishops win the heavyweight championship."

Even so, the big guy's mood wasn't exactly expansive when he showed up for breakfast. In the interview written immediately afterward, his boyish charm was mostly beneath the surface. Only in a few passages did his repartee sparkle. Once he said, "Uh." Later, expanding a trifle, he said, "No." And at last, taking off the conversational wraps, he said, "Unhuhn."

Colloquies like that spread an impression that he was scowling, sullen, suspicious and unmannerly. He wasn't always. To be sure, the first time he met Jack Murphy, the San Diego sports editor, Jack was smoking a cigar. When they were introduced, Sonny didn't offer a hand or say he was charmed or even hello. He said, "The cigar mus' go."

On the other hand, there was one afternoon at Aurora Downs, the abandoned racetrack outside Chicago where he trained for the first Patterson bout.

"Sonny," a guy said, "you're such a giant in the gym. You look so huge, in the shoulders, the arms, the hands, the chest. And yet you're about two hundred and fifteen pounds. Compared to the guys who play in the line in pro football . . ."

"Oh," he said, and his tone was downright diffident, "I'm too puny for that game."

When he was training in Dedham, Massachusetts, for the second performance with Cassius Clay—the one that eventually came off in Lewistown, Maine, I sat chatting with his trainer, Willie Reddish, whom I had known when Willie was a Philadelphia heavyweight and I was a reporter on the old *Record*. We rapped along about old Philadelphia days and at one point I said, "Yes, I did ten years hard in Philadelphia."

A little removed, Liston was sitting with his back to us and he hadn't appeared to be listening, but now his head swiveled around.

"Hard," he said. "No good time?"

"Not a bloody hour, Sonny," I said.

After the workout when I entered the tiny cubicle that was his dressing room he snatched a stack of towels off a chair to make a seat for me. With every evidence of confidence and candor he answered all my questions. At length I rose to leave, wished him luck, and we shook hands.

"Any time," he said cordially. "Any time." Obviously, any old con from Philadelphia was a friend of Sonny's.

Nor could anybody have been more at ease, or enjoying himself more obviously, than Liston was receiving the press the morning after he won the championship in Chicago. He sat up front at a long table like the chairman of the board and handled a microphone as though he had invented it.

A visiting author came weaving into the room, took the floor, and held it, making an ass of himself. Working stiffs tried to shout him down, but the new champion lifted a restraining paw.

"Leave the bum speak," he commanded, benevolence itself.

CHRIS CHENERY'S HORSES

IN THE stratosphere of big, big, big business, the president of, say, I.B.M. Corporation doesn't just pick up the phone and ring his friend, the chairman of the board at General Motors. Calls like that go through channels manned by operators, secretaries, expediters and maybe a junior vice-president or two. This tickled the public utilities magnate, Christopher T. Chenery, as far back as 1950 when he had Hill Prince, the two-year-old champion of 1949 who was destined to be Horse of the Year at three. That spring, when Hill Prince was coming up to the Kentucky Derby, there would be a deal of buzzing, ringing and scurrying until at last the president of Standard Oil would be connected with the board chairman of Southern Natural Gas.

"Hello, Chris?" an urgent voice would say. "How's the horse?"

Then there was this crusty guy who wanted to be a director of one of the corporations Chenery headed. The man held enough stock to qualify for a place on the board, but he was a crank who raised hell so insistently at stockholders' meetings that nobody wanted him around. One day he called on Chenery and after some perfunctory discussion of business matters, he said, "Mr. Chenery, you're interested in horse racing, aren't you?"

Oh-oh, Chris Chenery thought, *here it comes*. He was aware that in publicly held companies the extracurricular activities of officers can come under scrutiny, and that some investors grow uneasy when they see their leader mucking around gambling joints. Still, he wasn't going to back down.

"Yes," he said firmly, "I've always enjoyed racing."

"What do you think of Flares as a sire?" his visitor asked.

"Not a hell of a lot," Chris Chenery said, and they plunged happily into a discussion of breeding.

Memories of Christopher T. Chenery are brought back by news from Florida about Secretariat, who may be the finest horse this charming Virginia gentleman ever bred. The news is neither good nor bad. Secretariat is alive and well at Hialeah, but Mr. Chenery's death January 3, while not unexpected, threw plans temporarily out of joint and the chances are the colt will not be ready March 3 for the $100,000-added Flamingo Stakes, Hialeah's showcase event for three-year-olds with designs on the Triple Crown races of May and June.

Setting out as a sixteen-year-old assistant surveyor for the Virginia Railway, Chris Chenery made his way in business and finance. His beginnings in racing were equally modest. The first two stakes winners he bred were sired by Whiskaway, a stallion he bought for $125 when the horse was seventeen.

Later he paid $750 for a yearling filly named Hildene, who won only $150 on the track. To square herself, she went to work as a broodmare and produced the champion Hill Prince, winner of $422,140; First Landing, the champion two-year-old of 1968, who earned $779,577 and then sired last year's Derby and Belmont winner, Riva Ridge; Third Brother, Prince Hill and Manochick, all winners of major stakes; Satsuma, dam of the three-time champion, Cicada; and First Flush, dam of the stakes-winning Bold Experience, who in turn produced Upper Case, last year's Florida Derby and Wood Memorial winner.

Chenery was born in Richmond, Virginia, in 1886, and in 1936 he bought The Meadow, a 2,600-acre estate near Boswell, Virginia. The Meadow had been built by his family in 1810 but had passed into other hands. Here he started the breeding and racing activities that now are carried on by his daughter, Mrs. John B. Tweedy.

The $125 Whiskaway and $750 Hildene weren't the only bargains. There have been a dozen or more others, including Iberia, a $15,000 purchase who has foaled three stakes winners, including Riva Ridge. Up to now Riva Ridge alone has collected $898,895.

This brings us to Imperatrice, a mare that cost $30,000. Her children include three that won stakes and one that never got a cent. The latter is a daughter of Princequillo named Somethingroyal. One of Somethingroyal's sons is Sir Gaylord, the 1962 Kentucky Derby favorite who was injured the day before that race. He won $237,404 and is a top sire. Somethingroyal's daughter, Syrian Sea, won the Selima Stakes. Another son, First Family, won the Gulfstream Park Handicap. Then Somethingroyal had a son by Bold Ruler, and they named him Secretariat.

Both parents are bays, but Secretariat is a bright, burnished chestnut with three white feet and a star. He is a great big flashy dude, but more agile than might be expected of a youngster of his size. To be sure, he did get slammed at the start of his first race, which he lost. Nothing has beaten him since except the stewards at Belmont, who took his number down after he ducked into Stop the Music in the Champagne Stakes.

It has been mentioned before that Secretariat might not be flying the blue and white blocks of Meadow Farm if Mrs. Tweedy hadn't lost a coin toss to Ogden Phipps. When Bold Ruler was booked to somebody else's mare, it was usually a two-year deal, with the Phipps family getting one foal and the owner of the mare the other. In 1968 Meadow Farm sent Somethingroyal and another mare, Hasty Matelda, to Bold Ruler. Somethingroyal bore a filly and got in foal again to Bold Ruler. Hasty Matelda had a colt and the second breeding didn't take.

Phipps won the toss and took the filly. That left Mrs. Tweedy the colt and the foal Somethingroyal was carrying. The Phipps filly, named The Bride, couldn't beat a fat man. The colt from Hasty Matelda, called Rising River, was sold as a maiden for $50,000. Then Somethingroyal had Secretariat.

SLAPSIE MAXIE: EXIT LAUGHING

IT MADE news the other day when Muhammad Ali, already booked to box a British canvasback named Richard Dunn in Munich on May 24, agreed to take on Jimmy Young, a Philadelphia pacifist, in Landover, Maryland, twenty-four days earlier. Counting his tryst with Jean-Pierre Coopman in Puerto Rico February 20, that makes three title defenses, if you'll pardon the expression, in ninety-four days. To a generation that believes Ali invented boxing and will take it with him when he goes, it might come as a surprise that not many years ago a champion would defend his title three times in thirty days.

Maxie Rosenbloom used to do that between laughs. In 1933 when he was light-heavyweight champion of the world, he defended against Al Stillman in St. Louis on February 22, against Ad Heuser in New York March 10, and against Bob Godwin in New York March 24. To ward off boredom, he had twenty-six other fights that year, against heavyweight contenders like Young Stribling and K. O. Christner, against John Henry Lewis, one of his successors as light-heavyweight champion, against the indomitable Mickey Walker.

Less than twenty-four hours after Maxie slipped away in a rest home in South Pasadena, California, another figure from his era checked out less than twenty-four miles away. Teddy Bentham, a trainer out of Greenwich Village who was in the ring for thirty-five title fights and never took a punch, was found dead in the Beverly Hills home of a friend where he was a house guest. Maxie was seventy-one years old and wasted by illness. Teddy, still active at sixty-seven, apparently suffered a heart attack in his sleep.

Maxie had 289 fights and was stopped twice. He was a victim of Paget's disease, which attacks the breast and usually ends in cancer. The obituaries said his condition was the result of taking too many punches. Nonsense. Plenty of wives take more punching than Max ever did, and bury several husbands.

It may not mean much to say that Maxie started boxing as an eighteen-year-old and was still in there in his thirty-sixth year but the fact is that during his time in the ring the heavyweight championship passed from Jack Dempsey to Gene Tunney to Max Schmeling to Jack Sharkey to Primo Carnera to Max Baer to Jimmy Braddock to Joe Louis.

Slapsie Maxie, they called him, and his was truly the art of self-defense. Not everybody was enchanted with his hit-and-run tactics. The late Dan Parker wrote a parody of "Love in Bloom," a popular song of the day, which went in part

> Can it be the cheese that fills the breeze
> With rare and magic perfume?
> Oh, no, it isn't the cheese,
> It's Rosenbloom.

Maxie laughed. He laughed through seventeen years of warfare with battlers like Jimmy Slattery, Lou Nova, Bob Pastor, Tiger Jack Fox, Jimmy Braddock, Tiger Flowers, Dave Shade, Phil Kaplan, Leo Lomski, and up to a few years ago he was laughing through nightclub routines, movie scripts, Friars Club lunches, anywhere there was a crowd.

He was born to be a performer, and although he went only to the third grade in school he had an innate sense of class. He showed that back in the 1930s when he opened a club in Hollywood and, although money was tight in the Great Depression, insisted on a ten-cent cover charge to keep the riffraff out.

Teddy Bentham was a feisty guy who boxed a little as an amateur and fought a great deal as a trainer. If a manager sent his fighter out of town in Teddy's charge, he was confident that Teddy would bring both the fighter and the purse back, and probably a black eye of his own.

Billy Graham was a top welterweight who never held a world title but should have. He whipped Kid Gavilan, the champion, in Madison Square Garden one night but didn't get the decision. When he was an amateur weighing eighty-five pounds, he outpointed another boy his size, one Walker Smith, in a Police Athletic League tournament in Greenwich Village. Teddy Bentham was in Billy's corner, and when Walker Smith was riding high as Sugar Ray Robinson, Teddy always boasted that he had seconded Ray's conqueror.

Teddy worked with champions like Davey Moore, Jimmy Carter

and Carlos Ortiz, with Jerry and Mike Quarry, Danny Lopez, Oscar Bonavena and many others. He moved West years ago and always felt that he was camping out. Asked how things were going, he would shrug, "They got no trainers out here, no teachers like New York." A few years ago he said in an interview:

"They're gonna have to put me in a box to get me away from this, and you know what I want 'em to say when they're carrying me away? I want 'em to say, 'He done the job the best he could and he kept his mouth shut when he had to.'"

THE MAN WHO COULDN'T BUY PENNANTS

TOM YAWKEY was vice-president emeritus of the American League but in his late years he hardly ever attended either the business meetings or the boozy revels of the baseball hierarchy at All-Star Games, the World Series or the winter convention. He had little in common with other club owners and they were mystified by him, if not downright suspicious, because he was a strange fish who was in baseball not to make a buck or feed his ego but because he happened to love the game. Not many of the others could understand this, and it embarrassed them. When they were counting their money or posing for television cameras, Yawkey would be off somewhere fishing or hunting with a couple of his players, or in the summer when the game was over and the crowds had left Fenway Park he would put on spikes and baseball pants and a sweat shirt and get Johnny Orlando, the maitre de clubhouse, to pitch to him so he could hit line drives off that left-field wall.

His feeling for the game was rooted in his boyhood. When he was three years old his father died and he was adopted by an uncle, William Hoover Yawkey, who owned the Detroit Tigers from 1904 through 1907. Bill Yawkey, who was to die in Ty Cobb's arms at the age of forty-three, entertained some of the most famous players of his time on his estate near Detroit, and young Tom grew up in these surroundings.

Besides his devotion to baseball, another quality that set Tom Yawkey apart from the run-of-the-mill owner was his liberality. When the Red Sox were losing, critics tended to blame what they called a country club atmosphere induced by an overindulgent employer. When they won, their success was attributed in part to the players' loyalty to a generous boss.

Tommy McCarthy, the great man who presides over the press box in Fenway, had his own way of summing up. The exact numbers in his litany have escaped memory, but Tommy's testimony went something like this: "I have worked with fifteen managers, six general managers, four clubhouse men, seven public relations directors—and one owner."

On the sports pages Yawkey is often described as an owner who tried to buy championships and failed. To the extent that this had a slightly pejorative or unsportsmanlike connotation, it is a bad rap. Tom Yawkey wanted to win and he wasn't disposed to count the cost. When he hired a general manager he turned him loose to build the best team that could be put together. With no strings on them, several general managers reasoned that they could produce instant winners by just adding money and stirring. Yawkey's money.

The first of these was Eddie Collins, a patron saint of Yawkey's since young Tom enrolled in Episcopal Academy in New York. Collins, who had gone from Episcopal to the Hall of Fame, was a legend at the school and in 1933 when Yawkey bought the Red Sox from Bob Quinn for something like $350,000 his first move was to make the old second baseman his vice-president and general manager.

Collins charged headlong into the market place. He gave the St. Louis Browns $50,000 for Rick Ferrell, a brilliant catcher, and Lloyd Brown, left-handed pitcher. This, remember, was at the depths of the Great Depression when $50,000 was the equivalent of at least $500,000 today. For $100,000, Collins got George Pipgras, pitcher, and Bill Werber, infielder, from the Yankees. He was just beginning.

Eddie Collins had been a coach with the great Philadelphia Athletics of 1929–30–31. First he gave Connie Mack $125,000 for Lefty Grove, Rube Walberg and Max Bishop; then $150,000 for Jimmy Foxx and Footsie Marcum; later $75,000 for Doc Cramer and Boob McNair. Meanwhile he picked up Rick Ferrell's pitching brother, Wes, and Dick Porter, an outfielder, from the Indians. Yawkey's money got Lyn Lary, an infielder, Fritz Ostermueller, from the Cardinals.

By now Collins had spent well over half a million dollars, meaning $5 million or more in today's currency. Fans in Philadelphia and Cleveland grumbled a little when their favorites were sold but there wasn't a murmur out of the commissioner or the other owners. They considered baseball lucky to have a spender of Yawkey's stripe in the game.

At the end of the 1934 season Collins brought off his masterpiece. He called upon Clark Griffith, who in all his years with the Washington Senators had boasted, "I never sold a player for cash." When Griff got around to it, he didn't sell a mere player. He sold his manager and son-in-law. For $250,000 and Lyn Lary, the Red Sox got Joe Cronin, the shortstop who had married Mildred Robertson, Griff's niece and adopted daughter.

Clark Griffith's adopted son, Calvin, cried murder most foul this summer when Charley Finley sold Vida Blue, Joe Rudi and Rollie Fingers for $3.5 million. If Calvin's sense of history seems faulty, remember he was only twenty-two when Uncle Clark sold his son-in-law. Yet all that money never produced a pennant. When the Sox won in 1946, in 1967 and in 1975, their key players were homegrown players.

Tom Yawkey enjoyed fraternizing with his players, and perhaps this trait can be traced back to his boyhood when his foster father owned the Tigers. The team was on a losing streak, and after one especially galling defeat Bill Yawkey loaded the whole squad into a bus that took them to the nearest saloon. On the boss's order, the players lined up at the bar and knocked one back. They proceeded to another saloon and another and another and, at long last to a Turkish bath where attendants hauled them inside, gave them the works and tucked them to sleep. Next day at noon the bus returned them to the park. They won five straight.

POP WARNER'S GREATEST PLAYER

BACK IN New York for the opening of Yankee Stadium II, Joe DiMaggio reported that he had seen Ernie Nevers out on the Coast and the blond bull of Stanford's second Rose Bowl football team was in poor shape physically. That was less than a month ago. On Monday came news that Nevers had died of a kidney disorder in San Rafael, California. He was seventy-three years old.

By comparison with his contemporaries in college backfields, like Red Grange and the Four Horseman of Notre Dame, Ernie was a monster at six feet and 205 pounds. If memory can be relied on, he played tackle in high school in Superior, Wisconsin, and a big kid named Hancock was the star back. Hancock went to Iowa and was converted to tackle. When Nevers entered Stanford, Pop Warner put him at fullback.

Superior is in the northwestern corner of Wisconsin, about forty-five miles from Ernie's birthplace, Willow River, Minnesota. In 1920 Superior was undefeated and so was East High in Green Bay, where the left halfback was Jimmy Crowley, the same one who played left half for Knute Rockne in the backfield that Grantland Rice celebrated as the Four Horsemen. At the season's end, Green Bay challenged Superior to meet for the state championship at some neutral site like Madison, but authorities in Superior declined. They explained that the snow was already pelvis-deep there, but in Green Bay we knew they were just yellow.

We also knew that Jimmy Crowley, who could run, tackle, block, pass and dropkick, was beyond dispute the finest high school player in Wisconsin. It did not occur to the boys around Bobby Lynch's poolroom and bowling academy that Jimmy and Nevers might get together on the field some day in spite of Superior High's craven response to our challenge.

The field turned out to be in Arroyo Seco, that gulch in Pasadena where the Rose Bowl stands. The date was January 1, 1925. Notre Dame had never accepted a bowl invitation before then and never did again until the last few years, but the 1924 team was undefeated and Granny Rice's prose about the backfield had fired the public imagination. Jim Crowley, Elmer Layden, Don Miller and Harry Stuhldreher were midgets by today's standards—only Miller weighed more than 160 pounds and he didn't touch 170—but they were a marvelously synchronized unit, four little ballet dancers whose talents complemented one another perfectly. They were the biggest box office attraction in the game, an obvious choice for the Rose Bowl.

Stanford had played in the original Rose Bowl game in 1902 and had taken such a horrendous thrashing from Michigan, 49–0, that the Tournament of Roses Committee chucked football and made chariot racing the feature of its New Year's Day carnival for the next fourteen years. Now in 1924 Stanford went unbeaten and was chosen to represent the West.

Pop Warner had a fine team with a gaggle of fine players named Shipkey, Walker, Swan, Cuddeback, Lawson and Solomon, but these were only supporting actors around Nevers. He was a smasher of the Jim Brown type, a terror going straight ahead and fast enough to pull away from pursuers in the open. As fullback, he backed up the line on defense, getting in on half the tackles or more.

Nevers had broken one ankle early in the season and the other late, missing the final match with California altogether, yet Granny Rice still named him on his All-America team. As for Pop Warner, he insisted as long as he lived that Ernie was the greatest he ever coached, better even than a legend named Jim Thorpe, who had played for Pop at Carlisle.

"Ernie could do everything Thorpe could do," the old coach said, "and he tried harder."

Nevers went into the game with both legs taped to the knees. After some plays, his teammates had to help him to his feet. Yet he carried the ball thirty-four times for gains of 118 yards. He set up a field goal and put Stanford in position to score on a seven-yard pass play, and to this day Californians insist that he reached the end zone with a fourth-down plunge in the last period. However, when Ed Thorp, the referee, had peeled several layers of Notre Dame gristle off Ernie's back, he decided the ball was about a foot away from the goal line.

On defense Ernie intercepted a pass by Stuhldreher and was involved as a tackler in three-quarters of Notre Dame's running plays.

Layden scored three touchdowns, two of them on runs of seventy-eight and seventy yards after intercepting passes that Nevers intended for Ted Shipkey, the left end. The final score was 27–10 for Notre Dame, and that was about the only area where Stanford didn't dominate the statistics. Nevers and his colleagues led in gains from scrimmage, 298 yards to 179; on first downs, seventeen to seven; and in completed passes, eleven to three.

After the game, Warner proposed that the rules be changed to award a point or two for each first down.

"Good idea," Rockne said. "I understand that next summer baseball games in the American League will be decided by men left on base."

The American League hasn't adopted the suggestion yet, but don't bet against it. In a league of ten-man nines, nothing is impossible.

BIG JIM STOPPED ROTATING

AS DAMON RUNYON told the story, Bill Muldoon was chairman of the New York State Athletic Commission when Governor Al Smith appointed Jim Farley to the three-man board. Readers of W. O. McGeehan knew Bill Muldoon, Jim Farley and Bill Brown as the Three Dumb Dukes, and Muldoon considered his position as grand duke permanent until about a year after Jim's appointment. Then, Runyon related, Jim told Muldoon that he and Brown had agreed that the chairmanship should be rotated annually. Muldoon grumbled, but he knew he was outvoted, two to one, so he put up no active resistance and Farley became chairman.

A year and more went by and Jim was still chairman. "I thought we were rotating the chairmanship," Muldoon said to Farley. "We've stopped rotating it," Jim said.

Big Jim Farley was the only political figure who ever used the chairmanship of the boxing commission as the launching pad for a flight to national prominence, but because of his success, many others with political ambitions have tried to follow the same route. For small men with small talents, it turned out to be a small job. It worked for Jim because he was a big man and a master of his art. He could make a free ringside ticket or a job as boxing judge or deputy inspector go farther than any commissioner before or since his time.

He was the commission chairman in 1932 when he took over Franklin D. Roosevelt's campaign for the Democratic presidential nomination. Probably on Jim's advice, the New York governor was careful to avoid making enemies before the convention, and his reluctance to speak out on issues exasperated Heywood Broun, an Al Smith man. Broun called Roosevelt "Fearless Frank, the corkscrew candidate."

Jean Borotra, the French tennis star, was famous in those days as

the Bounding Basque. Broun, a reformed sportswriter who often lapsed
into the sports vernacular, wrote a fiery column about Fearless Frank
from the Democratic convention. "And who are his chief backers?"
he demanded. "Jim Farley, the Bounding Basque of the New York
Boxing Commission, and Huey Long, the basking bounder of Louisiana."

Later Broun came to idolize President Roosevelt. He had always
liked Jim Farley. It was impossible not to like the gracious, considerate
gentleman who was a New York landmark. Life in this city lost some
of its warmth when Jim died. It will not be the same walking the beat,
stopping at Toots Shor's or Gallagher's or "21," going to the fights and
the ball games, surveying the dais at sports dinners and not seeing the
shining dome, the ruddy, genial countenance and broad shoulders of
the old first baseman from Haverstraw, New York.

The obituaries told of his tenacious memory for faces and names, a
gift he refined to an art. Early in 1933 when Jim was postmaster general, my St. Louis newspaper assigned me to cover his visit to town. A
group of press and local pols met his train in Union Station, where
introductions were made swiftly and only once. From there Jim went
to the post office to shake hands with several thousand employees; to
Webster College for Women in suburban Webster Grove (some relative was a nun there) for a short address and another round of hand-
shaking; to a suite in the Coronado Hotel where party leaders from
all over Missouri shuttled in and out for audiences with the boss.

As each group departed and another was ushered in, lobbygows kept
trying to include me in the introductions but Jim would lift a palm: "I
know Smith." Eight years went by before we met again at the first
Joe Louis–Billy Conn fight. There were 55,000 in the Polo Grounds and
I was one out-of-town reporter among hundreds, but he called me by
name.

He remembered not only names and faces. He remembered to write
a note of congratulations if something good happened to someone, of
sympathy if it was something bad, of applause if he liked a story or
column. He remembered who did and who did not acknowledge these
notes, and he discovered that newspapermen were the sorriest correspondents of all. He forgave them.

"Politics," Jim said, "is the noblest of careers." He clung to that faith
in a time when many Americans had come to regard *politician* as a
dirty word. For him, at least, it was the true faith, for Jim Farley was
a tower of integrity. He was the most loyal of party workers and at the
same time a man of independence, prepared to stand up even against
"the boss," as he called President Roosevelt.

Once John Boettger, Roosevelt's son-in-law who was publisher of the *Seattle Post-Intelligencer,* quarreled with a postmaster in the Northwest who refused to bend the rules on mailing privileges in the paper's favor. Ordered to fire the postmaster, Jim found occasion to salute the man publicly for faithful performance of duty, saving the postmaster's job. Telling the story something like thirty-five years later, Jim remembered the postmaster's first name, last name and middle initial.

The *Post-Intelligencer* was a Hearst paper and although Boettger and his wife, Anna, were ardent New Dealers, the *P-I* ran syndicated features critical of Franklin and Eleanor. As radio commentator on a Texas network and a backer of John Nance Garner in 1940, Elliott Roosevelt actively opposed his father's bid for a third term.

About that time a representative of the Hearst organization offered Jim Farley a job, the policy at the moment being, "If you can't beat 'em, hire them over." Jim leaned back in the postmaster general's vaulted office. If, he said, his visitor stacked $1,000 bills from the floor to the ceiling, the answer would still be no, thank you.

When that story got out Jim was abroad and reporters reached Mrs. Farley. She confirmed it, adding something pointed to the effect that her husband couldn't be bought as easily as certain other individuals. "Oh-oh," Jim thought when he heard about it, "the boss won't like this." Still, as a boxing buff he knew that a bold attack was the best defense.

"Bess didn't say that, did she?" Mr. Roosevelt said the next time Jim saw him. "She was misquoted."

"Listen," Jim said, "Bess shouldn't have said it. I wish she hadn't said it. But she did say it, and I don't want to hear any more of it."

MONUMENT TO GEORGE LEVY

GEORGE MORTON LEVY had planned a gala at his home in Old Westbury for last night to entertain horsemen, press and others involved in Roosevelt Raceway's 19th International Trot, but the party had to be canceled when the host was called away unexpectedly. He will not be back, but the $200,000 race will go on tomorrow night with a field of nine horses from seven countries, and perhaps a few $2 players will pause on their way to the mutuel window to say a small prayer for the man whose vision, persistence, energy and gutsy willingness to gamble brought harness racing out of the sticks and onto the metropolitan sports stage.

There will be more here later about George Levy. For now, let us consider the race that has become the showpiece of his track, a race that stands as a monument to his memory.

The sudden death of the founder was the most recent calamity in a series of misfortunes besetting this year's International. First was the defection of Equileo, the defending champion. Last year's winner was expected to enable France to take dead aim on first money with a double-barreled gun, for he was returning along with Bellino II, three-time winner of Paris's premier Prix d'Amerique and twice the runner-up in the International.

Then came a cable from Pierre Allaire, the owner, advising that Equileo was ill and would be replaced by Fakir du Vivier from the same stable.

Next to take a fall was Jimmy Cruise, who has been a top trainer-driver at Roosevelt since the Raceway was a mewling infant. Jimmy drove there as early as 1946, and nineteen years ago he set a record that still stands by driving six races and winning them all. That was July 12, 1958. Seventeen years later Buddy Gilmour had six winners but he had seven mounts and one of his winners was moved up from second place by a disqualification.

Jimmy Cruise planned to compete in the International behind a steed named Kash Minbar, a five-year-old stallion he bought as a yearling for $2,500. Actually it was John Schroeder, a trainer and good friend of Cruise's, who bid the colt in at the Old Glory Sales. Minutes later Cruise arrived. "I'm late," Jimmy told his friend, "but this colt is the only reason I came. Would you sell him to me?"

Schroeder did but remained as trainer-driver until last summer when the horse went into a break and caused a pileup at Meadowlands. Jimmy took over but he, too, had trouble with the horse breaking stride.

Kash Minbar had shown speed from the start and after equaling the Roosevelt track record with a mile in 1:59.4 last summer he was regarded as a good thing for the American Trotting Championship. A break at the start cost him all chance in that Roosevelt stake, but Cruise put him back in this year's renewal last Saturday. Then Jimmy broke down. He wound up in Long Island Jewish Hospital for surgery on a double hernia, leaving the horse in the hands of his twenty-four-year-old son, Earl.

After the race a Roosevelt official telephoned the father. "Did we get a check?" Jimmy asked, hoping Kash Minbar had finished in the first five.

"Yes," he was told, "the biggest one."

Jimmy was incredulous.

"You beat Keystone Pioneer," he was told, "in one fifty-eight and three-fifths." That is a track record. Keystone Pioneer, with Billy Haughton up, is favored in the International at 3 to 1 on the morning line. With his father's approval, Earl Cruise had switched to the modified sulky and used a blind bridle (blinker) and the horse trotted a hole in the wind. He has now returned $446,202 on the $2,500 investment.

Kash Minbar is by Egyptian Candor from a daughter of Florican named Lambeth but his breeding doesn't account for the foreign flavor of his name. He was bred by the late Marty Tananbaum of Yonkers Raceway on his White Devon Farm in upstate New York. With a bow to his daughters, Minnie and Barbara, Marty ruled that colts foaled on the farm would have Minbar in their names and fillies would have Barmin. The other part of the name was chosen alphabetically, year by year.

This colt was born in Tananbaum's eleventh season as a breeder so the name starts with the eleventh letter. Marty likes cash, by any spelling.

Speaking of names, the Danish representative in the International is Tarok, driven by Jorn Laursen, son of the owner. Jorn (pronounced *Yorn*) is an amateur who grew up on the family farm at Skive (pronounced *Skeeve*) on the Jutland peninsula (pronounced *Yutland*), where the river Skive flows into an arm of Lim Fjord (pronounced *Fyord*).

Tarok is a fourteenth-century Italian card game played with seventy-eight cards, including twenty-two trump. The French call it *tarot* from the Italian *tarocco*. Tell that to the mutuel clerk.

A GAMBLING MAN

WHEN BOBBY RIGGS broke up with Priscilla, his second wife, he left their home in Golden Beach, just up the way a piece from Miami Beach, and that meant he lost George Morton Levy as a neighbor. "That's what really killed me," Bobby said. "I love that old guy." He told why.

Riggs was in his golfing phase then, an overage tennis player of inconsiderable stature with knobby knees and nothing striking about his swing. When a good bet had his adrenaline flowing, he could shoot in the upper 70s. George Levy was a little old guy in his eighties. He spoke in a cracked, querulous voice and he couldn't hit the ball out of his shadow, but he was steady as stone and could score consistently in the 80s.

For a guy with any appreciation, it was a supremely beautiful partnership. They would have a match going, and when negotiations reached just the right stage, one of the opponents would say, "Mr. Riggs, could we press it a little?" Bobby would go consult George Levy, whose voice would take on a new quaver. "Robert," George Levy would say, "you know I don't enjoy playing for that kind of money," but Robert would talk softly, urgently, and George would consent reluctantly, and they would wipe out the guys who had planned to rip them off.

If George Levy hadn't loved to gamble as he did, harness racing might still be a nickel-and-dime sport for farmers. When trotters and pacers raced for small change at country fairs, he invested most of his personal fortune and all of his energy and persuasive eloquence into bringing the game to the metropolitan scene by way of Roosevelt Raceway on old Roosevelt Field, the Long Island airport, where in 1927 Charles Lindbergh had taken off for Paris.

That was 1940, and in its first season Roosevelt attracted 75,175 customers, who bet $1,200,086. Thirty years later, betting on harness racing in New York State alone was $843,711,053 and the state collected $85,450,546 in taxes. If anyone else in George Morton Levy's lifetime made such an indelible mark on any sport, his name does not come to mind.

It didn't happen accidentally. When George had what he called "a little country law office" in Mineola, he had a client who promoted greyhound races at the Mineola Fairgrounds and kept getting arrested on gambling charges. They beat the rap by selling $2 options to purchase a dog, identified by a number on a saddle cloth. If the dog then showed enough speed to finish first, second or third, this naturally enhanced his value and the track bought back the options at $12.60, $7.40 or $5.20.

In 1939, New York legalized mutuel betting on horses. George convinced a group of associates that a license to gamble at night would be a permit to print money, but the group couldn't sell harness horsemen on trying to crash the big town. On the day of Roosevelt's scheduled opening, there weren't enough horses available to fill a card.

The investors were desperate. Should they invent some excuse to postpone the opening? Should they run with half a card? Should they swallow their losses and call the whole thing off? While they debated, it began to rain. It poured and kept on pouring for a week while emissaries of George Morton Levy fanned out though the East coaxing and cajoling horsemen into shipping to Long Island.

When the rain stopped at last, almost every stall at Roosevelt was occupied by a horse or reasonable facsimile. One of the latter, a kindly old mare named Martha Lee, won the very first race. A week or so later she made it once around the track and on as far as the backstretch, where she lay down and died quietly.

Then came World War II and wartime blackouts. Already suffering pernicious anemia, the racetrack struggled to make its impoverished way through that era, racing by twilight. Only artificial respiration applied constantly by George Levy kept it alive until 1946, when the postwar boom brought the beginning of prosperity.

Before he became a racing entrepreneur, George was a criminal lawyer who went years without losing a case. Then, when the track prospered, his fortunes kept pace. He had the money and made the time to indulge a passion for golf. When he couldn't play, he practiced hitting iron shots off his lawn. The lawn in Old Westbury was not an ideal fairway because his neighbor, Joel Jayson, had a greenhouse, but George said that was all right, he had arranged to be billed monthly for broken panes.

George was eighty-nine or ninety-one or ninety-two, depending on which of his friends are consulted. Last Saturday he played eighteen holes. Monday night he went to Roosevelt as usual, but became ill and left after the ninth race. If he knew he was having a heart attack, he didn't say so.

Carl Benevento of the Standardbred Owners Association drove him home and went into the house to notify George's son, Robert. They telephoned the Old Westbury police, who brought oxygen. With Robert applying oxygen en route, Benevento drove to Nassau Hospital in Mineola.

George was conscious, but his speech had thickened. He asked Robert to get the morning papers and Robert said he would. At the hospital George was placed on a stretcher. He waved.

"Goodbye," he said.

He died about an hour later.

JOHN PETER WAGNER

IN FEBRUARY of 1896 when Ed Barrow was running the baseball club in Paterson, New Jersey, he encountered an old sandlot player named Shad Gwilliam in a saloon. "I hear you're looking for players," Gwilliam said. Ed looked up from his beer. "I could use a few phenoms," he said indifferently.

When Ed Barrow was telling the story a few years before his death, repeating the dialogue word for word as though his encounter with Gwilliam had taken place an hour before, one was struck with the indestructibility of baseball jargon. *Phenom* apparently was as much a cliché in the Gay Nineties as it was in the atomic fifties.

"There's a fellow loose out in Mansfield, Pennsylvania," Gwilliam said, "who's going to be the greatest ball player in the world. All his actions are good; he's a pool player; he's good at anything he does. Name of John Wagner—Honus, they call him."

Ed knew about young Wagner, who had played with Steubenville, Ohio, in '95, but Barrow was under the impression that he had signed with Toronto. No, Gwilliam told him, that was John's brother Al.

"There were three Wagner brothers," Ed used to relate, "and the oldest was supposed to be the best ball player but he was so bowlegged he was ashamed to put on a uniform. He was an engineer on the old Panhandle line between Pittsburgh and Cincinnati. Al never made the major leagues. Honus was the youngest."

The tale of what followed the tip from Gwilliam has been told a hundred times. Let's have it just once more in Ed Barrow's words:

"I grabbed the next train to Mansfield, which is Carnegie now. I saw a red brick building with a sign, 'Wagner Bros., Pool Room.' A young fellow there told me Honus was down along the railroad tracks having a throwing contest.

"It was a winter day, but mild, with the snow melting. I walked along the right-of-way and here came eight or ten young fellows. One was carrying a big rock, big as my fist. He had a derby on the back of his head with a chicken feather stuck in the band. While I was coming toward them, he turned and fired that big heavy rock a good three hundred feet. I signed him then and there for one hundred and twenty-five dollars a month."

There are other famous Wagner stories, like the one about the time he was playing first base for Barrow and thrust his monstrous paw into a hip pocket for a wad of eating tobacco, and couldn't get it out until, catching an infielder's throw one-handed to retire the side, he could return to the bench and have the pocket cut away.

If you were a Johnny-come-recently who never saw Honus Wagner until his playing days were long past and he was a coach traveling with the Pirates, it was always those hands of his that you thought about when his name was mentioned. Those tremendous mitts and the twinkling good humor in his ruddy old face.

When he was past seventy he was still going around with the Pirates, still getting into uniform every day, and still outlasting the youngsters in the club-car sessions which brightened the hit-and-run exhibition tours from training camp in San Bernardino, California, to Pittsburgh.

Those barnstorming hauls can get more than slightly wearisome, and although it isn't recommended for the players there's no reason why coaches and manager and newspapermen and such can't shorten an evening with a few beers. If Honus ever missed one of those evenings, his absence somehow escaped notice, and if he ever backed off before the last round was served, that was a form reversal, too.

A stranger, not paying strict attention, might have got the impression that Honus was present only for company and not for refreshment, because it would appear that he alone wasn't holding a glass. Actually, he had his with the others but it was literally true that when he wrapped one of those paws around a tumbler of beer, the glass was entirely concealed.

As a shortstop, Honus got his throws across the diamond quickly and accurately, yet there was a common complaint about him among all the long parade of first basemen who passed through Forbes Field in his time. Catching a throw from him, they said, was like facing a firing squad, for along with the ball there would come a hail of dirt and pebbles. When Honus reached for a grounder he got it, along with a tract of infield as well, and everything went with the throw.

He was, of course, an early and automatic choice for baseball's Hall of Fame. In fact, he was the safest bet of them all, not excluding Ty

Cobb and Babe Ruth, because when the all-time All-Star selectors pick a team of the ages, they argue about eight positions but never about shortstop. Greatest of all shortstops in all opinions, he was also the greatest of all ball players in the judgment of men like John McGraw and Ed Barrow.

When you consider that Ed Barrow also handled a young fellow named Ruth, you have a measure of John Wagner.

TED HUSING

DEATH WAS a release for Ted Husing, and a sad relief for his friends. The end finds most of us unready, but Ted was waiting. He was blind, he couldn't walk, he couldn't work. For a man who has lived his life in the ceaseless activity of competitive sport, this is the hardest thing.

Ted died in Pasadena, where his mother and daughter live. The last time he visited the New York he loved was in April 1961, when he came on for the annual dinner of the Skeeters, an organization he created. The Skeeters are a small informal group named for New Jersey's redoubtable mosquitoes.

The club, if you could call it that, is one of those accidental things. About fifteen years ago some guys went down to Garden State to bet the races. "This was fun," somebody said. "Let's do it again." And that's how the Skeeters got started.

Last year they thought it would be a good idea to bring Ted east for the dinner. He came along but it wasn't a good idea. Everybody went home with a heavy heart.

Everybody realized then that it was only a question of time. So did Ted. Now the time has run out, and one can only feel that it is a mercy, though a sad one.

In the spring just past, a national Hall of Fame for sportswriters and sportscasters had its beginning in Salisbury, North Carolina. In a national poll, the only name that appeared on the required 75 percent of the ballots was Grantland Rice. Ted Husing missed by one vote. He'll make it in another year, of course, but this year he could have been told about it.

Ted may have been the first truly top-rate reporter to describe sports on radio, and he was one of the very best of all time.

Back in the days when radio was full of fakers straining dramatic license to the breaking point because they knew the audience couldn't see what was happening, Ted was reporting the facts accurately, expertly, with a cool detachment that underscored, instead of distracting from, the color and drama and excitement of the competition.

He had the great reporter's gift of telling exactly what happened and making you see and feel it. He didn't do this, as so many have tried to do, by cultivating a doomsday delivery or by hysterical screaming or by hoking up a fictionalized version of the facts.

He did it by study and application. Whether it was golf or tennis, boxing or baseball or football or horse racing, he learned the game before he tried to talk about it. If Ted said Monk Meyer shook off three tacklers making eighteen yards around end for Army, you could be dead sure it hadn't been Whitey Grove running on a reverse.

Before television made us a nation of armchair experts, Ted's football broadcasts struck some listeners as overtechnical. He was one of the first, for example, to identify the left halfback in a single-wing formation as the Number 4 or tailback, and "tertiary defense" was a coinage in which he took some pride.

He used such terms not to show off but because they had exact meaning. Compared with the gobbledegook heard today about "loaf of bread passes" and such, Ted's broadcasts were models of Stone Age simplicity.

Everything he did, he did well. He was ribbed for years about his call on the 1938 Kentucky Derby because the story got around that he had a winter-book bet on Lawrin.

Legend exaggerates the size of his bet and implies that he watched only one of the ten horses in the race. It doesn't happen to be true. He did mention Lawrin in every call, but he had all the others in their proper places throughout a first-rate broadcast.

If there was a good deal of the extrovert in him, as there surely was, it was part of his equipment as a showman. He knew his job and was aware that he knew it and didn't hesitate to call 'em as he saw 'em, even though his choice of an adjective like "putrid" might infuriate the holy joes at Harvard.

He called his shots boldly, even at the risk of offending a good friend like Red Blaik. Once, after an Army-Penn game in Philadelphia, the West Point coach chewed him out for what he considered second-guessing but softened his lecture by remarking at the end, "That's a nice tie you're wearing." Ted peeled off the tie and presented it to his friend, and the next week sent him half a dozen more like it.

Walter Kennedy, later mayor of Stamford, Connecticut, worked with Ted on a radio hookup called the West Point Network. When Army lost to Northwestern in Evanston in 1953, Walter was startled by Ted's merciless criticism of Blaik's strategy. "I'm afraid I was harsh," Ted said afterward. "I don't know, I don't feel so good."

The broadcast infuriated the West Point brass but Blaik said, "I think he's sick," and averted official complaint to the sponsor. Two weeks later, Army beat Duke, 14–13, in a thriller at the Polo Grounds. Ted's running account was a brilliant blend of accuracy and color.

He kept his emotions in check throughout, but when he was finished he buried his face and wept, drained and exhausted. Today Walter Kennedy remembers that autumn and those two games especially. It was then, he feels sure, that Ted first felt the effects of the brain tumor that ended his sight.

ST. NICK'S

THIS IS a one-question quiz for senior citizens only. What do the following names have in common? The Pelican, the Irving, the Pioneer, the Greenwood, the New Polo, the Atlantic Gardens, the Whirlwing, the Roman, the Princess, the Sharkey, the Houston, the Bleecker, the Washington, the Fairmount, the Lehigh and the Lion.

Give up? Well, all sixteen of them were neighborhood fight clubs in New York—there were many others, of course—and all of them are gone. All flourished as contemporaries of the St. Nicholas Arena, and as of today the St. Nick is gone too.

A couple of boys named Tony Fortunato and Stefan Redl, gladiators of limited renown, performed the obsequies for the old cockpit on Sixty-sixth Street last night. When the last punch was thrown, workmen dismantled the ring for the last time. The next blow struck there will be delivered by the wreckers' big iron ball, for St. Nick's is making way for a forty-story building.

It wasn't a spread-eagle funeral that the old joint had, although the services did draw a fairly distinguished company, including such eminent citizens as Abe Attell, Rocky Graziano, Johnny Dundee, Paul Berlenbach, Petey Scalzo. All fought in St. Nick's on the way to the championship of the world. Their return last night was, in a sense, formal, quasiofficial recognition of an era that is ended.

It comes as no news to anybody that the day of the small fight club is past. The closing of St. Nick's merely dramatizes the well-known fact. This was the last pocket of resistance, and its capitulation measures the extent of change that has come about in our time.

Once a single city was able to support as many as two dozen clubs operating on a regular schedule. There was talent to supply all of them in addition to the big shows in Madison Square Garden and the ball parks or old Long Island Bowl. Two main influences worked to reduce this flow of talent to a trickle.

One was the rising standard of living, bringing to millions of kids advantages that their fathers could win only with their fists. The other was television. Neighborhood clubs could compete successfully with one another—obviously, there were not enough nights in the week to go around—but they couldn't buck the free shows on TV, not only the fight shows but the shoot-'em-ups and quizzes and puppeteers and private eyes.

So, after more than half a century of boxing and ice hockey and bowling and roller skating and basketball and table tennis and ballroom dancing and union meetings, St. Nick's is dark.

The St. Nick opened in 1906, the year of the San Francisco fire, the year Captain Alfred Dreyfus was at last exonerated, the year Harry K. Thaw shot Stanford White dead. In Los Angeles, James J. Jeffries lifted Tommy Burns's hand after twenty rounds with Marvin Hart, and Burns claimed the heavyweight championship of the world.

Lillian Russell, then in her middle forties and maturely beautiful, attended the fights at St. Nick's with Diamond Jim Brady, who offered stickpins with tiny chip diamonds to the winners.

Sam Langford boxed there, and Jack Blackburn and Joe Jeannette and Barbados Joe Walcott and Kid Norfolk, not to mention Jim Driscoll, Terry McGovern, Stanley Ketchel, Mike and Tom Gibbons, Kid Chocolate.

In 1917, after Willie Jackson flattened Johnny Dundee in one round in Philadelphia, their return match in St. Nick's drew $10,444, a walloping figure in those days and getting to look better and better for these times. A decade later, Jack Delaney and Sully Montgomery set a record for the hall that stood for years—$15,000 for less than a minute of fighting. Delaney took Montgomery out with one punch.

Last night Tony Fortunato and Stefan Redl closed the hall. Another night, Jack Britton, Ted Kid Lewis and Harry Greb all fought there on the same card.

St. Nick's was popular with the Broadway crowd. Benny Fields and Bobby Clark were among the regulars. With customers in the gallery breathing down the necks of customers at ringside, it was a chummy joint and informal. Harry Balogh, the ring announcer, didn't even bring his tux.

One night early in World War II, the crowd spotted Milton Berle at ringside and set up a clamor for him. Balogh beckoned, and Uncle Miltie sprang through the ropes. Walking across the ring, he laid a palm upon the nude and shining skull of Billy Cavanaugh, the referee.

"I understand," he announced, "that his head has been declared an open city."

The clients howled. Balogh struggled vainly to recapture the microphone. Over the tumult rose the wrathful bellow of General John J. Phelan, chairman of the Boxing Commission: "Who is that man? Stop it! Stop it, stop it, I say! I demand that his license be suspended!"

JOSEPH FRANCIS PAGE

"IT WAS like thunder, rolling, and it made a cave of the vast Stadium. They rose as one, all their shouts and screams one great roar, and the gate of the low, chain-link fence would open, and he would come out, immaculate in those pinstripes, walking with that sort of slow, shuffling gait, his warmup jacket over his shoulder, a man on his way to work."

"That's how Bill Heinz remembered Joe Page coming in from the bullpen. There were almost always men on bases when he started in, and he confessed to Bill that he could feel his heart thumping clear up in his throat, but his manner never betrayed the inner unrest. When Joe Page was at the top of his game as a relief pitcher for the Yankees, his outward attitude was one of arrogant command that both infuriated and intimidated the hitter.

Revisiting old friends for the book *Once They Heard the Cheers*, Bill Heinz dropped into Joe Page's Rocky Lodge on Route 30 out of Laughlintown, Pennsylvania, about three years ago and found him wasted by throat cancer. Bill didn't believe Joe would live until the book came out, but he lasted another three years, and then it was a heart attack that killed him. Heart trouble was nothing new. An attack had knocked him out in 1970 when he was back in Yankee Stadium for an Old-Timer's Day, and that had led to open-heart surgery.

There were relief pitchers of note before Page's time, like Fred Marberry, Ferdie Schupp, Johnny Murphy, and since his day guys like Mike Marshall, Sparky Lyle and Bruce Sutter have come out of the bullpen to win the Cy Young Award. But it was Joe with his special flair—his swagger on the mound, his gift of laughter off the field and especially his left-handed smoke—who made relief pitching one of the lively arts.

"The Yankees beat the Dodgers in the Series," said Bucky Harris in 1947, "because I had an edge on Burt [Shotton]. I had DiMaggio and Page."

It might have been at that winter's New York baseball writers' dinner that an octet costumed as Brooklyn pitchers sang, "There Is Nothing Like Relief," a steal from Rodgers and Hammerstein. "We would play for half our wage," they chorused enviously, "just for anything like Joe Page."

In 1947 Page won fourteen games, lost eight and saved seventeen. In 1949 the figures were thirteen, eight, twenty-seven. The Yankees won the pennant again in 1950, but the hop was off Joe's hard one and he finished that season on the Kansas City farm. New York swept the Phillies in four games, played naively in daylight. The night after the last game, Toots Shor was chatting with a friend in the dining room of his restaurant when a waiter told him Joe Page had just come into the bar.

"Excuse me," Toots said, and hurried out. Soon the waiter came back, smiling.

"The boss gave him a hero's welcome," he said.

Eldest of seven children of a coal miner in Springdale, Pennsylvania, on the Allegheny River just northeast of Pittsburgh, Joe grew up playing ball on a field that was uphill to first and second base, downhill from third to home. The team traveled in a paneled truck owned by Lockerman's Meat Market. It needed new tires, which the kids couldn't afford, so they packed the old casings with sod and wired them to the rims. Joe worked in the mines two years before getting a chance in baseball.

Joe was one of the livelier spirits on the Yankees and another was John Lindell, the big outfielder. On the last weekend of the 1949 season, the Red Sox arrived in the Stadium holding a one-game lead. A split of the two-game series would have won the pennant for them, but they lost on Saturday and again on Sunday. On Saturday Boston made four quick runs and Page had to take over in the second inning with the score 4–1. He shut out the Sox the rest of the way, and a home run by Lindell finally won it, 5–4.

An hour later, they were still playing it over at the bar in the press lounge. Garry Schumacher, who had left the newspaper business to assist Horace Stoneham with the New York Giants, was there, his Flatbush accent growing more pronounced by the minute.

"Y'know what I liked best about this game?" Garry said. "D' rogues win it!"

If enjoying a drink, a lark and a laugh makes a ball player a rogue, then Joe Page qualified. A man named George DeRosa of Orange, Connecticut, might dispute the point. During one of Page's hitches in the hospital, DeRosa showed up at Rocky Lodge. He was told Joe was in the hospital and could not be seen.

"I have to see him," he told Mildred Page. "When your husband was pitching, I was five years old. I sold newspapers and one night I fell asleep when I was selling them. Your husband came along and he saw me there, and he woke me up and said, 'You have to go home and sleep.'

"I said, 'I can't, until I sell these papers.' Your husband bought all my papers and then he took me in and fed me. That's why I have to see him."

As a Yankee, Joe was a beautifully proportioned athlete, six feet, three inches and 215 pounds, a good-looking cuss with mischief dancing in his blue eyes. Maybe mining coal does something for a young left-hander's fastball, for in his first professional season Joe struck out 141 batters in ninety-eight innings for Butler in the Class D Pennsylvania State Association. He had one of the great left arms, he had the guts of a burglar and for emergencies he kept a supply of graphite oil on the inner side of his belt.

After the 1947 World Series, Mr. and Mrs. Bernard MacDougall named their infant son Joe Page MacDougall. Of course, they didn't know about the graphite oil.

EDDIE GOTTLIEB

EDDIE GOTTLIEB was a wonderful little guy about the size and shape of a half-keg of beer. When he died at eighty-one, the papers mentioned that he was a member of the Naismith Memorial Basketball Hall of Fame, which is a shrine on the campus of Springfield, Massachusetts, named for Dr. James Naismith, who invented the indoor game.

The late H. Allen Smith, a leading authority on genealogy, nomenclature and the medicinal properties of corn mash, wrote a scholarly monograph about people named Smith. It seems that ages ago the name was even more widespread than it is today but as civilization advanced, the clan was split into two factions according to moral standards. Those who lived clean lives and had pure thoughts were designated Yeasmiths; those who sinned against society by robbing poor boxes or perpetrating roundball became Naismiths.

Anyway, Eddie Gottlieb was one of the real pioneers of professional roundball. As early as 1918 he organized and coached the Sphas (South Philadelphia Hebrew Association), who dominated the Eastern and American Leagues through the 1930s. He helped form the Basketball Association of America, which became the National Basketball Association of today, and he owned, operated and coached the Philadelphia Warriors. For twenty-five years he was chairman of the NBA rules committee.

Now come a couple of Gottlieb stories from Bob Paul, a Philadelphia sportswriter who went square—or, at least, went to Florida. Bob writes that years ago when Gerry Nugent was operating the Phillies on a broken shoestring, Eddie interested Dr. Leon Levy in buying the team. Dr. Levy was owner of station WCAU and later he built the Atlantic City Race Track. However, Levy wanted assurance from someone like Ford Frick, then president of the National League, that there was no unwritten rule against Jews buying into the big league. Eddie asked Bob Paul to consult Frick.

"Ford assured me he knew of no rule about a Jewish owner," Bob writes. (Sid Weil had owned the Cincinnati Reds.) "When I asked for an appointment he said he had to catch a train for Chicago. He suggested I call him in two weeks. Eddie urged me to call Ford back and say I'd board his train at North Philadelphia and discuss what I had in mind on the way to Harrisburg.

" 'I've thought over what you said,' Ford told me, 'and I've come to the conclusion I cannot discuss anything about the sale of the Phillies. So don't bother meeting my train. Besides, I'll be very busy.'

"Ford's remarks just about killed Leon Levy's interest. I have often wondered what would have happened to the Phillies if Leon Levy and his brother Ike, instead of William D. Cox, had bought Nugent out and Eddie Gottlieb had become general manager." Cox was thrown out of baseball for betting.

Bob Paul's other story goes back to the winter of 1929–30 when Art the Great Shires, first baseman for the Chicago White Sox, was capitalizing on the reputation he had won by flattening the manager, Lena Blackburn, twice during the baseball season. Starting with a first-round knockout of one Mysterious Dan Daly, who turned out to be a teenager whose swan dive had been rehearsed, Shires was dropped three times by George Trafton, the Chicago Bears' center, but then stopped Bad Bill Bailey in Buffalo, took out a former minor league pitcher named Tony Faeth in St. Paul and got a technical knockout over Al Spohrer, a bald catcher, in Boston.

"I phoned Shires an invitation to the annual dinner of the Philadelphia Sporting Writers Association," Bob writes. "I told him we couldn't afford even to pay his expenses but he said, 'I'll be there. I'm getting mine, and the Philadelphia writers have been good to me.'

"The night of the banquet I mentioned to Eddie Gottlieb that Shires was the attraction that got us a sellout, and we felt guilty that we could only pick up his hotel bill to show our appreciation.

"Eddie said, 'I've read where Art claims to have played basketball at three colleges somewhere in the Southwest. Ask him if he'll stay over two days. I'll pay him $200 to appear with the Sphas against the Renaissance Big Five. Maybe he'll sell out the hall.'

"Booboo Hoff, who was trying to sign Shires for a Philadelphia bout, had filled Art's bathtub in the Adelphia Hotel with ice and beer. Art didn't mind staying over. When he practiced with the Sphas, his shots missed the basket by a foot or more. The players told Eddie not to start him.

"Fans who had paid to see Shires perform soon began to chant, 'We want Shires!' After five minutes of this, Eddie sent him into the game, but in a huddle he had told his players not to pass to Shires. Once a game started, Eddie wanted only to win.

"For four or five minutes, the Sphas made sure Art never touched the ball. The fans began yelling, 'Give it to Shires!' They were ignored until Renaissance took possession and called time out. On the first play after resumption they handed the ball to Shires. They only faked attempts to block his slow dribble. When he finally shot and missed, they tossed the ball to him again. Another minute or so of this and Eddie yanked Shires out of the game.

"During intermission Eddie handed me $250. 'Art proved he is no basketball player,' he said, 'but he certainly is a great gate attraction. I promised him $200. Give it to him with another $50.' Eddie made money and the sportswriters were able to pay Art for selling out their banquet.

"It was only a week later that Judge Kenesaw Mountain Landis, the commissioner, notified Art that 'hereafter any person connected with any club in this organization who engages in professional boxing will be regarded by this office as having permanently retired from base-ball.' "

LARRY GOETZ

IN AUGUST the Giants played a two-game series in Cincinnati and reporters covering the National League pennant race found Larry Goetz in the press box, as usual. Here was an umpire who was also a fan. Though he had been ill through most of the 1956 season he didn't want to quit the next year, when Warren Giles, the league president, nudged him out.

After his retirement he rarely missed a game in Crosley Field and he generally made the World Series and winter baseball meetings. Asked to list his offseason hobbies for the *Baseball Register,* he wrote, "Attend basketball and football games." His scrupulous honesty failed the next test, however. He gave his birthday as February 15, 1900. When he died in Cincinnati the obituary said he was sixty-seven, not sixty-two.

For many of Larry's twenty-two years in the National League he worked with Jocko Conlan and Beans Reardon, making up a team that had no rival for convivial loquacity, on the field or over a beer. Nor was there ever an umpire team who ran a game with a firmer hand than this cocky trio, or was any quicker to bow the neck and lift the imperious thumb at the first hint of mutiny.

Larry was the only member of the team working the Yankee-Dodger World Series of 1952, but Reardon was in New York as a spectator so there were two of them to speak their separate minds about an incident in the fifth game.

In the tenth inning the Yankees' Johnny Sain hit a slow grounder and the vote of witnesses was 70,536 to 1 that he had the throw beaten. The lone dissenter was Art Passarella, umpire at first base.

At dinner time a friend encountered Reardon in Toots Shor's. They exchanged amiable insults and the friend inserted a needle.

"One of your bums really kicked one today," he said cheerfully.

"Aagh," Beans said, "they don't pay umpires enough in a World Series. We work for a lousy $2,500 and some rinkydink sits on the bench and gets $6,000. Why—"

"You mean, Mr. Reardon, at these prices you're not supposed to call 'em right?"

"Correct!" Beans snapped.

This was good unclean fun, of course, but when Larry Goetz felt called upon for remarks on the same subject, he leveled with cold, Teutonic bluntness. While the Series lasted, the Yankees never did stop nagging about Passarella's error, as indeed it was.

In fact, when the bulldog editions hit the streets after that game, they carried photographs showing clearly that Sain had beaten the throw. Arthur Patterson, the Yanks press agent then, laid hold of a microphone in press headquarters and gave an exhibition of tasteless bellyaching that would have been considered bush in Horse Cave, Kentucky.

When the last game was over, Goetz spoke with unconcealed contempt: "The Yankees won the crying championship before they won the World Series."

Crybabies and "hot dogs," or show-offs, always earned Larry's contempt, and although he was genuinely fond of people he was capable of venomous dislike of a ball player who prolonged a protest or laid on the histrionics to show up the umpire before the fans. The players he detested had to be aware of it, for Larry was not one to disguise his feelings or reserve opinion.

Yet it would be burdening the obvious to add that he never let personal antagonism influence a decision by a millionth of one degree. His twenty-two years on the big time offer evidence enough.

Jocko Conlan subscribes to the Bill Klem credo—"I never called one wrong, in my heart,"—but Larry and Beansie were quick to disavow infallibility. Again the illustration involves Reardon rather than Goetz, but it could just as easily have been Larry.

Beans was behind the plate when Monte Pearson beat the Reds with a two-hit shutout in the second game of the 1939 World Series. In the clubhouse afterward, Bill Dickey, the Yankee catcher, volunteered a statement: "I'd like to say that guy worked one helluva game. Didn't miss a pitch."

Unsought praise from such a source seemed unusual enough to bear repeating to Reardon later. He accepted the compliment with proper modesty.

"I missed one," he said. "Pearson threw a fastball right down the pipe and I said, 'Ball.' Dickey stayed in his crouch and didn't turn around. 'What was wrong with it?' he said. 'Nothin',' I said.

"'I thought it was right over the middle,' he said. 'It was,' I said. 'Why ain't it a strike, then?' he said. 'Because I called it a ball,' I said. He said, 'Oh,' and threw the ball back to Pearson."

FOOTBALL TEAM

THIS ALL started with a news item out of Fitchburg, Massachusetts, but actually the story goes back to 1952 and a little earlier. In 1952 Boston University had a pretty good football team, not a great team but one with several superior athletes.

There was John Pappas, the center, an alert and suggestive line-backer. There was Tom Gastall, a quarterback by trade who played right end a lot of the time because he didn't want to sit on the bench watching Harry Agganis run the team. There was Agganis, whom they called the Golden Greek, and he was one of the very best. And there was Jim Meredith, also an end for Buff Donnelli, the B.U. coach of those days.

These four were probably the best on the squad, and there was another whom they all knew, though he was slightly older than they. Dick Fecteau, from Agganis's home town of Lynn, Massachusetts, was a tackle on the 1949 team when Agganis was a sophomore. After graduation, Fecteau went off to the Far East as an Army civilian employee. At last report, he was one of two Americans being held by the Red Chinese on espionage charges.

However, this piece concerns guys on the squad who were younger than Fecteau.

Agganis was a senior in 1952. He was Paul Brown's top draft choice for the Cleveland Browns. That year Stanley Woodward wrote, "Agganis may be not only one of the finest football players I've ever seen, but one of the greatest actors as well."

What had charmed Stanley was a two-point play that enabled B.U. to beat Andy Gustafson's good University of Miami team, 9–7. With the score tied at 7-all, Agganis intercepted a touchdown pass in the end zone and ran it out twenty yards. Three ground plays were smeared for losses, and the Golden Greek went back to punt from his end zone.

He got the kick away but was brushed by a Miami end. Agganis fell backward with a mighty crash, but what excited the drama critic in Woodward was that he didn't overplay the bit by threshing and writhing in mortal anguish. Officials, properly impressed, slapped a penalty on Miami for roughing the kicker, and four plays later Agganis punted out of bounds on Miami's one-yard line.

Perhaps flustered by this misfortune, Miami tried a double reverse in its own end zone. Jungle Jim Meredith and Marco Landon flattened the ballcarrier for a safety and the two points that won the game.

A week later, Agganis threw three touchdown passes and pitched out for a fourth as B.U. rolled it up in the first half against William and Mary, 27–7. In the second half, W. and M. made three touchdowns and led, 28–27, with two minutes to play.

Tom Gastall, the guy who played end because Agganis had his job at quarterback, called the next play in the huddle. It was a pass, Agganis to Gastall, that won the game, 33–28.

Agganis was a baseball player. The Red Sox gave him two seasons in Louisville, then brought him up. He was batting .313 when a blood clot killed him in June of 1955.

Before that, tragedy had put the finger on John Pappas. He was a class behind Agganis in school. In the first game of the 1953 season, B.U. astonished everybody by leading Syracuse, 14–0, at the half. Syracuse tied the score and was slamming for another touchdown. Pappas made two consecutive head-on tackles. After the second, he walked off unassisted. Before morning he was dead of a massive brain hemorrhage.

With Agganis graduated, Gastall became the regular quarterback. He steered B.U. to six victories in eight games in 1954, was captain of good basketball and baseball teams. The Baltimore Orioles gave him a bonus to play baseball. He had been in Air Force R.O.T.C. in school and had a civilian pilot's license. The engine of his small plane failed over Chesapeake Bay. Several days later his body was identified by his B.U. belt buckle.

And then there was Jungle Jim Meredith. After graduation he was commissioned in the paratroops. He had a bad landing in Germany and broke a leg. Cancer developed, and the leg was amputated.

Naturally, he couldn't fly or jump or fight anymore. They made him a wooden leg and he went back to Fitchburg and worked there as assistant coach of the Fitchburg High football team, stumping about on his artificial gam.

The news dispatch that started this whole piece was about him. It said that Jim Meredith, twenty-nine years old, had died of cancer in Fitchburg.

SIR WALTER

IF HE HAD lived, Walter Hagen would be celebrating his seventy-seventh birthday today (Sunday, December 21) and the fact that he isn't leaves everybody the poorer. There are always too few Walter Hagens in the world. This is a great pity, yet a thoughtful man might hesitate to argue that it would be better if there were too many.

The point is academic because there was and could have been only one Walter Christian Hagen. (Not until late in his life when his son dug up some old family records did The Haig know his middle name was Christian; he always went along with the biographers who called him Walter Charles.)

At any rate, he was unique, an original that couldn't be counterfeited. It wasn't merely that he was the best golf player of his time and, in the view of many qualified judges, the best of any time. It wasn't just that he had nerves of brass and a constitution that required neither sleep nor bicarbonate of soda. Rather, it was the fact—as John Lardner wrote—that he was "one who succeeded as few members of our meekly desperate species have done, in adjusting the shape, speed, and social laws of the world to his own tastes."

Maybe it was as simple as this: Nobody else lit a cigarette with the jaunty insouciance of Walter Hagen; nobody else had his Piping Rock swagger on the first tee; no other golfer walked the fairway with head so high.

When Walter Hagen was on a golf course, he always seemed to have his gaze fixed on a point some distance above the horizon. Perhaps it was this way of going that defeated him in the last match he ever played on the championship level.

It was in the Professional Golfers Association championship in Hershey, Pennsylvania, in 1940. Hagen was forty-eight but he had strutted into the third round, putting the hooks to big, young Vic Ghezzi in the second round with a combination of deadly putts and calculated gamesmanship.

His opponent in the third round, Jug McSpaden, pulled a shot into the rough and Hagen went to help hunt for the ball. You wouldn't see that happen today in a hundred tournaments, but friendly little courtesies like that were natural to Hagen. Suddenly Walter stooped, picked up a ball, and handed it to McSpaden.

"You win," he said.

"Why?" McSpaden asked.

"Because I stepped on your ball," Walter said. He had been carrying the head high again.

Of all his rousing matches—he won twenty-nine in a row against the world's best and gathered eleven American and British titles, including two U.S. Opens and four British Open championships—of all his triumphs the one most frequently recalled was the shattering conquest of Bobby Jones in a 72-hole match for the "championship of the world" in 1926.

Walter slaughtered Bobby, 12 up and 11 to play. Out of the $7,600 purse, he spent $800 for a pair of diamond-and-platinum cufflinks for Jones.

Years later Fred Corcoran sat watching while Walter shaved in his hotel suite in Boston. Hagen used a straight razor and shaved by the sense of touch, not bothering with a mirror. Idly, Corcoran asked: "If you were playing any two golfers in the world for ten thousand dollars, who would you want for your partner?"

"That's easy," Walter said, but because there were others sitting around he mentioned no name aloud. "Jones," he whispered in Corcoran's ear.

Walter Hagen, Fred Corcoran said one day to his friend Monseigneur Robert Barry in Boston, "has no religion and never goes to church and yet I'd rather be around with him than with any sinless man I know. Is that bad?"

"Don't worry about Walter," said the monseigneur, a fan. "He'll wind up in heaven, because he does charity."

Next time Corcoran saw Hagen he repeated the colloquy. Walter was delighted to hear that he had it made.

"So tonight," he told Fred, "you can buy the drinks."

PAUL KRICHELL

THEY BURIED Paul Krichell yesterday, that chunky, laconic little man whose calculating eyes measured much of the raw material that went into twenty-two championship teams for the Yankees. In 1920 Paul was a coach under Ed Barrow, manager of the Red Sox. That fall Ed told him they were moving to New York, Barrow as general manager and Krichell as scout.

"We're going to have to work," Ed said, "twice as hard as we've ever worked in our lives."

"I'm not afraid of work," Krich said.

"I know you're not," Barrow said.

Five years later, Paul worked himself into a physical collapse. In 1925 the Yankees were seventh, having won pennants in 1921, 1922 and 1923 and finished second in 1924. If you were a Yankee scout in Dover, Delaware, or Salt Lake City or Pittsfield, Massachusetts, you didn't dare go to sleep while there was another scout awake in the same town. You sat up and kept your eyes on your rivals, drinking all night with them if necessary.

It knocked Krichell out, but in 1929 he signed, among others, Tony Lazzeri and Mark Koenig, and the Yankees won pennants the next three years.

"If you don't make mistakes," Paul said, "you haven't got the nerve to pick up a ball player."

It required nerve to give five players and $50,000 of Jake Ruppert's money for Lazzeri. Krich followed the Salt Lake City team for three weeks, watching Lazzeri. Then he telephoned Barrow.

"This Lazzeri," he said, "takes fits."

"What do you mean?" Barrow asked.

"He gets epileptic fits or something," Krich said, "but he don't get them between two o'clock and six in the afternoon when you play ball."

When Charley Keller, a student in the University of Maryland, was playing summer ball in Kinston, North Carolina, Krichell arrived in Kinston at 7:00 A.M. and learned that four other scouts were registered in the hotel. He had visited Keller's home near Frederick, Maryland, and got his parents' approval of a Yankee offer. Carrying a note from the father, he got Charley out of bed in the rooming house, walked him around the block.

"I sign him against the wall of a building," Paul said. "I think it was a warehouse or a factory or something."

Krichell and two companions were riding down the New Jersey Turnpike, heading for a town in the Eastern Shore League. The spires of Princeton were visible on the horizon.

"You ever sign a player out of Princeton, Paul?" the driver asked.

"Charley Caldwell," Paul said.

"The football coach?"

"The sidearm right-hander," Krich said, putting first things first. "He hit Wally Pipp on the head."

Beaned in batting practice, Pipp was replaced as the Yankee first baseman by Lou Gehrig—for the next 2,130 games. How did Gehrig happen to be around? Krichell had seen him hit two home runs for Columbia against Rutgers in New Brunswick, and Krich had been watching on Columbia's South Field a few days later when Gehrig hit one against Pennsylvania that bounced up the library steps.

Because he got Gehrig, Paul didn't get Hank Greenberg. Krich was the first to spot Hank playing for James Monroe High in New York but Greenberg, a first baseman, wanted no part of a team that already had Gehrig. This is an occupational hazard for Yankee scouts and Krichell evolved a philosophy about it, though he conceded that Greenberg was an exception.

"A kid who thinks along the lines that it's too hard to make it couldn't make it anyway," he would say.

Paul Krichell signed Johnny Broaca in the writing room of the Hotel Garde in New Haven; he signed Hank Borowy in the Fordham gym; he saw Vic Raschi pitch an American Legion game in Elizabeth, New Jersey, and got him for an allowance of $250 a year for spending money in college.

On the advice of Kitty Bransfield, then manager in Waterbury, Connecticut, he bought the Hartford shortstop, Leo Durocher. After a tryout of schoolboys in Yankee Stadium, Paul said, "I'd like to see more of that Italian kid. He has a sore leg now but he has good hands." Phil Rizzuto's sore leg got better.

In Paul's years as chief scout, the Yankees lost men like Joe Devine and Bill Essick. Devine found Jerry Coleman, Gil McDougald, Andy Carey and Charley Silvera; Essick recommended Joe Gordon and a sore-legged outfielder named Joe DiMaggio.

"Our scouts die like anybody else," Krich said. "So we hire new scouts, and the Yankees keep getting ball players. You explain it."

BUMMY'S ANNIVERSARY

IT WAS ten years ago this week that Bummy Davis died. It was Thanksgiving week, like now, and if a preacher were looking for a Thanksgiving sermon all he'd have to do is tell about Bummy and wrap it up with "there, but for the Grace of God." This is no sermon, though.

It's just that Bummy's name came up at a bar and a fellow who was his friend said he didn't think people generally had ever got the whole, straight picture of Bummy, not while he was alive and not even now, ten years after those guns blew off in Dudy's Bar. He said that to see Bummy straight you had to know Brownsville and Beecher's Gym and the pushcart business and—well, there was even the matter of Bummy's name.

His square name was Albert Abraham Davidoff, and in Jewish, Abraham can become Ahvrom or maybe Ahvroom. The mother leans out the tenement window to call a kid to supper. "Ahvroom," she cries, "Vroomy, Vroomy," and with the kids Vroomy can become Boomy or Bummy. In some neighborhoods there may be half a dozen kids in one school called Bummy.

Later on, when the Davidoff kid got to be Al (Bummy) Davis, the fighter, the public accepted the nickname as a character sketch meaning he was a roughneck who fought dirty. Of course, he was a roughneck and at least once he did fight dirty, though not without provocation.

You don't have to be a roughneck just because you grow up in the Brownsville section of Brooklyn, but the odds are you will be if one of your brothers is Big Gang-gy and the other is named Duff, or Little Gang-gy, and you run with a mob called the Cowboys and enjoy fighting even as a very small boy. You get one kind of reputation and hardly anybody ever gets to see the other side of you.

There can be another side, though. There can be a kid who works very hard selling tomatoes and stuff off the pushcart and has a private collection of recordings by the better Hebrew singers. Al Davis used to sit playing his records by the hour, all alone, or maybe with some friend, and he ate in a little restaurant on Amboy Street near Pitkin Avenue favored by the Jewish actors, whom he admired greatly. Instead of that Al Davis, the public knew about the one in the candy store.

The public heard about that later after Bummy got to be a main-event fighter with a left hook that had brought him storming up through the Ridgewood Grove and Dexter Park and St. Nick's and into Madison Square Garden where he had stiffened Tony Canzoneri and Tippy Larkin. There was this argument in the candy store and Bummy beat up a guy and got pinched and Mike Jacobs had to get an adjournment for him so he could fight Lou Ambers, the lightweight champion of the world.

Of course, professional fighters shouldn't slug people in candy stores, and nobody ever asks how great the provocation may have been. To the crowd Bummy was a bully and a nogoodnick. The fans loved it when Ambers gave him a going-over.

That's how it was now with Bummy. He was a roughneck and a bruiser and a bully. The crowds came clamoring and paid to see him whipped. That night in the Garden with Fritzie Zivic there was nobody to take his side or even pause and consider that perhaps he did have a side.

Not that Zivic didn't have a reputation of his own, well earned and widely known. Nobody ever knew better than Fritzie what thumbs and laces were for. Another fighter might have been excused for retaliating when Zivic started giving him the business but this was Bummy Davis, the roughneck. When he lost his head and started belting Zivic low and kicked at the referee, the crowd practically rioted. Nobody stopped to ask, "Hey, wasn't it Zivic who started it?" It was Bummy they suspended, "for life."

Today, fifteen years later, everybody remembers the first Zivic fight and Bummy's disqualification. They forget the second one and what happened in between. In between, Bummy joined the army, taking Stutz and Mousie and the rest of his mob in with him. Then he got unsuspended so they could use him on furlough fighting Zivic back for Army Emergency Relief.

That was great, fighting out of shape for free. Zivic stopped Bummy in ten, putting lumps on him so that Bummy couldn't get his hat on afterwards. He stayed away from camp too long licking his wounds and when the army had to go find him to bring him back the Boxing Commission got sore and resuspended him.

That was Bummy, always in trouble right down to the day he was through with fighting and bought the bar on Rockaway Parkway. He ran it a while, unsuccessfully, and had only recently sold it when four hoods walked in. If they hadn't been jerks from the sticks, chances are they'd have known about Bummy Davis and never tried to heist that place, even though he was only there as a customer at the time.

He looked at their guns and said why didn't they give Dudy a break, the poor guy had just bought the joint and the till was practically empty. One of the punks said something and Bummy's hook broke his jaw but another shot Bummy in the neck. Then they ran and Bummy chased them, blood coming from his neck. He was running into a fight when more bullets got him. He died on the rainy sidewalk November 21, 1945.

DAN TOPPING: MONEY AND CLASS

THE WORLD Dan Topping lived in for almost sixty-two years wasn't exactly the same as the one where Yogi Berra grew up. Material things came more easily to Dan than to Jock Sutherland or Casey Stengel or many others who worked for him. In baseball he was a contemporary of Birdie Tebbetts, but there was a difference. Faced with a major expenditure, Birdie would remind himself, "This is money I saved sliding into second base." Dan never had to. Grandson of a tinplate king on one side of the family and a steel tycoon on the other, he always knew where his next yacht or private plane was coming from.

Dan Topping was not, in short, the hero of the standard American success story. But he was a man, and as John Donne tells us, any man's death diminishes us, for we are involved in mankind. When the former president of the Yankees died, mankind was diminished by two men—the public Dan Topping and the private one.

The public one was the wealthy sportsman with the most expensive toys. When he wanted a football team to have fun with, his mother bought him the Brooklyn Dodgers. When he was invited in as part owner of the Yankees, he got in on baseball's biggest bargain. Whenever the fancy struck him, he could afford to indulge a taste for golf or yachting or deep-sea fishing.

The private man was known to only a few. And it wasn't until after his death that some who had known him were willing to talk about the things they knew. Mentioning no names because names were always against the rules, they told of occasions when money in a plain white envelope had been entrusted to them for delivery to some guy who was having it tough, and never mind where it came from because he didn't have to know. Nobody had to know.

Along with his money, and not because of it or in spite of it, Dan

Topping had class, which is something money cannot buy. There was class in his private charities and class in his way of going. An incident of no importance comes back to mind.

When Dizzy Dean was hired as a member of the Yankees' broadcasting team, he declared that being on Topping's payroll was nothing new for him because he had been taking money from Dan for years. Dan Topping, he told the press, was his own special pigeon, and he regaled a news conference with tales of killings he had made on the golf course, where Dan had been his host and victim, and in the locker room playing gin.

Conservative members of one club found Dean's stories unsavory reading in the newspapers. There actually was a meeting of directors to discuss asking Topping to resign. No such request was made, and although Dan must have been acutely uncomfortable, he never mentioned it to Dean.

"I hope those stories didn't embarrass you," a newspaperman said later.

Dan grinned. "Considering that he was just going to work for me," he said, "I didn't think it was very bright on his part. But you know Diz. Forget it."

Baseball, like politics, makes strange bedfellows. Chances are there never was an unlikelier partnership than the group of three who bought the Yankees in 1945. The package was put together by Larry MacPhail, the promoter nonpareil: imaginative, aggressive, quarrelsome. Needing a bankroll, he brought together the swinging, sportsminded son of wealth and Del Webb, a former carpenter who had built a fortune with icy efficiency.

For $2.8 million they got the most valuable franchise in baseball, the best players in baseball, the most famous stadium in baseball and that part of the Bronx where it stood, together with the Newark Bears and their ball park, the Kansas City Blues and their park, and the lesser links in the empire. Two years later they bought out MacPhail for $2 million, so Topping's and Webb's total investment was $4.8 million.

They sold Yankee Stadium to one buyer and the land it stood on to another. They sold the real estate in Kansas City and Newark. Over the years their operating profit was more than $20 million. Then they sold 80 percent of the club to CBS for $11.2 million, and finally each sold his remaining 10 percent.

Before the deal with CBS was arranged, the partners planned to go public. This never came off because they couldn't get what they considered a satisfactory ruling on a capital gains tax, but it was believed that public demand would send Yankee stock up sharply. Six men whom Topping considered his "office team" were told they each could have $100,000 worth of stock at the offering price, and if necessary they could borrow the purchase price, interest-free, from his mother's estate.

"But is it legal," Dan was asked, "for you as executor to put out money from the estate without interest?"

"It is if I say so," he said.

SPIKE BRIGGS

A BAD THING happened to baseball in July of 1956. After four years, trustees of the estate of Walter Owen Briggs, Sr., got their way and the Detroit Tigers were sold for $5.5 million. So what's bad about $5.5 million? It moved Spike Briggs out of baseball, that's what.

To say that Spike's departure was a loss to baseball is no rap on John E. Fetzer, who headed the syndicate that bought the Tigers and thus won undying fame as the employer of Dennis Dale McLain. Fetzer is a businessman who had made his stack before he got into sport. Baseball was Spike's life until he was forty-four, and if he could have called the shots he would have stayed with it.

Career baseball men are painfully few in the ranks of owners. After you mention Horace Stoneham in the National League and Cal Griffith in the American you have only Phil Wrigley, who was rarely around the team until his father's death, and Buzzy Bavasi, who is president of the San Diego Padres but not the principal owner.

Spike was strictly baseball until sisters and lawyers intervened. The death of their father in 1952 had created a family trust shared by Spike and his four sisters. The ladies knew little of baseball and the trust's lawyers not much more, if any. A major league team, the lawyers said, was not a "prudent" investment. Spike tried to buy his sisters out for $3.5 million but they said it wasn't enough. In the end he had to sell.

The family connection with the Tigers had begun in 1920, when Spike was eight. Walter O. Briggs, Sr., a manufacturer of automobile bodies, bought 25 percent of the club for $500,000 from Frank J. Navin, a horse-playing entrepreneur who had got into baseball in 1903 via law school and the racetrack, where he had been sheet-writer for a book-maker.

A few years later Briggs bought another 25 percent from the estate of John Kelsey, who manufactured auto wheels. Though he and Navin were now equal owners, Briggs left direction of the club to his partner, an astute baseball man as venturesome as he was perceptive. (When Navin visited the track he carried a thousand-dollar bill for each race on the card, this being his normal bet unless he had something special in mind; in that event, he would bet up to $25,000 on a horse.)

In 1935 the horse player had a heart attack, fell off a horse and died. Soon after, Briggs paid about $1 million for Navin's stock and the Briggs era began for the Tigers. Spike was then fresh out of Georgetown, a bright kid and a pretty good swinger.

Father and son collaborated on a million-dollar reconstruction of the ball park. They made it the showplace of the American League, with triple-decked stands rising almost one hundred feet. Underground sprinkling and drainage facilities helped groundskeepers develop a velvet playing field set off by a border of red brick-dust at the foot of dark green walls unblemished by advertisements.

In those days it was customary to employ James M. Barrie or some other master of whimsy to announce the "official" attendance figures. Briggs Senior had the revolutionary notion that in addition to making the customers welcome and comfortable baseball could afford to tell them the truth. (He may have been influenced by the fact that Detroit is one town where the ball club has no cause to be ashamed of its attendance.)

It was an order that anybody who falsified the figures would be fired. Occasionally after that, one turnstile would be left out of the tabulation by accident, and it was wonderful to witness the frantic scurrying to rectify the error.

These are little things, but along with the owner's determination to present the best possible baseball no matter what the cost, they added up to an operation that was all class. Walter O. Briggs 2nd—his father gave him his nickname because he disliked "Junior"—was brought up in this tradition. He continued his father's policies until he was forced out.

Spike was one of two baseball men who died last Friday but the other is remembered best as a racing man. Wathen Knebelkamp, retired president of Churchill Downs, was involved in the operation of the Louisville Colonels of the old American Association from his graduation from Washington and Lee in 1921 until the team was sold to the Boston Red Sox in 1938.

Succeeding the late Bill Corum at Churchill Downs in 1959, Wathen ran the Kentucky Derby until his retirement last December. He made extensive improvements on the cruddy old plant. One of the nicest guys in the world, he wasn't a great executive because he tried to make everybody happy but he was a whale of an ambassador for the Derby.

From Kentucky to New York to California, he traveled the racing circuit tirelessly, making friends. A master distiller in his own right, he had the mellow warmth of old Kentucky bourbon, and even when toastmasters introduced him as Nathan Wabelkamp his smile didn't fade.

He seemed happy in racing, but never quite so happy as when he could hook up with an old baseball crony like George Weiss and just play the games over.

THE WORLD'S GREATEST FAN

WHEN HARRY RUBY, the songwriter, died in California, the obituary bestowed the title of "world's greatest baseball fan" on the composer of "Three Little Words," "Who's Sorry Now?" "Baby Face" and many other hits. The obit didn't tell the half of it. Harry Ruby felt deeply about music, yet given his choice of composing Beethoven's Third or ripping a line drive over second like Bill Dickey, he would have suited up on the spot. He loved the piano, but would infinitely rather have been Pete Rose than Artur Rubinstein.

In Hollywood he adjusted his working hours according to the Pacific Coast League schedule so he could be in the Wrigley Field or the old Hollywood Stars park early and work out with the professionals. When big league teams like the Pirates, Cubs, White Sox and Philadelphia Athletics trained in California, Harry was always welcome to shag flies in the outfield. In those days he wore the livery of the Washington Senators, a gift that he prized above any other possession. When the westward movement of the majors brought him into contact with other clubs he acquired other uniforms; before he died he could have fitted out an All-Star team from his own wardrobe.

There came a time—this was a good many years ago—when Harry felt a need for change. Nothing heretical like taking up golf or developing an interest in pro football, but some break in the routine that might broaden his outlook.

Travel, he decided, would do the trick. He would visit places where he had never been, view sights he had never seen, sample food and observe the customs of people in far lands, and come home with a fresh slant that would express itself in his work. He might even be able to provide his lyricist, Bert Kalmar, with a new rhyme for "eyes" or "moon."

After consulting travel agents, he fixed upon a Mediterranean cruise. This was early in the season, and all summer long he went about the studio lots with his pocket seven months gone with travel literature that he would break out and display with or without provocation.

"Did I tell you about my trip? Look, we sail from New York and the first stop is here in Gibraltar. Wait, I got something here tells about the Rock. Then it's Barcelona, Marseilles, and how do you pronounce it? Cannes? From there . . ."

His enthusiasm was infectious at first, but it was a long, hot summer. By the time Harry's friends had been twice through the itinerary they were ducking for cover or beating him to the conversational draw with "Harry, do you think this young Judnich with Oakland will ever play the outfield like Jigger Statz?" or "Hey, I see your friend Lefty O'Doul is leading the league again. Isn't he ever going to give up?"

If they could get Harry talking baseball they could usually escape without being shown another picture of the Acropolis, provided they were fast on their feet.

At long last the Coast League playoffs ended. (San Diego won four straight from Sacramento while Portland was beating San Francisco, then the Padres knocked over the Beavers in four.) Harry got to New York in time to see the Yankees defeat the Giants in the World Series. His ship sailed a few days later. In his luggage were several baseballs and a couple of fielder's gloves, and sneakers in addition to his spikes.

On the second day out, Harry found a deck steward who was a baseball fan. "Wait here," Harry said, and darted for his cabin. He returned wearing flannels and sneakers, carrying a ball and two gloves. That day, and every other day during the crossing, he and the steward played catch on the sports deck.

When the ship reached port, Harry and the steward were among the first down the gangplank. They found an open space on the pier, and, as eager sightseers streamed past, they played catch.

It happened at Barcelona, Marseilles and Cannes. It happened at Naples, Piraeus and Istanbul. It happened at Port Said, Algiers and Casablanca. Harry got home a rejuvenated man, and a traveled one. He had not seen a cathedral nor a museum. He had not bought a hookah in the bazaar in Istanbul nor a drink in the Casbah. But his arm was never so loose, his control never better.

WALTER ST. DENIS

TO ONE who knew him pleasantly, but not intimately, Walter St. Denis was a nice old guy with rheumy eyes and a cracked voice who could, when in the mood, spin yarns of oldtime fighters that might be meandering and frequently were rather pointless, but that somehow managed to capture and preserve the flavor of a day that is gone.

Now he has gone, too, following Jimmy Walker and Jimmy Johnston and Damon Runyon and so many others who, like Walter, were figures of some stature in the fight game of his time. It has been a hard winter in that dwindling company.

Today's fight writers, who rate as oldtimers if they can remember back to the era when the heavyweight champion's name was not Joe Louis, knew Walter as a press agent who had, in some vague yesterday, been sports editor of a couple of papers that are also gone now. Perhaps some remember an occasion when he did a bit of press agentry that must constitute some sort of record.

That was when Mike Jacobs was trying to get started as a promoter. The first show scheduled under Mike's direction was topped by a Barney Ross–Billy Petrolle match and it ran into assorted difficulties, including an injury to Ross that required a postponement. When it finally went on away up in the New York Coliseum in the Bronx there was every reason to believe the new promotional firm might lay a magnificent egg.

Walter handled publicity for the show. On fight night he bumped into Bugs Baer, who didn't have a ticket, and Walter said, "C'mon up with me. I haven't got a ticket either, but I'll okay you at the gate." A block from the arena they were halted by a policeman. The Coliseum was sold out, an estimated ten thousand were turned away and the cops were clearing the neighborhood of all who couldn't show tickets.

Walter identified himself, but the cop shook his head and said he didn't give a hoot who he was, orders was orders and nobody without a ticket was getting by. They didn't get by, either. Walter had sold that show so thoroughly that he press-agented the press agent plumb out of the neighborhood.

Thus Walter was a part of the world's most successful promotional organization from the day it started. Mike Jacobs has said that "St. Denis knows me better than I know myself," but it is unlikely that any one around knew Walter that well. Some thought him crotchety and short of temper, and the fact is he did age noticeably these last couple of years after his wife died, but he remarked one time that he and Harry Markson worked at desks three feet apart for ten years and never had the mildest sort of dispute.

He wasn't a particularly humorous man, nor one of those to whom antic adventure happen. He was amused by little things that mightn't have seemed funny to others. Like the time big Wilfred Smith, of Chicago, dropped into his office and said: "How are you, Walter?" and Walter said fine and Wilfred replied, "That's too bad." Walter howled with laughter and repeated the colloquy again and again.

It has been mentioned that he gave Bob Ripley and others their start toward brighter financial success than he ever enjoyed. His story about the start of Ripley's cartoon concerned the days when Bob worked under him in the sports department of the old *Globe*. Walter had saved in his desk a handful of news items about curious happenings in sports and one day he tossed 'em to Ripley with the suggestion that maybe he could make a cartoon out of them.

Ripley drew the cartoon which somebody captioned "Odd Events in Sports," or something about as lively as that. Dissatisfied with the caption, Walter remembered the phrase with which an old aunt of his in Canada had habitually begun any reminiscence: "Believe it or not." And that's how that began.

Walter liked to tell of his early days here working under the fierce and fabulous "Chapin of the *World*." He was left alone to make up the sports pages one day when there was a flood of news to be jammed into limited space, so he trimmed a lot of the stories to items and grouped them under the heading: "Roundup of Sports." Next day Chapin had him, trembling, up on the carpet.

"Who the hell did this?" Chapin said. "It's the first bright idea any one's had in this plant in five years."

Walter brought a lot of the Canadian country boy along with him when he came here from Pembroke, Ontario. He'd grown up there on the farm of his grandfather, a gruff and powerful and high-tempered man. The kid had a pet calf that he could manage, but the calf charged, billygoat fashion, at any one else who hove into view. Several times Walter tearfully dissuaded his grandfather from his avowed intention of butchering the animal.

One day grandpa was chopping wood and the calf was behind him. Grandpa stopped to pick up a stick. The calf charged. Subsequently the family dined on veal, but Walter wouldn't eat any. He never ate veal as long as he lived.

BOWL FOR CATFISH

WHAT WITH lawsuits, glacial contract talks and padlocked training camps, there is no telling when the game of baseball will get under way this year, but the business of baseball opens today in the Bronx. Starting this morning, tickets will be on sale at the Yankee Stadium box office for a game with the Minnesota Twins on Thursday afternoon, April 15, the first athletic contest scheduled for the rebuilt playpen. Maybe the players won't be ready by then, or the owners ready to pay them, but the ball park will be. That brings up a point that hasn't been mentioned out loud: What about the clubs' leases on municipal stadiums? From San Francisco Bay to Long Island, most of the teams play in publicly owned parks. In the improbable event that the owners made good their implied threat to call off the whole season, could their landlords still hold them responsible for a summer's rent?

However, this piece is about the new playpen at 161st Street and River Avenue, which is, as of today, better prepared than the team for the opening of the season. Fifty-three years ago Colonel Jacob Ruppert and Colonel Tillinghast L'Hommedieu Huston spent $2.5 million on a showcase for Babe Ruth. How much the taxpayers are spending to fix it over for Catfish Hunter is a question whose answer depends on who is doing the figuring. It is difficult to calculate the cost at less than $65 million, easy to show where $100 million is being spent, though not all of that comes directly from the local taxpayers' pockets.

In any event, when you consider that William H. Seward picked up Alaska for $7.2 million, the stadium figures are impressive. So is the stadium.

The House that You Built is roomier, handsomer, more comfortable and convenient than the House that Ruth Built, yet it is still Yankee Stadium. It is still the park where Don Larsen pitched that perfect

World Series game, without a windup and without sleep; where Ruth hit his sixtieth home run of the 1927 season off Tom Zachary, and Roger Maris hit his sixty-first in 1961 off Tracy Stallard; where Yogi Berra fell under the pop foul that should have completed Allie Reynolds's second no-hitter of 1951, whereupon Reynolds threw the same pitch to Ted Williams for another foul that Yogi caught. It is still the Home of Champions, the home of Joe DiMaggio and Mickey Mantle, or Miller Huggins, Joe McCarthy and Casey Stengel, the place where Max Schmeling knocked out Joe Louis and Louis knocked out Schmeling.

There were 65,010 seats in the old stadium, and not every one was behind a pillar. There are 54,200 plastic pews in the rebuilt stands, all wider than the old wooden ones, and there isn't a post in the joint.

A decade has passed since freeloaders gathered in numbers to watch games from the elevated station platform of the subway and the roofs of nearby apartment buildings. Even if the Yankees get good, those crowds won't be back, for that view is cut off by a scoreboard costing between $2.5 million and $3 million. It has a message board that can show instant replays, carry advertisements and wish the umpire a happy birthday.

If and when there are customers, color-coded escalators will carry them to the proper seat level. About three hundred can graze at one time in a cafeteria, the first public restaurant in any New York park, and the Stadium Club will accommodate around five hundred. The Stadium Club has two levels. The upper, which can be entered directly from the mall outside, is the bar; food is served below ground, and an elevator carries Beautiful People to sixteen luxury boxes with heat, air-conditioning, television and facilities for snacking and snorting.

Features most fans won't see include a private dining room for management, a television studio, the home clubhouse where the Yankees' lockers are done in red, white and blue, a sauna, a gymnasium, and a trainer's room equipped to cure anything short of a broken leg or lead in the bustle. There are air-conditioning vents in the home dugout.

The two questions most frequently asked about Yankee Stadium are "Did anybody ever hit a fair ball out of the park?" and "Which players are buried in center field?" The answers are "no" and "none." The monuments that stood in center field as memorials to Ruth, Huggins and Lou Gehrig now occupy a grassy little court between the bullpens in left, just beyond the low wall that bounds the outfield.

Ruth, Huggins and Gehrig. They made a ball park into a shrine. Indeed, it was so nearly a place of worship for some that more than one fan requested in his will that his ashes be scattered over the field.

Management never approved, sharing the views of Mrs. Ann Clare who used to be track superintendent at Saratoga. When a horse player from Gloversville, New York, left a request that his ashes be scattered over the homestretch, Mrs. Clare said positively no.

Next morning she asked, "What is that white stuff over near the rail?"

"Might be frost, Mrs. Clare," one of the track crew said. "It was pretty cold last night."

"In August? Here, you with the shovel and you with that broom, gather that up and bring it here."

They brought her a shovelful of pale dust with bits of bone and knuckle. She had them dig a hole in the infield, and as they smoothed fresh earth over the contents of the shovel, she said a silent Hail Mary.

"At least some of the poor man had a decent burial," she said later.

WAKE FOR A BALL CLUB

IN THE sixth inning the Pirates scored their seventh run and Bill Rigney walked out to call for a new pitcher. The crowd booed the Giants' manager, and this was the first time its voice was loud, though there had been decent applause before the game for Mrs. John McGraw and some of the old players.

Probably it is fanciful and sentimental to suggest that the quiet was that of a wake. Of course it was a wake. There were 11,600 customers for a game between the Giants, moored in sixth place, and the Pirates, tied for seventh. If it hadn't been the very last game that New York's oldest team would play in the hallowed Polo Grounds, the count might have been closer to Saturday's 2,768.

When they were simply the New York Club in 1883, they played down at 110th Street. It was there they received their name from their first manager, James Mutrie, who wore a top hat and frock coat and carried a gold-headed cane. "My big fellows!" he cried exuberantly. "My Giants!" It was 1891 when they took over Brotherhood Field and renamed it the Polo Grounds.

Here Amos Rusie fired the fastball that inspired a line which batters still use, probably believing they are coining it: "You can't hit it if you don't see it." Here a kid out of Brooklyn, Willie Keeler by name, broke in as a third baseman, not very good. Buck Ewing was good, though. Saloons all over town displayed a garish lithograph of "Ewing's famous slide."

There was a pretty fair cheer for Bobby Thomson when he went to bat the first time. He got a single but was trapped off base and was doubled on a fly ball. He was playing third base.

That's where Thomson was playing that unforgettable day in 1951, and he was having a time of it then, too. He messed up a promising inning by stealing second with a playmate already there, and when the Dodgers scored the runs that seemed to sew up the pennant play-off, it was through Thomson's position that their big hits whistled.

Then Bobby swung his bat, and the Giants were champions of the National League. Maybe they'll win other championships, some day, for San Francisco. Surely there'll be other home runs hit at timely moments, but will there ever be another scene like that? The season was over but the fans wouldn't leave. Thousands stood cheering beneath the clubhouse windows in centerfield, singing, sobbing, calling again and again for the heroes to show themselves. Twilight deepened, and still the clubhouse windows blazed with the flashes of photographers' lamps.

Yesterday's customers were equally reluctant to leave. Most of them sat it out as the Giants dragged wearily to defeat. Pigeons kept circling overhead, as though impatient to move in, and one could fancy Robert Moses, blueprints of a housing project in hand, waiting to pounce.

These Giants played as though they couldn't wait to get to San Francisco. They couldn't hit the ball or catch it, pick it up, or hold it, and Rigney kept calling the bullpen for another bull.

One day John McGraw handed Bugs Raymond a new ball and sent him out to warm up for relief. When Bugs got into the game he was loaded. Leaving the bench, he had hiked right past the bullpen to a gin mill across the street.

Pitchers with the old Giants got knocked out, too. After Rube Marquard arrived here as the "$11,000 beauty," it wasn't long before they were calling him the "$11,000 lemon." Rube Schauer had to relieve Ferdie Schupp so often that Sid Mercer wrote in the *New York Globe*, "It never Schupps but it Schauers." And there was even a Giant manager who tried Christy Mathewson at first base and shortstop and in the outfield because he said Matty couldn't pitch. Horace Fogel was the name of that genius.

In the ninth inning a Pirate named John Powers hit the last home run that will be struck in the Giants' New York home. It went clear over the roof and stirred scarcely a murmur.

The crowd shouted for Willie Mays on his next-to-last time at bat, when he beat out an infield single, and fans stood up to cheer him on his last, when he grounded out. A thunder of boos responded when it was announced that "after the game, patrons will not be permitted on the field until the players have reached the clubhouse."

The instant Dusty Rhodes hit a grounder for the last putout—remember the World Series of 1954 when he did everything but walk on water?—hundreds of kids rushed onto the field and Giants ran for their lives, fending off souvenir hunters who snatched for caps and gloves. Adults followed the boys.

Kids tore up the bases, clawed at the mound for the pitchers' rubber and dug for home plate. Boys scooped earth from the mound into paper bags and pulled outfield grass which they stuffed into pants' pockets. They ripped the green canvas from the screen behind home plate, gouged sponge rubber from the outfield walls, tore the roof off the bullpen bench in right field.

A man took a photograph of the plate. Another pried the number tag from the railing of a box. A woman walked off carrying a big cake of sod from beneath the plate. Below the clubhouse windows, a forlorn throng lingered. Somebody out there held up a sign. It read: "Stay, team, stay."

HE WOULDN'T DIE

BY RIGHTS, Your Host should have been dead more than ten years now. On January 13, 1951, the four-year-old chestnut son of Alibhai and a Mahmoud mare named Boudoir II started as favorite in the San Pasqual Handicap at Santa Anita. The favoritism wasn't merely a matter of mutuel odds. On form he justified his short price, for in two years of racing he had been unplaced only twice in twenty-two starts, and just a week earlier he had run the fastest mile and an eighth in Santa Anita's history.

Another factor, perhaps even bigger than form, was sentiment. Californians adored this horse as they hadn't loved one since Seabiscuit and wouldn't worship another until Swaps and Silky Sullivan. He'd been a precocious two-year-old, quick out of the gate with a brilliant turn of speed, who rushed off in front and stayed there. At three he could win on the front end or win from behind. He was swift and game and honest and biddable, a horse that would do what his rider asked, a horse to bet your life on.

In the San Pasqual he got into close quarters, fell, and smashed his right foreleg at the shoulder. It was a totally disabling injury, and an ordinary horse would have been destroyed on the spot. However, Bill Goetz, the movie man who owned him, was as daffy about the colt as any of the fans who mailed him Christmas cards and sent him sugar and wrote in asking for photographs. Goetz refused to have the colt "put down," as the euphemism goes.

"I remember when Goetz bought him," says Humphrey Finney, boss of the Fasig-Tipton Company, which runs the big throughbred auctions. "He was the last horse in that sale, and Bill paid twenty thousand dollars for him. He insured him for two hundred and fifty thousand dollars."

Because the colt was useless, Lloyd's of London paid off the quarter-million, and because Goetz wouldn't destroy him, Lloyd's took title. A veterinarian said he thought he could patch the horse up and George Stratton, believing him, took Your Host down to his Circle S Ranch at Canoga Park, California.

They tried putting the horse in a sling, but that was no good. More often than not a horse supported that way contracts pneumonia and dies. They fixed up a stall for him, bedding him in sand because he might have got tangled up in straw, and because he was tractable and intelligent and understood that these people were trying to help him, Your Host cooperated.

"I went out to see him," Humphrey Finney says, "and I must have spent two hours watching him. The right foreleg just swung loose, supporting nothing. They exercised him in sand on a lead, so he could let the rope support his weight and not put any on his bad leg. For the blacksmith he'd lie down and stick out his feet to be shod: they put shoes on three feet and kept the hoof pared down on the useless leg."

The horse should have died but he wouldn't. He got strong enough to serve as a stallion, and in his first crop of foals was the good stakes winner Social Climber. Your Host was off on a new and altogether pleasant career.

In 1951, the same year Your Host got smashed up, a stallion named Easton died on F. Wallis Armstrong's Meadowview Farm at Moorestown, New Jersey. Wally Armstrong was looking for a sire to replace Easton, and maybe the fact that his own right arm was withered from polio made him favorably disposed toward Your Host.

Anyhow, after a good deal of negotiation, Humphrey Finney bought Your Host for Armstrong from Lloyds, paying $140,000. Armstrong syndicated the horse, cutting him up into $7,500 shares, and Your Host went on having children. His best son was the smasher, Kelso, who would have been any sire's best.

The horse that wouldn't die outlived both George Stratton and Wally Armstrong. In all the years he stood at Meadowview, the Armstrongs never had to buy sugar, because it came through the mail to Your Host. Even as late as last Christmas he'd got thirty or forty greeting cards from worshippers in California.

Ten days or two weeks ago, Your Host threw a stifle in his right hind leg. Nobody knows how it happened: probably he got cast in his stall. In a sound horse that isn't necessarily serious, but now the old boy had only the two legs on his left side.

They did their best for him but it wasn't any good. The ankle of his left foreleg got sore and his spine began to go. The day before yesterday, Mrs. Armstrong gave permission to put him away.

TOM JENKINS AND THE TERRIBLE TURK

A SPECIAL mail delivery brought two communications from Colonel Red Reeder, who is known at the United States Military Academy as King of the Literary Frontier. He writes books and he also writes letters like this:

"West Point buried a great man the other day—Tom Jenkins. Tom 'commanded' the wrestling room in the West Point gym for years, and that is the right verb. Before that he coached cadets in boxing. Total time in the West Point gym: thirty-seven years.

"Tom looked like a grizzly bear on the prowl. He had a catch-as-catch-can style that barred only death by strangulation. He detested present-day wrestlers of the flimflam and faker school. He took to the mat in the days when matches were tests of skill and courage. He out-wrestled George Hackenschmidt, 'the Russian Lion,' and Youssouff, 'the Terrible Turk.'

" 'The Terrible Turk,' Tom said, 'was light as a feather. Weighed over 300 pounds and could jump on a piano as easy as a robin. Try it on your piano. The Turk wore a golden chain around his neck. When I got into the ring with him the first time, the Turk was drowsy, for he had just eaten a big meal. He got down in the middle of the mat on all fours and rested. I tried holt after holt but couldn't budge him. Finally my trainer, Harry Tuthill, give me some advice. "Break the chain," he yells. I done it and the Turk rose up and threw me out of the ring. It was his religion, that chain.

" 'Later, the Turk went home on a ship, all his money in coins on him in a money belt. The ship went down and the Turk sank like a stone.' "

"Tom had only one eye most of his life. He liked to give the impression that Frank Gotch had gouged out his eye in a match. Colonel John

Harvey Kane researched Tom's life and discovered that Tom had lost his eye in the explosion of a toy cannon in childhood.

"However, Tom told generations of cadets, 'Gotch! Humph! A gent that'll gouge out another gent's eye ain't no gent. So I broke his arm in two places.'

"Tom talked of his experiences in the dim past something like this: 'At eighteen I got a job as a puddler in a steel mill. Put a few callouses on my hands. Then I got a job picking up weights in a circus. What a cinch that was! Went over to London with a manager to make some money wrestling. Wrestled a fellow in the stable of a duke for 500 pounds. I threw the kid three or four times but they beat us out of most of the purse.

" 'I could hardly pay my hotel bill. It was the swellest hotel I ever saw. Golden chairs right in the heart of London. They brought your meals up on a golden tray. My manager had champagne for breakfast but I never touched the stuff. I forget the hotel's name!'

"When Tom was in his fifties he played professional football for Buffalo. He said the guy opposite him in the line in one game played dirty. (I think that was a very brave guy.) 'I just screwed his head back on,' Tom said.

"The cadets loved him because he was a competitor and because he had humor and a soft heart. Once a cadet ducked out of wrestling class. Tom saw him and reported him. The cadet had to reply by indorsement and he knew Tom would be called upon by the Tactical Department for remark. The cadet came to Tom and said, 'Sir, Mr. Jenkins, I'm sorry I left class without permission but I had a splitting headache. I especially admire you as an instructor. If I get a number of demerits out of this I won't get any Christmas leave and I haven't seen my mother in three years.'

"When Tom got the paper he tore it up. The Commandant office sent over a followup and Tom tore that up. Then the Assistant Commandant came over and asked Tom where the papers were about the cadet. 'The gent ain't guilty,' Tom said.

"Colonel John Corley, a star on the battlefield with the First Division, was one of Tom's cadet intercollegiate wrestlers. In the Battle of the Bulge Corley's battalion was outnumbered and surrounded. German artillery rained on the battalion day and night. An officer advised Corley to surrender.

" 'I was punchy for want of sleep,' Corley said. 'I went down into a dugout to think it over. I put my head down on a table and I must have dozed off. I was a cadet again in Tom's wrestling room. I could hear Tom saying to a cadet, "Mr. Dumbjohn, what do you weigh?" Then to another cadet, "Mr. Dumbjohn, what do you weigh?" Tom always ordered the two to wrestle, regardless of their weight.

"'I got the idea that you did not have to be as big as the other fellow to win. I did not surrender the battalion. General Bradley sent in tanks and rescued us.'

"That was Tom Jenkins paying off the United States."

OLD CHAMP

WHEN CHALKY WRIGHT was found dead in the bathtub in his mother's Los Angeles apartment, the news dispatches gave his age as forty-five, as it appears in Nat Fleischer's record book, but Nat had to take Chalky's word for that when he compiled the records. As featherweight champion of the world in 1942, Chalky used to tell people he was thirty, because he had been telling people that for a long time and saw no reason to change his story.

He was a great little man and a perfectly wonderful craftsman, and the chances are he fought on as late into life as Archie Moore or Jersey Joe Walcott. In 1942 Willie Pep, just turned twenty, stabbed and ran, jabbed and fled, and stole away with Chalky's title in fifteen rounds.

"I'd hate to win the championship of the world with a fight like that," a fellow said that night in Chalky's dressing room.

"If I was a kid like him," Chalky said, "fighting an old man like me, I'd box the same as he did."

After more than two hundred professional matches, Pep admired and respected Chalky above any other opponent. Many of the marvelous moves that, even today, Willie can make better than anyone else in the world, were learned in their forty-three rounds together. Four years after winning the title, having outpointed Chalky a second time in fifteen rounds and again in ten, Willie knocked him out in the third round in Milwaukee.

"Hey, boy," Chalky said, "you learned to punch."

"Learned to punch!" Willie said wryly afterward. "I knocked out an old man."

Whenever it actually happened, Albert Wright was born in Durango, Mexico. Once he remarked that he could speak two languages—"Mexican and American."

"Are you a Mexican, Chalky?" an interviewer asked.

"Do I look like one?" he said.

His father, a regular soldier in the United States cavalry, had jumped the border into Mexico and married the granddaughter of a slave escaped from Georgia. He left home when Chalky was a baby and Chalky barely remembered him, though in later years he heard that his father was working as a Pullman porter.

The boy grew up in Los Angeles, learning much that isn't found in books, like how to make eight the hard way. Though books never were a paramount interest—he found flaws even in a classic like Nat Fleischer's, which listed only 125 fights for him, whereas he reckoned he'd had at least three hundred—he was something of a scholar in his way.

When Chalky held the title, Harry Markson, then writing publicity for Mike Jacobs, confided in a press release that the challenger was devoted to great music. Around came a reporter from *Etude* for an interview.

"What do you think of Mendelssohn?" the long-hair asked.

"Who'd he ever lick?" Chalky said.

"How about Brahms?"

"A little too heavy for me," said the featherweight.

"Do you know Schubert?"

"I can't say I know him exactly," Chalky said, "but my actor friend, Canada Lee, introduced me to J. J. Shubert and his brother Lee, both."

"The guy stuck his pencil in his pocket and walked away like he thought I was crazy," Chalky told Markson reproachfully. "You got me in a lot of trouble."

About that time the whole fight game was heading for trouble, though Chalky and the others who had a hand in it didn't realize it. An old press release in Markson's file announced that Chalky's return match with Pep, in which he failed to regain the title, would be witnessed over television by wounded veterans in hospitals in the Philadelphia and Schenectady areas.

There had been experimental telecasts locally, but this, the announcement said, would be "the first time in history a fight will be shown on television on such an extensive scale." They didn't know the monster they were creating.

Chalky really did like classical music, but loved craps. Chances are he got about as much out of life as he expected. He never expected to wind up with money.

"Do you play the horses?" he was asked.

He said no, that game was too slow for him. Betting a race, a fellow had to wait too long to discover what happened to his money.

"The dice," Chalky said, "tell you right away."

ZUP

BOB ZUPPKE was a fierce, funny little man with a tongue that could peel the hide in long red strips off any 240-pound tackle who soldiered on the football field or saved his best play for after dark. He was a great favorite of Grantland Rice's, and because all of us are influenced in our judgments by the men we admire, this gave Zup a special place in the esteem of those who loved Granny.

At the top of his game, Zup was a giant in a company of giants—Knute Rockne, Pop Warner, Fielding Yost, A. A. Stagg, Bill Alexander, Tad and Howard Jones. In a profession in which slavish imitation is the accepted thing, he was an authentic original, imaginative, enterprising and resourceful. Though he scoffed at the notion that coaches ever won football games and refused to concede the superiority of any system (the player, not the play, was the thing in his mind), he was always out front with "flea-flicker" passes and other innovations.

Even more memorable than his contributions to a game was his warm humanity, his keen perception and sharp wit. In the truest sense of the word Zup was a philosopher, and when he spoke—with just a little blur of soft German accents—neither the thought nor the language was quickly forgotten.

It was he who wrapped up the whole subject of football upsets in words that have become the most threadbare cliché in the game: "You never can tell about a football game because the ball is a funny shape and it takes funny bounces."

In twenty-nine seasons at Illinois, Zup coached his share of players who won All-America distinction, yet the chances are not even Red Grange will be remembered longer than the coach's version of what makes an All-American. "A long run, a weak defense, and a poet in the press box."

Sharper still, and applicable to many fields outside of football, was his recipe for success: "If you can't do anything well, try to become an executive."

When a coach dies or retires or gets fired the papers always add up his teams' victories and defeats and make special mention of the unexpected triumphs, the upsets won but not those lost. There were many of these in Zup's life, as there are bound to be for any coach good enough to hold a job over an extended period. For the reason Zup phrased so aptly, the unexpected is fairly commonplace in football and those funny bounces have got to go both ways.

Zup understood people. He could be eloquent and persuasive and there were many times when he was able to stir a team to extraordinary effort. There must have been times too, when he misfired, for dealing with emotions can never be an exact science.

The classic example of a Zuppke dressing room spiel was a bewildering thing when delivered and the meaning and purpose are still unclear here after hundreds of retellings. The identity of the opponent eludes memory but it was a game in which the Illinois cause was regarded as utterly hopeless; might have been one of those famous meetings with Michigan.

A few minutes before kickoff time, Zup strode into the locker room, stood glowering silently until he had everybody's attention.

"I'm Louis the Fourteenth," he said. "After us, the deluge." And out he went.

What he meant, exactly, what he hoped to accomplish, still defies explanation. The players thought the old man had gone off his rocker entirely. They won in a smashing upset but nobody ever was able to support a claim that Zup's enigmatic call to arms was a contributing force.

It was, however, somehow characteristic of this odd, jaunty, muffin-faced, gray, lively, unpredictable little gamecock who, in his curious way, often came very close to genius.

THE MAN WHO RODE EPINARD

A TELEGRAM from Edna Haynes, in Inglewood, California, brought sad news. Edna's husband, Everett, is dead after a long illness. Silk Shirt Haynes, Epinard's jockey. He was a great and grand little man, a treasured friend.

His nickname dates him, more or less. At least it fixes the time of his widest renown. Remember the years just after World War I when the silk shirt was the plume of the cavalier, the mark of the man of parts? Perhaps a reticent lavender for every day, for special occasions something with half-inch pajama stripes in emphatic crimson.

Nobody was rolling higher than Everett in those days. He had been a first-rate rider in the United States and when weight began to catch up with him he went abroad. There he rode and trained horses for the great races of England and the Continent until, noting the rise of Hitler and foreseeing what it would mean, he and Edna smuggled what possessions they could out of Germany and slipped away after them.

Jockeys ride so many horses they are not, as a rule, identified with any particular one. Ten years from now nobody will speak of Eddie Arcaro as Nashua's rider or Whirlaway's or Citation's. Everett, though, was known as Epinard's jockey and he liked it that way. In his book there never was another as good and gallant and generous as Pierre Wertheimer's big, blaze-faced Spinach. The radiator ornament on his car was a running horse with the jockey wearing Wertheimer's colors.

When Epinard came to America in 1924 to take on all comers at six furloughs, a mile, and a mile and a quarter, Everett got the film rights as part of his fee as rider. The records say Epinard was second to Wise Counsellor at three-quarters, to Ladkin at a mile and to Sarazen at a mile and a quarter, but there was no photo finish then and Everett never went along with the record.

Well remembered is a sunny afternoon in Los Angeles in the house that was like a museum with Everett's scrapbooks and photographs and trophies and Edna's china and crystal and big carved pieces of furniture. Louis Feustel came over, Man O' War's trainer who saddled Ladkin against Epinard. He brought his own bottle of wine, loftily spurning his friend's hospitality.

Naturally, Everett and Feustel got to wrangling again over the race which the placing judges had given to Ladkin by a nose. Out came the movies. The pictures had been run so often and the projector stopped so often with the horses at the finish post, that the film was burned brown at that point and Everett didn't dare stop it again. He'd whisk it through and it did seem that Epinard, closing hard on the outside, showed a flash of his white blaze in front at the wire.

Then Everett would scream in triumph and Feustel, clutching the neck of his wine bottle, would growl like a dog over a bone. He had owned that bone for twenty years and he wasn't going to give it back now, even in friendly argument.

Later Everett and Edna moved to Phoenix, Arizona, to be near their two sons, who were jockeying jets in the Air Force. After a crash killed one of the boys they went back to California, to Inglewood hard by Hollywood Park. Perhaps it helped to have horses around.

HARDBOILED SMITH,
CABALLERO DE LOS ANDES

OUT OF the silence of years comes word of Hardboiled Smith, King of the Andes. Captain Warren B. Smith was a burly, jovial, generous, rugged, uninhibited pilot for Panagra, who made 1,634 crossings over South America's formidable mountain barrier—more than any flier before him and in all probability more than any will attempt in the supersonic age of tomorrow.

He was also one hell of a trout fisherman, and a companion who could do more good with a jar of Scotch than is dreamed of in Ron Teacher's philosophy.

Born in Minneapolis in 1903, the year Orville Wright got it off the ground at Kittyhawk, Warren barnstormed with the Gates Flying Circus in the 1920s and joined Panagra in 1931 when the Ford trimotor was the ultimate in aerodynamic design. Flying Fords and little Lockheed Vegas over the passes then was like riding a straw hat in a gale, squirming through chasms, dodging peaks, following railroad or river bed with no radio beam to point the way.

When he had made one thousand runs between Chile and Argentina, the Chilean government decorated Warren as a Caballero de los Andes. An avenue was named for him in Santiago. After Chile's great earthquake in 1939, he received the Order of Merit for his part in flying seven hundred *damnificados*, mostly injured children, out of disaster areas.

Fourteen years ago this week Warren took me trout fishing in the Andes. He had lived in Chile sixteen years and when a heart murmur reduced him to a desk job in Miami in 1952 he went back to fish for a month every winter.

A justice of Chile's Supreme Court encountered on the trip told me

Warren Smith was the best known *Norte-americana* in Chile, and that was easy to believe. Strolling the Avenida Bernardo-O'Higgins he'd be hailed by every other cab driver who passed.

We took the night train to Villarica, about five hundred miles south of the capital, and Warren seemed to be the pal of every crew member. If there were any he hadn't met before we got aboard, he remedied that swiftly. We sat all night in the diner with a couple of jugs on the table and everybody got fractured.

It's a mystery how we ever got safely to southern Chile's lovely land of lakes and volcanoes, where Volcano Villarica wears a perpetual plume of smoke above its snowy cap. We made it, though. What's more, because I had to get a column to New York every day, Warren arranged for the conductor to take my column to Santiago and turn it over to a Panagra representative who delivered it to the cable office.

It should not be inferred that Warren was a lush. He admired and respected grog not for the taste alone.

For an expedition to Laguna Maule, a lake a mile and a half high on the Chilean-Argentine border, he lined up a driver with a beat-up Chevrolet pickup. Lake Maule, sitting astraddle a mountain pass far above timberline in a desolation of volcanic rock, is populated by rainbow trout up to twenty-five pounds, evil brutes that lurk in the weeds and cut fishermen off at the pass.

The truck was crawling up a narrow shelf cut in the face of a sheer cliff, the mountain wall to our right and one thousand feet straight down on our left, the Rio Maule brawling west to the Pacific. On a hairpin bend Herman, the driver, muttered a Spanish curse. His brakes were gone.

When we could pull off the trail, Herman flagged down a truck carrying workmen to a dam site at the lake. They had no brake fluid, but one man said wine could serve as a substitute.

"Because it has alcohol in it?" Warren said. "We can do better. Get out the Scotch."

Then, seeing my face: "Don't worry. It only takes a thimbleful to a cylinder."

Damn if it didn't work. Shouting with laughter, we peltered onto the summit. It wasn't the best truck in Chile, but it had the happiest brakes.

So fourteen years have slipped by. Warren and I exchanged a letter or so after we parted, but our paths did not cross. Then when word came it wasn't good. Warren died in Miami last May. As requested in his will, his ashes were flown to Santiago and held until last month.

On December 12, Chilean Air Force Day, General Maximo Errazuriz

Ward, commander-in-chief of the air force, and Chile's highest officials of commercial and civil aviation conducted memorial services. Then the urn was loaded into an air force plane that headed east along the route blazed by the Caballero de los Andes.

Near Christ of the Andes, the bronze statue that stands at the 12,000-foot summit of Uspallata Pass on the Chilean-Argentine border, the ashes of Hardboiled Smith were scattered over his mountains.

THE 1906 MOTION

JUST BEFORE the opening game of a World Series, a fellow in the press box pointed down at an old pappy guy in a front-row box and asked Grantland Rice if that wasn't Cy Young. Looked like him, Granny said; yes, that was the old boy himself. In a moment Cy arose and, with cameras snapping, tossed out a baseball with a herky-jerky delivery stiffened by age.

"Oooh," Granny murmured, mostly to himself, "that's not the motion I knew in 1906."

This was two or three years ago, and Denton True Young was in his eighties, and all of us were older than we had been in 1906. As the noted philosopher, Dizzy Dean, observed in his latter days as a pitcher when Grant Rice asked how his arm felt: "It ain't what it used to be, Granny, but what the hell is?"

Now Cy Young is gone, but his departure merely closes a book he had finished writing long ago. Unchanged in his niche in the Baseball Hall of Fame in Cooperstown, reserved forever in his name, unchanged and unchallenged, are the records he put in the book—906 games pitched in the major leagues, 511 games won, 315 games lost.

Records are made to be broken. Roger Maris improved on Babe Ruth's sixty home runs in a season. Maybe a Joe DiMaggio yet unborn will hit safely in fifty-seven consecutive games. Perhaps a new Rube Marquard or Tim Keefe will pitch twenty victories without defeat. But Cy Young's 511 victories—nobody's ever going to threaten that, because it is impossible and it always was.

It is demonstrably unthinkable, an impossibility provable as much on the unimpeachable authority of mathematics. Figure it for yourself:

The twenty-game winner is the aristocrat of pitching society. Some seasons there'll be only one in a whole league; more often there are two or three; maybe once in fifteen years, as many as half a dozen will make it. Year in and out, one pitcher in four wins as many as ten games in a season.

Ten years is a good long career in the big leagues. The average is almost six years less than that. A Dizzy Dean gets in five seasons of regular work and hangs around doing part-time service four more seasons. A Carl Hubbell runs the string to sixteen years and is a twenty-game winner five times. These are great ones.

Now, make no allowance for a rookie's several summers of apprenticeship or for the declining years at the other end of his string. Say he breaks in winning twenty games and goes right on through his ten years with never an injury or illness or any other turn of bad luck to prevent him racking up his score of victories each season. What does he win? Two hundred games.

In the thirty-eight years since Grover Cleveland Alexander won thirty games, that figure has been attained once in the National League, by Dean in 1934. In the American League, Jim Bagby won thirty-one in 1920, Lefty Grove the same number eleven years later and Denny McLain [in 1968]. In the twenty-one years prior to 1955 close to thirty thousand games have been played in the majors, probably three thousand pitchers have had employment, but not one has brought off a thirty-game season.

So let's create a wildly fictitious Paul Bunyan who can win thirty every year, never slumping to a miserable twenty-nine, and we'll let him go on at that pace not ten but fifteen years in a row. He'd do all right. He'd score 450 victories and be only sixty-one behind Cy Young.

Want to make it twenty-five victories a season for twenty years solid? We're doing better now. That way our guy would win 500 games and the chances are some owner would pay him regularly.

There are three snootily exclusive clubs in baseball, tougher to crack than Fort Knox. There are the .400 hitters; twenty-nine have qualified in seventy-seven years. There are those who made three thousand hits in a lifetime; that club has seven members. There are the pitchers, twelve of them, who won three hundred games.

Cy Young, for heaven sake, lost 315, and they don't keep you in the majors for twenty-two years because you're good at losing.

His record is safe. The old boy may rest easy. He won't, though. He always did insist that he really won 512. Wherever he's gone, he'll be looking for the official scorer who gypped him out of that one.

A FAN NAMED BOB SHERWOOD

SOME INTELLECTUALS deem an interest in games evidence of arrested development. They seldom miss an opportunity to boast that they are utterly uninformed about sports and wouldn't know Conn McCreary from Rocky Marciano. Theirs is a foolish snobbery that exposes their own inability to see a whole, round world in which games have a part along with politics and science and industry and art.

Robert Sherwood once confessed, "I have been an avid reader of the sports pages since childhood. In fact, when I first went to work after the First World War, I tried to get a job as a sports columnist myself. I wrote out some sample columns and submitted them to the *Boston Herald* and the *Boston Post*. I got a job on the latter paper, but not in the sports department. I was a reporter for Sunday feature stories. The job lasted two days, when I was fired, and that was the sum total of my career as a reporter until I went to work on *Roosevelt and Hopkins* twenty-seven years later."

It is a little frightening to consider what undiscerning irresponsibles the *Boston Post* had as sports editor and Sunday editor—one man who didn't consider Bob Sherwood worth a trial and one who discarded him after two days. Probably they did the world a favor, for if they had known their jobs we might never have had a *Petrified Forest* or *Reunion in Vienna* or *Idiot's Delight*, but Lord how the literature of the sports page would have been enriched.

It's not good to lose a reader. It is a hard thing to lose a friend who is also an idol. As Maxwell Anderson wrote in the eulogy Alfred Lunt read at Bob's funeral, "We wish the dice could have fallen the other way."

As Jimmy Cannon has written, Bob Sherwood was one of our guys. He belonged to the theater and politics and history and literature, but he also was one of us, the sports mob, though he didn't get to the games and fights and races as often as he would have liked. He was frequently in Toots Shor's, not because it is one of the places where celebrities go to be gawked at, but because he had friends there and wanted to be with them—guys like Eddie Arcaro and Joe DiMaggio, who worshipped him, and Toots himself and just about all of the regulars.

Bob was a Pulitzer Prize winner, a great man in the world, but he wasn't there as a celebrity. He was there as one of the guys, a tall, quiet gentleman of limitless kindness who had a way of making it seem that your friendship was a favor to him.

We all have to come to terms with death, Maxwell Anderson wrote. Sometimes they seem unnecessarily harsh terms, though. It would be presumptuous to say there are others whom we could have spared more easily. Better simply to say there is no one whom we could less afford to lose.

A CLASS GUY

THE YANKEES' organization lost more class on the weekend than George Steinbrenner could buy in ten years. Elston Howard, former catcher, outfielder, first baseman, coach and lately administrative assistant to Steinbrenner, died in Columbia Presbyterian Medical Center. He was fifty-one years old and had been handicapped by a heart condition the last two years.

Ellie Howard was the Yankees' first black player. By the time he arrived in training camp as a twenty-six-year-old rookie in 1955, eight years after Jackie Robinson had broken the color line in the major leagues, it was suspected that the Yankees didn't want blacks and would stall as long as possible before accepting any. Most other teams had blacks, most of whom shared the gift of exceptional speed afoot. Howard was six feet, two inches tall and weighed two hundred pounds. He batted .330 in Toronto in 1954, with twenty-two home runs and 109 runs batted in.

"They gave me the one that can't run," Casey Stengel said. When he converted Howard to catcher from the outfield, some suspected the Yankees of contriving an obstacle.

Probably there was no basis for such suspicions in the first place. If Howard shared them, they didn't diminish his determination to make the team. For hours every day, he worked on the field with Bill Dickey, a great catcher turned coach, and after dinner they met again in Dickey's room to practice more. Yogi Berra was still going strong behind the plate and Howard played most of his baseball in the outfield for three years, but by 1960 Ellie was firmly established as a catcher. In 1963 he was voted the Most Valuable Player in the American League.

Nine times a member of the American League All-Stars, Ellie helped the Yankees win nine pennants. In his first time at bat in a World Series, he nailed Don Newcombe for a home run with Joe Collins on base. That was 1955. Five years later, he hit a homer as a pinch-hitter against the Pittsburgh Pirates, and in the next game made two hits in one inning. He batted .462 that Series. In 1967 the Yankees sent him to Boston in time for him to help the Red Sox win the pennant. The World Series that year was Howard's tenth.

Returning to the Yankees, Ellie became the first black coach in the American League. He was a warm man and a gentleman whose quiet dignity made racial prejudice impossible. There is no reason to suspect that Bill Dickey would have been turned off by a man's color in any case, but it is worth noting that Dickey, born in Bastrop, Louisiana, and a resident of Little Rock, Arkansas, was Howard's first instructor in the big leagues.

Sometimes Ellie was disgusted by performances he witnessed in the "Bronx Zoo," but he managed to stay aloof from clubhouse politics and disputes.

His single unfulfilled ambition was to manage a team in the majors. He had that job once. In fact, he was the first black manager ever hired in the big leagues, but the job was shot out from under him before he could start. It must have been 1968 when Bill Veeck made one of many attempts to buy the Washington Senators. This time he was so confident he had the club that he went looking for a manager.

During the World Series he met with Howard in the Jefferson Hotel in St. Louis and offered him the job. Ellie accepted and they shook hands. Veeck went back to Washington and found that the club had been taken off the market.

Howard would have been a fine manager. Technically, he could do it all as a player; as a catcher, he ran major league games for fourteen years. He handled pitchers with a quiet confidence that imbued the pitcher with confidence.

As a gentleman, he would have been trusted by his players. He wasn't one to make speeches about fair play, about the right of all players to the same treatment, about anything, for that matter. He didn't have to make speeches. He only needed to be himself.

Whether he ever could have been manager for George Steinbrenner is something else again. It has yet to be shown that anybody can manage a team for Steinbrenner for more than a short time. Yet it is conceivable that some of Elston Howard's class might have rubbed off on the owner of the Yankees.

That possibility makes his death a greater loss than ever. He was a loyal friend, a polished professional in his job, a cool judge of whisky and a man of simple honesty. The world will be poorer without him, the Yankees immeasurably poorer.

MAX HIRSCH

A THREE-YEAR-OLD maiden named Koryo ran in the first race at Aqueduct Wednesday not very swiftly, and the program identified his trainer as Max Hirsch. The doyen of American horsemen didn't saddle the colt, though, and wasn't there to watch the race with the liveliest blue eyes on the Eastern seaboard.

In the eighty-ninth year of his life, little Max is seriously ill in Long Island Jewish Hospital and racing, the sport he has dignified for three-quarters of a century, is holding its breath and praying.

Others will write about the barefoot twelve-year-old in jeans and cotton shirt who stowed away with a carload of horses leaving Fredericksburg, Texas, and arrived half-starved and freezing almost a week later in snow-covered Maryland, to be wrapped in blankets, thawed out, fed, and started off as a jockey.

Others will write of the famous trainer and the horses he brought out, horses with names that are a litany today—Grey Lag, Vito, Sarazen, Bold Venture, Dawn Play, Stymie, Assault, High Gun, Middleground.

I prefer to write about a friend, one of the most patient and considerate men I have ever known, the most gracious of hosts and warmest of companions, bubbling with mischievous laughter, great with wisdom, an inexhaustible well of information and anecdote.

Thinking of Max brings back memories beyond counting. Mornings on the back side of Saratoga with Max putting his black dog Homely through his paces climbing trees and retrieving coins—the visitor's coins—flung over a six-foot wall into an empty stall.

Breakfast in Max's cottage in the Belmont stable area or at Saratoga, with Virgie, the cook, shoveling out hotcakes and bacon and eggs in quantities that would founder an ocean liner.

A week on the vast King Ranch in Texas hunting turkey and quail and geese and the fierce wild pig the Mexican call *javelina* and listening while Max traded insults with Sam Chesshir, a little old Texas Ranger gifted at training dogs and shooting things. "All right, go drag him back," Max ordered a visitor who had shot down one pig in a pack that stood glowering over the dead brother, ready to tear any enemy to ribbons. When the guest obediently started to walk toward the critters, Max's laughter shook nuts and bolts off the hunting car.

Mornings around the barn with Max patiently going over and over the points to look for in the conformation of a race horse. "Look at those straight legs. See that hump on the withers, that's muscle. When you want a horse that can stay a distance, look for that hump."

There was a May morning in 1950 when the mail brought a package to the cottage at Belmont. It turned out to contain a blanket of roses Middleground had won in the Kentucky Derby about ten days earlier, but it had been delayed in transit and the red flowers were a moldy black. Max laughed and hung it in the sun to dry and then sat down and told why he had dared to put Bill Boland, an apprentice, on Middleground.

Eddie Arcaro had promised to ride if Max said the word, and after Middleground finished second to Hill Prince in the Wood Memorial with Arcaro on the winner, Bob Kleberg, Middleground's owner, wanted to confirm the assignment immediately. "We'll see," Max said, and they went around to the jockeys' quarters.

"Boss," Arcaro said, "I'm still hearing about 1942 when I picked Devil Diver instead of Shut Out and passed up the Derby winner. If I take myself off Hill Prince after today and he wins the Derby, I'll never hear the end of it."

"Even then he would have kept his word if I had said so," Max related, "because that's Arcaro. But this kid Boland is a fine horseman. I knew he wouldn't hurt my horse's chances."

Max was born either July 12 or July 30, 1880, but he preferred to celebrate his birthday in August when the clans were gathered in Saratoga and he could sling a chili party for hundreds at his barn. This practice brought a faintly derisive sniff one recent August from Alfred Vanderbilt.

"Anybody can be eighty-six," Alfred said, "if he has two birthdays a year."

By that count, Max is in his 178th year and still going strong, on the racetrack, at least. Koryo did nothing in the first at Aqueduct Wednesday, but the feature race struck a delightfully familiar note. It went to Heartland, a four-year-old filly trained by Max Hirsch.

WHEN MAX GOT TOUTED

MEMORIES OF Max Hirsch filled this space the other day when the great little horseman's fight against endocarditis was in the last round. Now it is over, and the heart remains heavy with thoughts of the first gentleman of the American turf, the warmest of friends, and merriest.

Did Maximillan Justice Hirsch have an unerring eye for a horse of quality? You'd better believe it. One afternoon at Saratoga Max stopped to greet two ladies before the last race and their companion said, "These gals haven't had a winner all day, Max."

Max said he'd been so busy he hadn't even looked at the entries, but the other insisted, handing him a program. "Wait'll they come out," Max said, and as the field paraded, his improbably sharp blue eyes measured and weighed the horses one by one. At length he turned to the next box where a younger trainer, Woody Stephens, sat. "What d' you like here?" Max asked.

"I like my mare real well," Woody said, and Max reached for a pocket.

"Here," he said to the ladies' companion, "bet me fifty win, fifty place on Woody's horse." The mare won in a photo and the profits were delivered next morning to that matchless judge of horseflesh, Max Hirsch.

Max won the Triple Crown with Assault in 1946 and sent the gallant clubfoot off as a four-year-old with five straight handicap victories, with more than scale weight up every time. After a classic series against Stymie and Armed, Assault was retired to stud.

That would have been enough for Max, who had no interest in working an honest horse for the last dollar of purse money. What he loved, Max explained, was to bring an untried horse along through the important stakes for two-year-olds, to realize his full potential in the classics at three, then get the mature animal ready for the burdens of weight and distance in the handicap division. "After that," he said, "I'd just as soon somebody else had him while I go back and start with another young one."

However, Assault proved incurably sterile and was returned to training. "It runs in his family, you know," Max remarked casually on the day of the comeback race. An hour later a man in the press box leaped up from his typewriter with a cry. "That old horse thief," he told Joe Palmer, "told me sterility runs in Assault's family."

What Max meant was that Assault's sire, Bold Venture, had been a "shy breeder" who got few foals.

The names of wealthy owners whose horses Max handled would fill several volumes of *Dun & Bradstreet*. Most were accustomed to giving orders and being obeyed, and this made it edifying to notice how their manner changed when they'd come around the barn in the morning to inquire after their horses. Max treated them almost as though they were his equals.

"Has that thing of yours any chance?" a friend asked Max before a big stakes.

"The owner thinks so," he said, with not quite enough emphasis on the second word to make it an obscenity.

"And you believe in humoring owners once in a while?"

"Very seldom," Max said.

He was always courteous, though, except when bandying insults with an old friend like Willie Knapp, who rode Upset to beat Man O' War, or Clarence Buxton, who used to run the training tracks in Columbia, South Carolina, where Max wintered his horses. (This was before Mrs. Tad Legere, called the Latonia Thrush out of respect for her singing voice, took on the job of operating the track in addition to her other duties as Max's assistant, companion, and conscience and as a professional seamstress specializing in jockey silks.)

Reporting from Columbia during the Buxton regime, Joe Palmer explained that under the one-horse, one-vote principle, the more livestock a trainer had on the grounds the more overbearing he was entitled to be around management. With much the largest stable, Max abused Buxton hideously, and was repaid in kind.

"Trainers," Joe wrote, "were talking of odd stable pets they had had. This one had a bulldog that would take a lead-shank in his mouth and walk hots, and that one had a monkey that would jog horses under the shed, and another had a chicken that would fly to the top of the stall and drop eggs over a bran mash. Truth, in a phrase, was being crushed to earth.

" 'I think we had the strangest pet of all,' said Max's son, Buddy, trying to raise her again. 'It was down at Juarez when we were kids. We had a wolf for a pet—a real, full-grown wolf.'

"Mr. Buxton leaped to his feet, bristling with exclamation points.

" 'Wolf?' he shouted. 'That was no wolf—that was your father!' "

A MAN WHO KNEW THE CROWDS

WHEN THE iceman cometh, it doesn't make a great deal of difference which route he takes, for the ultimate result is the same in any case. Nevertheless, there was something especially tragic in the way death came to Tony Lazzeri, finding him and leaving him all alone in a dark and silent house—a house which must, in that last moment, have seemed frighteningly silent to a man whose ears remembered the roar of the crowd as Tony's did.

A man who knew the roar of the crowd? Shucks, Tony Lazzeri was the man who made the crowds and who made them roar. Frank Graham, in his absorbing history of the Yankees, tells about the coming of Lazzeri and about the crowds that trooped into the stadium to see him, the noisily jubilant Italian-American crowds with their rallying cry of "Poosh 'em up, Tony!"

"And now," Frank wrote in effect, "a new type of fan was coming to the stadium. A fan who didn't know where first base was. He came, and what he saw brought him back again and again until he not only knew where first base was, but second base as well."

It was a shock to read in the reports of Lazzeri's death, that he was not yet forty-two years old. There are at least a few right around that age still playing in the major leagues. One would have guessed Lazzeri's age a good deal higher because his name and fame are inextricably associated with an era which already has become a legend—the era that is always referred to as the time of "the old Yankees."

You can't think of Tony without thinking also of Babe Ruth and Bob Meusel and Herb Pennock and Waite Hoyt and Lou Gehrig and Mark Koenig and Benny Bengough and Wilcy Moore, all of whom have been gone from the playing fields for what seems a long time.

And you think of Grover Cleveland Alexander, too, for it was Lazzeri's misfortune that although he was as great a ball player as ever lived the most vivid memory he left in most minds concerned the day he failed.

That was, of course, in the seventh game of the 1926 World Series when the Yankees filled the bases against the leading Cardinals, drove Jess Haines from the hill and sent Rogers Hornsby from his position at second base out toward the Cardinals' bullpen where Alexander drowsed in the dusk.

Everyone knows that story, how the St. Louis manager walked out to take a look at Alexander's eyes, how he found them as clear as could be expected and sent Old Pete in there to save the world championship by striking out Lazzeri. Come to think of it, Alex wasn't a lot younger then than Tony was when he died.

It was after that game that some one asked Alexander how he felt when Lazzeri struck out.

"How did I feel?" he snorted. "Go ask Lazzeri how he felt."

Tony never told how he felt. Not that it was necessary, anyway, but he wasn't one to be telling much, ever. He was a rookie when a baseball writer first used a line that has been worn to tatters since. "Interviewing that guy," the reporter grumbled, "is like mining coal with a nail file."

Silent and unsmiling though he was, Lazzeri wasn't entirely devoid of a taste for dugout humor. Babe Ruth, dressing in haste after one tardy arrival in the stadium, tried to pull a shoe out of his locker and found it wouldn't move. He didn't have to be told who had nailed it to the floor.

When other players found cigarette butts in their footgear or discovered their shirts tied in water-soaked knots or were unable to locate their shoelaces, they blamed only one man.

Lefty Gomez used to tell of the day, long after Lazzeri's experience in the 1926 World Series, when Gomez lost control and filled the bases. Lazzeri trotted in from second base to talk to him. Lazzeri always was the man who took charge when trouble threatened the Yankees. Even in his first season when he was a rookie who'd never seen a big-league game until he played in one, he was the steadying influence, the balance wheel. So after this incident Gomez was asked what words Lazzeri had used to reassure him in the clutch.

"He said," replied Lefty, who didn't necessarily expect to be believed, " 'You put those runners on there. Now get out of the jam yourself, you slob.' "

They chose Lazzeri Player of the Year after one of his closing seasons. They could just as well have made it "Player of the Years," for in all his time with the Yankees there was no one whose hitting and fielding and hustle and fire and brilliantly swift thinking meant more to any team.

Other clubs tried to profit by those qualities of his when he was through. He went to the Cubs and the Dodgers and the Giants. None of these experiments was particularly happy; none endured for long. He managed Toronto for a while and then just before the war he went back home to San Francisco. That was the last stop.

YARNS OF A GRAND OLD SOLDIER

THEY WERE spinning yarns, thirteen to the dozen, along Jacobs Beach yesterday and they'll be spinning 'em for a long time to come, because it will be a long time before the hero of their tales is forgotten.

Probably "hero" isn't the happiest possible word for General John J. Phelan, for the role he played so long as chairman of the New York boxing commission was seldom heroic in the accepted sense. The performance of the old soldier and brassiere importer was more a comic-opera success, or at least it was pictured as such by the fight mob and the fight writers, all of whom had a real respect for the general and most of whom ribbed him with a genuine but not always gentle affection.

The picture that emerges from all the stories now is slightly confused and yet fairly accurate. A picture of a man who was himself often confused but always honestly confused, a man of monumental integrity and equally monumental rages, a man who could be completely charming and utterly baffling, who was gentle and excitable and sincere and conscientious and so thoroughly decent he seemed oddly out of place among the devious characters who people the sport he governed.

By and large, he governed it intelligently and well, and those who made the most raffish fun of him never disputed that. But they couldn't resist guying him, because he did seem so incongruously cast in his job.

A justice of the State Supreme Court noted the incongruity when the general came before him in connection with an abortive libel suit filed by Phelan and his fellow commissioner, Bill Brown, against Jimmy Johnston. Some irreverent remarks by the "Boy Bandit" prompted the commissioners to sue, but the case was settled swiftly and amicably when it reached John E. McGeehan's court. Announcing the settlement, McGeehan observed that Johnston was the waggish sort who'd say almost anything for publicity purposes.

"One sees the rakish leer in his eyes," the justice said, "and gathers that he has a wayward wit and must have his laugh. He picked on refined, sensitive men, honest public officials with unsullied reputations. A pungent tongue rasped tender ears. Ruffled feelings have been smoothed out. The case is closed."

It was mostly when the general's feelings were ruffled that he made with the magnificently mangled syntax the fight mob treasured. They loved to remember the time he shouted defiantly, "There's no man alive who can accuse me of being honest!" And the time he was annoyed by some rear-seat chattering during a prefight meeting attended by Joe Louis's handler, Jack Blackburn.

Interrupting his own rambling lecture on the rules and ethics and principles of the manly art, the general snapped, "A little less quiet, please, Mr. Blackbird."

There is no malice, no intent to ridicule in the yarns they're spinning about him now. Because in the next breath they tell stories of another sort.

They tell of how he devoted all his time to the boxing job, to the ruination of his own business. How he was in the office by nine o'clock each day and how on dull Monday nights he could be seen at ringside in Rochester or Syracuse or Albany, checking on the state of the sport in those outposts. And in Buffalo, too, although it is recalled that he once expressed astonishment at the discovery that Buffalo was in New York.

They remember that at the height of Henry Armstrong's reign as triple champion, the general persistently referred to him as "Henry Jackson." But they also remember how swiftly he charmed Bill Brown when the latter was made a commissioner and the railbirds were saying that these two, temperamental and political opposites, never could get along. Within two weeks Brown was calling the general "Boss," was referring to him as "The Chief," and was faithfully voting with him on all issues.

There's a story of a session prior to a Barney Ross–Jimmy McLarnin bout when Ross's manager, Sam Pian, raised a fuss about "rabbit punches." The general set out to describe legal and illegal punches, ran out of words and sought to demonstrate. He swing a mighty left, fetched himself a resounding smack in the features, and broke his glasses.

Then there was the time he visited Stillman's, watched two boxers in light sparring, then rushed down to ringside to clutch the manager of one boy and demand, "Make your man quit holding!"

That was the same bitter winter day when he decided the gym was too stuffy and insisted that Lou Stillman fling open every window. The fierce blasts were cruel enough to the unclothed boxers in training. Breathing fresh air was a far more scarifying experience for the non-boxing denizens of the place. The windows have not been opened since.

AS HE SEEMED TO A HICK

IT SEEMS presumptuous to be writing of Jimmy Walker now, after all that has been written with honest affection by those who knew him longer and more intimately. And yet we hicks out in the Middle West knew the man, too, and perhaps our long-range view of him was as sharply defined and as accurate as the closer slant.

Probably there are many serious-minded New Yorkers who resent the repeated statement that Jimmy was the symbol of his city and his era, feeling that there is a great deal more to the world's greatest city than the things he represented. But the fact is that if Jimmy was a symbol to his townsmen, he was ever so much more than that to us in the hinterlands.

To us he was New York. He was the New York we had come to know, or to think we knew, through the columns of Winchell and O. O. McIntyre. He was the Broadway of George M. Cohan and Texas Guinan, the Polo Grounds of John McGraw, the Madison Square Garden of Tex Rickard and Jimmy Johnston. He was the New York of Babe Ruth and Tammany Hall and Tin Pan Alley.

He was the fiddler who called the turns in a dance which we pictured as never-ending. He was the debonair prophet of gaiety and extravagance and glitter. He was the embodiment of all the qualities which hicks like us resented and admired about New York.

Little things like this made a lasting impression on a visitor to New York in those days:

The crowd was in the Long Island Bowl for the second Sharkey-Stribling fight and the preliminaries were stumbling to a close and there came the rising whine of sirens from outside. A stir and a babble ran through the crowd and heads turned away from the ring and it seemed everyone was standing and craning. Down an aisle swept Jimmy with his retinue, with a hand uplifted in jaunty response to the shouts that greeted him. And that entrance was more exciting than any of the fifteen rounds of brawling that followed.

Afterward, the cab coming back to Manhattan was halted on the bridge by the warning of sirens. A big black limousine hissed by, weaving through the jammed traffic behind its escort. Ahead and below through the darkness the lights of Manhattan glowed. The two hicks in the cab sighed.

"Golly!" one of them breathed. "But they do it big in this town!"

Jimmy hadn't built the bridge, of course, or the towers or turned on the lights, and he hadn't staged the fight or drawn the crowd. And yet, somehow, he seemed to stand for all the things that they did so big in this town.

New York was the perfect background for him. New York set him off. But he was no less a figure of distinction when he crossed the Hudson or the Atlantic.

Al Laney recalls how he took France by storm on his first visit and how his speeches created a schism in the scholarship of the country. Jimmy used the expression "these good-time Charlies," and writers for the French literary journals worked up a fearful sweat trying to translate the term, composing long and ponderous essays defining its hidden meanings.

Jimmy also brought the expression "the cocktail hour" to France. Indeed, he represented that pleasant institution in Parisian eyes. And again the scholars quarreled, practically fighting duels over the comparative merits of the Anglicized spelling and the French *coquetele*.

Mr. Laney remembers, too, how lonesome and homesick Jimmy was in his later exile in southern France. And how often of an evening, out of loneliness and boredom, he would telephone the *Paris Herald* and just sit there shooting the breeze with any American who happened to answer the phone.

To us out in the country there seemed nothing shocking about the disclosures made or hinted at in the investigation which drove Jimmy out of office and out of the country. So he hadn't been an efficient administrator. Well, whoever said he was? What we felt was a sincere regret in his passing from public life; we'd rather have lost our dearest bootlegger.

Jimmy wasn't supposed to be a statesman. He didn't pretend to be. He was a bandleader, and the most charming one that ever swung a baton. His charm, his urbane graciousness, were his trademarks to the end. To any who had the good fortune to know him, the facts published in his formal obituaries were of small interest. The essential thing about Jimmy was something you hardly ever read on the obituary page, the simple fact that he was the most charming man you ever met.

WHO'S ON SECOND?

AT A PARTY in Hollywood a year or so ago where introductions were casual, a newspaper stiff found himself face to face with a smiling redhead whom he recognized instantly though they hadn't met.

"Who played second base for the Browns of 1929?" the redhead asked without preamble.

"Oscar Melillo, is that right?"

"I don't know," Danny Kaye said. "I just thought it would be a good way to open conversation."

If the question had been easier, like who played second for the Tigers in 1961, chances are the working stiff couldn't have come up with the name, but it just happened that 1929 had been his first season as a baseball reporter and the Browns were the first team he accompanied to training camp.

The memories of youth are long, long memories. Today that bat-eared young baseball writer, now grown pretty shiny in the seams, can still rattle off every name on the roster of the team Dan Howley was training in West Palm Beach that year—Lu Blue at first base, Red Kress at short, Frank O'Rourke at third and so on. The rookie writer admired them all, and Oscar Melillo more than most.

The Browns of 1929 weren't a great team, though they had a few top men like Heinie Manush, Alvin Crowder, Sammy Gray, Rick Ferrell and Kress.

Melillo would have been great if he could have hit like Frank Frisch or Charlie Gehringer or Rogers Hornsby, for he was a scampering marvel on the infield with wonderfully sure hands and more competitive zeal than you'd believe a little man could contain.

His manual skills were considerable but it was his indomitable spirit that won the admiration and affection of his colleagues and the odd nickname "Spinach." He got that handle by beating a rap that would have put a lesser man on his back for life.

In the mid-1920s Oscar fell gravely ill of Bright's disease, an ailment that threatened to end not only his playing days but his life. "Not this dude," Oscar told his doctor. "Just spell out the rules of this game."

They put him on a diet that would have made a Spartan warrior whimper. For the next two or three years he subsisted mostly on spinach, a noxious weed which mothers of that day tried vainly to stuff into small offspring not because it had any muscle-building properties or food value but because it was supposed to build character.

If memory is reliable, Otis Brannon became the Browns' regular second baseman while Melillo was ill, but in 1928 or thereabouts Oscar was back to recapture his job by force.

He broke all records for errorless play at second base, he marched up to the plate day after day to take his licks against pitchers like Lefty Grove and George Earnshaw and Herb Pennock, and there wasn't a stouter competitor in the league going up against a sirloin medium-rare, never mind the vegetables.

Muddy Ruel, a craftsman of Melillo's time, was no great hitter either. His special gifts were dexterity, fortitude and brains. Not a large man, he had in abundance the qualities demanded today by Jake Gaither, the coach at Florida A & M, who wants his football players "mobyle, agyle and hostyle."

A perceptive student of hitters and crafty handler of pitchers, Muddy set endurance records for catchers, who are prone to all the ills of the flesh plus split fingers and broken hands.

He was also a lawyer licensed to practice in the Supreme Court and in 1945 when the club owners discovered they had bought a turkey when they chose Happy Chandler for commissioner, it was to counselor Ruel that they turned for rescue.

In Chicago during the World Series of 1945, the first under Chandler's administration, they held a kangaroo court to consider firing the Duke of Versailles, Kentucky. Cooler, and possibly flatter, heads prevailed and a compromise was reached.

Instead of canning Chandler they appointed Muddy as his baby sitter to lead him by the hand, show him where first base was and try to keep Happy's big fat foot out of Happy's big fat mouth.

Cool, gracious, intelligent, dead-panned and infinitely amused, Muddy did the best he could. If he wasn't altogether successful in making Chandler over into the image of Abraham Lincoln, he was in good company. Neither was the Creator.

DEATH OF "THE ICEMAN"

THE FATAL injury of Georgie Woolf in a spill at Santa Anita Thursday is a reminder of something which race fans forget with the greatest of ease when they boo and sneer and rail at some dusty kid who has just finished out of the money astride the horse they're betting. That is, that every time one of these little guys scrambles into the saddle for a race he is literally taking his life in his hands.

Nothing could illustrate this truth with more shocking clarity than the circumstances of "The Iceman's" death. Here was one of the genuinely great riders of our time, conceded without argument to be right up there alongside Eddie Arcaro at the very top of his profession. Here was one of the most nearly perfect craftsman alive, famed among fans and respected among jockeys for his cool skill and daring. He had ridden in every stake of importance in America and won virtually all of them at least once and it is not recalled that he ever had a serious fall from the time he was seven years old and riding his father's horses on the hayseed tracks of Alberta, Canada.

There was no jamming or interference of any sort in his last race. He had a tight hold on his mount, Please Me, and was in the clear behind the field. The horse stumbled, flinging Georgie over his head, and that was all.

It was ironic that a fellow who rarely accepted mounts in any but the major events should be killed in an ordinary $3,500 allowance race.

Because he declined assignments in the minor events, some of the public got the impression that he was high hat. Now he is dead, there is no reason to conceal the fact that he wasn't physically able to ride complete cards day in and day out.

He was diabetic and didn't dare train down below 115 pounds or ride too often. A quiet little blonde who took few people into his confidence, he didn't advertise what watchful care he had to exercise in order to work at all.

He would sleep most of the morning on the day of a race and shortly before saddling he would drink a Coca-Cola spiked with spirits of ammonia. His wife supervised the rigid diet he had to keep, traveling with him from their home in Arcadia, near Santa Anita, where they had invested in a restaurant in anticipation of the day when Georgie would quit the track.

Georgie Woolf was a bit of a hero in the jockey rooms, personally popular with the other riders and respected as a competitor whose tactics were fair but whose temper permitted no liberties. More than one jockey got a whip across the face for trying to rough up "The Iceman."

He came fast on the big wheel, for it was less than fifteen years ago that he first wandered into Saratoga wearing dusty jeans and a big white cowboy hat. They laughed at the "Montana cowboy" then and guyed him, until they saw him on a horse.

He'd been riding almost as soon as he could walk. His father, a rider and stagecoach driver in Montana before he settled in Cardston, Alberta, taught him racing on the backwoods tracks of southern Alberta and in 1926 the fifteen-year-old Georgie rode his first race on an organized track, a horse named Catch Me at Chinook Park, Calgary.

Once he reached the big leagues, he rode the best in the biggest and scarcely any big prize eluded him except victory in the Kentucky Derby. At Churchill Downs he never got closer than a second on Staretor in 1941.

He took his greatest personal satisfaction in winning the first $100,-000 Santa Anita Handicap with Azucar, a reformed steeplechaser from Ireland. In that race Woolf drove Azucar up from fourteenth place and won by two lengths, with the beloved favorite, Equipoise, far back in seventh place.

Others, however, remember more vividly his ride on Whirlaway in the Massachusetts Handicap in 1942, when Whirlaway broke Seabiscuit's earnings record. Red Pollard, Seabiscuit's jockey, sat in the press box and watched as Woolf restrained his horse frighteningly far behind the pacemaking Rounders.

Pollard was the first to spot the flash of devil's red when Georgie began to move on the far turn. The redhead leaped to his feet, yelling, "Here he comes! Here he comes, the son of a bitch!"

And there was the golden afternoon at Pimlico when, with Pollard in a hospital, Woolf got up on Seabiscuit and stole the start and the horse race from Charley Kurtsinger in the unforgettable match with War

Admiral, whose owner had dictated all the conditions right down to a walk-up start.

"Didn't think I could do it, did you?" Georgie shouted when Seabiscuit broke ahead of War Admiral. "Get that whip ready, because I'm going to make you run," he said when Kurtsinger drew even with him on the backstretch.

On the stretch turn Georgie spoke once again. "Goodbye, Charley," he yelled. He didn't wait for an answer.

HOWARD EHMKE

OF ALL the stories Connie Mack used to tell at dinners, and he had a routine as fixed as any in vaudeville, his favorite concerned Howard Ehmke. It never varied by so much as a syllable in the telling. Late in the 1929 season, Connie would explain, it had become evident that nothing could stop the Athletics' drive to a pennant. Just before the last tour of the West, Connie called Ehmke into his tower office in Shibe Park in Philadelphia. Ehmke's days in the major leagues were ending. He sat on the bench almost all summer watching Lefty Grove, George Earnshaw, Rube Walberg and others younger than he handling the chores on the mound. This was the scene as Connie described it:

" 'Howard,' I said, 'the time has come for us to part.'

"He looked at me. 'Mr. Mack,' he said, 'I have always wanted to pitch in a World Series.' He lifted his arm"—here Connie would raise his own thin right arm, fist clenched—" 'Mr. Mack,' he said, 'there is one great game left in this old arm.' That was what I wanted to hear. 'All right, Howard,' I told him. 'When we go West I want you to stay here. When the Cubs come in to play the Phillies, you watch them. Learn all you can about their hitters. Say nothing to anybody. You are my opening pitcher for the World Series."

There was a sidelight which Connie omitted from his tale, but Al Simmons supplied it. When Ehmke started to warm up for the opener with the Cubs, Simmons snorted with consternation. "Are you going to pitch *him*?" he demanded incredulously.

"Is it all right with you, Al?" Connie asked.

Simmons gulped. "Oh, well—er, well, if you say so."

Skipping that bit, Connie would go on to tell how the Cubs lunged and stabbed at Ehmke's soft stuff. He would recall the strikeouts in order—Rogers Hornsby, Hack Wilson, Kiki Cuyler, Riggs Stephenson,

Gabby Hartnett, Hornsby again, then Wilson—until the total reached thirteen for an alltime World Series record.

Connie attached a lot of importance to the secrecy surrounding his plan. He made it clear that in his opinion the element of surprise was a major factor in Ehmke's success. Chances are he never knew of a conversation which Ring Lardner repeated a year later.

Lardner was writing fiction and plays by 1929 but he had many friends in baseball after his years as a sportswriter. Joe McCarthy, the Cubs' manager, was one.

"I was chatting with Joe a little before the season ended," Lardner said. " 'I'm not afraid of Grove and Earnshaw,' he told me. 'We can hit speed. But they've got one guy over there I am afraid of. He's what I call a junk pitcher'—but Joe used an indelicate expression. 'His name,' he told me, 'is Howard Ehmke, and he's the sucker we're going to see in this Series.' "

So maybe the Cubs' surprise wasn't quite so great as Connie liked to believe. He did enjoy telling the story, though, and today it all comes back because the morning paper reported the death of Howard Ehmke at sixty-five.

He was a big, handsome, light-haired man, head of a successful tarpaulin and awning firm in Philadelphia, and a pretty good horse player. He used to get to Miami every year during the Hialeah meeting and it was a pleasure to encounter him there, a quiet man of warmth and charm. This season he wasn't there.

Howard lived to see his strikeout record broken by Carl Erskine, pitching for Brooklyn against the Yankees. He wasn't in the stands when it happened, though. He and Mrs. Ehmke were taking a drive in suburban Philadelphia, listening with mild interest to the radio broadcast of the game.

At first it was just another game to Howard, but as Erskine turned back one Yankee after another, it took on a special interest. When Erskine got his ninth or tenth strikeout, Howard said, "Let's park and listen to the rest of this." He pulled off the road and cut the motor.

Another Yankee struck out. Then another. Now Erskine tied Ehmke's mark but the game wasn't over. Mrs. Ehmke was watching her husband. The fourteenth Yankee went down—it could have been Don Bollweg. Howard smiled quietly.

He said nothing as the game drew to an end. The record he had held for a quarter of a century was gone. He stepped on the starter. Nothing happened. The radio had drained his battery.

THE MAN WHO BET HIS TONSIL

CLIFF MOOERS, the man who bet his tonsil on a horse, died of a heart attack on November 13, but the news didn't reach me then. Consequently, it was a painful shock to read that the "executor of the estate of Clifford L. Mooers" had sold the horse, Traffic Judge, for $362,345.67. This week the sense of loss was renewed by a story about eighty-seven other horses from his stable going at auction for $781,300.

He was a grand little guy and a delightful companion, spinner of incomparable yarns, gold prospector, cowboy, wartime fighter pilot, mining engineer, Texas rancher and oil man, breeder, owner and sometimes trainer of thoroughbreds and a sportsman to enrich any game.

The tale has been told here before about Cliff as a kid holding out $25 and a tonsil on a doctor who had agreed to snatch both of them for $50 and putting the money on a winner at Bay Meadows. As a twig is inclined, et cetera. Many years later, young William Woodward came to know Cliff Mooers and to recognize the challenging spirit that could inspire an investment like that.

"If that fellow had a mouse," Bill Woodward said, "and you had a great big tomcat, he would bet you anything his mouse could whip your cat."

Over the years Cliff was encountered fairly often on the racetracks, in New York and California and Maryland, and—whenever he had a mouse that he considered a match for the tomcats—at the Kentucky Derby. He liked to see his old rose and blue silks in the big heat and he put them in whenever possible, though all he ever took out was Old Rockport's $2,500 in fourth money in 1949.

Between meetings there was occasional correspondence with him. The last direct word came by telephone in August. He and an associate, he said, had just completed a big pipeline and had had a little ceremony over driving the golden spike, so to speak, and now how about joining him for a couple of weeks of loafing and fishing in the Pacific Northwest?

Guys who operate like Cliff, they work hard on a big deal and then have time to go off and play hard. It doesn't always occur to them that there are working stiffs who have to stay chained to the spelling machine. Well, he said, think about it and give him a call at this number.

"Is that the Seattle Yacht Club?" he was asked.

"No, it's the marine phone on my boat. Just tell the operator and she'll find me."

The invitation had to be declined, with deep regret because there would have been a fortnight of yarns that could be spun only by Cliff Mooers, like the one about his penguins.

A friend had brought a gaggle or so of these overdressed birds to California from the Galapagos and sold or given them to Cliff, who started to fly them to his Texas ranch in another friend's plane. When they were airborne Cliff let the penguins out of their crates in the passenger compartment.

One ambled over to a window and took a gander below. "He saw how high we were," Cliff said, "and I'll swear he shrieked with horror. He covered his eyes with his wings like *this*, shrank back from the window and never went near it again."

Weather put them down for the night somewhere in Texas. Cliff hauled his crated cargo into town in a couple of taxis, bribed a bellhop to smuggle them up the freight elevator while he engaged connecting rooms, then filled a bathtub and turned the birds loose. Now how about dinner? If penguins want live fish, how do you accommodate them in a Texas city?

At the five-and-ten, Cliff bought up a stock of goldfish in bowls. Back at the hotel he found his new pets splashing happily. In went the goldfish. The penguins looked, "turned pale," and fled from the tub in panic.

Then there was the story Cliff told Joe Palmer about his prospecting days when Jack, the champion dog-team driver, lost the big sled race from Dawson to Nome. Among bettors who had dropped their pokes there was some pretty ugly talk about drivers who pull their dogs but after a month or so most of it had died down. Jack lived over a saloon in Nome with a lady who, Cliff said, could have been his wife.

"One morning the boys at the bar heard gunfire upstairs. The couple quarreled a lot and for a while nobody paid much attention. But all of a sudden here came Jack down the stairs hitting every fifth step. Every time he lit she took another shot at him. She couldn't shoot worth anything, but she was throwing .45 slugs into the walls pretty freely.

"Jack hit the floor, skidding a little in the sawdust, and straightened out for the swinging doors. As he went to them a man at the bar called out:

"How about it, Jack!" he said. "Are you trying this time?"

NAPOLEON LAJOIE

IT COULDN'T possibly happen today. Baseball has no backwoods today, no frontiers, no dark continents. Stop in at 745 Fifth Avenue in New York and ask George Weiss who's the best ball player in Australia; he'll tell you all about a cricketer named O'Neill.

Olanta, South Carolina, is a nodule on Highway 301 six miles north of Turbeville and about equidistant from Florence and Sumter. On the day Don Buddin finished high school, representatives of fifteen major league clubs waited at his home in Olanta. For *lebensraum,* he took them to the funeral parlor next door and interviewed them one by one before selecting the bonus offered by the Red Sox. That's how baseball's intelligence service works today.

In August of 1896 Bill Nash, a scout for the Philadelphia Nationals, went up to Fall River, Massachusetts, to look over an outfielder named Phil Geier. He saw a strapping twenty-year-old playing second base, and forgot all about Geier. The kid was leading the New England League with a batting average of .429 but scouts had not heard about him yet. Charley Marston, the Fall River manager who had signed the rookie on the back of an envelope, sold him to Nash.

That is how Napoleon Lajoie reached the big leagues en route to the Hall of Fame. In those days, it could happen.

Nap Lajoie had been a hack driver in Woonsocket, Rhode Island, playing ball between fares, when Marston picked him up. In his first season as a professional, after only eighty games with Fall River, he got to Philadelphia in time to play thirty-nine games and bat .328. That fall he went back to Woonsocket and his job as a hack driver.

The next year he hit .363, went back home and climbed into the hack again. The following season his average dropped back to .328 but he led the league in doubles and topped all second basemen in putouts. He was in the hack again as soon as he got home. Wasn't sure he could stick in the big leagues.

As it turned out, the baseball job wasn't permanent. It lasted only twenty-three years. When he was forty-two and finished in the majors, he went up to Toronto, where he played 151 games and batted .380. The Enos Slaughter of his day, they call him.

That wasn't bad for a washed-up antique, but the chances are Lajoie didn't regard it as a noteworthy season. He would compare it with 1901, when he batted .405 and led the American League with 220 hits, 145 runs, forty-eight doubles, thirteen home runs and 403 putouts. When they built the Hall of Fame in Cooperstown, he came with the deed.

Considering the excitement that was stirred when Stan Musial became the eighth player in history to make three thousand hits, it would be interesting to know whether anybody even noticed it when Lajoie attained that figure. That was in 1914, his last season in Cleveland. Two years later, when he left the majors after his second tour of duty with the Athletics, he had 3,251 hits, fifth in the all-time list.

These days when a club gets a hitter like Lajoie the club keeps him, as the Yankees kept Joe DiMaggio, the Red Sox Ted Williams, the Cardinals Musial. Lajoie moved from the Phillies to the Athletics to Cleveland to the Athletics, but there were special circumstances.

When the American League moved into Philadelphia, Lajoie jumped to the Athletics for $2,400, which was double his National League salary. His ingratitude infuriated the Phillies, for whom he had averaged only .349 over four seasons, and they sued. The courts were making curious decisions even then. Lajoie was enjoined from playing in Pennsylvania but he wasn't restored to the Phillies. Cleveland got him instead, letting him sit on the bench when the club played in Philadelphia.

He managed Cleveland from 1905 until midseason of 1909. The team was called the Napoleons in those days, and Lajoie's roommate on the road was a young sportswriter covering the club, name of Grantland Rice. It is indicative of Lajoie's disposition that when Jim McGuire succeeded him as manager it wasn't deemed necessary to trade him away. In 1910 he played 159 games, led the league with 227 hits and fifty-one doubles, and batted .384. Must've been sulking.

After his death in Daytona Beach, the obituaries mentioned the minor scandal of 1910, when the St. Louis Browns, playing Cleveland a doubleheader on the last day of the season, tried to hand Lajoie the batting championship because they did not love his rival, Ty Cobb.

In spite of their efforts, Cobb won. Chances are Ty regarded Lajoie with something less than cuddly warmth thereafter. At any rate, he dissented from the popular estimate of Lajoie as a demigod of picturesque grace.

Choosing Lajoie on his All-Star team in 1908, the Reverend Billy Sunday wrote, "He works as noiselessly as a Corliss engine, makes hard plays easy, is great in a pinch, and never gets cold feet."

In a letter to E. J. Lanigan, Hall of Fame historian, in 1945, Cobb put Eddie Collins at second base. "Lajoie," he wrote, "could not go out, nor come in, and did not cover too much ground to his right or left."

MOSEY KING, FINANCIER

MOSES KING, called Mosey by Yale students over half a century, was a tough and agile little man who grew up fighting for money in the backrooms of saloons and became the elder statesman of the athletic department in New Haven. He lived seventy-two years according to the records and seventy-four according to his friends, and then one night about a month ago a car clipped him as he was crossing Whalley Avenue.

This is the street that Charles Loftus, Yale publicity man, used to point out to visitors as the official proving ground for nifty halfbacks. If they reached the far curb alive, they were on the team. Mosey King didn't make the curb, and about four hours later he died.

What would you say a man's top salary would be over forty-six years as boxing coach at Yale? Five thousand dollars a year, maybe $7,500? Well, now it comes out that Mosey King left an estate of nearly half a million to relatives scattered through New England.

This isn't unprecedented. Jock Sutherland never made more than $12,000 a year as football coach at Pittsburgh, and when he died he left something between $750,000 and $800,000. He invested wisely. So did Gene Tunney and Eddie Eagan, who were friends of Mosey King and probably got advice from the same source that guided Mosey through the financial jungles. Devote your life to advising young Yales, and when they're old Yales they can advise you.

When he was in his seventies Mosey could have weighed in close to the limit of the lightweight division in which he fought as a boy. He never wore an overcoat in a New Haven winter and never owned a car. He walked ten miles a day, and on each New Year's Day, which was his birthday, he took a swim in Long Island Sound. It was on one of his nightly walks that he was hit by the car.

He was Eddie Eagan's coach when the former chairman of the New York State Athletic Commission was heavyweight champion at Yale. Perhaps because Mosey himself had been a skillful boxer, he always regarded his friend Gene Tunney as the greatest of all heavyweight champions, not such a hitter as Jack Dempsey or Joe Louis but a dedicated man who trained faithfully, planned his fights intelligently and made the most of a fine physique, a facile brain and wonderful legs.

The obituaries didn't mention this, but the story is that when Mosey started at Yale it was not as a boxing coach but as a quasiofficial member of the football staff. Because he was deft and light of foot, it was felt he could teach the New Haven backs some tricks of coordination.

Anyhow, he went to work as boxing coach the following year, and stayed on after his retirement about four years ago. He was a sort of unofficial troubleshooter in his last years, seeking out students who might have emotional or financial or family difficulties, taking them out to dinner, trying to talk them into balance and a sense of proportion.

He was, it should be remembered, a product of what is sometimes called "boxing's dirty business." Born in New York but brought up in New London, he started fighting when he was fourteen, and his first instructor was James J. Corbett. He fought nine years, won the New England lightweight championship, never was knocked out.

When Mosey was eighteen or so he and a boy from Wallingford, Connecticut, named Shorty Gans were claimants to the state lightweight title. A match was made in the backroom of a saloon in New Britain with the winner to get 65 percent of the gate, such as it might be, and the loser 35 percent.

Backers of Shorty Gans were laying 4 to 1 on their man, and even that price looked good when Gans dropped Mosey in the fifth round. Mosey got up fighting and floored his man.

In fact, he floored Gans seven times, but by the most curious of coincidences every knockdown was scored in the last nine seconds of the round. Dick Howell, for many years afterward a Bridgeport newspaper man, was the referee. Every time Gans went down, Howell started counting. Every time he reached nine, the bell rang.

Years later Howell wrote that "the bell should not have come to Gans's rescue just to the second so many times," but that is another story. The referee was not a man to impugn either the competence or the impartiality of the timekeeper.

Anyhow, in the fourteenth round a right to the jaw dropped Gans for the seventh time. For the seventh time, the bell ended the round at the count of nine. The fallen gladiator's handlers scraped him up and carried him to his corner.

The fifteenth round started but Gans didn't. He couldn't get off his stool. Mosey always said it was a real tough fight.

SIC TRANSIT GLORIA

A FEW YEARS ago when Gerry Nugent was trying to hold the Phillies together with spit and hope in lieu of money, he was forced to hock another player, as he had to do almost annually in those days. This time the guy to go was Bucky Walters or Dolph Camilli or Kirby Higbe or somebody of that stripe, some guy who was both good and popular and whose departure outraged the fans.

There was the usual public outcry: "Ah, the bums! I'm through. Never another dollar of my money do they get." There was a man around who'd always been a devoted baseball fan and, just to make conversation, he was asked, "Well, Tom, what's your feeling about the latest deal?"

"Me?" he said, mildly surprised. "I have no feeling. I quit 'em in 1917 when they sold Alexander and Killefer."

The iron must have gone deep, for he had never been back. If twenty-odd years seems an elephantine time to hold a grudge, well, that's how the fans at the time of World War I felt about Grover Cleveland Alexander. There may even be people in Philadelphia who remember, bitterly, the names of the other players in the deal that sent Alex and Bill Killefer to the Cubs.

Alexander and Killefer were the greatest battery of their day, one of the greatest ever. Alex had won twenty-eight games as a rookie with the Phils and, in subsequent seasons there, nineteen, twenty-two, twenty-seven, thirty-one, thirty-three and thirty. So they peddled him and his catcher for—*sic transit gloria!*—Mike Prendergast, Pickles Dilhoefer and $60,000.

What they all remembered and wrote about after Alex's death was the seventh game of the 1926 World Series against the Yankees, when he shambled out of the Cardinals' bullpen and struck out Tony Lazzeri with the bases filled. That was his hour of glory, but he had other hours, too.

There was the time in 1929 when young Billy Southworth, all full of beans and righteous ideas as the rookie manager of the Cardinals, suspended the poor old guy for "breaking training" while the club was on the road and sent him home in disgrace. Young managers have to learn, too, same as young ball players; Southworth wouldn't do a thing like that to a guy like Old Pete today.

Back in St. Louis, Alex found understanding in the office of Sam Breadon, the Cardinals' owner. Sam couldn't undo what his manager had done, but he did the next best thing. He announced that Alex was taking a vacation for the remainder of the season, that he was going home to Nebraska to fish bullheads and get ready for the following year.

After their conference newspapermen dropped around one by one to visit Alex in the Fairgrounds Hotel, near Sportsman's Park. Sid Keener, then of the *St. Louis Times*, found Alex alone and, by right of long friendship, read him a temperance lecture:

"You know, Pete, you're your own worst enemy." . . . "You're right, Sid, and I'm off the stuff for life." . . . "You never hurt anybody but yourself, Pete, but you know what that paint does to you and you're not getting any younger." . . . "I know, Sid, and I mean it. Never again, so help me." . . . "You've still got a few good seasons ahead if you'll only take care of yourself, Pete." . . . "Sid, the arm never felt better. You'll see a different man in spring training." . . . "I'm glad to hear you say it, Pete. Good luck now, and don't forget your promise." . . . "So long, Sid, and don't worry, I won't forget. Look—"

From under his mattress, Alex dug out a half-filled bottle.

"Before you go, Sid," he said, "how about us having a drink on that?"

No. Not all the old boy's days were days of glory. One remembers him barnstorming with a bearded team called the House of David nine, a sleazy little outfit touring the tank towns with portable flood-lights for night games. Old Pete was the only player without full whiskers, although he may have shown up to pitch with a bit of stubble on the jaw if he'd had a bad night. The press agent insisted there was a special clause in his contract allowing him thirty-five cents a day extra for shaves.

There was a time when he made his living as a freak in a flea circus. There were the days he depended for his bed and meals on an old friend who ran a combination saloon and hotel in southern Illinois.

At the end he was getting a pension. From baseball? Not exactly, although he thought so because the checks came through the National League office. He never knew it, his former wife said, but the money came from Sam Breadon. Sam is dead, too. When he was alive they called him Singing Sam, the Cut-Rate Man.

HERBERT J. PENNOCK

FROM THE moment Bob Carpenter became president of the Phillies—which was the day Bob's father bought the club from Bill Cox, who was out in the alley where Judge Landis had dropped him on his shell-pink ear—it was a foregone conclusion that Herb Pennock would run the organization.

Young Bob, living in the country behind Wilmington, Delaware, had been a friend and neighbor of Herb's as long as he could remember. More than that, the kid had always been plumb whacky about sports, and among all his personal heroes the greatest was this slender squire of Kennett Square, Pennsylvania. In his early teens Bob went along with Herb on a Yankee road trip. It isn't difficult to imagine what that meant to a boy, traveling under the wing of the great pitcher with the likes of Babe Ruth and Lou Gehrig and Tony Lazzeri and Joe McCarthy.

Later on, as Bob grew up, he and Herb rode to the hounds together until, a comparatively few years ago, Herb decided the proper mount for a guy rising fifty years of age was the cushioned seat of a car following the hunt. But the two friends continued to see a good deal of each other, and when Carpenter got the club it was just a question of how soon Herb could get his release from the Red Sox organization before he would move in as general manager of the Phillies.

The business association wasn't very old when Carpenter had to go see a man about a war, leaving Pennock to run the club alone. Herb used actually to shudder and his sharp features would go pink when he contemplated the sort of ball clubs he had to put on the field during the war. Just watching them was torture to a guy who'd pitched in front of Connie Mack's "$100,000 infield" in 1914 and had shared the World Series fame of Ruth and Gehrig and Meusel and Hoyt and Bush and Lazzeri and Koenig and Dugan with the Yankees.

But even then Herb was laying the foundations of a farm system, building toward the future. Since the war the Phillies have shown a flash or two of promise. There was hope that this year, maybe, the farms would begin to pay some small dividends in playing talent. Herb was high on a young pitcher named Curt Simmons, whom he called "another Waddell." Now, he and Carpenter figured, they were just about ready to get going.

And now Herb is dead. He died suddenly on a visit to New York for a National League meeting. He would have been fifty-four on February 10.

Perhaps it is a banal thing to say that a man was just about as gracious and charming and decent a person as ever lived. The obituaries never say that, so maybe it isn't the sort of line to put in a newspaper. But nothing else could be said of Herb Pennock that would be so true.

He must always have been the same. He broke into baseball when it was still more or less a game for roughnecks, a rather rowdy sport for a kid with his background. He was still a high school student when Connie Mack heard about a promising left-hander who was pitching for the Kennett Square town team and arranged for an offer from Ed Bader, former mayor of Atlantic City, who had a semipro club called the Atlantic City Collegians.

The offer of $100 a month and board sounded fabulous to the kid, but it disturbed his father. The elder Pennock wanted Herb to remain in school and go on to the University of Pennsylvania. Acceptance of the job, he pointed out, would professionalize him. But he made it clear he wouldn't stand in his son's way.

Years later Herb told how he wrestled with that decision. He sat on a dusty curb with his chum, Roy Freck—whose sister is Mrs. Pennock now—and they dreamed and talked and debated and dreamed again. At last Herb went home and told his father the answer had to be yes.

The rest of the story is in the record books, or most of it. With Connie's son, Earle Mack, as his catcher, Herb won a no-hit, no-run game, 1–0, for the Collegians, and then he was with the Athletics and then the Red Sox and then the Yankees and, finally, the Red Sox.

Twenty-two seasons in the American League. Eight times a World Series pitcher and never once defeated. In 1923 he gave the Yankees what they hadn't had in earlier championship battles with the Giants— a completely solid left-handed starter. In 1926 he battled little Bill Sherdel and whipped the Cardinals, 2–1, with a three-hitter.

In 1928 he became the first man ever to pitch two 3-hit World Series games when he smothered the Pirates, 8–1, for the third of New York's four straight victories. And in the last championship won by the Yankees of that era, 1932, it was Pennock on the mound at the finish of the fourth straight triumph over the Cubs.

Class showed in everything he did. It was in his manner, his speech, his courtesy, his very walk. And there was never anything to surpass his class on the mound. Connie Mack often had said the greatest single mistake he ever made was to let Herb go to Boston. Connie lost his temper with Herb one day; decided, he said afterward, that the guy had no ambition. Perhaps it was Pennock's style that created this impression, the exquisitely graceful ease with which he worked.

Anyhow, Connie sent him to the Red Sox and then, year after year, had to watch the guy win and win and win, still pitching exactly as he always had. In his fourteenth season, still working with that fluid grace, he won twenty-three ball games.

Herb was a grandfather when he died. His charming daughter, Jane, married Eddie Collins, Jr., son of Herb's old teammate. They will not grieve alone.

BART SWEENEY

THE IRISHMAN of tradition and fiction and belief is a merry lad and carefree, hot-tempered and humorous, quarrelsome and poetic, moody and mercurial and impetuous and irresponsible. "For the great Gaels of Ireland," Mr. Chesterton wrote, "are the men that God made mad, for all their wars are merry, and all their songs are sad."

Bart Sweeney was a Gael out of Tipperary. He was a quiet, courteous, reserved gentleman, slightly above the average in height, stoutly built as an oak is stout, graying more than a trifle. All the poets notwithstanding, the qualities that distinguished this Irishman were unwavering faithfulness, meticulous attention to detail, utter and absolute reliability.

In the thirty years from the day he got off the boat until he died of a heart attack in Miami, he had one employer and one job. If he had a title, nobody ever mentioned it. He was the right hand of James E. Fitzsimmons, the great horse trainer.

"He was the man," said young Jim Fitzsimmons, Mr. Fitz's grandson, "whom you gave the job that had to be done at 2:10 P.M. or A.M., knowing it would get done at 2:10, plus or minus no seconds."

Over the years there has been a succession of young Irishmen who, wanting nothing but to work with horses, shipped out of the homeland and went directly to Mr. Fitz for jobs. Joe Donelan is one of them, and Tommy Wynn, and Tommy Quinn, who gallops Bold Ruler.

Bart Sweeney was one. He was met at the dock by a man named Dick Goff—in 1927, according to the best recollection around the barn —and he went to work that same day as a stablehand.

Mr. Fitz had been training for William Woodward's Belair Stud since 1924, and in 1926 had taken on the horses of the Wheatley

Stable, formed that year by Mrs. Henry C. Phipps and her brother, the late Ogden Mills. There were some fine horses in the barn—Distraction, Diavolo, Swizzle Stick, the unbeaten Dice. Bart mucked out stalls and rubbed the lesser members of the string.

He was still a groom in 1930, but now he was rubbing Gallant Fox, and when Gallant Fox shipped to the Kentucky Derby to win the second of the three races that brought him the Triple Crown—he had already won the Preakness—Bart went along.

That was the year Mr. Fitz couldn't get through the crowd to the winner's circle, but he didn't have to worry about the horse. Bart would be there with a hand on the bridle, not posing for pictures, just taking care of the horse.

After 1935 and Omaha, Bart would have been called a junior foreman if he'd been known by any title. From 1940 on—that would be after Johnstown—he was The Man. He was never stable foreman officially; he was simply the man who took care of things. In effect, he was the out-of-town trainer, too, though they never called him that.

When a horse shipped out of Chicago or Kentucky or Florida for a race, Mr. Fitz didn't always go along, but Bart always did, riding in the horse car or van, right up to and including this year. For a big race out of New York, Mr. Fitz's son, John, went to supervise the overall operation; Bart went to take care of the horse.

Once Bart had a sort of vacation. In 1936 William Woodward sent Omaha to England for four races—he won two and was beaten a head and a neck. You wouldn't expect that the Irish groom would have a great deal in common with the millionaire banker and president of the Jockey Club, but Belair's owner wanted to do something for Sweeney. So, Bart took the horse across and, afterward, had time to visit his Tipperary home.

If Bart had one favorite among the horses, he never mentioned it. He may have had a special affection for Gallant Fox, the first big one that was "his horse." There were so many, though—Granville and Dark Secret and Melodist and Apache and Nashua and Misty Morn and Misty Flight.

Trainers will tell you that it's easy to handle cheap horses; it's the good ones that cost you sleep. Mr. Fitz didn't seem to worry especially when he had Nashua standing in his barn, a million dollars on the hoof. Bart Sweeney was in charge.

Bart was ailing last winter in Florida. He did a hitch in the hospital, but he was too nervous away from the horses to rest satisfactorily. He went back to work. This fall he took Bold Ruler down to Garden State for the big race with Gallant Man and Round Table, then took Misty Flight to Baltimore for the Pimlico Special, then took seventeen or so to Florida. The last one he had in charge was Bold Ruler, the Horse of the Year.

CASWELL ADAMS

WHEN CASWELL ADAMS was going around and about he had a running gag that might have seemed macabre to a stranger unfamiliar with his flair for impudent nonsense, though when Cas was in the company it was odds-on nobody would remain a stranger very long. The gag grew out of Cas's habit of poking fun at his own physical appearance; he was so thin as to be almost spectral.

Every day when he awoke out home in Port Washington, Long Island, Cas used to say, he called for the morning paper and read the obituary page. If his name wasn't on it, he got up and shaved.

One certainty offers a little comfort now to hearts made heavy by his death; nobody ever got more fun out of life than Cas Adams. At least, his friends are telling themselves, he enjoyed every moment of this hassle and, although he was only fifty when he died, he would have been the last to feel that he was being short-changed.

Cas may not have been the most widely known sportswriter in America since Grantland Rice, but certainly there was none with more and warmer friends in more widely varied fields—actors and authors and artists and businessmen, bartenders and doormen and hack drivers and waiters, lawyers and cops and politicians and the pro in the men's room, and maybe even a banker or so, though as a rule bankers aren't gaited like Cas.

Leaving the Waldorf one day, Cas and two friends found that a howling rainstorm had broken during lunch. Crowds huddled under the marquee, waiting vainly for taxis. At the curb was a big, black limousine with chauffeur.

"This'll do," Cas said, and led a three-man boarding party to the gaping astonishment of a little man in the rear seat. "Toots Shor's," Cas said to the driver, and to his involuntary host: "What's your name? Where you headed?"

"James C. Petrillo," the man said. "Got to make a train at Grand Central."

"Great. Shor's is practically on your way."

The boss of the musicians was one guy who hadn't known Cas Adams up to then, but he did before the car halted on Fifty-first Street.

In sports, of course, Cas knew everybody and everybody knew him, for although he tried his hand at a few other dodges like public relations, television and freelance writing, he was a sportswriter first and last, over a span of twenty-eight years. He started on the *New York Herald Tribune,* did a hitch with King Features, wrote boxing for the *New York Journal-American.*

The gift of laughter was with him always, in a crowd or at the typewriter. He delighted in deflating the self-important, yet it always came as a surprise to him when a needle that he had slipped deftly into some stuffed shirt's hide brought screams of indignation. He never consciously hurt anybody in his life, and when he was poking fun it was usually so gentle that the victim didn't realize he was being had.

At the time of Grace Kelly's wedding, a celebrated lady columnist devoted her column to a catalogue of the wardrobe she (the reporter) had assembled for the assignment in Monaco. On the day the piece ran Cas was going to Washington for a fight of no special distinction. His advance story on the match was a description of the attire he would be wearing at ringside—baggy tweeds, frayed shirt, brown shoes with rundown heels.

Amused readers waited for the lady to retaliate, but she never did.

Relations are generally cordial between sports figures and sportswriters, yet truly warm friendships are the exception, for a natural barrier exists between the public performer and the critic of his performance. After Cas's stroke, Archie Moore, the light-heavyweight champion, stopped over in New York en route from Europe to San Diego.

"I hear Cas is sick," Archie said to Al Buck. "What can I do?"

"Write a check," Al said, and Archie did on the spot.

Al tucked it away without reading it until he encountered Bob Kelley. "By the way," he said, "there's a contribution to the Cas Adams Fund."

The check was drawn for $1,000.

DEFENDER OF THE STRONG

BILL ALEXANDER was a gallant gentleman and an intractable fighter for the football player's inalienable right to sign checks with an X. If a good defensive tackle wished to carry a book under his arm when he strolled the campus, Bill did not offer serious objections, although he disliked ostentation. He was, however, unalterably opposed to eye-strain.

That, at least, was the attitude he delighted to take among his friends in coachly circles. Chances are that if the occasion demanded he could whip an audience into a froth with an honor-of-the-old-school oration, for he had a facile tongue and a nimble mind and a bald, bland face of almost outrageous innocence.

But when he relaxed he was a bundle of chuckling irreverence, an easy-going homespun philosopher poking fun at the character-building dodge with disarming good nature. He would drawl extravagant tales about an athlete whose thirst for knowledge kept him in college fighting valiantly for alma mater under a succession of aliases, until hardening of the arteries set in.

During his twenty-five years as coach at Georgia Tech, Bill developed a philosophical turn of mind virtually unparalleled in his profession. He actually learned not to worry.

In 1928, for example, when Georgia Tech was plowing through a season toward the Rose Bowl game that Roy Riegels transmuted into legend, Grantland Rice got to town a day or so before a vital game and asked Bill how his team was shaping up.

"Tell you the truth, Grant," Bill said, "I been so busy scratchin' up tickets for alumni, I haven't seen the team this week. Reckon they'll be all right, but I cain't honestly say."

Naturally, Georgia Tech won. That year Georgia Tech smashed nine scheduled opponents, including Notre Dame, and beat California in the Rose Bowl.

When Jim Thorpe, Joe Guyon and their bloodthirsty tribesmen finally finished at Carlisle, Bill was pleased to discover that Carlisle was, in the eyes of Georgia Tech, merely a preparatory school. It was a view not shared by the universities whose teams Thorpe had trampled, but Guyon was permitted to enroll as a freshman in Georgia Tech, and play there through another career.

Bill used to speak with admiration of the technique Guyon developed for blocking punts. Guyon would storm through the line and thrust a leg out stiffly, heel down, in front of the kicker. If the "stiff-leg" worked properly, the punter's foot never touched the ball: instead, his instep brought up with shattering impact against Joe's cleated heel.

The obituaries this week, reporting that Bill was only sixty years old, stirred a faint sense of surprise. Not that he looked any older, but one always thought of him as a link with football's golden past. His name was bracketed with the elder statesmen—Pop Warner, Tad Jones and Knute Rockne.

He was, in fact, the junior member of that great company—Rockne would be sixty-two today if he had lived. They were friends and sometimes rivals and they served together on many committees. In the '20s, when Jones was the greatest name in the East and Rockne in the Midwest and Warner on the Pacific Coast, Bill Alexander was top guy in the South.

Even after he retired as coach, he remained the most active of the group. Three winters ago when purity, like a worm in the bud, was making inroads into college football, Bill attended the National Collegiate Athletic Association convention here and engineered a joyous jape.

The N.C.A.A. was installing its celebrated chastity code at that meeting, and the holier-than-thous were tottering around under the weight of their halos, dropping pointed remarks about the sanitation conditions in Southern schools. Bill picked a morning session which he knew would be poorly attended, and packed it with Southerners.

Then when everybody save the conspirators was napping, Colonel William Couper, of Virginia Military Institute, dropped in a casual motion to outlaw all postseason games.

There was a chorus of inattentive "ayes" and the motion was carried. For the next few minutes, panicky puritans from the Midwest and

Pacific Coast scoured through the corridors recruiting reinforcements. Rules of parliamentary order were flung out the window, the motion was dragged up for reconsideration, and tabled.

Bill Alexander just sat there and chuckled. He'd always had fun with the puritans. Years ago there had been thought of establishing rules in the South that would permit the trapping of athletes within a college's normal territory but would not, a man explained to Bill, let a coach travel, say, fifteen hundred miles to ensnare a rookie.

"You're crazy," Bill said, "some of the best players are more than fifteen hundred miles from Atlanta."

MAX BAER

THERE IS a handsome book almost thirty years old now called *The American Sporting Scene* with illustrations by Joseph W. Colinkin and text by John Kieran. One full-page drawing shows a grotesquely muscled gladiator, instantly recognizable as Primo Carnera, hung by the middle over the second strand of rope, his head and upper torso outside the ring.

Right behind him stands the man who has done this mischief. His feet are planted wide apart, his weight on the right leg. Both hands are low and the closed right glove is out here, wide of the hip and a trifle behind it, ready—if that sprawling galoot gets up—to whistle around in a sweeping arc with every ounce of its owner's weight and strength behind it. You can cover three-fourths of the picture, concealing everything but that right shoulder, arm and glove, and there is no mistaking identities.

This has to be Max Baer winding up that old Mary Ann which no other fighter of any time could throw with quite the same gaudy and destructive and altogether unforgettable flourish.

When the news came that Max had died suddenly, the book was taken off its shelf and opened to this page. It was good to see Max Baer again at twenty-five, crackling with health, winding up to pitch the high hard one in from deep center field.

Max was on television refereeing a Zora Folley fight recently and he looked a little paunchy, though this may have been due to the cut of his working clothes or the tricks the camera sometimes plays. Certainly he looked great in San Francisco when Gene Fullmer fought Carmen Basilio there. Handsomely groomed as always, flat-waisted at fifty, straining the padded shoulders of his elegantly tailored jacket, he was full of bounce and full of a practiced patter about a heavyweight named "Johnson" who had recently won the championship from "Peterson" who had previously defended against an amateur named "Rutabaga."

When he died the papers told how he had won the world championship from Carnera June 14, 1934, clowned through exhibitions for a year and lost to Jim Braddock in his only title defense. Some papers described the wild and gory spectacle with Carnera, who was smashed down twelve times before Arthur Donovan stopped it in the eleventh round, and some told of his post-Braddock match with Joe Louis, when Max took the count on one knee in the fourth round.

He was savaged as a quitter after the Louis bout and he never denied that he could have gotten up, merely remarking that "if they want to see the execution of Max Baer it'll cost them more than twenty-five dollars a seat." To the best of my knowledge he never offered further explanation, but yesterday a man telephoned with a story which, if true, puts that incident in a new light.

The man had heard the tale years ago from Bayard Bookman, who was accountant for Max and his manager, Ancil Hoffman, and was in the dressing room on the night of the fight. It goes this way:

Max broke his right hand in training camp, but the injury was kept secret and the hand dosed with Novocaine to protect the million-dollar gate. This is neither incredible nor unprecedented; other fighters have concealed injuries for far less money.

There was a threat of rain on the evening of September 24, 1935, and the fighters were sent to Yankee Stadium early to be ready in case the main event went on ahead of schedule, which sometimes happened in pretelevision days.

Actually, the bout didn't start until ten o'clock, but the fighters dressed and had their hands bandaged well ahead of time, too early to use Novocaine beforehand, for the effects would have worn off. During the bandaging, of course, there was a watcher from Louis's corner in Max's room and he remained until fight time. As the hour neared, Max and the doctor slipped into the men's room where the doctor inserted the needle beneath the bandages.

Apparently the needle went in up near the wrist. At any rate, instead of merely numbing the hand, it deadened the whole right forearm. Within ten minutes Max was a frantic wreck, not far short of collapse. His friend Jack Dempsey almost literally had to drag him out for the fight.

"I knew Bayard Bookman well," said the man on the phone, "and there was no point in making up a story for me. If it was the truth, I can imagine what Max went through, and I saw the fight. Max had the intelligence and imagination to know what Louis could do to him, and here he was going in with his main weapon—the only weapon, actually —useless.

"Afterward they called him a coward, but I've always wondered."

FREDERICK C. MILLER

FREDDY MILLER, "the world's most honored football coach," was perhaps the most persistently enthusiastic sports fan in Wisconsin, and a sure touch for almost any athletic enterprise that needed financial backing.

Fred was designated "honorary coach" of the Notre Dame football team and held the same title with the Green Bay Packers of the National Football League. It's an unusual title, but then his position was a bit unusual, too. If Notre Dame got licked, no wealthy alumni were going to holler for Fred's job; he was a wealthy alumnus, himself. If the Packers fell upon hard times, he was the first to go into his pocket to help bail them out. Coaches like this are difficult to come by.

Actually he did little coaching. His connection with the Packers was financial rather than athletic; when they needed money he bought stock—nonredeemable, non-interest-bearing and innocent of dividends —to help them out. He was the Milwaukee Braves' radio sponsor and whenever a new rumor was circulated to the effect that Lou Perini was going to sell the club, Fred Miller was mentioned as the buyer. Chances are he was ready to buy at any opportunity.

Fred played tackle at Notre Dame in 1926, 1927 and 1928, and was team captain in his last season, when the late Walter Eckersall gave him honorable mention in his All-Star selection. He was rough and reliable and rich, but only the first two attributes were noticeable.

After graduation he returned to the campus in the autumn, often helping out as an unsalaried instructor in line play. Friends ribbing him about his "honorary" status used to call him assistant coach-in-charge-of-flying Frank Leahy to out-of-town games. He didn't mind. One never got the idea that he was interested in titles.

Chances are nobody will ever know how many individuals received help of one sort or another from Freddy Miller, or how many acts of kindness and generosity he performed for kids at Notre Dame, especially. Where there were debts of gratitude, he did not keep books.

The plane crash that killed him was not his first. He was aloft a good deal of the time, as pilot or passenger, on business or pleasure, and not every landing was smooth. He told of one adventure that made an impression on his hearers not so much because it could have been disastrous, but more because of his matter-of-fact tone.

It happened during one of those years when he was a volunteer member of Frank Leahy's staff. Business called him home one weekend and he invited two or three members of the football squad, who lived in Milwaukee, to ride along for a visit.

Weather closed down on them as they flew across Lake Michigan, and when they neared the Wisconsin shore Fred realized he'd have to turn back. Night and a violent storm caught them on the return trip.

"I shut off the radio for fear it would attract lightning," Fred said, "and we went bucking along in the dark with nothing to guide us. The ship was pitching and bouncing. All I could do was grip the wheel, try to hold her level, and hope we could ride out the storm.

"After a while I figured we must be over land again—Indiana, I hoped—and I told the kids to watch for some landmark like the lighted dome of the administration building at Notre Dame."

The kids were praying. Fred was fighting the wheel and fuel was running low. With the gas virtually exhausted and only darkness below, he took a chance. They came down in a plowed field some miles south of South Bend, hit hard, bounced once and stopped. They walked out of the wrecked plane, unscratched.

"Next day," said Fred, "I went out and measured the distance we'd bounced. Then I got to thinking what I might have done to the team. Those were good players I had up there in the dark."

They were, too. One of them was a halfback named Terence Patrick Brennan. He lived to do some coaching.

BABY DOLL

THE PLACE is Checotah, Oklahoma, on the Katy line between Muskogee and McAlester. It is a town of about 2,700 and it looks like every other town of that size in that country—flat, dusty, hot; a few shabby business blocks flanking the patched pavement of the main street; paint peeling under a merciless sun.

On the sunburned lawn in front of the Odd Fellows' Hall, four or five cowboys stand in earnest conversation. They have negotiated a perpetual lease on a plot of this brown turf, big enough for a memorial to a horse named Baby Doll, a blocky little bay mare with a white stripe down her face.

Now they are arguing about the form the memorial should take. Some favor a plain tablet with a bronze plaque. Several want "art work," a statue by a good horse sculptor. The cost? None of these men ever has a spare dollar, but—

"Willard," says Jim Painter, a great big young guy out of McAlester, "how much do you say she win in her life?"

Willard Combs is a big man, too, a professional rodeo hand who has been bulldogging for twenty years, has a ranch near Checotah that is unofficial headquarters for steer wrestlers. There is no sentiment in his face. "In her life?" he says. "Just shy a half a million dollars."

"Well," says Billy Hale, "that's it about the cost, ain't it?"

Man O' War, maybe the greatest and certainly the most famous American thoroughbred, raced two years and earned $249,465. Exterminator won a quarter million in eight years. Racing was four hundred years old before Seabiscuit became the first horse in the world to win as much as $400,000.

Seabiscuit raced for and won purses as great as the Santa Anita Handicap's $100,000. Baby Doll made hers carrying steer wrestlers

four or five times a night, year after year, in rodeo arenas in Dead-
wood and Colorado Springs, Vinita and Chickasha, Casper and Nampa
and Abilene. She was still working an hour before she died.

It was in Salina, Kansas, on August 31. Combs, Painter and Hale all
rode her that night, and two of them won money off her. Her owner
was the last to get off her back. ("I guess she was in real bad misery
then. I didn't know when I ran my last steer. I'm sure she was.")

Combs led her back to the trailer, noticed she was breathing hard,
and called a vet. She stood on her feet until three minutes before she
died of a ruptured intestine. When she lay down, Combs took her
head in his lap and bawled.

There was never a rodeo horse like Baby Doll. In bulldogging, the
horse is all-important. The steer comes out of a chute and is given
a head start on the dogger, whose "hazer" rides to the steer's right to
keep him on a straight line. The dogger rides hell-bent to overtake
the steer from the left, slides his right hand along the bull's neck until
he grips the right horn, then drops off the horse and flops the steer on
its left side.

The drop from the horse is the secret. As the rider starts down,
his mount must pass the steer and veer away from it, whipping the
dogger's legs out to the left. If the horse doesn't know exactly how
and when to "widen," the dogger's legs flop behind and the steer
just drags him along.

Combs had been bull-dogging for years, doing nothing outstanding
until he bought Baby Doll in 1952 for $3,200, having used her on
lease that season. In 1955 Willard won $13,042 off her, losing the na-
tional championship to his brother Benny by $700. He also mounted
other cowboys, and Baby Doll's earnings for the year were $56,000.

When another dogger rides your horse, you get an eighth of his
winnings; if you also haze for the cowboy, you get one-quarter.
Combs would have put Big Daddy Lipscomb or Kate Smith on Baby
Doll if there was prize money to be had. "So many things can happen
to a horse," he said, "you might as well keep going while you can."

Baby Doll taught cowboys how it was done. Big Jim Painter
started on her as a pro, won $9,270 in his first year and up to the night
she died he had won $10,740 off her back this year for second place
in the race for national honors.

In 1959 Billy Hale, a high school track and basketball star in
Colorado Springs, went to Checotah to study steer-wrestling under
Combs and Baby Doll. She and Billy had won $6,730 for the year when
she died.

One night in McAlester she all but tore a foot off. "She caught the steer just as good with her foot crippled and bleeding as she would if it wasn't," Jim Painter said, "and she won all four holes in the average (the first four places). Willard win it and I was second and Billy Hale win a third and Bill Murray fourth."

Baby Doll got in foal a couple of years ago, said Lex Connelly. "They used her at Tulsa the first week in May, took her home: she had her foal in the third week in May and they won the first go-round at Fort Smith on her three or four days later."

WILLIAM TATEM TILDEN II

IN WASHINGTON, thirty-eight of sports's finest had luncheon with President Eisenhower. Rocky Marciano was there, and Joe DiMaggio and Helen Hull Jacobs and Lefty Grove and Jack Scarbath and Bill Dudley and Tris Speaker and Gene Sarazen.

Three thousand miles away on the Pacific Coast, a man who should have been there died in his Hollywood apartment. Bill Tilden, who lived among the crowds, died alone. So it ends, the tale of the gifted, flamboyant, combative, melodramatic, gracious, swaggering, unfortunate man whose name must always be a symbol of the most colorful period American sports have known.

Bill Tilden was a tennis player, maybe the best ever born. He would have been great in any age; he lived in the age that was exactly right for him. He was one of the company of giants whose personalities transcended their own narrow fields and left an indelible mark on their time—Babe Ruth and Red Grange, Ty Cobb and Bobby Jones, Tommy Hitchcock and Walter Hagen, Gene Sarazen and Man O' War, Jack Dempsey and Earl Sande, and Bill Tilden.

There never was another troupe like this riot squad of the roistering '20s. We shall not see its like again.

Bill Tilden turned professional with three Wimbledon singles and one doubles championship, seven United States singles, five doubles and four mixed-doubles titles, seventeen singles and four doubles victories in eleven challenge rounds for the Davis Cup.

When he was done, only three men lived to say, "I beat the guy in the National finals." They were René Lacoste, Little Bill Johnston and R. Lindley Murray, who did it in 1918 when Tilden was a kid fresh out of Germantown Academy in Philadelphia.

Later Johnston would come off the court gasping with weariness: "I just can't beat that big bum."

Later still, Vincent Richards would meet Francis Albertanti, the little sports editor turned publicist, and Francis, beaming, would pump his hand. "It's nice to know you. You remind me of a headline we always kept set in type in our composing room."

"What was that?"

"TILDEN BEATS RICHARDS AGAIN."

It wasn't merely that Big Bill could play better than anybody else: he could put on an infinitely better show. In a time that probably provided more top-class competition than any other—there were Johnston and Richards and Murray and Norris Williams and Francis T. Hunter and Cochet, Lacoste and Borotra—they used to say Bill was simply too good. They said he deliberately let down at times, teasing his adversaries until the moment he saw fit to destroy them.

Certainly that seemed to be the case in the opening match of the Davis Cup Challenge Round at Forest Hills in 1921. For the first and only time, Japan got into the act, sending two tireless little guys in round Panama hats to claim the cup that Tilden and Johnston had brought from Auckland the year before.

Ichiya Kumagae sat peering through steel-rimmed spectacles watching his comrade, Zenzo Shimizu, go scampering off with the first two sets, 7–5, 6–4. The hustling little invader led in the third set, too. He was two strokes away from match point.

Then it started—the cannonball service, the forehand chops, the paralyzing backhand slices. There are still men around who will tell you there's never been anything like that, before or since. Tilden took the third set, 7–5, the fourth 6–2, the last 6–1. Thereafter, Japan won one set from Johnston and one in the doubles.

There was an air of grandeur about Tilden on the court, which he made no special effort to dispel. In the warm-up before a match, he moved with leisurely majesty. He would slam a couple of serves across, volley a few, and permit himself a just perceptible sigh.

"I'm ready when you're exhausted, partner," he would announce.

In his eldering days as a pro, when he could still play one set as well as any man alive and talk a better match than all of them put together, he was discussing Frank Kovacs, who was then clowning through the matches in a fashion that amused some and offended others.

"Trouble with Frankie," he said, "is his timing. He doesn't know when to play tennis and when to play the bloody fool."

"He should take lessons," it was suggested, "from you." Mr. Tilden nodded benignly.

JOHN LARDNER

ST. PETERSBURG, FLORIDA. It was the eve of the great grease festival at Sebring. There had been a barbecue out in the bush and now, during the drive back, the eleven o'clock news came in on the car radio. "Names in the news," an impersonal voice said. "John Lardner, the sportswriter—"

Those in the car froze. Two days earlier Sterling Bottome, managing director of the Vinoy Park Hotel in St. Pete, had received a phone call from Walt Kelly, Pogo's father, and John Lardner's great friend. Walt and John had reservations at the Vinoy but couldn't make it because John had suffered a heart attack, not his first.

"—died in New York of a heart attack," the voice went on. "He was forty-seven." The radio was snapped off.

Whenever a man of prominence dies, his associates make statements for the papers describing his death as a loss. A loss to the nation, a loss to art, a loss to the bagel industry. This is a loss to the living, to everyone with a feeling for written English handled with respect and taste and grace, a tragic loss to the world of laughter, an irredeemable loss to the friends who loved John Lardner and will miss him as long as they live.

Contemporary literature is left immeasurably poorer—especially the literature of sports, but also that of the theater and television and all the other fields his gift enriched—for there is nowhere now a talent like John's. He was wonderfully funny but ahead of that he was informed on a range of subjects from left hooks to Australian rhyming slang to popular music to the rules for an unfriendly game of craps. He was the finest of reporters and the most meticulous and thorough of researchers.

The true humorist has a mind that functions differently from most and eyes that see past the horizon to discover wondrous things. Thus

John, the one true humorist of his time on the sports beat, watched dreamily through two fights between Ezzard Charles and J. J. Walcott.

In the first, an inconsequential rigadoon for the heavyweight championship which Joe Louis had relinquished, Charles won on points and when the decision was announced his manager, Jake Mintz, swooned in the ring. Later, in Pittsburgh, Walcott fetched Charles a swat in the chops and Ezzard swooned, but Jake remained upright.

"This," John wrote thoughtfully, "is my idea of the perfect partnership—always one man on his feet to count the house."

John had a connoisseur's appreciation of the larcenous guile of his old friend, the bald and crafty and bat-eared Dr. Jack Kearns. Writing of Archie Moore's first match with Yvon Durelle, John described how Dr. Kearns, after seeing Durelle flatten his man three times in the first round, hastened up the steps to Archie's corner, "his ears flapping intelligently."

Ring Lardner was a lugubrious wit, taciturn and mournful. His son inherited the economy of speech but he was convivial in a monosyllabic way. His eyes were merry behind owlish glasses, he had a small, sweet smile, and when he spoke it was usually a quip, sometimes wry, always penetrating, often pointed but almost never barbed.

I think the only people he disliked were the self-important and the bad writers. He considered bad writing a hanging offense.

We were never close, as John was close to Walt Kelly and Mitch Rawson and Morrie Werner and Hugh Beach and Dick Maney and Leo Corcoran and some others, but I never encountered him without a thrill of pleasure and I rejoiced in his company. Profited by it, too.

A few years ago, for instance, Bill Heinz discovered a small but dauntless English eater, Harold Mayes, of the London sporting press, and sought to eat him against Herman Hickman in an international match. John was frankly skeptical but set the project into motion with a column in *Newsweek*. Bill Heinz was Mayes's manager, John was chairman of the New York State Eating Commission and I was the promoter, which probably explains why the promotion fell through. Still, it kept us supplied with columns through a hard winter.

Being Ring Lardner's son must have been a burden for a young guy starting to write sports. Readers who still idolize his father took a stiff view of a kid trying to write funny like his old man. Their resistance melted fast.

John really was funny, but not like his old man. He wasn't funny like anybody else. He was funny like John Lardner, a bona fide original. There is dreadfully little laughter in this world, at best, and now a great big irreplaceable lot of it has been lost.

BOXING'S ELDER STATESMAN

EVEN WHEN the man was seventy years old they still called him the Boy Bandit, which was a form of compliment by the reverse English standards of the profession he dignified, because in the fistfight dodge a talent for banditry is considered stock equipment but youth is a coveted attribute. When the fight mob applied the nickname to James Joy Johnston they used it in envious tribute to a man who not only could be as bold and guileful a brigand as the best of them but could also remain, at heart, younger than the youngest.

Actually, Jimmy Johnston died before the title he preferred for himself won public acceptance. He would have liked to be known as "boxing's elder statesman," which was the role in which he really fancied himself. It was a well-earned title, too, for there never was another ambassador who could carry the cauliflower gospel into such unlikely quarters with such unfailing grace as he. It was his pride and his delight that he could appear before the Browning and Fancy Needlework Guild of Mount Vernon, whose members obviously expected to see a man in a turtleneck sweater and checkered cap, and charm the bridgework out of their mouths.

He affected a cynical attitude ("Legitimate business," he said, "is a figure of speech"), and it was said that he was unhappy in his last days because nobody hated him any longer. But as a matter of fact he was always at his best among friends, and the fight mob never has known such amiably social salons as he used to conduct in Charlie's Restaurant.

That was the feedbox in the Madison Square Garden Building where Jimmy held a tea party every afternoon at four o'clock when he was the Garden promoter, gathering the mob about him and spinning yarns hour upon hour. It was the greatest school for young fight writers this town ever knew, and some who attended it for three or four years hand running will swear Jimmy never had to repeat a story.

One of the tales concerned a day in his old office in what is now the Paramount Building, where there materialized in the doorway a tremendous hunk of man who said he wanted to be a fighter.

"How did you get up here?" James demanded.

"By the elevator."

"That," snapped Mr. Johnston, "is a good way to get out."

"Which was a good enough retort," Jimmy related years later, "except that when I next saw the young man he was Jess Willard, heavyweight champion of the world."

This wasn't, of course, the only mistake he ever made. He used to tell of another time when he and Charley Harvey were partners and decided to import a phenomenal English boxer named Jem Driscoll. He and Harvey met the ship on which Driscoll was to arrive and scanned the debarking crowd without finding anyone who looked like the fighter. They were about to depart when a snaggle-toothed stranger with hideously cauliflowered ears introduced himself as Driscoll.

Knowing Driscoll's reputation as a defensive genius, Jimmy instantly tabbed this damaged derelict as an imposter. A reformed boxer himself, Jimmy took him to a gym and set out to expose the imposter by getting into the ring with the newcomer.

"I let go with one punch," Jimmy used to recall, "and landed outside the ropes. I put two or three pros in with the guy, and they haven't touched him yet. It turned out he had such wonderful reflexes he could dodge a punch by a sixteenth of an inch, and that's how he got his ears torn up."

Generally speaking, Jimmy didn't talk up the good fighters he handled, knowing their performances would speak for him. He was at his best building up a Phil Scott or some other essentially peaceable citizen, and he was unrivaled in the art of transmuting a knock into a boost. Thus when his Bob Pastor ran away from Joe Louis, Jimmy boomed him from coast to coast as "Rapid Robert" and "Bicycle Bob."

A personal recollection concerns a night in Hollywood when Pastor appeared with one Turkey Thompson. There were either seven or nine knockdowns, although not that many punches, and once Pastor was floored by a left jab. This is a difficult feat in any circumstances, and even more so when you're in with a man who can't throw a left jab. After Pastor won, Jimmy was asked to explain how this knockdown came to pass.

"I was hollering at my Robert to stay down and take the full nine count," came the unhesitating answer, "and he misunderstood me to say 'fall down.' My Robert is very obedient."

Jimmy knew for years that his heart was unsound. His physician pleaded with him not to work in Pastor's corner in the second Louis fight in Detroit, and when Jimmy insisted, the doctor compromised by giving him a bottle of pills for use if the ticker misbehaved.

It was a perilously exciting bout, with Pastor down several times in the first round, then coming on to belabor Louis stoutly in the eighth or ninth and finally succumbing in the eleventh. Jimmy had to feed the whole bottle of pills to the doctor.

THE ONLY RUNYON

THE WAITER in Shor's said, "That's bad news in your business, eh? About Mr. Runyon?" That was how the word came. It wasn't unexpected, of course, because everyone knew how sick the guy was and only a little earlier in the evening there'd been a question asked as to how he was doing and somebody had said, "He's at the top of the stretch." Which, by the way, the guy himself wouldn't have deemed a proper answer because he was a reporter who believed in getting the score right, and the fact was he was at the seventy-yard pole.

To say Damon Runyon's death is a loss to his craft would be like saying breathing under water is inconvenient. Perhaps it should not be said there'll never be another like him. There just never has been up to now.

Runyon could do things with the alphabet that made a fellow want to throw his typewriter away and go dig coal for a living. He was one of the few men of our time with genuinely original ideas about what words were for. He created a new language and enough characters to people a fair-sized town. He could take an essentially dull person like Mr. Frisco Legs of Philadelphia and make him a man of distinction by putting him into a story. (The belief here is that Runyon coined the appellation "America's Guest" to identify Mr. Legs, although it has been borrowed a good many times and applied to a good many others.)

Not many people could write more agile light verse than Runyon. His sports column was as good as a sports column can be. There ought to be a special library for his fiction because there isn't any other fiction quite like it, even though he took an ancient formula and adhered to it rigidly. His collaboration with Howard Lindsay, *A Slight Case of Murder*, became, in this book, the funniest movie ever made.

But above all, he was a reporter. Perhaps the world at large will remember him longest for his short stories, but the men in his own business will remember the job he could do on a news assignment, whether it was a heavyweight championship or a political convention or a trial of Al Capone or an appearance of J. Pierpont Morgan, with or without midget attached, before a Senate committee. (One of those Morgan pieces, written in the days when everyone was playing the market, sketched an unforgettable picture of the lawyers hanging breathlessly on the financier's words in the hope that he'd drop a tip.)

It has been said that Runyon was one guy in this business who never wrote an indifferent story. It isn't possible to go along with that all the way. There was a period after he moved out of sports when his fiction and film work didn't leave him time enough to do legwork, and many of the columns he wrote then were ordinary. Now and then he'd do a tenderly nostalgic piece, redolent of lavender and old lace, about the dear, dead days when mobsters were taking one-way rides. But he wasn't getting around enough to keep his comments on current affairs fresh.

So he came back to reporting. Although he knew he was dying, the column he was writing up to his last illness was just the best column-about-town ever done anywhere. That's one man's opinion.

The obituaries listed some of the fictional characters he created but didn't mention the stockpiles of standard writing goods he left on the sports shelves. There was a time when most of the top guys in sports were identified automatically by names Runyon gave them—the Manassa Mauler, the Wild Bull of the Pampas, the Beezark of the Basque.

Books could be written in an effort to isolate the qualities that made Runyon's stuff so superbly and inimitably Runyonesque—and it remained inimitable in spite of the fact that no other newspaper man had so many imitators—but the books wouldn't do the job half so well as a paragraph of his own.

One remembers, for instance, a report of the deathbed advice an old gambler gave to his son. It went, more or less, like this:

"Son," the old man said, "as you go around and about this world, some day you will come upon a man who will lay down in front of you a new deck of cards with the seal unbroken and offer to bet he can make the jack of spades jump out of the deck and squirt cider in your ear."

"Son," said the old man, "do not bet him because just as sure as you do you are going to get an earful of cider."

It is laboring the point to insist that no matter how closely you imitate style, there will be something lacking because you can't duplicate the mind that made the style.

BERT BELL

AS THE train for the Jersey Shore pulled out of Philadelphia that Saturday evening, a passenger turned to the young stranger sharing his seat. "See the game today?" he asked. The young man nodded. "Isn't that Bell the lousiest thing you ever saw?" the other man said, and launched into a diatribe against the University of Pennsylvania, its faculty, its athletic policies, its football team and, above all, its 155-pound quarterback.

"That Bell," he said, "is a safety man that can't catch a punt! A punter that kicks backwards over his own head! You know why he's on the team, don't you? His old man's got all this dough and he's a trustee of the university and head of the athletic committee.

"If it wasn't for pull, that little bum couldn't buy his way into the park."

The young man held his peace, and a silent audience was all the speaker required. He was still talking, and still on the same topic, when the train reached his station.

"Enjoyed talking to you," he said, rising. "My name's So-and-So, what's yours?"

"Bert Bell," the young man said.

It was characteristic of de Benneville Bell that he told that story on himself, with laughter raucous in his ripsaw voice. A man of buoyant joviality, he had a rough and ready wit whose target was almost always himself. At the weekly football luncheons of the Maxwell Club in Philadelphia, which Bert served for many years as chairman and toastmaster, it was sally, parry, thrust and riposte all through the meetings, with the toastmaster making himself the butt of every joke.

That is why the tales that come most readily to mind are yarns of the same sort, the ones he enjoyed with special relish because they made him the patsy. This was neither affectation nor disguise. It was a real and endearing quality in a warm, endearing man, a man of laughter and genuine humility and an honesty clearly innocent of pretense or pretension.

As he had been for twenty-four hours a day over thirteen years, Bert was on the job as commissioner of the National Football League when he collapsed at Sunday's game between the Eagles and Pittsburgh Steelers in Philadelphia. "A great loss," said coaches and club owners throughout the league and they meant it, for every one of them knows it was Bert's tireless leadership that won for professional football the prestige and success it now enjoys.

They meant what they said and some meant much more than they could say, for some had known Bert in his roistering youth as a player at Penn, as a coach at Penn and Temple, as owner, president, coach, press agent, ticket-seller, gateman and janitor with the starveling Eagles before and during World War II, when he even solicited advertising for the program, scouted, recruited, signed and traded the players, all in exchange for abuse and financial loss.

There must be alumni of those old Eagles who wanted to cry when they heard the news, yet found themselves chuckling fondly as they recalled tales of the sort Bert enjoyed so much. Like the one about his heart-rending eloquence in Brooklyn. . . .

In those days, Brooklyn may have been the only town where it was possible to find a pro team as bad as the Eagles. Dreadful as he knew his team to be, Bert was confident of victory in Ebbets Field, and desperate when the first half ended with the Eagles trailing.

Addressing the players in the locker room, he strove for sweetly reasonable restraint. They all knew, he said, how much this game meant to him, and he had no doubt it was equally important to them, for this was their livelihood and they were honest men of honest pride. Many of them had wives and children dependent on them.

"I just want you men to ask yourselves how you would feel," he said, and now the husky organ tones were swelling, "how you would feel tonight if you went home and leaned over the crib, and that little fella lying there looked up and said: 'Daddy, did you lay down in Brooklyn?' "

The Eagles were big, strong men, but they collapsed. Weak with laughter, they tottered out for the second half and were slaughtered.

It was a while before Bert could laugh about that one, but that time arrived ultimately, as it always did. If he missed anything in his sixty-five years, it wasn't a chance for laughter.

Chances are he was laughing and enjoying himself when the bell rang for him. He was watching the Eagles, the team he had created with his own sweat and tears and money, playing his other team, the Steelers, which he operated with Art Rooney during the war. They were playing on Franklin Field, where forty years earlier a little Penn quarterback had played the game that was to become his life.

It was almost as though he were allowed to choose time and place.

THE O'MALLEY, PRO AND CON

WITH A cigar in one hand and a Scotch in the other, Walter O'Malley ambled about World Series headquarters in the basement of Brooklyn's Bossert Hotel, a suitably genial host. He stopped to exchange pleasantries with a pair of newspapermen, and as he moved on, one of them gazed after him. "Nice man," he remarked. His companion agreed with reservations. "Yes," he said, "a little too much the grand seigneur for my taste."

The second reporter had met O'Malley for the first time at the end of the 1951 season, the year the New York Giants closed a gap of 13½ games to finish in a first-place tie with Brooklyn. In fact, New York had taken a half-game lead by beating the Braves in Boston in the last game of the schedule, and the Dodgers had to go fourteen innings with the Phillies to get back on even terms. Jackie Robinson had saved that game with an implausible diving catch in the tenth inning and won it with a home run.

On the train from Philadelphia, the reporter had been introduced to O'Malley, Branch Rickey's successor as Dodger president. Walter was telling a story about seeing Robinson play before Rickey bought him from the Kansas City Monarchs. From that evening on, the reporter had reservations.

By 1951, O'Malley was not disposed to give Rickey credit for discovering Robinson, or for anything else. The two had become partners in 1944 when Rickey, president of the Dodgers, O'Malley, the club's attorney, and John L. Smith, head of the Charles Pfizer Chemical Company, had bought the 25 percent of the Dodger stock held by the estate of Ed McKeever. The next year the trio bought the 50 percent owned by the estate of Charles H. Ebbets, so each had 25 percent. With Rickey's contract as president expiring in October 1950, O'Malley and Smith let him know the contract would not be renewed. Not eager to become an unemployed minority stockholder in an organization that paid no dividends, Rickey wangled an offer of $1,050,000 from William Zeckendorf, the real estate tycoon, for his 25 percent. To keep control, O'Malley and Mrs. Smith—her husband had died— had to meet the price. Zeckendorf received $50,000 for his trouble, Rickey got his million and O'Malley's enduring hostility.

That may have been the only time O'Malley was outmaneuvered in a deal, for his financial acumen was legend. It was this talent that ultimately made him the most powerful figure in baseball, where no other quality is held in such reverence as the ability to make one and one equal three. His acuity is also the reason he has not been widely mourned in Brooklyn.

When other baseball men could see no farther west than the Mississippi River, O'Malley recognized the immense profit potential of a major league franchise in swiftly expanding Southern California. To realize the profit, he despoiled the most fertile baseball territory in the National League.

For half a century, major league baseball franchises were fixed and immovable. Though they were private commercial enterprises and some were profit-making, they had a quasipublic character, a strong sense of community identification. Then in the 1950s, the Boston Braves moved to Milwaukee, the St. Louis Browns to Baltimore and the Philadelphia Athletics to Kansas City. All were distressed properties seeking greener fields. In those same years, the Brooklyn Dodgers had the greatest net profit in baseball. No other team was more closely identified with its community, none had more passionately devoted fans and not even the Yankees made as much money.

Ebbets Field was old and inadequate. O'Malley wanted a new stadium at Atlantic and Flatbush avenues, the commercial hub of the borough. He was willing to pay a substantial share of the construction costs if he could get the land. He couldn't. Robert Moses, commissioner of parks, proposed Flushing Meadows as a site but O'Malley wasn't interested. At the same time that he negotiated with city and state officials in New York, he was talking with the city fathers of Los Angeles. By 1957 he had resolved to move West, but all he would say for publication was "I can only urge Brooklyn fans to continue to support the club as loyally as they have in the past."

So of course he did move and he persuaded Horace Stoneham, whose Giants were in straits in the Polo Grounds, to go to California with him. In many ways it was good for baseball. It opened vast new territory, tapping sources of income that had been ignored. It paved the way for the big leagues' expansion to the South, Southwest and Canada. It made many millions for O'Malley.

Though the Yankees now had the entire metropolitan territory to themselves, that was no windfall. They won a fourth straight championship in 1958, but their attendance declined in the first year of their monopoly. In 1957, not a great year for the Dodgers and a desperate one for the Giants, the three New York teams drew a total of 3,179,315 customers. In 1958 the Yankees drew 1,428,438. Almost two million fans had vanished.

In Brooklyn there was something approaching heartbreak. The inescapable fact was that O'Malley, making large profits in Brooklyn, took Brooklyn's team away to make even bigger profits. You didn't have to be a Dodger fan to be affected by the move. It had always been recognized that baseball was a business, but if you enjoyed the game you could tell yourself that it was also a sport. You quoted William Wrigley's dictum that baseball was too much a sport to be a business and too much a business to be a sport.

O'Malley was the first to say out loud that it was all business—a business that he owned and could operate as he chose, and the community the team had pretended to represent for almost seventy years had no voice in the matter at all. From that day on, some of the fun of baseball was lost.

O'Malley sweet-talked Los Angeles out of four hundred acres near the heart of town. He built the handsomest outdoor park in baseball, where he drew more than 2 million customers a year, getting parking revenue and the other concessions as well as box-office receipts. As the most successful operator in the game, he became the dominant power in the game, working mostly behind the scenes. Bowie Kuhn was regarded as his handpicked commissioner, and it was believed that his advice influenced many of the commissioner's decisions. When Oakland's Charlie Finley led a palace revolution that almost unseated Kuhn in 1975, O'Malley galloped to the rescue and won over the key votes that saved Bowie's job.

He built supremely well and contributed greatly to the game's financial health.

As long as he had his way he was an affable man, a social person who loved a drink, a smoke and a friendly poker game. He was devoted to his family. When his wife, Kay, died last month, he was under treatment for cancer in Rochester, Minnesota, and wasn't told right away. One can hope he wasn't told at all. Theirs was a life-long love affair.

HUTCHINSON NOW PITCHING

ONE NIGHT Carl Sawatski of the Cardinals beat the Reds with a home run in the ninth inning. Fred Hutchinson is a manager of few words. Head down, his shoulders hunched, he trudged into the clubhouse with the rolling gait that inspired his nickname, "Big Bear."

There he laid hold of a chair, and heaved it through a window. The window was closed, but it was a libel when they said that Hutch, as a pitcher with the Tigers, couldn't break a pane of glass on the best day he ever saw.

"The smile of Fred Hutchinson," wrote Jim Brosnan, the literate martini-shaker, "is a treasured one. His ballplayers vie hopefully for it. By playing well and winning they earn it. (Hutchinson snorts at plain luck.)

"Miserly with his laughter at all times, Hutchinson is miserable in defeat. The depth of his frown is in direct proportion to the length of his losing streak."

Yesterday there was a news photo of Hutch wearing a crooked grin. It was snapped while he told newsmen that he had cancer.

The news struck home with shocking impact and then two thoughts occurred. It was characteristic of this blunt, honest man that when he got word, he made the plain hard fact public, mincing no euphemisms. It was also typical that the announcement would be accompanied by one of his rare grins.

In his book, *The Long Season*, Brosnan quotes a conversation with a sportswriter. The pitcher says of his manager, "He makes his pitchers believe in his decisions. Probably the rest of the team thinks the same way. What the hell, you gotta think twice before arguing with him. They don't call him The Bear for nothing.

"Everyone who ever played with him calls him a nice guy, though."

"I wouldn't describe him as a nice guy myself. Which doesn't mean I don't like him. I've known managers I would call nice guys but I didn't even respect them, much less like them."

"Look at it this way," Brosnan says, "most ballplayers respect Hutch. In fact, many of them admire him, which is even better than liking him. He seems to have a tremendous inner power that a player can sense."

Four days later the Reds were leading the Dodgers by six runs in the ninth inning. With the bases filled Brosnan walked Junior Gilliam, forcing in a run.

"Hutchinson stormed out of the dugout. I didn't wait for him to chew me out. Tossing the ball at him as we crossed paths, I headed for the clubhouse. But he got to me with a contemptuous snarl. 'That was the worst exhibition I ever saw!'"

When the season ended, Brosnan and his manager said so long. "He looked up from the trunk into which he had packed his equipment, shoved a huge bear paw at me and said, 'Good luck. You did a good job for me. Have a good winter.' And he almost smiled."

This is a man, this Bear. When Detroit bought him from Seattle, the word on the Pacific Coast was that he didn't have what it took, even though he had led the Coast League with twenty-five victories and seven defeats when he was only nineteen.

What they meant was he didn't have the real good fastball. What he did have was courage, control, intelligence and a competitive spirit nothing could daunt. He was a consistent winner in the American League, with one eighteen-game season. The war cost him four years at his peak, yet his career won–lost record was 95–71.

In 1961, when Cincinnati blew a six-game lead inside two weeks in July, the word was that Hutch's club didn't have what it took. In truth, outside the pitching staff the Reds weren't much; they had only fair hitting and a dim infield that couldn't make the double play.

Yet they recaptured first place from the Dodgers in the classic fashion—by smashing the leaders three times in a row—and never looked back. No manager in our time has got finer results with fewer tools.

Hutch expects to be ready to take charge when the Reds open training camp in March. He has, as Jim Brosnan says, "inner power."

THE LATE BILL HEWITT

BILL HEWITT, whose football style may very well have suggested the original idea for jet propulsion, drove an automobile off a Pennsylvania highway the other day. He was found unconscious inside a culvert and two hours later he was dead. It must have been a stout culvert.

If Bill was driving the way he used to play end, it is easy to understand what happened. Caution never was his dominant characteristic on the field or elsewhere. You could tell that even if you never saw him play, by one glance at his features, which looked as though they should bear a sign reading: "Danger. Closed for repairs. Advance at your own risk."

As the monsters of professional football go, Bill wasn't big. In fact, until his junior year in high school he was a little squirt in short pants who couldn't get a tumble from the coach. But he wound up there as regular fullback and end, went on to the University of Michigan, then to the Chicago Bears and finally to the Philadelphia Eagles.

On defense he had a trick of lurking a couple of yards behind the line of scrimmage and starting his charge just before the ball was snapped so he'd roar across the neutral zone in full stride. If his timing was wrong the Bears would lose five yards, but if it was right the ballcarrier would lose ten, and maybe his senses to boot.

His football instinct made him right far oftener than he was wrong, but his rush took him into the enemy backfield so swiftly the fans couldn't believe he wasn't offside.

"Offside Hewitt," they called him, and up in Green Bay, Wisconsin, in particular, he was held in a curious sort of esteem. Even in the darkest days of the Depression, when lots of folks hadn't enough to eat, it was a poor Packer fan who couldn't spare an obsolete egg or weary turnip or melancholy legume for Bill when the Bears came to town.

After fourteen years of high school, college and pro football, Bill quit because he couldn't stomach the idea of playing at a slower gait. When he announced his retirement he was asked what prompted it, and he said, "I've discovered that I'm flinching away from punishment, easing up just before a shock that I wouldn't even have felt ten years ago. I used to laugh at the old gaffers waiting for a rub in the training room after a game. Now I'm first in line, and then I go around to the door and get in line again."

Two or three years ago he collaborated on a *Saturday Evening Post* piece that offended many of his old friends, who misconstrued it as an argument that pro football made bums. It wasn't that at all.

Speaking from experience of the days when $100 a game was a respectable National League wage, he argued that pro football couldn't serve as a career and could offer no more than financial aid toward getting a kid started in life. He warned that it would make a bum out of the fellow who tried to live on the game alone.

Using himself as the horrible example, he told of loafing through the offseason his first half-dozen years out of college, living on a $100-a-week standard during the fall and snooting the lesser jobs that would have helped out. He insisted he was at least an apprentice bum until, at Bert Bell's insistence, he took a filling-station job at something like $22 a week.

A restless night got him out of the oil business. He was sleepless one night, thinking, "All these years in football and not a nickel to show for it," and he got up and started writing a speech. The theme was, "Drink milk and grow up to be All-America." The dairy council paid him to deliver the spiel before school kids, and he wound up with a pretty good job with one of the dairies.

He used to wince when that speech was mentioned, for he had a humorous contempt for such corn and no use at all for affectations. When he was trying to sell stuff to magazines he said, "I'm no crusader and I want to accomplish no reforms. I want the dough."

During the war Bell talked him out of retirement to rejoin the Eagles at $400 a game. (Rising prices and competition have done even better for players since then.) Bill lasted part of one season and afterward said with typical honesty that he hadn't been worth $100.

The Green Bay fans who used to throw things might have enjoyed meeting the Hewitts at home. Once when they talked of moving, Edie, Bill's first wife, protested.

"Who'll take care of my boys?" she asked, puzzling friends who knew they were childless. Turned out their house was headquarters for a flock of neighborhood kids who played football with Bill, trooped through the place and made a lodge of the living room.

Bill closed the house when Edie died. He remarried less than a year ago. He was only thirty-seven when he died. He lived 365 days of every year, though. In the first draft of a magazine piece, his collaborator had him say something like, "So all I could do was say, 'Yes, Mr. Halas,' and be a good boy."

"That's got to come out," Bill said, reading the copy. "I wasn't a good boy. I was a very bad boy." But a very swell one.

JIM AND HIS BAUBLES

ONE OF those voices that crowd into the living room out of the unoffending air was talking about the death of Jim Thorpe. All its owner could think of to say was that he hoped those men were satisfied now, those men who had made a career of depriving Jim of the medals he won in the Olympic Games of 1912. The inference was that by taking his baubles away from him forty years ago, the amateur athletic authorities had hastened old Jim's death.

Jim Thorpe never was happy making speeches and in recent years when he had to make a public appearance he would settle for a line that must have been fed to him by a movie press agent or some such. He would get up and say he was glad to be present and he only wished he could have his medals back. Then he would sit down.

The speech was all right. It did nobody any harm, least of all Demosthenes. Nor did it convince anybody that Jim, a burly, simple, wonderful gent in the maturity of his middle sixties, gave a whoop in a rain barrel about that long-lost hardware.

He was the greatest athlete of his time, maybe the greatest of any time in any land, and he needed no gilded geegaws to prove it. The proof is in the records and the memories of the men who knew him and watched him and played with him—especially those who tried to play football against him in a day when football was not, according to President Butler of Columbia, one of the "games decently played by decent young men."

As a matter of fact, Jim's gold medals, if he had kept them, would merely have borne false witness, testifying that in 1912 he was an amateur eligible under the rules for competition in amateur sport. He was not.

He had played two summers of professional baseball at Rocky Mount and Fayetteville in the Eastern Carolina League. Then he had returned to the Carlisle Indian School to make All-America in football in 1911 and 1912; and to win the pentathlon and decathlon in the Stockholm Olympics.

When the facts came out in 1913, Jim wrote to James F. Sullivan, secretary of the Amateur Athletic Union: "I hope I will be partly excused by the fact that I was simply an Indian schoolboy and did not know that I was doing wrong."

It was an age of innocence, indeed. Of course Jim did nothing wrong. If playing professional baseball was even a venial sin, Stan Musial's hope of heaven would be dim. But the Olympics are restricted to amateurs and Jim wasn't an amateur and wasn't entitled to the medals he won.

Amateur or professional, however, he was richly entitled to the accolade he received from King Gustav of Sweden. "Sir," said the king, heaping hardware upon him in Stockholm, "you are the greatest athlete in the world."

In the pentathlon, Jim had won the broad jump, the 200-meter hurdles, the discus throw and the 1,500-meter run. He was third in the javelin throw.

In the decathlon he was first in the high hurdles, the shotput, the high jump and the 1,500; he was third in the 100 meters, the discus, the pole vault, and the broad jump; he was fourth in the 400 meters and the javelin.

That's the sort of thing remembered by the men who knew him, rather than the nonsense about metal trinkets. Nobody who saw him on a football field could ever forget the wild glory of that indestructible Indian.

There's a man in the White House today who must retain a vivid memory of an opponent's 185-yard touchdown. Playing against a West Point team that included a cadet named Dwight Eisenhower, Jim raced ninety yards to the goal line but Carlisle was offside. On the next play he went ninety-five and this one counted.

Jim didn't need medals to assure him of his rank in any game. He understood his place clearly, and explained it clearly to Knute Rockne when the Notre Dame graduate tackled Thorpe in a professional game. "Don't do that," Jim warned. "All those people paid to see old Jim run."

When Jim played football, serious thinkers like Chancellor Day, of Syracuse University, were saying that "one human life is too big a price to pay for all the football games of the season."

That attitude puzzled Jim. As a baseball player with the Giants, he was puzzled when John McGraw said he didn't want to hear of Jim playing football after the season closed. Jim protested.

"Why not, Mac?"

"You might get hurt."

"How can you get hurt playing football?" Jim asked.

THE MAN WHO BEAT DEMPSEY

WHEN TONY GALENTO was fighting they called him Two-Ton Tony, and a tidy tubful of old world charm he was, indeed. But, the man was saying, you should have seen Willie Meehan thirty-odd years ago. Thirty-odd years ago, the man was saying, a fellow couldn't really claim to have been around unless he had seen Niagara Falls, the Woolworth Building, the Grand Canyon, a dead whale on a flatcar and Willie Meehan in the ring.

The man had read an item on the obituary page beginning "Willie Meehan, old-time prize fighter who won a decision over Jack Dempsey in 1918, died in a San Francisco hospital last night at the age of fifty-nine."

It was in San Francisco that Willie was born, on Christmas Day, 1893, under the good fighting name of Eugene Walcott. The original Joe Walcott of Barbados was in his nineteenth year of fighting when Willie took a nom du glove into the ring, and ambitious kids were borrowing the old man's name. In 1912 Willie was to fight a boy called Young Walcott, whose real name might have been Meehan for all anybody knows today. Willie stiffened him in three, for his presumption, probably.

The obit said Willie began as a bantamweight but discovered fairly early in life the body-building qualities of San Francisco beer. The record book has him down as five feet, nine inches tall, weighing 185 pounds.

"That was before he got his growth," the man said. "Maybe he just looked big to me, because I was young and small then, but I remember him as the fattest man I ever saw in the ring, fatter by far than Galento.

"He used to stand there with his hands down and stick out his bay window and invite the other fellow to hit it. I saw him box Bill Brennan in Philadelphia in 1930 and Bill kept hitting him in the giblets and I'll swear Bill's glove would go clear out of sight.

"As I remember it, Willie whipped Brennan, but those were the six-round no-decision days in Philadelphia and I couldn't swear now that the newspapers voted for Meehan.

"Anyhow, Willie was a pretty good fighter. He was the windmill type, both hands whirling as he bored in. Sometimes he'd stop and take a full wind-up, like a pitcher with nobody on base, and even if the other guy hit him in the middle of the wind-up it wouldn't stop Willie."

It was natural that the man writing the obituary should mention the decision over Dempsey. It's a distinction few men could claim. Not long after he came out of Manassa, Colorado, fighting under the name of Kid Blackie, Dempsey was beaten by a guy named Jack Downey, and of course there was his one-round knockout by Fireman Jim Flynn.

At the time he boxed Flynn, Dempsey was young and hungry—"a moral, physical and financial wreck" in the happy phrase of Dr. Jack Kearns. This circumstance has prompted some historians reviewing the Flynn bout to suggest that necessity is the mother of invention.

At any rate, until he lost his title to Gene Tunney in 1926, Dempsey never again finished second, except to Willie Meehan. Their first meeting was Jack's first bout after the Flynn affair and his first under the direction of Dr. Kearns, who had found Dempsey working in a San Francisco shipyard.

Willie was by then a veteran of eight years of battling against such agreeably named citizens as Jockey Ludwig, Young Joe Grimm, Bow-wow Flanagan, Racehorse Monroe, Young Ketchel, Jew Goldberg, Hobo Doughtery, Indian Joe Gregg and innumerable Kids, Sailors and Soldiers.

He lost his first bout with Dempsey on a four-round decision, drew in four rounds later that year (1917) and won a four-round decision a year later.

"I hear he smacked Dempsey all over the ring," reports Mr. Dumb Dan Morgan, "but I didn't see it. Only time I ever see him, he came here to work out in a gym and I seen him then. He was clever enough and one of the fastest punchers around, but strictly a four-round fighter.

"You get those heavy men with the big stomachs and they rely on you hitting 'em there because whenever you punch for the body you got to leave your head uncovered.

"This guy was what we call a freak, but he was one of the biggest freaks we ever had in boxing."

THE SHRINE

THE DAY after Jack Kearns died there was one flag flying in Shelby, Montana. It was in front of the post office and it flew from the top of the staff.

"I should think it would be at half-mast," a tourist remarked to a leather guy who was addressing a letter. "Doc Kearns died yesterday."

"That so?" the man said. "I didn't hear about it."

"Jack Kearns, Jack Dempsey's manager. The man who stripped this town bare forty years ago, almost to the day."

"Oh." The cordovan face lost its vague expression. "Those were great days when they had that fight here. Busted all the banks and that fellow—Kearns, you say?—ducked out in a railroad caboose, with the money. And half the town after him, from what I hear."

"You weren't around here then?"

"Yes, but I was a kid. I got to see the fight free. They had this wooden area with a six-strand wire fence. It's torn down now but you'll see a sign just west of town on Highway 2 showing the place.

"A man handed me a pair of pliers to cut the fence but I was a kid and a-scared. I was starting to leave when somebody else cut the wires and we all piled in without paying."

The man hefted the letter he had addressed. "You know what air-mail has to weigh before you pay extra?"

"No, but the man at the window will weigh it."

The man hesitated, then slid the envelope into the slot, taking his chances. So they still live dangerously in Shelby, the only town that ever sold its birthright for a prize fight.

Of course, it wasn't just any old prize fight, the match between Jack Dempsey and Tommy Gibbons on July 4, 1923. It was a fight for the heavyweight championship of the world, and there's something about a heavyweight championship that—well, it's instant history, that's what.

Let any one who doubts this visit Shelby today, forty years after Jack Kearns plucked the town clean as a Christmas turkey. When the late doctor caught that caboose out of town, his bat-ears flapping in triumph and sticky fingers gripping a satchel holding $250,000, three banks folded.

Shelby had built a stadium for forty thousand customers and the fight drew 7,966 who paid $201,485 at $20 to $50 a seat. The group of young boosters who promised Kearns $300,000 to bring Dempsey to Shelby had put the town on the map—oil had been discovered in 1922 and the boom was on—but they were middle-aged before their city staggered back to fiscal health.

Yet, because a heavyweight title fight is the special event that it is, the boosters accomplished what they set out to do. Shelby today enjoys a fame undreamed of in other Montana towns like Havre and Chouteau.

Even the road map you pick up in the filling station notes that Shelby was the site of the Dempsey-Gibbons fight. The postcards sold in the drugstore on the main stem boast of disaster. As far away as Great Falls, there is a saloon called the Dempsey Inn that advertises, even after forty years, "where Jack Dempsey trained."

In 1962 the July fourth edition of the *Shelby Promoter*—a newspaper happily named—carried a Page One spread of pictures and text under the banner headline: "IT ALL HAPPENED 40 YEARS AGO." Referring to the tens of thousands of words written about the Sack of Shelby, the paper observed that "if all this free space was totalled as advertising inches, we think that throughout the years Shelby's investment in 1923 has paid for itself twice over."

RED KRESS

IN 1929 the two finest young shortstops in baseball were both in St. Louis, and this is a claim that many-splendored city never made again, or ever will.

The Cardinals had Charley Gelbert, and except for a hunting accident he would be remembered today as one of the greatest of them all. Playing his second season for the Browns was a wide-ranging redhead just turned twenty-two, a line-drive hitter who had everything—speed, dash, sure hands, a tremendous throwing arm.

This was Ralph Kress, a name that was mentioned sadly again and again yesterday among the baseball men gathered at the winter meetings in the Roosevelt. The morning paper had told how Red Kress, only fifty-five and apparently as superbly fit as always, had died of a heart attack in California.

It was hard to believe and harder to take. At fifty-five, with the once-bright hair faded and thinned, Red was the youngest, busiest, most tireless, cheeriest figure in flannels on any big league field last summer. He was a coach with the Mets and an absolute marvel, who could run the legs off every pitcher and outfielder with his fungo stick, hit grounders until the infielders collapsed, then trot to the mound and wear the hitters out in batting practice.

In his fifties and in his twenties, here was a guy who loved life and reveled in baseball. There was in him a happy ebullience one could sense from afar: a fan in the deepest bleachers somehow knew that that kid at shortstop was having the time of his life, that there was no place in all the world that he would trade for this.

In his first big league year, which was only his second in baseball, he played 150 games for the Browns, and in 1929 he batted .305 and led American League shortstops in fielding and double plays.

He had a notion he ought to get paid for this, though on the Browns in those days such an attitude amounted to subversion.

Phil Ball, the millionaire who owned the club, lost money cheerfully on his hobby but he had an office staff dedicated to pinching the boss's pennies. (At the second-rate hotel that was spring training headquarters in West Palm Beach, the $1.50 table d'hote offered a choice of ice cream or pie for dessert. Players were warned in writing that any one who ordered pie á la mode would be expected to get up the additional dime.)

In the circumstances, Red's suggestion that his salary be raised in 1930 was poorly received. So he held out, until Ball himself sent a telegram beginning, "You have been temporized with too long and this has caused your head to swell." The owner added an ultimatum: sign the contract in hand or the figure would be cut by $500 for every twenty-four-hour delay.

"What else can I do?" Red wired . . . and signed. He was justifiably bitter over this treatment, and by holding out he had cut to a minimum the time he needed for training.

So that year he played all 154 games for the Browns, filling in at third base as well as shortstop, batted .313 and drove in 112 runs. Even with good cause, he couldn't sulk on the field.

"I've always believed," a guy in the Roosevelt was saying yesterday, "that Red would have made the Hall of Fame if he'd been allowed to stay at one position. But the Browns started moving him around and after they traded him to the White Sox he played the outfield and every infield position including first, and even pitched if I'm not mistaken."

"You aren't," Birdie Tebbetts said. "Just after the war, when he must have been in his forties, he went back on the active list and pitched for the Giants."

"It seems to me," the guy said, "that bouncing from one job to another like that has to take something out of a player. What a shortstop he would have been if he'd done nothing else, because what a shortstop he was as a kid."

"All I know," Tebbetts said, "is that when he was with Washington they told him he was through and they were sending him out the next day, to Minneapolis, I think. That day the shortstop got hurt and Red went in and got three hits and they didn't get him out of town for years."

"And when they finally did," Al Lopez said, "he played shortstop for Minneapolis, hit over .330 and led the league in total chances.

"I was playing in Macon, Georgia, when I first heard about him.

There were hitters in the American League like Ty Cobb and Harry Heilmann and Al Simmons, and a name I'd never heard, Kress, was on top of the league with an average over .400.

"He didn't win the championship but he had a fan in Macon rooting for him all summer, even if he didn't know it."

JIM NORRIS

LONG AFTER Jim Norris got out of the boxing business a fight manager whom he liked had a heart attack. Visiting her father in the hospital, the manager's daughter brought along the mail, which included a statement from the bank. There was too big a balance in the checking account.

"There's one deposit here," the girl said, "for thirty-five hundred dollars."

"They're telling me I put thirty-five hundred dollars in the bank and never knew it?" the sick man said. "It's not my heart that's gone haywire, it's my head. Look, honey, you call Mr. Halloran at the bank and ask him to check for us, will you?"

When the girl came back she said, "Mr. Halloran says the statement is correct but you didn't make that thirty-five-hundred-dollar deposit. It came in the mail from a Mr. Norris in Chicago."

When the fight manager was able to speak he said, "I see. And he wasn't taking bows. He thought maybe I'd never know about it."

The guy got better. Back home from the hospital, he wrote his thanks to Jim Norris and enclosed a check. The letter that came back said, "I'm not accepting this as a repayment, my friend. I'm holding it for you. I hope you never need it but if you ever do, remember the money is here and it's yours."

A few mornings later, the manager awoke with a start.

"Good lord!" he said to himself. "I really am off my rocker. It was thirty-five hundred dollars Jim sent me and the check I wrote back was for three thousand. He must think I'm the cheapest chiseler ever lived."

He rushed off a second check with a note of explanation and abject apology. "I take it a little bad," he wrote, "that you never mentioned the five-hundred-dollar oversight. What did you think I was trying to pull?"

Norris was traveling and that letter followed him around, catching him at last in someplace like Winnepeg. He didn't write a reply. He wired.

"You're a nut," the telegram read.

So all right, Jim Norris had millions and could afford to do that sort of thing. But now that he has died, it ought to be known that he did do that sort of thing and he wasn't looking for applause.

When Jim ran boxing in this country, you hardly ever heard or read anything good about him. He was the octopus whose stranglehold on the big arenas and the network television shows was killing the game. He was the rich ogre, the playboy associate of mobsters, the promoter who did business with the underworld and let boxing fall into mob hands.

Maybe some of it was true but a great deal wasn't. Mob guys were in boxing long before Norris came around. He took over as a new boy from Chicago, a fan with financial interests in other sports like hockey and horse racing, and he soon discovered that many of the champions and top contenders were owned by guys like Frankie Carbo, Blinky Palermo, and Eddie Coco.

With contracts for two national TV shows a week all around the year, Norris needed these fighters. To be sure, he owned the big halls, Madison Square Garden, Detroit Olympia, Chicago Stadium and the St. Louis Arena, and with his personal fortune he could have starved the mob guys out.

Perhaps that's what he should have done, though of course without the top fighters he would have blown the TV contract and failed to do the good job of fight promotion that he wanted to do. Instead of crusading, he accepted conditions as he found them. He dealt with the Carbos and Palermos and Cocos.

He took pride in the fact that he put big fights in the big arenas all over the country and through TV brought boxing the widest popularity it has ever known. His shows were run efficiently and on schedule. He had good fights and for the most part they were on the level. And afterward, all the bills got paid. Boxing never had it so good, before or since.

Like most of us, Jim was neither a plaster saint nor an evil man. He suffered deeply from the abuse he took. I liked him, which isn't necessarily a testimonial. I have known rogues and reformers and generally preferred the rogues.

DAN WARNED 'EM

DAN DANIEL, a newspaperman to the end and maybe past it, wrote his own obituary to be used "in the event of my death, which is scheduled within the next fifteen years." Dan was ninety-one when the event came to pass, within the time frame he had scheduled. He was always meticulous about those details.

Daniel M. Daniel didn't go by that name in 1910, when he was sprung from City College and got his first newspaper job. He was Daniel Markowitz. Anti-Semitism hadn't gone into the closet in those days; the paper refused to use "Markowitz" as a byline and Dan's stuff bore the line, "By Daniel."

As time went by he came to be known as Dan Daniel, he was introduced by that name, mail was addressed to him thus. He told his immigrant father that it would make life simpler if he changed his name legally but he wouldn't consider it if his father had any objections. Would he mind?

"Not at all," Dan's father said. "Markowitz isn't your real name, anyway."

It could be that Dan never did know what the family name was before it was shortened but that seems improbable. He was too good a reporter to let an obvious question go unanswered.

Dan was a sizable man, rather heavyset, and if he wasn't a trifle round-shouldered he somehow gave that impression. He had a gravel voice that, together with an almost perpetual scowl, made him seem a perpetual grouch. In truth, he was warmhearted and generous with a quick, if somewhat astringent, wit. As a deadpan toastmaster who could discourage bombast at sixty paces, he was unexcelled.

Professionally, he specialized in baseball coverage although he wrote college football and handled many other assignments in sports. He and Nat Fleischer founded *Ring* magazine; Dan said he staged the first college basketball games in Madison Square Garden, not Ned Irish, who is usually credited with that promotion.

Though he was an all-round newspaperman, Dan regarded himself primarily as a baseball writer, and he was respected as such by his contemporaries. He had excellent news sources. There was a stock line in baseball press boxes that was heard almost any time a reporter came up with a scrap of news: "Daniel had it last week."

As a writer, Dan did not subscribe to the Hemingway school that prefers the simple "he said" to "he declared" or "replied" or "remonstrated" or "cried" or "growled," etc. Dan coined his own verbs: "he exuberated," or "he vehemed."

His frown may have been myopic; his rasping tone probably was the voice he was born with; his emphatic, dogmatic manner of speech was an acquired gift. Sometimes when he was holding forth on some subject his friend Frank Graham would say, "Oh, Dan, stop veheming."

In 1946 the American League won the All-Star Game, 12–0, with Bob Feller, Hal Newhouser and Jack Kramer combining on a three-hitter. "The events that transpired yesterday in Fenway Park," Dan wrote, "make it clear that the National League is in imminent danger of becoming a minor league and unless immediate steps are taken . . ."

That fall the Cardinals whipped the Red Sox in the World Series, and although it went the full seven-game distance, St. Louis was clearly the superior team. "The autumn classic," Dan wrote, "demonstrated once again that the National League has a distinct margin of superiority over the junior circuit. It is imperative that the teams in Will Harridge's organization look to their farms for new and exciting talent. . . ."

"Hey, Dan," a friend protested. "In July you stick it to the National League and in October you kick the Americans around. What is this?"

"I've warned them both," Dan said. "Now they're on their own."

During the Great Depression, when a loaf of bread cost a nickel and everything else was priced accordingly, Dan of the *World-Telegram* and John Drebinger of the *Times* caught a cab at the Englewood Station in south Chicago to check into the Del Prado Hotel with the Yankees. They had just come from Detroit.

"Look," Drebby said as they passed a market. "Tuna fish, sixteen cents a can."

"Fourteen in Detroit," Dan said.

That's why "Ask Daniel" was one of the most entertaining features in the *World-Telegram* sports section. Readers sent in questions, mostly about baseball, and Dan replied. Chances are he knew the answer most of the time. He responded all the time, in terms that left all doubt dead and partly decomposed.

STEVE O'NEILL

ALL THROUGH September 1944, the Browns and Tigers were at each other's throats. Again and again they awoke to find the teams tied for first place in the American League, and in that last feverish month there was hardly ever more than half a game between them. When the last week of play began with the leaders all square, Sportsman's Park in St. Louis and Briggs Stadium in Detroit were two big pressure cookers threatening to blow up.

A visiting baseball reporter arriving in Detroit to cover the finish was not surprised to find an abnormal quiet in the Tigers' dugout. Steve O'Neill, the manager, and Stubby Overmire, a pitcher, sat together on the bench, talking in low tones. They were steeped in gloom.

"Still a young guy, too," O'Neill was saying.

"Cut off in his prime," Overmire said.

"What a way to go!"

"Horrible!"

Tactful inquiry disclosed the nature of the bereavement. Manager and player were mourning the untimely passing of Flat Top or the Mole or whichever miscreant Dick Tracy was pursuing at the time, who in that morning's strip had leaped, fallen or been pushed from a high window and had been fatally skewered on a flagstaff many stories below.

This gift of dead-panned nonsense in the midst of a nerve-wracking race was an outstanding quality in Steve O'Neill as a manager. To this tough-looking, muffin-faced old catcher out of the anthracite mines of Minooka, Pennsylvania, Einstein and e. e. cummings and the Bolshoi Ballet were strictly for the birds, but he could sniff out baseball talent in the heaviest cover and he had a rare knack for keeping players relaxed.

When Steve died, obituaries gave his age as sixty-nine, though old record books give July 6, 1891, as the date of his birth, which would make him seventy. Anyhow, he was in baseball in one connection or another from 1910 on, outlasting his brother Mike, a pitcher with the Cardinals and Reds in the early years of this century; brother Jack, who caught for the Cardinals, Cubs and Braves; and brother Joe, a shortstop with the Senators.

Steve managed Cleveland, Detroit, the Red Sox and the Phillies. Old catchers are regarded as authorities on the care and feeding of pitchers and that's the chief reason so many of them are hired as managers, though being brave enough to turn their backs on the fans may have something to do with it. Anyhow, Steve was noted especially for his success with pitchers.

In 1944, for example, when the Tigers were nosed out by the Browns on the last day of the season, Hal Newhouser won twenty-nine games for Detroit and Dizzy Trout twenty-seven. Paul Richards, then catching for the Tigers, had a lot to do with taming the temperamental Newhouser, who had won only eight games and lost seventeen a year earlier. But Steve was the guy in charge.

Steve was managing the Indians in 1936 when Cy Slapnicka brought in a seventeen-year-old plow jockey named Bob Feller. Fast and wild, the kid was booked for the New Orleans farm, but Steve pitched him three innings of a July exhibition with the Cardinals and he struck out eight of nine hitters. From that day on, Feller was headed for the Hall of Fame.

In 1938, Cleveland had a rookie third baseman out of the University of Illinois named Lou Boudreau, and a bachelor of science from Case Institute named Ray Mack. Boudreau was on a Three-I League farm in Cedar Rapids, Mack was playing shortstop and the outfield with Fargo and Moorhead in the Northern League.

The Indians sent both kids to Buffalo in 1939, because Steve O'Neill was managing that farm. "You're my second baseman," Steve told Mack. "You're the regular shortstop," he told Boudreau. Boudreau hit .331 and Mack .293 and before the summer was out both were called up to Cleveland, which was one reason Buffalo finished no higher than fourth in the International League.

For the next half-dozen years, there wasn't a finer second base combination in the American League than Boudreau and Mack.

In thirteen seasons as a manager in the big leagues, Steve had only one pennant winner. That was the Detroit club of 1945, which beat the Cubs in a World Series witnessed by the largest, and most horrified, crowds any Series had drawn up to then. "The richest of all World Series," it was called, "and the poorest."

It was six or seven weeks after V-J Day, and only a few of the big-leaguers had returned from the war. Before the Series when a wire service reporter polling the press sought a forecast from Warren Brown, of Chicago, Warren told him gloomily, "I don't see how either team can win."

Steve's boys managed it. That was the year when an American League team, making its last visit to Cleveland, stood in a knot in front of Terminal Tower.

"Take a good long look at it, men, so you can remember," a realist among them said. "The pros are coming back."

SAM BREADON

WORD COMES from St. Louis that Sam Breadon is seriously ill. He started for a Florida vacation, fell sick and had to return home for treatment. During his illness he has had a lot of mail, much of it from baseball men who knew him, in one capacity or another, when he was president of the Cardinals.

If a fan could read some of these letters, especially from players and former players, the chances are he'd be surprised and bewildered. The sentiments they express would not coincide with the picture of Sam Breadon as it was commonly drawn during his baseball days.

Sports-page readers frequently got a distorted notion of the Cardinals' owner, colored by ignorance and provincialism. He was pictured —more often than not by someone who knew the man only casually if at all—as a skinflint sweatshop operator, a bad sport who exploited his stars and then callously discarded them, a nickel-nurser whose guiding business rule was greed.

Even today you hear the statement that if Stan Musial were playing for, say, one of the New York clubs, he would be making twice as much money as the Cardinals give him. Perhaps if a star of Musial's magnitude played in a town where receipts were bigger than in St. Louis, some of that difference might be reflected in his bank account.

But the fact is that when Musial was playing first base for Breadon's Cardinals he was, with a single exception, the most highly paid first baseman in the history of the National League. That was the year Hank Greenberg, the single exception, was with the Pirates. And although a superficial reader of the sports pages would have assumed—from the publicity broadcast from Pittsburgh while the Cardinals held their silence—that Hank's wages were at least $50,000 greater than Stan's, the actual difference in base pay provided for in their contracts was $7,500.

Moreover, it has only been in recent seasons that Musial's opposite number in New York, Joe DiMaggio, received more money than Stan has been getting in St. Louis.

A true picture of Sam Breadon would not depict him as a Scrooge or a Lady Bountiful or a sucker. He is, in fact, a smart and able businessman whose business situation compelled him to operate on a narrower margin than some other owners, who tried to treat his help fairly, who admires ability and appreciates loyalty, who made friends on all levels of baseball society, and has kept them.

He was, of course, incomparably the most able and successful owner the Cardinals ever had. With money he had earned for himself he bought into a bankrupt organization, reorganized and refinanced it, and made it the dominant club of the league. Under Breadon, the Cardinals were the best team in their league and the chief source from which rivals purchased major-league material.

National League faces grow pink when modern World Series records are mentioned. They would be purple if it weren't for the clubs Breadon built. From 1926 through 1946, the National League had eight world champions. Six of them represented St. Louis. In nine consecutive seasons, the Cardinals did not finish worse than second. Then Breadon went out of baseball.

Strictly speaking, Sam didn't drop entirely out of baseball right away. He retained personal interests in the game, represented by guys like Mort Cooper. It is, perhaps, worth noting that when big Mort got himself jammed up with some funny checks, it was not an active baseball man who came to his help and picked up his tab and got a job for him. It was Sam Breadon.

A MAN OF DISTINCTION

HARRY S. SHARPE was a dressy little walking-stick of a man, immaculate in a tweedy sort of way, scholarly of speech, with classic features and the wavy iron-gray hair favored by whisky distillers in their photographs of men of distinction. Chances are he didn't always have that Roman senator's profile, for he remarked once that when he returned to St. Louis after boxing Frank Crosby seventy-seven rounds near Nameoki, Illinois, his best friends didn't recognize him, Crosby having put in five hours and eight minutes rearranging his facade.

"I had a letter from him not five weeks ago," said Bow Tie Jimmy Bronson when he heard the news that Harry had died in St. Louis at the age of seventy-eight. "Isn't that awful? He was a great man."

Although he has been more places and knows more people than most, Bow Tie Jimmy wasn't born in time to see Sharpe and Crosby box the longest match ever fought to a knockout under Marquis of Queensberry rules. He knew Harry later, though, when Jimmy was a kid out of Joplin getting a start in the fight business out West and Harry was hustling around selling insurance, serving as president of the Typographical Union, writing pleasant little essays on boxing for the *St. Louis Post-Dispatch*, and refereeing bouts.

They were together in France, too, helping out as referee and judge in the A.E.F. and Inter-Allied championships of World War I. Matter of fact, the impression is that Jimmy was the referee and Harry a judge when Eddie Eagan, now head of the New York Athletic Commission, won his heavyweight title in the Inter-Allied bouts.

At any rate, anyone who ever messed around in sports in St. Louis knew and liked Harry Sharpe and heard him tell of his rowdy afternoon and evening in Mr. Crosby's company. He used to make a lively yarn of it, with his elegant turn of speech.

"I recall," he would say, "that a little later when I read of James J. Corbett engaging in a match at a limited number of rounds, with five-ounce gloves and padded ringposts, it was the fruition of a dream."

Sharpe and Crosby used three-ounce gloves, which were not such satisfactory cutting tools as, say, a hatchet, but were not far inferior, either. Yesterday's obituaries told some of the details of the fight, but not all.

In 1893 Sharpe and Crosby were rival contenders for the lightweight championship of Missouri. Crosby was a boy out of Wisconsin working as boxing instructor in St. Louis's Pastime Athletic Club. Sharpe was a typesetter. Prizefighting was illegal in Missouri and Illinois then, but after several efforts to arrange a site for the match had failed, a friendly sheriff was turned up in Madison County, Illinois.

In fact, the sheriff was more than friendly; he was a real aficionado. Unwilling to miss the fun, but reluctant to give it quasiofficial sanction by his presence, he attended wearing long phony gray whiskers. In addition, there were about three hundred sports from St. Louis, who had ridden a special train over the Eads Bridge to the east side of the Mississippi, where the ring was pitched in a picnic grove near the Wabash tracks.

This was on February 5, a cold, rainy day. Starting at 4:00 P.M., the boys fought until dark. Then a man running the show—memory suggests that his name might have been Allen—shouted that he would pay $10 for ten flares. While somebody was getting flares, the special train's locomotive was run up close to the ring so the fight could go on in the light of its headlamp.

The boys fought through rain that changed to sleet. These were regular three-minute rounds. Other oldtime bouts you read about which went one hundred or more rounds were fought under the old London Prize Ring rules when a fall or knockdown ended a round, and a boxer could gain respite merely by dropping to his knees.

At 9:18 P.M., Sharpe pinned Crosby to the ropes with a left hook, hit him again, stepped back and let him fall. Crosby didn't get up. He didn't even wake up until the special train was nearly back to St. Louis.

Sharpe got the purse of $500, Crosby got nothing, and everyone connected with the affair was indicted for "aiding, assisting and abetting" a prize fight. Sharpe and Crosby, whose faces bore fairly convincing evidence, got a year each.

It would be pleasant to report that the officer who served the papers was the same friendly sheriff, minus the crepe whiskers. Actually, though, Harry never mentioned that angle one way or the other.

HAZEN SHIRLEY CUYLER

"HAZEN CUYLER, fifty," read the dispatch from Ann Arbor, Michigan, "coach of the Boston Red Sox and former star in the major leagues, died tonight of heart disease in an ambulance that was taking him from his home in Harrisville to the University Hospital here."

At first there was only a sense of shock and the thought: *Not Kiki Cuyler, surely.* . . . Why, he was around with the Red Sox the day the season closed here only four months ago and in another three weeks he would have been with them again in training camp in Sarasota, Florida, harrying and hustling the ball players in that shrill voice of his.

Memory sketched a picture of a dark, vivid face with a big nose; of square shoulders that gave the effect of stockiness to a middle-sized figure that moved in a blur of speed across National League outfields and around the bases.

Then gradually the picture began to fill in. You remembered Hazen Shirley Cuyler for the exceptional ball player he was, a combative kid of twenty-one—with a bit of West Point schooling in his background— playing the outfield for Bay City, Michigan, in 1920, and a combative man of forty-two managing Chattanooga and choosing himself as a pinch-hitter just once that year and making a single and scoring a run thus wrapping up a twenty-one-year career with a batting average of 1.000.

You remembered him as a player with the Pirates and the Cubs and the Reds and the Dodgers, a guy who played in three World Series and should have been in four. A guy who played winning baseball in all of them, although he was with a winner only once.

Mostly you remembered that only twice in the whole history of baseball have the Pirates won a world championship, and that once it was Cuyler who won for them.

That was in 1925, when the Pittsburgh club broke the pennant monopoly the Giants had held for four years. Cuyler played 153 games that season, batted .357, stole forty-one bases, led the National League and set an all-time Pittsburgh record by scoring 144 runs. He was in the big number-three slot in the batting order when the Series opened against the Washington Senators, defending champions of the world.

It was a memorable Series for a lot of reasons. It was the first time a club lost three of the first four games and then won three in a row for the title. It was the year Roger Peckinpaugh, Washington shortstop and the American League's Most Valuable Player, set a record by making eight errors. It was a Series of unprecedented slugging, with a total of twelve home runs. It was the year John McGraw stomped into the Pirates' clubhouse when Pittsburgh was trailing, three games to one, and persuaded Bill McKechnie to bench his first baseman, George Grantham, and put in the eldering Stuffy McInnis, a hero of the last three games.

On the first day, Walter Johnson pitched a five-hitter for Washington and won, 4–1. Cuyler got one of the hits. Next day Vic Aldridge pitched for Pittsburgh against Stan Coveleskie. Washington got a run in the second inning and Pittsburgh tied it up in the fourth on a homer by Glenn Wright. The score was still tied in the eighth when Cuyler came up with a runner on base and slammed one out of the park for the ball game.

Cuyler doubled and scored in the third game, but the Senators won, 4–3. Johnson pitched a shutout in the fourth. Cuyler had two hits and batted in a run as Aldridge won the fifth, 6–3. When the Pirates took the sixth behind Ray Kremer, 3–2, the series was squared.

The Senators bolted out of the gate in the seventh game, scoring four times in the first inning. The Pirates kept pecking at Johnson, though, tied the score in the seventh at 6-all, then yielded another run in the eighth. It was raining and evening was closing down on Forbes Field when Cuyler came up for the last time, with the bases filled. He'd already doubled home one run. Now he sliced another double into the right-field corner. Two runs came home. The Pirates were champions of the world.

Baseball people still speculate about the reasons why Donie Bush kept Cuyler on the bench in the World Series of 1927. One version is that Kiki had quarreled with Barney Dreyfuss, the owner, and Bush acted on orders from upstairs. By then Pittsburgh had the two Waners and Clyde Barnhart in the outfield, but Kiki had played in more than half the games that season and batted .309.

When the situation demanded a pinch-hitter, Pittsburgh fans called for Cuyler and booed when Earl Smith or Fred Brickell or Heinie Groh batted instead. The Yankees won four straight. Six weeks later Kiki was traded to Chicago for Sparky Adams and Pete Scott.

As a Cub, Cuyler played a World Series for Joe McCarthy in 1929 and played one against Joe in 1932. He went on to Cincinnati and Brooklyn and then back to the Southern Association, whence he'd come up to Pittsburgh in the first place. Down there they still tell a story about 1923 when he was a swift kid coursing up and down Goat Hill, the steep terrace that swept up to the right-field fence in Nashville.

Babe Herman was with Atlanta then, or thought he was. He didn't know his manager, Otto Miller, was carrying his release in his pocket. Each morning Miller would resolve to turn the Babe loose, and each afternoon Herman would belt a big one in the clutch. Miller would stuff the pink slip back in his pocket and bide his time.

After six days of this, Atlanta and Nashville locked up in a game that went into extra innings. With two out and runners on in the fourteenth, the Babe aimed a howler at the right-field wall, Cuyler scurried up the slope like a mountain goat, whirled as he reached the crest, leaped and stretched high. The ball smashed into the glove and stuck. Kiki trotted to the bench, picked up a bat, and won the game with a home run.

That night Herman was on his way.

THE HOUSE ON DELAWARE AVENUE

ITHACA, NEW YORK. The house they built at 101 Delaware Avenue for Gil Dobie is occupied by Lefty James now, but it will be a long time before the guys around Cornell tire of talking about the lean scarecrow who coached their football teams for seventeen years. Funny thing, though, the guy they talk about isn't the glum old piece whose persistent pessimism made *Gildobean* an accepted adjective describing the ultimate in gloom. The man they mourn was a tough gaffer during business hours, but actually a gay companion when his job was done.

"I never knew," Bob Kane, Cornell's athletic director, was saying, "whether his habit of getting names mixed up was a gag or due to a real blind spot. He did it all his life, though. As recently as a year ago, for instance, the Cornell coach was 'Lefty Jones' to Gil.

"Before we took movies of games, Gil used to scribble pages of notes all Saturday afternoon and the next day he'd get the squad together for Sunday school. He was giving 'em a going-over one Sunday and he started working on a halfback with a name like Kasparian or something. He called the kid Burns.

"According to Gil, the kid hadn't done anything right. On this play Burns had missed his block. On that one Burns had hit the wrong hole. On defense Burns had let a pass receiver get past him. Mostly the players didn't talk back to Gil, but this one thought he was being pushed around and got mad enough to be reckless. He interrupted.

"'Listen, Mr. Dobie,' he said, 'for three years you've called me Burns. My name is Kasparian.'"

"Gil shoved his dime-store glasses farther down his nose and glowered over 'em. Then he said very quietly, 'I know your name is Kasparian but I like Burns better. Now, Burns, where did you think you were going on the 168 crossbuck?'"

The yarns go on. There was an evening during Prohibition when Ace Leonard and Bill Reid, of Colgate, visited Dobie. Gil took their hats and turned and stalked into the kitchen. When he came back he had three tall glasses filled with something wet and colorless. The standard poison of the time was gin and lime and lithia water.

Gil lifted his glass. "Cheers," his guest said. "Lookin' atcha," they dipped their beaks deeply. They came up gasping, sputtering, strangling.

"What the hell's in that glass?" Reid demanded.

Gil looked disgusted.

"Damned if I traipse out to the kitchen for you every two minutes. That's alcohol and water, it'll hold you all night."

It's an old story that the University of Washington teams that he coached from 1908 to 1916 played sixty-one successive games without defeat, and never received a hint from Dobie that they had any reason to be proud of themselves.

Navy lost once in three years under his direction. When he came to Cornell, he started off with a winning streak of twenty-one games. Yet next Saturday always was the day of doom, and last Saturday was a tragedy of unforgivable errors.

If his players squirmed under what seemed to them unfair and unnecessary criticism, their fear of the forbidding old martinet was stronger than their resentment. If they grumbled, it was not in his hearing. At least one of them chewed over his grievances in silence for a quarter of a century.

When this guy—call him Eddie Kaw, because it wasn't he—finally spoke up it was at a reunion of Cornell's undefeated teams of 1920 to 1923. All but two or three members of those squads made it to Philadelphia for the Penn game of 1947 and that party was Gil's last public appearance.

They were milling around the room cutting up touches when the guy we're calling Kaw plunked down on a sofa beside Gil. He got a fistful of lapel, but the old man sat studying the carpet, paying no attention.

"Listen, you old bastard," the guy said. "I was afraid to talk back to you when I was playing, but you don't scare me now. Plenty of times you kicked me around when you didn't know what you were talking about. I was in the play and I knew what happened, but would you ever listen? Well, you'll listen now."

Did Gil remember the Penn game in his senior year? Well, he had thus-and-such. And then there was the Dartmouth game where, in the kicked about such-and-such a play, but what actually happened was second quarter, this happened but Gil had claimed it was that. And then, after the Syracuse game, and also before the Penn State game and furthermore and on the contrary. The guy went on and on, making it a good rib.

At long last Dobie glanced up. His eyes and his voice were sleepy.

"Kaw," he said, "you ain't a damn bit smarter than you were twenty-five years ago."

FRANK WHITMAN HAYES

AS THE years pile up, this happens more and more frequently but it is difficult to believe that a fellow ever gets accustomed to it. A fellow picks up the paper at breakfast, and the headline is blunt as a club. "FRANK HAYES, EX-CATCHER, IS DEAD AT FORTY."

What could anybody say? Another friend is gone.

How could Frank Hayes die at forty? That's no age at all, and he was an indestructible guy.

He caught 312 consecutive games. Maybe that doesn't seem a great number, if you're familiar with records and recall that Lou Gehrig appeared in 2,130 consecutive games. If you're that conversant with records, then chances are you are aware that Gehrig wasn't quite thirty-eight when he died.

Frank Whitman Hayes was tall and wide of shoulder, with features set straight up and down, so to speak, in a pear-shaped face. He liked to laugh and he loved a party. He never seemed to get tired. Though he grew up in New Jersey just outside the metropolitan area of Philadelphia, his interests were mostly those of a country kid—fishing, hunting, bird dogs. During World War II when the ball clubs couldn't go far from home for spring training, he'd beg time off from camp to work his dogs in field trials.

The impression is that it was Lena Blackburne, a coach with the Athletics who also lived in Jersey, who discovered Hayes for Connie Mack. At any rate, Lena had a special interest in the boy from the time Frank came out of prep school in 1933 and joined the Athletics as a seventeen-year-old.

Lena was all whalebone and whipcord, himself. He could stand for hours batting tall fungoes straight up in the air, and if you think that doesn't take it out of your thighs and back and shoulders, try it sometime for five minutes.

Lena hit 'em and Hayes chased 'em, learning to judge the direction a foul ball would take as it came off the bat, to wheel with it, whipping off the mask and shielding his eyes from the sun; learning to follow a ball against a high sky with a billion wiggletails in it; learning to move lightly on his toes so as not to joggle the catch; learning to keep the descending ball in front of him and move in with mitt ready at the last instant. They did it thousands of times, and then there was nobody surer on foul balls than Frank Hayes.

Before Hayes was nineteen, he toured the Orient with an all-star troupe of American League players. He was an added starter; all of a sudden a catcher was needed and Frank was flown out to the Pacific Coast in time to take ship for Japan. The baby of the company, he was thrown in by chance with a traveling companion who wasn't exactly an infant in arms, although he was called Babe Ruth.

Afterward Frank would tell how idolatrous Japanese trailed Ruth by the thousands wherever he went, trooping behind the man and screaming, "Baby Roos! Baby Roos!"

Getting a start like that at his age may have made Hayes a bit cocksure. Some thought it did. At any rate, he served out the following summer in Buffalo and Albany, and that was the only minor league ball he ever played.

From 1936 on he was a big leaguer, catching and hitting the long ball for Philadelphia, St. Louis, Philadelphia again, Cleveland, Chicago and the Red Sox.

As one looks back now, it seems unlikely that Frank ever gave much thought to setting records and getting his name into baseball's history books. Catching some of the pitchers who worked for the Athletics in the 1930s, he reckoned himself lucky whenever he got through a game alive. In the war year of 1944, a guy with a job in baseball had to work at it every day because, like as not, there was nobody to take his place. Frank was just going along doing his job and thinking nothing of it until somebody discovered he was close to doing something that had never been done before. He was catching every game his team played.

Twenty-four years earlier, Ray Schalk had set a record by catching 151 games in a season for the White Sox. Fifteen years earlier than that, George Gibson had performed the even more remarkable feat of working 133 consecutive games behind the plate for Pittsburgh. (It was remarkable because a catcher can't go that far without being chopped up by a base runner sliding into the plate or having a finger broken by a foul tip; Schalk's great year had interruptions.)

Hayes, who had never worried about records, began to sweat in the last weeks of the season. "Fifteen days to go," he'd say, and then "fourteen. . . thirteen." Now that the record was in sight, he wanted it bad. He made it, but not alone. Unbelievably, after all the years when nobody could do it, two men caught right through the same season—Hayes and Ray Mueller, of Cincinnati. More incredible still, both teams played an extra game that year, so that Hayes and Mueller caught 155 games each.

The race went on but there's no use stretching out the tale. Hayes kept going through 312 games. Mueller's string ended at 233. Baseball records being as numerous as they are, it doesn't matter much. Certainly it doesn't to Frank Hayes, any longer.

DR. EDWARD KILROE

THE KILROE family made news two ways, with the death of Dr. Edward P. Kilroe, a grand and gracious gentleman, and the announcement of weights for the first Experimental Free Handicap drawn by his son, Jimmy. As always, life ends and life goes on, and it could not have displeased Dr. Kilroe that his sons' lives were to be bound up with racing.

His life was. One thinks of the doctor not so much as a physician but rather as a charming, smiling man about the racetracks. He was both. When he finished his internship as a young man he became personal physician to Pierre Lorillard and traveled the world with the tobacco king.

This was back in the 1890s, when Lorillard was laird of Rancocas Farm, those lovely acres near Jobstown, New Jersey, now known as the Helis Stock Farm. Rancocas was then, as it is now, a showplace among Eastern breeding establishments, with its green paddocks and white fences, its indoor and outdoor training tracks, its magnificent barns and—crumbling away now but still standing in a bosky dell—the impressive pile of neo-Roxy architecture that Lorillard built to house a marble-and-tile swimming pool.

Later Rancocas passed to Harry Sinclair and achieved its widest renown, among bookmakers if not among breeders. Up from those rolling pastures, Sinclair and Sam Hildreth brought a mighty company —Grey Lag, Zev, Bracadale, Mad Play—their names are a whispering today, but then they were a panic in the betting ring.

Between them, Sinclair and Hildreth terrorized the books. When the word went 'round that the pair was sending it in on a long shot, bookmakers turned green and white to match the Rancocas silks. Down went the odds in a dizzying spin, and at one time Hildreth found it advisable to employ a "beard," a man who had no visible connection with him and could bet for him without stirring rumors. He selected as a reliable agent for this purpose one Frank James, elder brother and sometimes partner of the redoubtable Jesse James.

Meanwhile, Dr. Kilroe's medical practice led to active association with Eastern racing. He was physician to Eugene D. Wood, promoter and plunger who was a major stockholder in the Jamaica track where the Wood Memorial used to run each spring. Through Wood, Dr. Kilroe became a director at Jamaica and Aqueduct, then president of Jamaica, and he was treasurer and chairman of the board at Aqueduct when he died.

The late, great Jack Campbell trained Jimmy Kilroe in racing and when Mr. Campbell died last summer, Jimmy succeeded him as New York racing secretary and handicapper. One of the jobs he inherited was the assignment of weights in the Experimental.

As everybody ought to know now, it was Jack Campbell's winter custom to issue rankings reflecting his judgment of the leading two-year-olds of the season just completed. He rated them not necessarily off their form in short races as two-year-olds but according to his opinion of their probable class as three-year-olds at distances beyond a mile.

This is a chancy business, for horses change between their second and third years at least as markedly as people develop when they grow up. Year after year, however, Mr. Campbell's amazing prescience was demonstrated in the Experimental Handicaps run at Jamaica in the spring under the weights he assigned.

Taking over this job, Jimmy Kilroe lost no time establishing himself as a young man with strong convictions. This year, he puts Mrs. Russell Firestone's Summer Tan on top with 128 pounds and Belair Stud's Nashua second with 127.

"So all right," he is telling the world, "so Nashua beat Summer Tan three times in four meetings, over Belmont and Saratoga at five and a half and six and a half furlongs. I still like Summer Tan."

What's more, he liked them both exceedingly well, for with the exception of Native Dance (130 pounds) two years ago, it's been ten years since any horse got as much as 127 pounds in the Experimental. Mr. Campbell put 128 on Lord Boswell after 1945.

Before Summer Tan and Nashua, only six horses were assigned more than the three-year-old's scale weight of 126, and only once before did two get more than the scale in the same year. That was the winter of 1942–43, when Count Fleet drew the biggest package of them all, 132 pounds, with Devil's Thumb second at 127.

In a way, Jimmy seems to be saying that he considers both Summer Tan and Nashua better than Citation, not to mention Tom Fool, Middleground, Hill Prince, Blue Peter and Pavot, for none of these stars drew more than 126 pounds.

On the other hand, he may merely be saying, "If I'd been doing it then, those others would have got higher weights. Mr. Campbell was too kind-hearted." Owners and trainers will swoon in platoons.

JOE LIEBLING

"IT IS through Jack O'Brien, the *Arbiter Elegantiarum Philadelphiae*, that I trace my rapport with the historic past through the laying-on of hands. He hit me, for pedagogical example, and he had been hit by the great Bob Fitzsimmons, from whom he won the light-heavyweight title in 1906. Jack had a scar to show for it.

"Fitzsimmons had been hit by Corbett, Corbett by John L. Sullivan, he by Paddy Ryan, with the bare knuckles, and Ryan by Joe Goss, his predecessor, who as a young man had felt the fist of the great Jem Mace.

"It is a great thrill to feel that all that separates you from the early Victorians is a series of punches on the nose. I wonder if Professor Toynbee is as intimately attuned to his sources. The Sweet Science is joined onto the past like a man's arm to his shoulder."

The words are from A. J. Liebling's *The Sweet Science*. Chances are A. J. Liebling, the roving reporter for *The New Yorker* and the sometimes salutary, sometimes smart-alecky critic of the "Wayward Press," was more widely known than Joe Liebling, the boxing buff and Pierce Egan of his day. Yet he did his best work in the latter field because that is where his liveliest enthusiasm could be stirred.

He was, in the literal sense, a student of boxing. As a boy he had some instruction in the use of his maulies from several teachers, including Philadelphia Jack O'Brien, who taught the rudiments of self-defense to a whole generation of Sunday school pupils in Philadelphia and also ran a gym on Broadway.

Later Joe became a devoted reader of Pierce Egan, the great historian of Boxiana in England (1818–24). In his own essays he continually referred to Egan and quoted from him, and when writing to a friend in The Fancy he occasionally allowed himself the small conceit of signing the letter "Pierce Egan."

A gay and witty writer with a remarkable ear for the speech of a Whitey Bimstein or Al Weill, Joe Liebling did memorable work ranging from a profile of George Nicholson, a veteran sparring partner for Joe Louis, to an analysis of Sandy Saddler, "a protracted terra-cotta colored prize fighter whose physique and profile remind me of a praying mantis."

The Sweet Science was published years before fatal injuries to Benny Paret and Davey Moore raised a clamor for laws to ban boxing, but the book contains passages pertinent to that commotion:

"If a boxer ever went as batty as Nijinsky, all the wowsers in the world would be screaming, 'Punch-drunk.' Well, who hit Nijinsky? And why isn't there a campaign against ballet? It gives girls thick legs.

"If a novelist who lived exclusively on apple cores won the Nobel Prize, vegetarians would chorus that the repulsive nutriment had invigorated his brain. But when the prize goes to Ernest Hemingway, who had been a not particularly evasive boxer for years, no one rises to point out that the percussion has apparently stimulated his intellection. Albert Camus, the French probable for the Nobel, is an ex-boxer, too."

Joe tells of a "resonant old gentleman, wiry, straight and white-haired," walking into the Neutral Corner bar on Eighth Avenue and inviting the proprietors to his ninetieth birthday party.

"The shortly-to-be nonagenarian wore no glasses, his hands were shapely, his forearms hard, and every hair looked as if, in the old waterfront phrase, it had been drove in with a nail. On the card of invitation he laid on the bar was printed: 'Billy Ray. Last surviving Bare Knuckle Fighter.'

"Mr. Ray would not let anybody else in the Neutral buy a drink. As he shared his bounty I thought of all his contemporary lawn tennis players, laid away with their thrombosis, and the golfers hoisted out of sandpits after suffering coronary occlusions. If they had turned in time to a more wholesome sport, I reflected, they might still be hanging on as board chairmen and senior editors instead of having their names on memorial pews.

"I asked Mr. Ray how many fights he had had and he said, 'A hundert forty. The last one was with gloves. I thought the game was getting soft, so I retired.'"

HERMAN

WHEN A man of prominence dies, people who knew him make little statements for the press saying, "He will be sorely missed." It is about all they can say for publication. Probably they'd feel they were being mawkish or affected or something if they said that the world has so few men like Herman Hickman that we can't afford to lose one of them.

On Friday the word came that he might not last through the day. All day long phones were ringing, friends of Herman calling one another—Dave Camerer, Jack Lavelle, Charley Loftus, Frank Graham, Bill Heinz, Walter Kennedy. There was one who heard the news when he got home from his office, and he cried. Perhaps many did.

It was not a football coach whom they were mourning, nor a television performer, nor an athlete, nor a gourmet or wit, or writer or raconteur or poet, but a great and dear friend. The thing about Herman was his goodness. He was talented and versatile and warm and funny and fun to be with, but above all he was a truly good man in the spiritual sense, genuinely sweet and pure.

Everybody knew about his collapse of a month ago but the report was that last Monday's operation had been a success. Toots Shor had telephoned him in the hospital afterward: "Say, Fat Boy, I hear you're weighing less than me. Now, listen—"

Thursday night, maybe twenty hours before Herman died, Charley Loftus was saying he was pretty sure that when Herman got out of this he would give in and go down to Florida and take it easy. He wanted to go on working on radio and *Sports Illustrated* but last year had been tough, with both him and Helen in the hospital.

"How about Helen? How is she?"

In his life Herman never had another girl. He was a freshman in the University of Tennessee and he was standing on a street corner in

Knoxville all dressed up—a new tweed suit with plus-fours, two-toned shoes, black stockings, a black knit tie. A couple he knew came along in a car and stopped to offer him a lift and there was another girl in the back, a girl with big eyes and dark hair in coronet braids.

He was just a kid, a schoolboy elocutionist and football player out of Johnson City, Tennessee. When they dropped him off and he made his manners, he was excited. He forgot the textbooks he'd been carrying, and so of course he had to see the dark-haired girl again, and after that it was every night for four years.

Helen was a town girl and her mother was a wonderful cook. She lived clear across Knoxville from Herman's quarters, and after a date he would catch a late trolley that took him through the heart of town.

General Bob Neyland, Tennessee's football coach—he was Major Bob then—used to prowl the downtown streets at night on the lookout for athletes who were supposed to be keeping careful hours. The trolley conductors and motormen got to know Herman well and didn't object when he rode through the business section lying on the floor.

Last time Herman and Helen were encountered in Shor's they both looked wonderful. Herman was down to 240 pounds and was positively svelte, though a little mournful about the diet and being on the wagon and all. What he missed most were the condiments, the hot, peppery dishes and spicy stuff that don't go with ulcers.

He loved to cook almost as much as he loved to eat. When the Village Green Reading Society met in New Haven, Joe Stevens would bring the steaks and when Herman would go to work at the broiler he was a priest at the sacrificial altar.

The Village Green Reading Society never had but eight members and never was a real society, for that matter. Now there are six but they won't meet again, not formally, that is. Grantland Rice was the first to go and after that nobody had the heart for another meeting.

JACK LAVELLE

ONE EVENING when television was comparatively new, with sets located mostly in bars, a convertible with the top down drew up to the curb on Lexington or maybe Third Avenue in New York. In the car were Herman Hickman, the new football coach at Yale, weight about 315 pounds; Jack Lavelle, somewhere around 300; Steve Owen, coach of the professional Giants, maybe 265 at that time; and Charley Loftus, the Yale publicity man, a mere 220 or so.

"Look, Hymie," said a fellow standing at the door of a tavern. "Wrestlers!"

To picture that quartet together now is to realize with a pang what a great deal of laughter, what an immensity of fun, has gone out of life on the sports side of our town. Herman Hickman is gone and Steve Owen, no longer with the Giants, is encountered rarely on the daily round. Charley Loftus has left us. The other evening a party leaving Shor's was intercepted near the door by Joe Harrison, the maitre d', who had just got a phone call.

"Jack Lavelle dropped dead," Joe said.

There was a moment of aching silence. Then without signal or suggestion the group moved back to the bar. There never was a sadder toast.

The obituaries identified Jack Lavelle, correctly, as a scout for the football Giants. They mentioned other activities, recent and not so recent—sports director for the Catholic Youth Organization, official starter of races at track-and-field meets, raconteur, wit and incomparable afterdinner speaker, Eastern scout for Notre Dame assigned especially to watch the Army team in the years these schools met at football.

The obituaries had the facts and missed the truth, which is not surprising. Jack was my friend from college days on and I have been sitting here a long time groping for the words to tell about him and the words won't come. How can you say in a newspaper that a man had a beautiful soul? You can't begin to document it.

He was, in the best and cleanest sense, a wonderfully funny man, a matchless storyteller. An extraordinary thing about his stories was that you never heard one of them until you heard it from him. You'd hear them often later, for other speakers borrowed his yarns and used them over and over, but Jack was always first.

"He could have been a professional entertainer," Bill Heinz said, "and a great one, but he was happy in sports. When you think of the thousands and thousands he brought pleasure to, when you think of the hundreds of times guys went to dinners expecting to be bored and had a wonderful time because Lavelle was there—well, how can you measure that?"

Before he went out to Notre Dame as a freshman, Jack was by his own account a New York City kid who thought all travel west of Paoli, Pennsylvania, was by covered wagon. He knew trains ran to Philadelphia, for he'd been born there. His traveling companion was another New York kid who considered Newark the frontier.

"Think we'll see Indians out in Indiana?" the kid asked nervously. Jack jeered at the yokel.

"So the train pulled into South Bend early in the morning," he related afterward, swearing it was true, "and what did we see? Indians. A Wild West show was coming or going."

He was a shot-putter on the track team, played at football, traveled with the team and his idol, Knute Rockne. He knew or invented more Rockne stories than anybody else in the world. It was Rock who gave Jack his first scouting assignment, back about 1929. As Jack told the story, he got trapped in traffic and never reached the game, so the next morning he bought all the papers and drafted an exquisitely detailed scouting report calculated to deceive the keenest critic.

Rock telephoned from South Bend. "Jack," he said, "you may not believe this, but I can read the papers, too—all except the big words."

From the beginning, he became a scout respected by coaches everywhere, though not even he could devise tactics enabling war-riddled Notre Dame to beat Army's great Blanchard-Davis teams. As the next best thing, he proposed a slogan to replace the campus war cry, "Beat Army!" He recommended "Beat the Japs!"

When Herman Hickman went to Yale he asked Jack to scout for him, and this connection brought Jack a lot of pleasure. His first assignment was at a Wisconsin game, where he found his press box seat already occupied by a stranger with binoculars, notebooks and charts.

"Plenty of seats down at the end," the trespasser told him brusquely. Jack insisted, and the man stiffened.

"Maybe you don't know who I am," he said. "I'm Ernie Godfrey, scout for Ohio State."

The reply was swift and succinct. "Lavelle. Yale. Beat it."

It's dreadfully hard to believe he is gone. Almost the last thing he did was get a friend a pair of tickets to a football game that was sold out. Almost certainly, a quip went with the tickets. If Jack could have written stage directions for himself, they would have been brief:

"Exit laughing."

STEVE OWEN

ON THE eve of a game for the National Football League championship the Law grabbed a punk named Alvin Paris for trying to bribe the Giants' Frank Filchock and Merle Hapes to fix it for the Chicago Bears. As it turned out, the Bears needed no help but the punk wasn't smart enough to foresee that.

Steve Owen, the Giants' coach, pleaded for a chance to question Paris in private. Reluctantly the district attorney said no, not because Steve lacked legal authority but because the DA wanted something left to prosecute. Steve was past fifty then, and his waistline had undergone alterations since his days as an All-League tackle, but his interrogation would have started where the Spanish Inquisition left off.

That Saturday night was the blackest in his life. Nothing else that ever happened to Steve—not even getting fired after twenty-three years as the Giants' coach—hurt him so deeply as the discovery that somebody was trying to play footsie with two of his guys.

There was no evidence that the players ever tried to help Paris win a bet, but they had listened to his proposition without blowing the whistle and had let him pick up the tabs in nightspots.

"I knew that Indian, Hapes, was war whooping around town," Steve said, "but nobody could have told me Filchock would pull anything like that."

The Giants' owners dusted off an armchair for Steve after the 1953 season, and walking the sports beat in New York hasn't been the same since. Nobody ever had more friends than Steve, but memory brackets him with two in particular. Jack Lavelle and Herman Hickman.

This was a mighty triumvirate indeed, close to nine hundred pounds on the hoof and every ounce pure thought. Standing together on a football field they looked like something by Gutzon Borgum. Sherman left no such desolation from Atlanta to the sea as these three could wreak at table or bar.

Jack Lavelle, a raconteur and scout, was the first to go, sitting in front of the television set in his Long Island home. Herman Hickman, poet and Yale coach, was stricken at the wheel of his car in the back country of Maryland and died a few days later.

Steve, who had survived a heart attack two years ago, was taken to the hospital in Oneida after suffering a cerebral hemorrhage, the papers said. Eight days later the last of the Big Three was dead.

Steve came out of Oakland to join the Giants in 1927, their second year of existence, and took over as head coach in 1931. Thus he spanned the formative years of pro football in New York, gave the game aid and comfort when it was clawing for a foothold, helped it achieve major league status, and departed just before the balloon went up.

Since his day a whole new breed of pro football fans has grown up. The Giants today have countless camp followers who never heard of Steve Owen. Others, who only know by hearsay that his teams excelled on defense, will tell you the Giants' success began when they got rid of him.

They couldn't be less informed. Steve's teams won eight divisional titles and two league championships. He adapted his game to his material. When he didn't have the horses to trample the opposition, he figured out how to keep the enemy from scoring. When it came to laying out a plan and getting a team ready for one game that had to be won, he had no superiors and few equals.

In 1953 the Cleveland Browns flogged the Giants, 62–14. "Good thing I'm a defensive genius," was Steve's only comment.

That was his way of going. When his employers didn't provide him with what it took to win, and this was known to happen, he didn't whimper.

He never wanted sympathy. One day, driving up to the Polo Grounds, he stopped for a red light and another driver pulled up on his left to snarl, "Where'd you learn to drive, Fatso?"

"Watch me mousetrap that *indelicacy*," Steve told his passenger. Just before the light changed, he raced his motor in a false start. The hero on his left, who couldn't see what Steve could, leapt ahead to prove his valor. A truck roaring across from the right to beat the light nailed him amidships.

Steve bellowed with joy. He never asked for quarter. He figured out a way.

TOM MEANY

TO A CUB reporter breaking into sports in St. Louis thirty-five years ago, the New York writers were godlike creatures. The kid was, to be sure, almost incredibly naive, but being accepted by the top guys in the dodge was enormously important to him, and with a busher's bat-eyed innocence he regarded anybody who got his stuff published in a New York paper as a top guy per se.

He never forgot or ceased to be grateful to the two who first bothered to discover his name and to treat him as an equal. They were Ken Smith, of the *Mirror,* now director of the Baseball Hall of Fame in Cooperstown, and Tom Meany, of the *World-Telegram.*

Going out of his way to make friends with a busher was the least of Tom Meany's good works, something he did without thinking because friendship came as naturally to him as breathing. He even managed, without trying, to breach the wall that separates the baseball player from the baseball writer.

Usually that wall is invisible, for peaceful coexistence is the general rule, but it stands between writer and player just as the nature of the job keeps the drama critic and the actor at arm's length. Yet after they had toured the Mediterranean theater together entertaining troops in World War II, Nick Etten, the big first baseman, named a son for Tom Meany. This was the equivalent of a Hatfield marrying a McCoy.

During the years of our friendship, Tom moved from the *World-Telegram* to *PM* to the *Star* to the *Morning Telegraph* to *Collier's* to the A. S. Barnes publishing house to the Yankees to the Mets. His talents enriched and his wit brightened them all, though in private he compared a couple of those jobs to "writing for a time capsule."

He possessed in abundance two talents that seldom go together—a phenomenal memory and a flashing wit. Most memory experts are dullards with room in their heads for little or nothing besides their freight of facts and figures, names and dates. Tom's remarkable memory was a mine of anecdote, illumined by his sometimes double-edged wit.

When Toots Shor closed his old joint on Fifty-first Street, the sports mob had a spread-eagle party with, naturally, Tom as toastmaster. It was every man for himself and no holds barred, and as Tom called the shots the accomplished old pro, Jack E. Leonard, sat fascinated by this amateur. "The greatest," he kept saying. "The greatest toastmaster since Jimmy Walker."

Yet Tom could be topped. Before one World Series we appeared together on a television show with two kids of eleven or twelve, whose knowledge of baseball records and averages prompted one viewer to predict, "When those kids learn to type, Meany and Smith are out of work."

The obituaries mentioned Tom's biggest sports scoop—the retirement of John McGraw and appointment of Bill Terry as manager of the Giants. It goes without saying that anytime Tom mentioned this, a story went with it. He would tell not of his own news beat, but of Lou Gehrig and how the big first baseman lived in Babe Ruth's shadow through all his years with the Yankees. One day, June 3, 1932, Lou did what the Babe never accomplished, hitting four consecutive home runs in one game against the Athletics and barely missing a fifth.

That day Tom broke the McGraw story, and again Lou ran second in the headlines.

Characteristically, Tom preferred the story about the scoop he didn't get. On February 15, 1933, Tom visited the Miami city jail by request of a traffic cop. During his brief stay he was aware of a commotion surrounding a wild-eyed character who arrived under heavy guard. Even if he had known that the man was Guiseppe Zangara, the name wouldn't have meant anything. In the pokey he hadn't heard about Zangara taking a shot at Franklin D. Roosevelt and killing Mayor Anton Cermak of Chicago.

Starting on the *Brooklyn Daily Times* in 1923, Tom covered Notre Dame and Army in Ebbets Field when no spotters in the press box fed details of every play and compiled substitutions and statistics to reporters. The reporter toted his notebook among the sidelines and found out for himself who carried the ball.

From these beginnings he "rose"—though he wouldn't describe it so—to be top man in the *Star* sports department. When they shoved that job on him he refused the title of sports editor, so the paper carried his byline as "sports director."

"Sounds like the fellow who thinks up deck games on a cruise," said Clara, his wife.

Clara and Tom traveled the sports beat together and names like Ruth and Grange, Tilden and Jones and Earl Sande and Bronco Nagurski became part of her vocabulary, too.

Late one night Tom came home to Brooklyn slightly the worse for wear. Undressing in the dark so he wouldn't wake Clara, he tried to step out of his pants, tripped on the suspenders and plunged headfirst against a chest of drawers. He staggered back, holding his bruised knob, and listened. No sounds from Clara.

He tried again, tripped again—*bash!* Now there was a voice out of the darkness.

"Okay, Nagurski, this time let's try a pass."

MR. FRANK

IT HAS been written that "many small make a great." Small things like peanuts, scorecards and lemon pop were Frank Stevens's business, but large kindnesses were his career. He was a truly great man.

When Frank Mozley Stevens died at eighty-four, he had been president of Harry M. Stevens, Inc., for thirty years, heading the catering empire that serves hotdogs in ball parks and turkey á la king at racetracks "from the Hudson to the Rio Grande," and beyond.

More importantly, after the death of his father in 1934, he was head of the wonderful Stevens family, an extraordinary clan. Some day it may be possible to say that one Stevens works harder than another, that this one is more generous, more thoughtful, more gracious or more fun than another, but up to now nobody has invented a photo finish camera that could split them out.

They are the finest people alive, they marry the finest girls and raise kids who run exactly to their breeding. Mr. Hal, who was the first of the brothers to go, Mr. Frank, Mr. Joe, Mr. Bill and their sister Annie, their children and their children's children—they are a closeknit family bound by undisguised affection. Thirty years after their father's death, just to mention Harry M. Stevens to Mr. Frank or Mr. Joe would bring tears.

There was the time the late Colonel Matt Winn asked them to take over the catering at Churchill Downs. He and their father had been friends and business associates even before they opened the old Juarez track in Mexico together in 1900—for a highly flavored clientele peppered with bandit chieftains like Pancho Villa and their followers—and he had known the boys most of their lives.

Joe appreciated the business value of a showcase like the Kentucky Derby and was eager to take it on, in spite of the fantastic burden of work it would put on him.

Frank, though, had many valid objections. He was determined to confine operations, at that time, to the Eastern Seaboard. No one-day operation could justify the investment of manpower, money and toil the Derby required.

Colonel Winn argued and Frank said no. He fancied himself as a hard-headed businessman and he could be wonderfully stubborn.

"Well," the Colonel said, sighing, "I didn't want to bring this up. But I once did a favor for your father."

All of a sudden Frank dissolved in tears.

A job in the Stevens organization is like a commission in the army, except that officers aren't shifted from post to post the way these troops move from Rockingham Park in New Hampshire to Hialeah in Florida, from New York to San Francisco, always with a member of the family on the spot.

Mr. Frank, as he was called by all employees, was the commander-in-chief. A ruddy, handsome, immaculate man with blue eyes twinkling behind his dark-rimmed glasses, he was a prodigious worker, yet he always had time for his friends.

He knew everybody and he could tell stories about most of them—about the wild days in Juarez, about the mornings in Saratoga when Harry Sinclair might bring a party to the track still in evening clothes after an all-night whirl in the Casino, and more champagne would be consumed at breakfast than the clubhouse bar sells in a whole meeting today.

At the races Frank was a sucker for any tip. Lacking advice from Max Hirsch or Mr. Fitz or Preston Burch, he would buy two daily double tickets on the 1–3 and 3–1 combinations. It was surprising how often those numbers came up, but they didn't at Saratoga on August 10, 1955, his seventy-fifth birthday. That afternoon 7 and 5 paid telephone numbers. Frank had 'em. That night the 7–5 double hit, again for boxcar figures, at the harness track. As usual, Frank was working the day-and-night shift. He had 'em.

He would keep such winnings in a separate pocket and exhibit the roll with delight. The money meant nothing; it is impossible to describe his unaffected joy in winning.

At any track or ball park where the firm operates, there is always a corner of the Stevens office open to friends for a drink and a yarn at the day's end. Once a newcomer was brought into the office in the Polo Grounds, where the day's receipts were being counted. Banknotes were stacked on a long table and silver whirled in coin-sorting machines.

"What'll it be?" Frank asked, bringing bottles out of the safe.

"Well I'll be damned!" the newcomer said. "This is the first place I've ever seen where they leave the money around in the open and keep the whisky in the safe."

PEACE, AT LAST, COMES TO THE BATTLER

BARNEY ROSS needed some new threads and was impatient when his friend Ira Colitz said, "I want to get some things, too. Wait till I can go with you."

"The Man's going to tap me on the shoulder any day," Barney said. "How can I wait?"

The tap came at a veterans' hospital in Chicago and those closest to Barney at the end—Ira Colitz and Barney's wife, Cathy, and Sam Pian and Art Winch, the pair who managed him when he was lightweight, junior welterweight, and welterweight champion of the world—could not truly mourn. At fifty-seven, Barnet David Rasofsky had suffered more than any man should.

Barney was a week less than fourteen years old when his father was murdered by a pair of punks trying to rob Isidore Rasofsky's little grocery in Chicago's Jefferson Street ghetto and from that day on the boy's life was a battle.

He fought men like Billy Petrolle and Jimmy McLarnin, Ceferino Garcia and Henry Armstrong in the ring. He fought the Japanese in the Guadalcanal jungle and came out loaded with shrapnel and weak with malaria. He fought the narcotics habit in the Public Health Service hospital in Lexington, Kentucky, and he fought cancer to the end.

Barney was a lightweight giving away close to ten pounds when he challenged McLarnin for the welterweight title and punched his baby face off. A few months later they met again and McLarnin got a split decision. In their third match Barney broke his left thumb in the sixth round. For nine rounds he couldn't use the hand without blinding pain, but he punched out a unanimous decision.

After McLarnin came Ceferino Garcia, who would later knock out Fred Apostoli for the middleweight championship. In their first match,

Garcia's bolo punch caught him in the first round. Next thing Barney knew he was in his corner and Art Winch was shaking him.

"What round is it?" Winch asked.

"End of the first," Barney said.

It was the end of the fifth.

Barney woke up in time to win the decision in ten rounds and spent the rest of the night in a Turkish bath trying to cook out the pain.

He whipped Garcia in another ten-rounder, then signed for a third bout at fifteen rounds in New York. It was one of four title matches on Mike Jacobs' Carnival of Champions card.

Three days before that fight, Barney broke his left hand on a sparring partner's skull. Pian and Winch wanted to call it off but Barney told them he wasn't going to spoil Mike's big show. The truth was, he had earned half a million dollars in the ring and blown it all on the races. One afternoon he went for $18,000 at Washington Park in Chicago. It wasn't only his hand that was broken.

Because he couldn't afford not to, he went in and fought Garcia with his right hand, trying to use his left only for defense. There were times when he was forced to punch with it, though, and then he almost fainted.

Garcia was a good fighter, as tough as anybody in his time, but he couldn't lick one side of Ross. Barney won ten of the fifteen rounds.

On May 31, 1938, Barney was only twenty-nine years old but he had been boxing more than twelve years as amateur and professional and had been through eighty-one pro fights, most of them small wars. Still, he was sure he could take little Henry Armstrong, the featherweight champion moving up two divisions.

Barney was right for five rounds. Then the legs quit on him. After the tenth round Pian told him he was through, but Barney screamed at him and answered the bell. After the eleventh Arthur Donovan, the referee, said, "Sorry, champ, I've got to stop it."

"Let me finish," Barney pleaded. "It's the last favor I'll ever ask of you. I'll never fight again."

He was still on his feet at the last bell. "A champion," he said, "has the right to choose how he goes out."

GOODBYE, HARRY

A STORY Harry Stuhldreher liked to tell concerned the days when the Goodbye Harry Club was a going concern on the University of Wisconsin campus. The old quarterback of Notre Dame's Four Horsemen was athletic director and football coach at Madison then, and his dark, intelligent features were not displayed in oil in every home in the state.

Like all teams, Wisconsin had years when it couldn't win for losing. Unlike all football fans, the undergraduates and alumni and taxi drivers in Madison are exceedingly knowledgeable. When the team lost, they knew the reason and the remedy: The coach was a boob; throw the bum out.

So they unfurled their banners reading "Goodbye, Harry," in the stands. They screamed for the coach's pants. They threw things long overdue for the garbage pail. The papers were full of it, of course, pro and con.

One day the *Capitol-Times* or *State Journal* published a letter to the editor. It pointed out reasonably that there was no sense in firing Stuhldreher unless the college had a better man to take his place. It reviewed the football records of the local public high schools; Madison East had an enviable reputation for imaginative, effective attack. Madison West almost always came up with a defense that was virtually impregnable.

The solution to Wisconsin's problem seemed obvious to the writer. Bounce Stuhldreher and hire the two specialists as cocoaches.

That evening the Stuhldrehers' eldest son, Skippy, was waiting with the paper in his fist when his father got home. Skippy, already bigger than Harry had ever been, was the regular quarterback at the third high school in town, Central Catholic. He was livid. Had Harry read this—this rag?

Harry felt a pang. He'd been around long enough to know it was always open season on coaches and he could shrug off abuse. Sometimes a particularly vicious attack would make Mary cry, though, and now the kids were getting old enough to be hurt, too. It was time for a heart-to-heart talk.

Yes, he told Skippy, he had read the letter. It hadn't bothered him and he hoped Skippy wouldn't let these things get under his skin. It was part of the game. After all, this was a free country and who were they to say the man didn't have a pretty fair idea. . . .

"But," Skippy protested fiercely, "Madison East and Madison West, those bums! My coach at Central Catholic is the guy should have your job!"

The Goodbye Harry Club was disbanded after the 1948 season when Wisconsin got a new coach. It was reconvened yesterday for the last time, not only in Madison but in every city in the world where there are two or more football fans over the age of forty-five. Harry Stuhldreher had died suddenly in Pittsburgh, the first of the Four Horsemen to go.

"Outlined against a blue-gray October sky, the Four Horsemen rode again. . . ." That was how Grantland Rice began his story of Notre Dame's victory over Army in 1924, and the magic of the catchwords transformed a gifted, exciting, wonderfully coordinated pony backfield into a quartet of immortals.

Harry Stuhldreher, the 154-pound leader and passer; Jimmy Crowley, left halfback, sallow, flat-chested, with the mincing, deceptive gait and fluid hips; Don Miller, swift and rugged at right half and the biggest of the four at something like 170 pounds; Elmer Layden, the 162-pound fullback who shot through the line like a Comanche's arrow—never in the history of football did a single group enjoy such undying fame, not even Fordham's Seven Blocks of Granite, whom Crowley coached.

They had Granny Rice to thank for that and thank him they always did as long as he was alive. Fame goes to the heads of a lot of college kids who get to believing their press notices. These guys never forgot their debt to Granny.

Don Miller coached only briefly while in law school but all three of the others made substantial contributions to football after graduation. Harry, who stayed in the game longest, was a great director of athletics.

Yet it was as a unit, and as undergraduates, they made their greatest contribution. They gave the game something special and precious that can't be coached and can't be manufactured. People call it romance.

Harry, who insisted in later years that none of them was big enough to make a major college team of more recent vintage, used to chuckle about the excitement they stirred. The backs got all the publicity, as backs usually do, although a good, game effort was made at Notre Dame to give the linemen equal billing as the Seven Mules. (Actually there were eight, with two right guards splitting duties about equally.)

"Knute Rockne," Harry would recall, "worried that the linemen might resent all the attention showered on us, so he had the team vote on which was the more important, the backfield or the line.

"The line won, seven to four."

DASH OF PEPPER

JOHNNY KEANE, a Cardinal from his first day in baseball until he managed the world champions thirty-five years later, was reminiscing about last year's struggle for the National League pennant when Joe Reichler of the Associated Press came into the Yankees' dugout.

"Sorry to bring bad news," Joe said, "but Pepper Martin is dead."

Keane's gray, lined face was stricken. It is unlikely he and Pepper ever were intimate, for when John Leonard Martin was the biggest name in the game John Keane was nineteen, going on twenty, and had just completed his second season as a bush league infielder. In a baseball sense, the towns where Keane had played—Globe, Arizona, Waynesboro in the Blue Ridge League and Springfield, Missouri—were a million light years from Sportsman's Park.

But as a kid in St. Louis Johnny had been a card-carrying member of the original Knothole Gang, sitting in left field and screeching, "We want a homerrr!" whenever Rogers Hornsby or Chick Hafey or Jim Bottomley went to bat. Then in Globe and Waynesboro and Springfield he was a member of the family. And for any kid in the Cardinal chain in those days, the beau ideal, the model, the hero larger than life, had to be Pepper Martin, the Wild Horse of the Osage.

"Oh, my," John said at Reichler's news. "Oh, my, I saw Pepper just—well, maybe it was at the World Series. He was in St. Louis and he looked fine. What a sweet guy, and what a ball club that was! Do we have them as tough as that today? These were guys who just hated to play in clean suits."

Perhaps that was a curious way of expressing it, but the words brought memories back in a flood—a hundred memories of the cutting, slashing desperadoes who were the Cardinals of 1931, and most vivid of all the image of a rawboned, ungainly country boy who couldn't play one inning without looking like something dug out of a potato field.

They could send Pepper Martin out of the clubhouse all scrubbed and combed and laundered and pressed, though there never was a tailor who could cut flannels to look natty on those preposterous shoulders. Then he'd go busting down to second base with one of those headlong, belly-whopping slides and up he'd come out of the dusty whirlwind that was his native habitat with his sweat-soaked haberdashery blacked with loam, a glistening film of grime on the homely face with its great, beaked brow.

Pepper Martin wasn't the greatest hitter of all time, or the greatest fielder or thrower or base runner, but he did everything well and no more fiery competitor ever lived in any sport.

In the highly colored judgment of one who was a young sportswriter at the time covering the Cardinals and all wrapped up in the team's fortunes, Pepper was, for at least one ten-day span in his life, the most exciting ball player of human history. That was in the 1931 World Series, when he was a living flame laying waste to what may have been Connie Mack's greatest team.

This was the team of Lefty Grove, George Earnshaw and Rube Walberg, Al Simmons, Jimmy Foxx, Mickey Cochrane and the rest, overpowering favorites to win their third straight world championship. Almost literally, Pepper broke them between his soiled and reddened hands.

He didn't hit everything Grove and Earnshaw threw and he didn't steal Cochrane's underwear. It only seemed that way. By the time the Series was three games old, newcomers arriving in the park were asking first of all, "Which one is Martin?"

In enemy Philadelphia, the hotel lobby was a maelstrom with Pepper its center. "Pepper, how do you account for the way you're going?" "I dunno. I'm just takin' my natural swing and the ball is hittin' the fat part of the bat." "Mr. Martin, where did you learn to run the way you do?"

"Well, sir, I grew up in Oklahoma, and once you start runnin' out there there ain't nothin' to stop you."

In Philadelphia's Broad Street Station Judge Kenesaw Mountain Landis, the commissioner who never was unaware of an audience, bellowed above the crowds, "Young man, I'd like to change places with you right now."

Quoth Pepper, never unaware of salary discrepancies, "Well, Judge, seventy-five thousand dollars against seventy-five hundred dollars—I'll swap you."

After the World Series Pepper toured in vaudeville for more money than he had collected in baseball—people would fill theaters just to see and hear a ball player in those days of innocence. Then he loaded his shotgun and his midget racing car and other necessities of life into the pickup truck that was his idea of a wealthy young sportsman's equipage, and took off for Oklahoma.

He never changed. He played the big cities and he managed in the top minors but in all his travels he never found anything more beautiful in his eyes than a tractor. There was passionate honesty in him, and an almost ministerial sincerity, yet on a team of indefatigable merry-Andrews he had a hand in every prank.

He was one of those who, disguised in white coveralls and carrying paint buckets, marched into a dinner in a Philadelphia hotel and began redecorating the room, somewhat to the consternation of the speaker. He was maestro of the Mississippi Mudcats, a jug-and-washboard band in the Cardinal clubhouse. When the team was tossed out of a Boston hotel for shooting pigeons from the windows, Pepper was there.

He did not clown in the field, though. An umpire in the minors found that out when Pepper, then a manager, dissented from a decision.

"Pepper," the league president asked later, "when you had your hands on that man's throat, what could you have been thinking?"

"I was thinking I'd choke the son of a bitch to death," Pepper said earnestly.

BIG POISON

PAUL WANER had been one of baseball's finest hitters for a dozen years before a chance remark dropped in the dugout disclosed that he couldn't read the advertisements on the outfield walls. He never had been able to read them from the bench and he hadn't given it a thought, for in his philosophy fences were targets, not literature.

Naturally, steps were taken immediately. With his weak eyes, Paul was batting only about .350. It stood to reason that with corrected vision he'd never be put out. So the Pirates had him fitted with glasses and he gave them a try.

He hated them. For the first time in his life, that thing the pitchers were throwing turned out to be a little thing, a spinning, sharply defined missile no bigger than a baseball. He had always seen it as a fuzzy blob the size of a grapefruit.

Near-sighted millions read about the experiment and chuckled in sympathetic appreciation of his disgust. We in the myopia set see the world as a rather pleasant blur where vaguely outlined objects any distance away appear larger than life, like a street lamp in fog.

The point is, Waner had been whacking that indistinct melon in exact dead center ever since he left the town team in Harrah, Oklahoma.

When Paul Waner died, the obituaries cited the statistical proof of his greatness as a ball player, mentioned his election to the Hall of Fame in 1952, and, of course, referred to the nicknames he and his kid brother Lloyd bore in the game—Big Poison and Little Poison.

Both were small men physically but Paul, with a batting average of .333 for twenty big league seasons, was somewhat more poisonous to pitchers than Lloyd, who hit .316 for eighteen years. Actually, though, Paul's nickname was neither a tribute from the pitchers' fraternity nor a reference to his preference in beverages, appropriate though it would have been in either case.

"Poison" is Brooklynese for "person." A fan in Ebbets Field was supposed to have complained, "Every time you look up those Waner boys are on base. It's always the little poison on thoid and the big poison on foist."

Maybe the quote is apocryphal but the facts support it. Between them, the brothers made 5,611 hits, about four times as many as a whole team gets in a season. Since Eve threw the first curve to Adam, only eight men have made more than three thousand hits. Paul's 3,152 put him ahead of some pretty fair batsmen named Rogers Hornsby, Ted Williams, Lou Gehrig and Babe Ruth.

By rights the records should credit Paul with 3,153 hits or else there should be a separate page in the book for him alone. It would read: "Most Hits Rejected by Batter Lifetime—1, P. Waner, Boston NL, June 17, 1942."

When the second game of a doubleheader started that day, Waner had 2,999 hits. He had opened the season with 2,955 and had struggled through fifty-two games toward the shining goal of 3,000. In twenty-five games he'd been shut out, but now one more hit would do it.

With Tommy Holmes a baserunner on first, the hit-and-run was on. Holmes broke for second on the pitch and as Eddie Joost, the Cincinnati shortstop, started over to cover the bag, Paul hit toward the spot Joost had vacated. Joost slammed on the brakes, spun back and got his glove on the ball but couldn't hold it.

In the press box the official scorer lifted a forefinger to indicate a single, which it was. A roar saluted the three-thousandth hit. Beans Reardon, the umpire, retrieved the ball and trotted to first base with the souvenir.

Waner was standing on the bag shaking his head emphatically and shouting, "No, no, no!" at the press box. Reluctantly the scorer reversed his decision. Two days later Paul got number three thousand off Rip Sewell, of Pittsburgh, and this was a clean single to center.

Because his hitting overshadowed everything else, Waner's defensive skill is rarely mentioned, but he was a superior outfielder, one of the swiftest runners in the National League with a wonderful arm. One season he threw out thirty-one baserunners to lead the league.

"He had to be a very graceful player," Casey Stengel has said, "because he could slide without breaking the bottle on his hip."

Casey was Waner's manager with the Braves and he knew it was a myth that he enjoyed his nips between games. Most of the tales told of him around the ball parks tell how he might show up somewhat bleary after a night of relaxation, strike out three times, then triple the winning runs home on his fourth trip.

The late Bill Cissell, an American League infielder, spent some time with the Waners and their friends in Sarasota one winter. They had a field baited for doves, but not every shot fired there came out of a 12-gauge. In fact, Bill reported—and he was an excellent jug man himself—sometimes the safest place in the county was out in the field with the birds.

BOY FROM PARNELL

WHEN JIMMY JONES was growing up in Parnell, Missouri, his father Ben was gypsying through the West and Southwest trading horses and beads with the Indians, not entirely for their benefit. By the time Jimmy got to be mayor of Parnell and president of the bank, his sire was racing on big wheels and doing well enough to send back substantial deposits for his savings account.

Now, nothing much can happen in a town like Parnell without word getting around to all four hundred inhabitants, if not clear across Nodaway County. So after a while Jimmy scribbled a note to his father.

"Dear B.A.," he wrote. "I'm certainly happy that you're doing well, but I'd suggest that you send in your deposits in smaller chunks. The folks back here think you're stealing it."

It is paying small homage to the memory of a great man to say that Benjamin Allyn Jones honestly earned and richly merited every good thing he got in his seventy-eight years. He didn't steal money and he didn't steal horses—but ah, my foes, and oh, my friends, the horse races that he stole!

There was a morning at Churchill Downs when a couple of visitors dropped into the tack room, which Ben, and Jimmy too by that time, used as an office in the Calumet Farm barn. The stable area was a-boil with the excitement of Kentucky Derby week but for once the Jones boys didn't have a colt they considered good enough to start in the big one.

"It just doesn't seem right, Ben," a guy said, "to be sitting here with you with another Derby coming up and you not in it."

"I know," Ben said. "I miss it, too. I love the excitement of the Derby, and getting a horse ready, and all."

"Last year," he said, and his blue eyes were happy, "last year I had

Hill Gail so sharp for this race that there wasn't a three-year-old in the world could've beat him at a mile and a quarter. And before that, what a kick I got out of putting little old Ponder over in '49!"

"Yes," a visitor said, "I'm sure you did." For he was remembering the refrain that Ben had sung all week long before the Derby of 1949: "That poor little old horse of mine, he ain't got no more chance'n a Shetland Pony."

Herbert M. Woolf, whose horses Ben trained for a while and for whom he won the Derby with Lawrin in 1938, complained that Ben talked too much to newspapermen. In that respect the trainer knew what was good for the owner's business better than the owner did. Ben made that clear in 1948, though he didn't have Woolf in mind at the time.

It was Friday, the day before the Derby. Calumet's twin favorites, Citation and Coaltown, had finished their work and cooled out and were back in the barn when along came a newsreel crew to set up cameras and sound equipment and Kleig lights in Coaltown's stall, having cleared it with the trainer, of course.

Ben went in with the horse and moved him around here and there, posing him this way and that, doing everything asked without protest while the cameras ground on and on and the colt began to tremble and sweat under the hot lamps. Afterward Ben was worried, because breaking into a sweat like that just after cooling off could have knocked the horse out of the race. Never again, Ben confided, but not in the newsreel men's hearing, would he take such a chance with a good horse so close to a big race.

"I marvel at you, anyway," a friend said. "I simply can't see how you keep your patience at all with all this mob getting underfoot all week when you're trying to do your job."

"If we don't have publicity," Ben said simply, "we can't have racing." Maybe others would recognize this truth, perhaps even Herbert Woolf, but most of them would say, "Sure, but why pester *my* horse? Somebody else, not me."

Then there was Whirlaway's year, 1941, when Ben was going for his first Triple Crown. The Jockeys' Guild was just getting organized and the riders arranged their first annual dinner as a big testimonial to Earl Sande, taking the ballroom of the Lord Baltimore Hotel for the night after the Preakness and bringing in Bernie's orchestra.

The Preakness Ball was on the same night, and the racing brass gave the riders the back of their necks. It was a painful affair—a great long dais peopled with little guys wearing black ties, the band trying to make like a festive occasion, and not more than two or three parties at all those dressed-up tables on the floor.

The strain of trying to pretend that the party wasn't a flop was becoming downright suffocating when here came a passel of escapees from the Preakness Ball—Ben Jones, trainer of the winner; Eddie Arcaro, rider of the winner; and their pal Don Ameche, whom the gang was calling "Whirlaway's Mascot" that spring.

If he could, Ben would have brought Whirlaway himself.

"The best horse in my barn," Calumet's late Warren Wright called his trainer, and Jimmy is cut from the same cloth.

WESLEY BRANCH RICKEY

WHEN THE Library of Congress gets around to offering its facilities as a repository for the bills, dun letters and picture postcards of Golden Gate Bridge that make up the collected papers of this department, it won't be necessary to throw out Groucho Marx's correspondence to make room. Of all the goodies that Joe the Mailman has delivered over the years, only two personal letters have been saved for posterity.

One is a note from a jockey and the other a scrawl in the hand of Wesley Branch Rickey. The latter is treasured for its closing line: "I think you understand me better than most, perhaps."

That has to be the most undeserved compliment of the century. To respect Branch Rickey is as easy as breathing. To hold him in warm personal esteem is easier still. But to understand this brilliant and complicated man, to follow confidently the workings of his mercurial mind, to reconcile the paradoxes of his personality—this is a boast never made here.

Branch Rickey is, as they used to say in Brooklyn, "a man of many facets—all turned on."

To say that Branch Rickey has the finest mind ever brought to the game of baseball is to damn with the faintest of praise, like describing Isaac Stern as a fiddler. From the day in 1903 when Branch signed as a catcher for LeMars, Iowa, at $150 a month, he was a giant among pygmies. If his goal had been the Supreme Court of the United States instead of the Cincinnati Reds, he would have been a giant on the bench.

His contributions to the game have been catalogued too often to bear repetition. He changed the structure of organized baseball more completely than Babe Ruth changed the strategy of play. And though he was not a great manager—chances are his blackboard lectures only confused the players—he never turned his hand to a job on the executive level without total success.

In St. Louis he built the bankrupt Cardinals into an empire that dominated the National League. In Brooklyn he got the Dodgers out of hock and installed them as the power that displaced St. Louis. In Pittsburgh his "youth movement" was derided, but it flowered in a world championship after his departure.

Success and personal popularity do not always go hand in hand. Rickey made many baseball men uncomfortable. They feared him in a business deal because he was smarter than they. Some suspected him because he never drank. He was pictured as a hypocrite who would outslick you in a trade on Saturday but considered Sunday baseball immoral.

He did no such thing, and it always bothered him that his reason for refusing to play ball or count the house on Sunday was widely misunderstood. It wasn't sanctimony and it wasn't, as the popular notion went, that he had "promised his old lady."

The profoundest influence in Branch's life was his deeply religious mother. His affection and admiration for her were such that when he left Scioto County in Ohio to play professional baseball, he wanted to pay a tribute to her.

She never asked him not to play on Sunday and he never promised he wouldn't. He just didn't. He thought it would hurt her if her son desecrated the sabbath. Years later he realized that she must have been hurt more when she discovered that she was the cause of the ridicule he invited.

So it was a deeply personal thing, yet Branch could chuckle at a joke that was current in St. Louis during all his years there. The windows of the Northside YMCA overlooked the center-field fence of Sportsman's Park and big Sunday doubleheaders always had spectators there. "That one's Rickey's room," somebody in the press box invariably said, pointing to a high corner window.

Also misunderstood were his motives in breaking baseball's color line by hiring Jackie Robinson. To be sure, the motives were mixed, but he was not, as charged, trying to shape himself in Abraham Lincoln's image.

When he was baseball coach at the University of Michigan in 1910, he shared the pain of a black player named Charles Thomas on encountering discrimination in a hotel in South Bend, Indiana. "Tommy," he promised, "someday we'll change all that."

From that day on, he waited for the chance to strike a blow against prejudice. Yet, when he got Robinson, he was trying primarily to make the Dodgers a better team.

A baseball man above all, he could not sit by and let a great reservoir of talent be wasted. How great that reservoir was is shown by the big league batting averages any day during the season. Blacks monopolize the top lines, and the National League excels the American because, thanks to Rickey, the Nationals got to this talent first.

That must gratify the baseball man more than anything else.

ARTHUR NEHF

JUST ABOUT a year ago there was a word-of-mouth report that Arthur Nehf had died. It wasn't true, but it wasn't the sort of "exaggeration" that could be brushed off with Mark Twain's classic comment, either, for Arthur had undergone an operation for cancer and it had been a desperately tight fit.

A man of quiet dignity and rawhide resolution, he made a remarkable recovery. Or so it seemed. In early March there was an opportunity to visit with him in his pleasant home in Phoenix, Arizona. It was a happy hour or so on a lovely, sunny afternoon.

Art moved sprucely about the house, seeming wonderfully fit. He poured a drink and had one himself, his first since entering the hospital. He chatted of old friends and old days, of the long-ago days when—as his teammate Larry Doyle said—it was "great to be young and a Giant."

He winced when he heard how the Polo Grounds had come to look, with an asphalt auto track around the field and weeds growing on the basepaths. But memories brought laughter, memories of Shuffling Phil Douglas and the keeper John McGraw hired to supervise Phil's drinking, of Jess Barnes and Fred Toney and Beauty Bancroft and Frank Frisch, of young guys named Waite Hoyt and Bill Terry, and a man named McGraw.

Now there is news again from Phoenix. This time it is true. Arthur gave it a tussle, and lost the battle that no man can win.

They called him "Little Arthur" when he was the best left-handed pitcher in the National League but he was a full-grown man, all class. He might have been a church organist as his mother hoped when he was a kid in Terre Haute, Indiana; he might have practiced engineering, as his family expected when he was an undergraduate at Rose

Polytechnic; but baseball was his destiny, and a tougher, more honest competitor never honored the game.

If he never had another distinction, Art Nehf would still be unique as the only rival pitcher who ever started against Walter Johnson feeling sorry for that mighty man. It is a measure of his understanding that he knew what Johnson was feeling when they started the first game of the 1924 World Series, Johnson's first World Series after eighteen heroic years in Washington.

"Walter was so nervous before the game I felt sorry for him," Arthur said that night to Frank Graham, who reported it in his history of the Giants. "He knew that millions of people were pulling for him. When we shook hands for the photographers, his hand trembled."

It is not to be imagined that Arthur's compassion embraced Bucky Harris or Sam Rice or Goose Goslin or any other Senators. He went twelve innings against Johnson, and beat him, 4–3.

If Arthur could understand how Johnson felt before the game, he also knew from personal experience how Walter felt after. On October 6, 1921, Arthur had made his first World Series start against the Yankees' Waite Hoyt. Pitching to Babe Ruth, Bob Meusel, Wally Pipp and that mob, he allowed three singles. Hoyt allowed two, and errors beat Nehf, 3–0.

The teams were all square at two victories each when Nehf and Hoyt hooked up again. This time the Giants got to Hoyt for ten hits. Arthur pitched a six-hitter and lost, 3–1.

Three days later the pair went at it for a third time and this was the payoff. The teams were square again, nine innings away from the fifth victory then required for the championship. Hoyt yielded six hits and one unearned run, Nehf four hits and no runs whatever.

That was thirty-nine years ago. Then, as now, the standard of World Series pitching perfection was Christy Mathewson's three straight shutouts in 1905. Matty held the Athletics to fourteen hits in twenty-seven innings; Nehf gave the Yankees thirteen in twenty-seven.

In 1926 Arthur had neuritis and couldn't pitch. McGraw asked waivers and Cincinnati put in a claim. The Reds were better than the Giants that year and would finish second to St. Louis. Catching on with them was a rare break for a man with a sore arm, or so most players would feel.

Arthur didn't see it that way. When he discovered that the Reds hadn't been warned of his condition, he was furious at McGraw for making him part of a swindle. They didn't speak until six years later when Art walked into training camp towing a big kid outfielder named Hank Leiber.

It was the Boston Braves who had given Art his start in the majors and he had also played for Cincinnati and the Cubs. Yet when he found a kid who looked like a live one, there was only one place to turn. Little Arthur was a Giant.

CAPPY WELLS

THERE WAS a time not many years ago when an autumn Saturday in New York could bring an atmosphere of happy excitement that you could sense away down in the bowels of the subway. Notre Dame would be playing Army at football in Yankee Stadium, or perhaps it would be Fordham and St. Mary's in the Polo Grounds or Fordham–New York U. Anyhow, the town would be jumping and this, you felt, was the way it should be in the greatest of all sports centers, the city of John McGraw's Giants and Joe McCarthy's Yankees, the city that had all the big fights, the finest racing, the international polo matches and, indeed, just about every event that qualified as big league.

When changes came, they came with bewildering speed. It is shocking to realize that when Army plays the Air Force in the Stadium Saturday, it will be the city's first big college game—Columbia at Baker Field hardly meets that description—in six whole years. Inducements had to be offered—the city is picking up the tab for $15,000 in amusement taxes and the Yankees cut the Stadium rent in two to get the show—but here it is, and the joint is sold out and for one day, at least, all will be as it used to be.

By the sorriest sort of coincidence, it had to be this week that Cappy Wells died. Nobody had a bigger part in New York's great football days and nobody lived through them more fully and joyously, than Colonel Walter H. Wells.

Cappy was the prophet of Army football and probably the finest goodwill ambassador West Point ever had, though he never attended the military academy as a cadet, never got there until he was a captain who, starting as an enlisted mn in World War I, had won his commission in combat in France.

Cappy was the public information officer in the late 1920s and early

1930s. Phil Fleming was graduate manager of athletics then and Biff Jones and Ralph Sasse did the coaching and among them they thawed out the icy reserve that had characterized the brassbound military caste up the Hudson.

Even in sports there had been a noticeable stiffness in Army's press relations before their time. Either the press reflected the public attitude or vice versa, but there was a fairly widespread notion that West Point cadets were supercilious poppinjays in bellhop suits. Cappy dedicated himself to breaking down this feeling, with resounding success.

He made the press welcome. Particularly in regard to football, he managed to establish the Army team as the home team in New York, and it has retained this identification even through these last half-dozen years when Army never played in the city. He created friendships that have endured, friendships for himself, incidentally, but primarily for the academy.

About the time of Cappy's arrival Army and Navy had a spat over eligibility rules. They didn't meet in football in 1928 and 1929. Cappy sweet-talked both sides, and it is generally agreed that he did more than anybody else to get them together again.

Prohibition's parched paw was on the land in those days, but no guest with proper upbringing was going to stick a hydrometer into the lime juice served in the privacy of an officer's quarters. Not, at least, if the officer was also a gentleman.

In his five years at the Point, Cappy built enough goodwill to survive the stupidity of some of those who held the job later. Perhaps there were periods when the climate tended to cool but then another guy would come along to restore the old warmth, a guy such as Ockie Krueger who was very much like Cappy and, together with Red Blaik, General Jerry Counts, Red Reeder and a few others, preserved the traditions of the Wells-Flemming-Jones-Sasse days.

Cappy was a soldier before he served at the Point, and a soldier afterward. In World War I, he and an enlisted man armed with .45s cleaned out two German machine-gun nests. In World War II he was a full colonel and hoped for combat command but was sent instead to Rio de Janiero as chief of staff in the South Atlantic Theater.

Visited there by members of the Brazilian cabinet, he showed the guests through the installations, including the code room. Next day, discovering an order forbidding such exposure of secret material, he promptly turned himself in. No harm had been done, but he was busted to lieutenant-colonel and shipped to the Pacific Theater.

Maybe that was the reason he never made brigadier.

LITTLE FELLAS

JUST AS vacation started, Eddie Gaedel died. Eddie Gaedel was the midget who went to bat once in major league baseball, if you could call the St. Louis Browns of 1951 a major league team. The plot was written years before that by Jim Thurber, but Bill Veeck, who signed Gaedel to a contract, always swore the idea was original with him and said he hadn't read Thurber's yarn until after he had arranged for life to mirror art.

Both in fiction and in fact, the deed was done in St. Louis. In Thurber's story, "You Could Look It Up," a midget named Pearl du Monville, signed to a proper contract, was sent to bat with two out in the ninth inning and the bases filled, the tying run on third. Pearl's orders were to get a base on balls and force in a run, but after throwing three balls the pitcher eased one up with an underhand lob, so soft and tempting that the midget swung. He grounded out, ending the game.

On August 19, 1951, Eddie Gaedel went to bat for the Browns against the Tigers and did draw a walk from Bob Cain, who couldn't find the tabloid strike zone. Eddie was replaced by a pinch-runner. Amidst screams of "Sacrilege!" from baseball's stuffed shirts, Will Harridge, then president of the American League, voided Gaedel's contract, but never did define legal size limits for players. Eddie measured three feet, seven inches.

Well sir, Eddie's death reminded Dick Reynolds, of Providence, Rhode Island, of still another case in which a fingerling pinch-hitter won renown.

Seems there's a little squirt out of Providence who is the world's midget rassling champion right now, though this is a fairly fuzzy title, and will remain so until somebody answers the question: How big is a midget? Suppose Conn McCreary or Willie Shoemaker were to switch from the racetrack to the rassling mat?

Anyhow, the midget rassling champion of the world performs under the name of Sonny Boy Cassidy, but his square name is Larry Tattersall. He's a trifle over four feet tall, about six inches longer than Eddie Gaedel.

In 1948 he was hailed as the smallest pinch-hitter on the globe after he had won a game for North Providence High School. This was three years before Eddie Gaedel burst onto the big league scene.

Tat is a natural athlete who played high school hockey and basketball as well as baseball. He was on the bench that day in 1948 when North Providence loaded the bases against Woonsocket in the last of the ninth with the score tied, two out, and a weak hitter due at the plate. Dick Flynn, the North Providence coach, waggled a finger at Tat, who leaped down from the bench, picked up a bat approximately as long as himself, and shaped up for instructions.

"You're on your own," Flynn said, "but keep away from that umpire. He's so blind he'll trample you to death."

The umpire was Hank Soar, now an American League veteran but then a refugee from the New York football Giants, coaching the Rhode Island State College backfield and trying to break into organized baseball.

When Soar saw Tattersall, he said, "Get behind the backstop, kid. You'll get killed out here."

"I'm the hitter," Tat said.

Soar wheeled to bellow toward the North Providence bench: "Get this kid outta here, Flynn. He's too low for an umpire."

"Don't be silly, Albert Henry," Flynn said. "There's nothing too low for an umpire."

The Woonsocket pitcher did his best, but the first three deliveries were too high for Tat's tidy little strike zone. Gus Savaria called time. He was coaching Woonsocket. He is a solid baseball man, justly respected for sending Clem Labine to the big leagues.

Savaria spoke to his catcher. "Kneel down," he said, "and give him a target." The catcher knelt, and the pitcher got two strikes over. The count was three and two when Flynn called time.

"Go into a crouch," the coach told Tattersall.

"Lie down and give him a target," Savaria told the Woonsocket catcher.

Everybody gave it his best Sunday try, but the Woonsocket pitcher missed the strike zone. Hank Soar said "ball four," and the winning run crossed the plate for North Providence.

"Everybody in the littlest state," writes Dick Reynolds, of Rhode Island, "is still mighty proud of the littlest athlete who has converted his handicap into an asset that makes him his living."

PORKY OLIVER

NEWS OF Porky Oliver's death brought deep sadness but no great sense of shock, for everybody knew how it was with big Ed, including Ed himself. It is said that the Lord never lays a burden on one whose shoulders aren't big enough to bear it. Ed Oliver's shoulders were huge. They needed to be.

For the last two years this great, warm-hearted bear of the fairways knew he was dying of cancer. He never complained and he never stopped working as long as he was out of the hospital, where he went for two operations and for the inevitable end. He had to give up golf but he refused to give up the public appearances and travel in behalf of cancer research, for which he helped raise something like $20,000.

I think it is literally so that anybody who met Ed Oliver, even once, remembered him thereafter with genuine affection. There was warmth about him as enduring as it was endearing.

He didn't look like an athlete, unless your idea of the perfect athletic build is a smooth oval measuring 5 feet, 9½ inches at its greatest length and weighing 225 pounds. Yet he was a splendid golfer—lowest competitive round, 60 at Hornell, New York; best 72-hole score, 265 in the Virginia Beach Open—and he was a gallant competitor, lacking only the merciless quality that makes a champion.

When Byron Nelson was at the top of his game, he looked like a big hungry cat debating whether to play with his victim a little longer or swallow him at a gulp. In the course of a championship tournament, Ben Hogan's tan face would grow haggard, his lips stiff and pale.

Then you'd see old Porky come swinging down the fairway, a jolly fat man with a wide, infectious grin, swapping jokes with the gallery and playing beautiful golf that seemed plenty good enough to win but somehow never got him more than second money in the major championships.

Once he might have won the United States Open. That was in 1940 at Canterbury outside Cleveland when he turned in a 287, the same score as Lawson Little and Gene Sarazen. However, he was disqualified for starting the final round ahead of schedule, so instead of a three-way tie there was a two-man playoff that Little won.

Six years later at Portland, Oregon, Ben Hogan beat him in the final match for the PGA title. He was runnerup in the Open in 1952, with 285 to Julius Boros' 281. In 1953, his twentieth year out of the caddy ranks of Wilmington, Delaware, when he was rising thirty-seven, Ed rolled jauntily around the Augusta National course for a 279, tying the Masters' record shared by Ralph Guhldahl and Claude Harmon. That was the year Hogan chose to shoot 274 for a record that still stands. Once more Porky finished second.

A caddy at eleven, Ed turned pro before he was eighteen, but army service kept him away from golf from 1941 to 1945. At least it kept him away from tournament golf, though he did have one memorable match during the war which he loved to tell about later.

He'd been assigned to some camp in the South, maybe Fort Bragg, when his old friend, Joe Louis, came through on a boxing exhibition.

"What you doin' way down here, Porky?" Joe asked, "whyn't you come up to Camp Shanks where we could play some golf together?"

Porky conceded that the suggestion had merit, but he was reluctant to bring it up with General Marshall, the Chief-of-Staff.

"Hell," Joe said, "I know the guy. I'll fix it."

Sure enough, a day or so later Private Oliver was ordered transferred. "Whyn't you take a weekend off?" Joe asked when Porky arrived at Shanks. "Go over to New York or maybe down home to Wilmington?"

"Look, Joe," Porky said, "there's a war on, or hadn't you heard? I've just got here and I've got no pass."

"I'll give you a pass," Joe said. "I'm the sergeant."

Army life could be beautiful after all, Porky decided. His sergeant was and is daffy about golf, and he had a knack for making opportunities to play. One day they had some duty but Joe said there'd be time for eight holes before they had to shape up. "But you gotta start me two-up," he said.

Porky hollered. Two-up for an eight-hole match! How bloodthirsty could army life make a guy?

"You gotta," Joe said. "I'm the sergeant."

So they played, and with his handicap Joe won. With such grace as he could muster, Porky paid off.

"Tell you what, Porky," Joe said, conscience-stricken, "now we'll box four rounds. I'll give you the first three."

THE WESTROPE BOYS

IN THE winter of 1931–32 when Eddie Arcaro was an apprentice at Agua Caliente who had never ridden a winner, one of the horsemen who occasionally gave him a mount was W. T. Westrope, whose son Tommy was a rider at the meeting. Tommy's kid brother, Jackie, was there too, serving mostly as exercise boy and hot-walker, though with his fourteenth birthday coming up he considered himself a veteran jockey. He had ridden his first winner in Lemon, South Dakota, when he was twelve. He wouldn't score on a recognized track until he was fifteen.

From the jockey's quarters on the clubhouse turn, riders could watch the races in which they were not employed. They were there, Arcaro among them, when Tommy Westrope was thrown. The race was over and he was pulling up his mount right in front of them when the horse stumbled. Tommy landed on the point of his chin, and died instantly with a broken neck.

"I'm not sure," Arcaro said yesterday, "but Jackie might have been watching with us that day. He probably was. He was always around the jocks' room."

They were talking about Jackie in the jockeys' quarters at Belmont. He was winning the Hollywood Oaks in California with a filly named Well Away when she bolted and flung him into the rail. He died two hours later, following his brother after twenty-six years.

"If the mare threw Jackie," Arcaro said, "she'd toss anybody, because he was as good a horseman as you could find. In the morning he'd handle the rogue horses that nobody else could work. You never saw him with a pony boy taking his horse to the post. Jackie could take care of his own mounts.

"We were always friends, from those first days. I broke my maiden in that 1932 meeting at Caliente and it was the next year in Havana he got his first winner on a big track. His big race? Gosh, now you ask me like that, I can't seem to recall any in particular. He rode so many stakes and won so many races. I can't pick any of 'em out."

"I remember one," Ted Atkinson said. "I'll never forget it. He was on Royal Vale in the Suburban of 1953 and I had Tom Fool. We hooked up at the three-eighths pole and were noses apart all the way to the wire.

"Tom Fool won by a short head but it was so short I wasn't sure we had won. Two-three times in that three-eighths I thought I was getting away from him but he always got back to me. He could get everything out of a horse that the horse had in him, if not more."

"He was a strange guy," Eddie said. "He had a manner—it was kind of a complex. I don't know how to describe it but when you first met him you didn't like him. Then when you got to know him, you liked him very much."

Two or three valets murmured assent.

He was a strange guy, aggressively militant and full of resentments and outspoken. He rode with a fierce combativeness and he was frequently in trouble with the stewards and he fought their rulings angrily.

In 1952 he was winning the Santa Anita Handicap for Buddy Hirsch with Intent when Johnny Covalli forged up inside with Michie. Intent banged Michie against the rail and went under the wire first but Michie collected the $104,000 purse and Westrope got thirty-four days on the ground. That evening Arcaro had a little dinner party in Beverly Hills.

"I'm seating Jackie between you," he told a pair of late arrivals, "because I know you'll be kind. He feels bad."

Strope, as the jocks call him—he was christened Jack, not John—was a bit hard to handle that night, morose and moody and sullen. He defended his riding, insisting young Covalli had tried to get through a space that was too narrow. At one point he stated the creed of his craft.

"For ten thousand dollars," he said, referring to the rider's share of the purse, "I'm giving nobody room."

THE PRIEST WAS AMBIDEXTROUS

THERE MAY have been an instant's hesitation on Frank Frisch's part when the name of the Reverend Harold J. Martin was mentioned. Then came recognition. "Uncle Judy," the Dutchman said, "oh, sure. He was a right-handed pitcher, a left-handed pitcher, and he played left field. A terrific guy."

There had been stories in the papers about Father Martin. As a student at Fordham he played ball with Frisch before Frank went to the Giants en route to the Hall of Fame. In the obituaries he was identified as a right-handed pitcher.

"He could throw both ways," Frank said, "and he did. He was truly ambidextrous."

"Did he ever switch over during a game?"

"I think he did," said Al Lefevre, who played on the same Fordham team. "I remember him particularly pitching for our freshman team when I was on it, and it seems to me he switched a few times. He was best as a right-hander, though.

"Seems to me he batted from both sides of the plate, too. He was a pretty good hitter, though he wasn't very big—about five-eleven and kind of skinny. That name—Judy, we called him—I don't know how he got it. He was from Boston, you know, and he brought the name down with him."

Between Fordham and the seminary, Judy Martin pitched professionally for New Haven and Albany. When he was pastor of a church in Ogdensburg, New York, the parish needed money for a playground. Under the name of Doc O'Reilly, the priest went to work pitching for a semipro team and achieved a local renown that eventually brought him to the attention of Bishop Joseph H. Conroy, who put on a storm.

The idea of a priest giving scandal, putting off collar and cassock for a ball player's flannels! A man of God appearing in public as a professional athlete! And for what?

"Seventy-five dollars a game," Father Martin said.

"Seventy-five dollars!" His Excellency said. "Do you think they could use a third baseman?"

With Bishop Conroy's permission Doc O'Reilly kept on pitching until the children of his parish had their playground.

"That was Uncle Judy, all right," Frisch said. "I used to see him at the minor league meetings in the winter. You know, he was president of the old Canadian-American League and he organized the Border League and the Northern New York State League. On top of that, he was part-owner and vice-president of the Utica club in the Eastern League. How about that?"

"A priest owning part of a ball club? How did he ever manage that?"

"I don't know," Frisch said. "I expect he just pitched into community affairs and the club needed backing and he raised money somewhere and said, 'All right boys, stand back. I'm going to keep this league alive.' He was that kind of guy.

"Three winters in succession I made arrangements to go up and see him in his parish near the St. Lawrence River. I was spending my winters in Lake Placid then and I was going to drive up from there. Every time we had a date, I'd get up that morning and look out the window and I couldn't see my car, the way it was snowing.

"I'd get on the phone. 'Judy,' I'd say. 'I know all about it,' he'd say, 'it's the same up here. Never mind, we'll do it another time.' But we never did."

"As a student, did he show an inclination toward the priesthood?"

"We would have May devotions on the quadrangle around the statue of Our Lady," Al Lefevre said. "Each day a student would be appointed to conduct the services. I remember Judy preaching an outstanding sermon, the very finest."

"I wonder where he got that name, 'Doc O'Reilly,'" Frisch said. "While we were in school I played as 'McCarthy' with pick-up teams, semipros. Lefevre was 'Lenihan' in those games. You know, McGraw wanted to send Lefevre to San Francisco but Al went for the law instead. He was one of those guys, good field, no hit the curve.

"We were playing the Lincoln Giants up on the old Catholic Protectory Grounds in the Bronx. I was playing third and a fellow in the front row kept saying, 'Hey, McCarthy, they'd love this up at Fordham. Oh, McCarthy, what college you playing for next week?' I was mumbling, 'Lay off, will you please? I'm only getting a buck and a half for ice cream.'

"After those games some of the other guys would pool their pay and buy a barrel of beer. I'd walk another block and a half and get a double malted."

"As an undergraduate, did Judy ever play with you bums on the sly?"

"I don't think so," Frisch said, "he was a good student. Me, I was a good hitter."

CHUCK KLEIN

IT USED to be said in jest that the Philadelphia newspapers of the early thirties kept a headline standing in type to eliminate the expense of constant resetting. It read: "KLEIN HITS TWO AS PHILS LOSE."

Philadelphia readers didn't have to be told that the number "two" referred to home runs, not singles. With Chuck Klein it was generally double or nothing, two or no-count. Curiously, he never once hit three in a game, though once he hit four. Chances are the Phillies lost that day, too.

Out of all the oddly assorted hundreds who wore Phillies' uniforms in the days between Grover Cleveland Alexander and Robin Roberts, Chuck was the reigning deity. Habitués of fusty old Baker Bowl adored him as Babe Herman was worshiped in Brooklyn.

As a matter of fact, one realized in retrospect that Chuck and the Babe had a good deal in common, for both were mighty left-handed hitters whose defensive skill fell a trifle short of genius. Not that Klein was a bad outfielder. He had good speed and could steal bases—when he wasn't jogging around tipping his cap to idolaters—and he became accomplished at playing caroms off the tin-faced wall in right field. If it is true that practice makes perfect, then improvement was inevitable in that department, because when a left-handed hitter failed to hit the wall against Philadelphia pitching it was scored as an accident.

A strapping, smiling, clouting kraut from Indianapolis, Chuck was ogre-in-chief in what must have been the most frightfully destructive batting order ever presented in matching flannels. In the lineup of 1930, for example, Klein batted .386, Lefty O'Doul .383, Pinky Whitney .342, Barney Friberg .341, Don Hurst .327 and Spud Davis .313. The identity and average of the center fielder has eluded memory, but the weakling of the squad was the brilliant shortstop, Tommy Thevenow, who hit a mere .286, three points under the figure sustained last summer by the American League's finest shortstop, Gil McDougald. It wasn't until a couple of years later that Dick Bartell succeeded Thevenow and improved the attack with a .308 average.

You read the figures and you ask how, by all that Doubleday made holy, could such monsters lose ball games. Well, there was a line that the announcer in Baker Bowl repeated even oftener than the papers proclaimed the divinity of Klein. It went: "Willoughby now pitching."

No matter what name was borne by Philadelphia's starting pitcher, sooner or later his burden would shift to the shoulders of Claude Willoughby. Trudging wearily in from the bullpen, Willoughby would cast a wistful glance at the scoreboard. It would read something like this:

        VISITORS . . . 3 5 1 4 2 3
        PHILLIES . . . 4 4 1 1 4 2

Chuck had played barely one hundred minor league games when the Phillies bought him from Ft. Wayne in 1928 for $7,500 or thereabout. In what was left of his first full season, he ripped into National League pitching for an average of .360.

For the next five years his average ranged from .337 to .386, he drove in as many as 170 runs in a season and smashed as many as forty-three home runs. Twice chosen the Most Valuable Player in the league, he established a hatful of records yet never won a batting championship. (The year he hit .386, Bill Terry hit .401 for the Giants.)

It broke Jerry Nugent's heart to peddle Chuck to the Cubs after the 1933 season. Still, the club president's heart wasn't the only thing busted in those days, and he was getting $65,000 and three players in the deal. Jerry got Chuck back after two comparatively ordinary seasons in Chicago, and got to keep the $65,000 to boot.

That was one of the earliest deals in a series that earned the Cubs a distinguished reputation as the prize gulls of the game. Six months after getting Klein, they gave the Phillies cash and Dolph Camilli for Don Hurst, who repaid them by hitting .199. The Phils got four fine seasons out of Camilli and sold him to Brooklyn for $45,000 and an outfielder.

Chicago gave up the fine pitchers Curt Davis and Clyde Shoun plus $185,000 to get Dizzy Dean's dead arm, and then had to pay a taxidermist to mount it. In another maneuver they landed the admirable Claude Passeau but a rookie tossed in to bind the deal was sold later by the Phils for three Brooklyn players and $100,000. Rookie named Kirby Higbe.

Just last fall the Cubs bribed the Braves to take Bob Rush—but that's getting away from Chuck Klein. Except for part of a season in Pittsburgh, he went on and on with the Phils into the season of 1944, then stayed on as a coach. He was a sweet guy.

THE DAZZLER

THERE WAS a photograph next to the obituary of Dazzy Vance. It was the great man, all right, in characteristic pitching motion, canted back on his hind leg with the ball in his fist behind him, his gloved hand pointed skyward, left foot in the batter's face. Yet there was one false note. Where the laundered sleeve of his uniform ended, the sleeve of his sweat shirt showed neat and tidy, clinging to the contours of the mighty right arm.

That wasn't the Dazzler's real business attire. When the greatest of all Brooklyn pitchers was fogging them over for the Dodgers, the right sleeve of his sweat shirt was an unsightly rag, a flapping thing of shreds and tatters. Daz would hide the ball until the last instant, and then if the batter was lucky he would see something white rocketing toward him out of a distracting flutter of drygoods.

Ultimately the umpires discouraged Dazzy's experiments in camouflage, which he didn't need anyway. There was smoke on his fastball and smoke in his highball, and surely nature intended him from the beginning to be just what he was—the gifted, gregarious, gaily unrepentant leader of the merry andrews who played baseball, when the spirit moved them, as the Dodgers of Uncle Wilbert Robinson.

Dazzy went south to Homosassa Springs, Florida, many years before the Dodgers went west. Today Brooklyn fans have only their memories. For those too young to have known the days of Daz, then the next best thing is to read about them in Tommy Holmes's classic *Dodger Daze and Nights* and Frank Graham's history, *The New York Yankees*.

When Larry Sutton, the scout, recommended Vance after seeing him pitch for New Orleans in 1921, Charley Ebbets, the Dodgers' president, wanted no part of him because he had failed in trials with the Yankees and Pirates. He took him only because Sutton arranged a package deal including Hank DeBerry, a catcher whom Ebbets did want. A few years later Ebbets was disgorging $25,000 a year to the highest-paid pitcher in baseball.

This was untold wealth in the eyes of a country cousin of Dazzy's who went into Atlanta to see his famous kinsman pitch a spring exhibition against the Yankees. In the hotel before the game, cousin Arthur—Dazzy's real name was Clarence Arthur but he pretended it was Arthur Charles—amused himself by introducing his visitor to the Yankee stars.

"This is Lazzeri," he said. "I'll strike him out. This is Combs. He'll pop up. Meet Babe Ruth. He'll break his bat swinging at my stuff."

Leading off in the first inning, Earle Combs did pop up, to the cousin's delight. Then Mark Koenig doubled, Lou Gehrig tripled, Ruth hit one out of sight, Bob Meusel tripled, Tony Lazzeri knocked small boys out of a tree beyond the left-field wall, and the lad from the country saw no more of his cousin until he got back to the hotel. His chagrin cooled by now, Dazzy asked him how he had enjoyed the game.

"Cousin Arthur," the boy said, "that's the easiest way to make twenty-five thousand dollars I ever saw."

In those days prominent citizens like Representative Andrew Volstead and Scarface Al Capone were divided on the wisdom of St. Paul's advice to "take a little wine for thy stomach's sake." Dazzy was founding father of an inner circle of Dodgers who subscribed to Capone's view.

Dazzy named his more or less secret society the Big Four, though membership was not so strictly limited, and Tom Meany, then covering the Dodgers for the *Brooklyn Times*, contributed the club motto—"One for all and four for oh." Fined for being out after hours, the pitcher Jess Petty was notified in writing that the crime of getting caught merited expulsion from the Big Four but he would be permitted to submit a written appeal. Hailed before a kangaroo court, Petty perspired through a letter he had Joe Gordon of the *New York American* write for him.

"The inner council of the Big Four," Dazzy told him sternly, "is endowed with infinite wisdom. It is a simple matter for us to ascertain whether you actually wrote this brief for yourself. You have used the word *ignominious*. What does it mean?"

"It means," said Petty, "I was cold sober."

After the culprit was dismissed in stony silence and the roars that followed had subsided, Vance wrote out the sentence: "It is the unalterable judgment of the council that inscribed beside the name of Jesse Lee Petty in the immemorial archives of the Big Four shall be the following notation: 'Tried—and found wanting.'"

Curiously, the games Vance pitched that seem most vivid are games he lost. In 1931 he and Paul Derringer, a Cardinal rookie, were scoreless into the ninth inning, when George Watkins bunted safely, reached third with two out and another Cardinal on first base. Dizzy liked to give a runner a false sense of security by lobbing several soft throws to first base before firing for a pick-off. After a couple of slow tosses, Watkins called for time.

Kneeling, ostensibly to tie a shoelace, he told Gabby Street, coaching at third, to have the runner draw another throw to first. The runner took a lead, again Vance tempted him with a lazy toss, and Watkins stole home with the winning run.

Dazzy had had an even more trying experience the previous September, for then the Dodgers were leading the league by half a game over the Cardinals, who were starting a three-game series in Ebbets Field. This time he and Bill Hallahan went into the tenth without a score, though except for Dazzy's quick thinking Sparky Adams would have swiped the game before that. Trying to steal home, the St. Louis infielder appeared to have it made but the Dazzler thoughtfully aimed at and potted the batter, Chick Hafey. The pitch was ruled dead and Adams returned to third.

In the tenth the Cardinals scored on a pinch-double by Andy High, then choked off the last Brooklyn threat with a phenomenal double play. St. Louis took over first place and Dazzy lost the only chance he ever had to lead the Dodgers to a pennant. With the great man beaten, they didn't win another game that year.

THE BRAVEST MAN

THE BRAVEST man Ray Arcel ever knew was Bob Olin, who won the light-heavyweight championship of the world in a travesty of timorous sparring and then, hag-ridden by fear, lost it in the most wantonly reckless fight of his life. Ray Arcel has handled hundreds of fighters and fifteen world champions, and none of the others was so tortured by fear.

"He used to give up inside," Arcel once told Bill Heinz. "He'd be so sick before some fights that you could hardly get him out of bed. You'd have to scream at him and holler at him and abuse him. Yet if ever a man had courage, he had it."

Olin took a decision and the title from Maxie Rosenbloom November 16, 1934, and eleven months later Arcel took him to St. Louis to fight John Henry Lewis, who had whipped him in a nontitle match in April. Four nights before the bout, Ray and the sparring partner, Marty Sampson, were awakened by frantic pounding on the door between their hotel room and Olin's.

They found the fighter up, wearing overcoat and trousers over his pajamas, white and sweating. "I'm gonna die, I'm gonna die," Olin babbled. "I don't know what's the matter. I'm gonna die."

Ray got some warm milk into him and got him back to bed and sat stroking his forehead, telling him the fight was off, there was nothing to worry about, just to go back to sleep. In the morning the trainer telephoned their room-service waiter, a brother of the old lightweight, Joe Ghnouly, and said, "I'm sick. I need a doctor." The waiter got them an appointment.

"My name is Marty Sampson," Ray told the doctor, "and," pointing to Olin, "this is Ray Arcel. Ray doesn't feel well."

The doctor went over Olin for an hour. When he was finished, he said, "Mr. Arcel, if I had your physical condition—your build—I'd be a prize fighter."

When Olin was out of the room, the doctor turned to Arcel. "Mr. Sampson," he said, "what did you do to frighten that man?"

Ray said he didn't understand.

"Mr. Sampson," the doctor said, "that man is afraid of something. He's suffering from extreme nervousness and nervous indigestion. That's all that's the matter with him, and if I were you I'd watch him very closely."

One day Olin had been scheduled to box and had not gone to the gym. Another day when no work was planned he sparred three rounds. The newspapermen were puzzled and suspicious. Harried by doubts that he'd ever get his man into the ring, Arcel kept assuring them everything was just peachy.

There was no mention of the fight in Olin's presence. Arcel and Sampson stayed with him around the clock, keeping him in the hotel, babying him.

They got him to the arena and into his fighting clothes. He had been training for two months and his body was fit, but in the dressing room sweat poured off him. They led him down to the ring.

"It was one of the greatest fights I ever saw," Arcel says.

Olin walked out and ripped into Lewis, who was a first-class fighter then. John Henry teed off. He gave Olin a good licking, yet in round after round Olin kept coming in. Round after round, they dug in and punched.

John Henry's great friend, Joe Louis, was at ringside. Mixed bouts were uncommon in St. Louis then. There were many in the crowd who had come to root for Lewis and before it was over they were cheering Bob Olin. So was Joe Louis.

In the corner after the thirteenth round, Arcel said, "Bob, don't let this guy take your title." Olin didn't answer. He stood banging his gloves together and glaring across at John Henry, waiting for the bell for the fourteenth. They battled through the fourteenth and fifteenth and Lewis earned the decision and got it, with the title.

Crowds clamored outside Bob Olin's dressing room. There was an old Negro woman in the mob. "Let me look at that man," she kept yelling. "Let me see that man. I got to see a man's got guts like that."

THE DUKE OF MILWAUKEE

THIS MAY have been Al Simmons's last time at bat in a major league baseball game. At least, it was right around there, for by this time Al was a coach with the Philadelphia Athletics and the only reason for keeping his name on the active list was his hope that he might make the few more hits he needed to achieve a lifetime total of three thousand. He had, like many other ball players, a deep reverence for records. And the three-thousand-hit club is one of baseball's most exclusive fraternities.

Anyhow, he went up as a pinch-batter this day in Boston, with one out in the ninth inning and the game on the bases. He hit the ball as well as a man could, and it went straight to the shortstop for a double play that ended the game. A rookie who came face to face with him as the play ended was startled beyond the limits of ordinary diplomacy.

"Hey," said the kid, brand new with the club, "what's the matter with you? You're white as a sheet."

"Don't worry about me," Al snapped furiously.

If the rookie was so ignorant he had to be told that Al Simmons didn't choke up in the clutch, then there was no use trying to explain the fact was that to Al baseball was so close to war it affected him as war affects some men; it filled him with a cold, bloodless fury which literally turned him pale.

"When I was hitting," Al said after he was through, "I hated pitchers." This was one of those hit-and-run jumps during spring training like an all-night ride from Los Angeles to Yuma, when the athletes were in bed and their elders sat up over a last beer.

"Pitchers," Al said. "I wanted them dead. Them so-and-so's were trying to take the bread and butter out of my mouth."

He never killed a pitcher, but he made a lot of them wonder why they'd been born.

He never got his three thousand hits, either, but he blamed no pitchers for that, only himself. "If I'd only known as a kid what I know now," he said. This was when he was a coach clinging to the active list and reaching hungrily for a bat whenever Connie Mack nodded his way.

"If I'd ever imagined I could get as close as this, three thousand hits would have been so easy. When I think of the days I goofed off, the times I played sick or something and took myself out of the line-up because the game didn't mean anything, I could cut my throat."

Al was a truly successful man, for he knew he was a great player and a bona fide celebrity and he relished being accepted among them on even terms. The Duke of Milwaukee, they called him, and he had a swagger befitting the rank. He was proud of the title and proud of his hometown, used to boast about other celebrities from Wisconsin like Alfred Lunt and Don Ameche and Pat O'Brien.

Yet he had the gift of self-appraisal. When he started out in baseball he set a financial goal that, having attained it, he raised several times. "When I finally decided I had it made," he said, "I was never again the ball player I was when I was hungry. The only man I ever knew who never lost his fire when he got rich was Ty Cobb."

If Al lost his fire, only he knew it. One summer when a very poor team of Athletics was having an unaccountable hot streak, Connie Mack was asked which player he deemed chiefly responsible. Connie glanced at the only photograph of a ball player that he kept in his office. It was a picture of Simmons at bat, one of those standup jobs mounted on wood and cut out with a scroll saw along the outline of the figure.

"I wish I had nine men like Simm," Connie said, disconcerting his questioner by mentioning a coach instead of a player. "Just coaching there on third base, he does more for the spirit of this club than anybody else on the field."

At a winter meeting in Chicago, Connie told Simm there would always be a place for him in the Philadelphia organization.

"I appreciate that, Mr. Mack," Al said, and he hesitated. "Of course you"—he had started to point out that Connie was getting along in years and wouldn't be around forever. "That is," Al said. "I—well, we don't know how long—"

Connie was chuckling at his embarrassment. "I think my sons know how I feel about it," he said.

"Maybe they do," Al said dubiously, "but would you mind telling them?"

Laughing, Connie said he would. Seems odd, somehow, and sad. Al lived only a few months past Connie's death.

GEORGE KREHBIEL

THE EIGHTY-SECOND Kentucky Derby was the last for George Krehbiel, racing editor of the *Detroit News*. He was in the Churchill Downs press box watching Needles run over his field, and he shouldn't have been. Everybody knew he shouldn't, including George, but nobody could have induced him to back off a job he had been doing for a quarter of a century.

George had been having dizzy spells. One of them knocked him out two days before the Derby, but on Saturday he was back, feeling rotten. He would do his job and then go home to Detroit and enter a hospital for a check-up.

Sunday morning, the day after the Derby, George and his wife, Lenore, got into their car to start home. "What's that noise?" The noise was in his head. He was having a stroke.

Lenore got him to a hospital and they called a brain specialist. On Monday they hoped they would be able to fly him home but he never rallied. He died Thursday morning.

He was sixty-four, a glorious guy. He and Joe Palmer were special friends when Joe was writing racing for the *Herald Tribune*. In 1952, when Joe died of a heart attack, George broke up at the funeral. Mourning George now, it is perhaps sentimental, but comforting, to believe that Joe is rejoicing.

A year or so before Joe died, George had a slight heart attack. He was on the wagon for a while after that. One night he startled Lenore by coming home from a party about ten o'clock.

"Look," she said, "I know about Man O' War in the Sanford Stakes and Jim Dandy in the Travers, but a form reversal like this! George, what gives?"

"Honey," George said, "the jokes aren't funny any more."

After a while he got to feeling better and living better. He would come out to the track with his eyes sparkling, a glow of health in his round cheeks. He had discovered vitamins. He took a capsule every morning and it did wonders for him.

Joe Palmer didn't accept much on faith. Inquiring about this wonder drug, he established that it was George's daily custom to chase the capsule with a couple of muscular slugs of bourbon.

"The bum!" Joe said indignantly, "he's giving Squibbs the credit that belongs to Brown-Forman!"

One of the last columns Joe wrote, and certainly one of the most memorable, was inspired by a jug of jellied whisky that was a gift from George, whom he had encountered in the Lafayette Hotel in Lexington. They met fairly often there, for it was Joe's hometown and George, who raced horses besides writing about them, had a farm in Kentucky.

The two of them held some prejudices in common and they took a lot of pleasure in them. Joe is a native Kentuckian and George as a Kentucky breeder affected a lofty contempt for horses bred in outlandish places like California, and they united in baiting West Coast turf writers at Derby time. Later George added Florida-breds to his list of unspeakables.

"They're all the size of Shetland ponies," he said, "because they got nothing to eat down there except coconut husks."

His own best horse, probably, was Golden Man, a stakes winner that ran for him over six seasons and earned about $10,000 a year, give or take. To see George stall-walking in the press box when Golden Man was going to the post, to hear him talking to himself, talking to the jockey (who couldn't hear him), talking to the Lord (who probably could), was an object lesson for any neophyte who might imagine it would be fun to own a thoroughbred.

At a Detroit meeting when George was calling the feature for the radio, he put Golden Man in a race he didn't think he could win, intending merely to tighten the horse for later engagements. Golden Man broke on top but that meant little to George, who was confident his horse would soon come back to the field.

Coolly dispassionate, he described the running for the great unseen audience. Golden Man at the start. At the quarter, Golden Man, So-and-so, This-and-that and Such-and-such. At the half, Golden Man by two lengths. This-and-that by a head.

They were coming around the stretch turn. Through his binoculars, George could see that the jockey had a good tight hold on his horse. Golden Man was leading by two lengths and drawing out, and there was a purse of $5,000 waiting at the wire.

"Excuse me, ladies and gentlemen," he said into the microphone, and now there was a hoarse note in his voice. "That's my horse in front, and if you don't mind, I'm gonna do some rootin'.

"Come on with 'im boy! Come on! Come aaahhh! EEEEyah!"

That's how the broadcast ended. From the stretch run on, the listeners got no description, and they flooded the radio station with phone calls and letters. They had loved it. It was honest.

AFTERWORD

IN ONE OF the columns collected here, my father recounts a funny tale about Stanley Woodward, his editor and great friend, and a dinner party that ended in a good-humored, marvelously drunken wrestling match on the floor. Defending this apparent irreverence in an obituary column, Pop wrote: "I realize that's no kind of story for a time like this, but some of us must laugh, lest we cry."

That was his philosophy. He always wanted to talk about life rather than death, joy rather than sadness, the art of living rather than the act of dying. A reader could get the wrong impression from the theme that links the columns in this collection, the impression that the author was preoccupied with dying and those who had gone before him. Nothing could be further from the truth. He meant it when he said in a eulogy for a friend: "Dying is no big deal, the least of us will manage that. Living is the trick."

My father mastered that trick admirably in his seventy-six years. If living well is the best revenge, then living life exactly the way you want, doing whatever it is that you like most and do best until the last hour, that was his idea of fulfillment.

In the last three years of his life, when his health and strength were fading, my father and I talked a lot about what he might do with the time that was left to him. Concerned that he would tire himself out, I kept urging him to slow down. It was an unrewarding task. He wanted nothing so much as to keep traveling the beat and writing his column. No surprise then, that conversations that began about dying turned quickly to living.

He knew, of course, that his time was running out. But he seemed genuinely at peace with the thought. "I can't complain," he said during one late-night conversation in front of the fire at his home in Martha's Vineyard. "I've had a very good run."

Others of us can complain, to be sure, on the grounds that he went too soon. But I take comfort from the fact that his "good run" continued until the very end. Writing his column and writing it well was the ultimate proof to my father that he was still alive, really alive. His last column appeared on Monday of the week he died. It had a vaguely valedictory quality to it, although I doubt he realized as he wrote it that it would be his last. But it was good—that's the point—and it looked ahead, to writing more columns in the future and to living rather than dying.

TERENCE SMITH
Washington, D.C.
March 1, 1982

WALTER W. (RED) SMITH *was born on September 25, 1905, in Green Bay, Wisconsin. He graduated from Notre Dame in 1927, and went to work as a reporter for the Milwaukee* Sentinel. *He then became, in rapid succession, a copyreader, rewrite and assignments man, and sportswriter for the St. Louis* Lone Star, *the Philadelphia* Record, *and in 1945 the sports columnist for the* New York Herald Tribune. *Not long after the Trib's demise, Red became the primary sports columnist for* The New York Times, *where he worked until his death in January 1982. Among his many awards over the years were an Honorary LLD from his alma mater, Notre Dame, the George Polk Award, and in 1975, long overdue, the Pulitzer Prize.*

Quality Paperbacks from PLUME and MERIDIAN

(0452)

☐ **LET THE TRUMPET SOUND: The Life of Martin Luther King, Jr. by Stephen B. Oates.** The magnificent recreation of the great civil rights leader's life from birth to his tragic death. Through this brilliant examination of the forces that shaped King—parental, cultural, spiritual, and intellectual—and of the forces he became at a crucial moment in America's history, we see the real Martin Luther King, not an abstract symbol but a very human and great man.

(254426—$8.95)

☐ **ALBERT EINSTEIN: CREATOR AND REBEL by Banesh Hoffman with the collaboration of Helen Dukas.** On these pages we come to know Albert Einstein, the "backward" child, the academic outcast, the reluctant world celebrity, the exile, the pacifist, the philosopher, the humanitarian, the tragically saddened "father" of the atomic bomb, and above all, the unceasing searcher after scientific truth.

(252636—$4.95)

☐ **THE ORIGIN by Irving Stone.** A master writer's magnificent saga of Charles Darwin. Spanning half a century and the entire globe, it tells a story of epic proportions, dealing with the life, times, and destiny of the man whose ideas changed forever human-kind's view of itself.

(252849—$8.95)

☐ **LIVING MY LIFE by Emma Goldman.** Edited by Richard and Anna Maria Drinnon, with index, biographical essay, and critique of Goldman's life after 1919. An historical document as well as a biographical one. "Through it we get marvelous first-hand accounts of major events in late 19th-and early 20th-century American social life, and as such the book is a valuable classroom addition . . . also presents us with a clear exposition of anarchist philosophy."—*Teaching History*

(006694—$9.95)

All prices higher in Canada

To order, use the convenient coupon on the next page.

Quality Fiction from PLUME

*Not available in Canada

All prices higher in Canada

To order, use the convenient coupon on the next page.

Ⓟ